D1245131

BEAN BUSINESS BASICS

The Definitive How-to Manual
for Starting & Operating
a Retail Specialty Coffee Business

Second Edition

Ed Arvidson

Victor Bogart

Bruce Milletto

Illustrations by James Cloutier

Bellissimo Coffee InfoGroup | Eugene, Oregon | www.espresso101.com

Dedication

This book is dedicated in loving memory to Brandy
Brandenburger—mentor, associate, and friend.

COFFEE INFOGROUP

1501 Pearl St. Suite B
Eugene, OR 97401 USA

Tel: 541-683-5373
Fax: 541-683-1010
ciao@bellissimocoffeeinfo.com
espresso101.com
coffeeuniverse.com
virtualcoffee.com

January 2. 2002

Dear Coffee Entrepreneur,

When the first edition of *Bean Business Basics was* published in 1997, we had no idea how successful the book would be. We wondered if we would even be able to sell the few thousand books we ordered. We also had other concerns—should we give away tens of thousands of dollars worth of information that took us years to acquire for such a small price? Would the book undermine our consulting services? Our fears proved groundless. *Bean Business Basics* has given Bellissimo more credibility and shown not only our knowledge, but our commitment to the specialty coffee industry. In fact, our consulting services have flourished as a result of this book.

In 1997, we felt the time was ripe for a book written specifically for those interested in specialty coffee retail. We believed the people who would read it would find the answers to the 1000 questions they had and obtain the insight to ponder 500 new and important ones they had never considered.

Most in the industry would agree that *Bean Business Basics* is the definitive start-up and ongoing operational manual for anyone interested in specialty coffee retail. Almost all of the top coffee experts, presidents of coffee-related companies, directors of our national organizations, and editors and publishers of industry trade publications say there is no finer book available for the specialty coffee entrepreneur. We agree.

Now we offer you the 5 Bs: The Bigger and Better *Bean Business Basics*. This second edition is an up-to-date offering that will help you in your ongoing quest for the knowledge you need to succeed and profit in the coffee industry.

I promise anyone who purchases and reads this book a wealth of information obtained from our hands-on experience in opening and running our own successful operations and the lessons we have learned from working with thousands in the industry over the last 10 years.

We at Bellissimo, Inc. wish you the best and thank you for truly understanding that "knowledge is profit".

Respectfully,

Bruce Milletto
President, Bellissimo Coffee InfoGroup

About the Authors

Ed Arvidson

Ed Arvidson is an independent coffee-industry consultant. Mr. Arvidson is a former partner in Bellissimo, Inc., and he continues to work alongside Bruce Milletto as a Bellissimo consultant. He has accumulated over 20 years experience in the food-service industry while working for national and regional restaurant corporations. He has also owned his own successful restaurant. During his career, he has held positions at a variety of operations as: corporate food and beverage director, corporate management trainer, and owner/general manager. He has managed high-volume units with annual sales approaching $3 million and has supervised staffs in excess of 100. He is an expert in all aspects of restaurant operations and menu research and development. His experience, creativity, people skills and problem-solving ability qualify him as an authority. Arvidson has written for several coffee-industry periodicals, and has been a frequent speaker at industry trade shows on product preparation and business operations. He is co-author and co-developer with Bruce Milletto of many Bellissimo products, including the start-up manual *Opening a Specialty Coffee Drive-Thru a*nd the award-winning training video "Espresso 101."

Bruce Milletto

Bruce Milletto is president of Bellissimo Inc. His early involvement and insights into the American gourmet coffee movement have been written about in numerous national and international industry trade publications where Mr. Milletto has been hailed as a pioneer of the American espresso industry. He was also dubbed "Mr. Espresso USA" by an Italian trade journal. Mr. Milletto holds an undergraduate degree from Northern Arizona University and a master's degree from the University of Oregon. He has worked for various corporations and government agencies in marketing and teaching positions, and has also created and owned multiple retail businesses. He has owned three successful retail gourmet coffee operations, and has assisted numerous clients in creating new coffee start-ups worldwide. Mr. Milletto serves on and is the former Vice Chair of the Specialty Coffee Association of America (SCAA) Communications Committee. He writes frequently for such trade publications as *Fresh Cup Magazine*, *Fancy Food Magazine*, *Coffee Culture Magazine* (Canada), and *Speciale Caffé* (Italy) and *Coffee Net* Hellas (Greece). He was the recipient of the 1999 Award for Distinguished Author in the Specialty Coffee Industry presented by the SCAA.

In 2000, Mr. Milletto was nominated to serve on the prestigious editorial board of the *Specialty Coffee Journal*, covering the marketing segment of the specialty coffee industry, and a coffee-product review panel for NSF International, an independent, not-for-profit, third party standards development and certification organization specializing in public and environmental health. Mr. Milletto is a frequent speaker at national and international coffee conferences and tradeshows.

Numerous Bellissimo projects have won awards and been recognized at prestigious film festivals, including The New York Film and Video Festival. Bellissimo was a winner at the 1997 Summit Awards, and was presented the Award of Distinction at the 1997 Communicator Awards and The 1998 Videographer Award of Excellence, as well as three *Fresh Cup Magazine* Spressy Awards.

In 2001, the Bruce Milletto/Kenneth Davids production, "The Passionate Harvest," won Best of Show at Coffee Fest Las Vegas and Best New Product at the 2001 Specialty Coffee Association of America Conference and Exhibition. The film won an award at the 22nd Annual Telly Awards, a Silver Award at the 2001 Summit Awards, and the Award of Distinction at the 2001 Videographer Awards. At the largest independent film festival in the world "World Fest Houston 2001," the film was awarded one of only 16 Platinum Awards out of almost 5000 entries. Bellissimo's "Everything BUT Coffee" also won a Telly Bronze Award in 2001.

Victor Bogart

Mr. Bogart collaborated on the first edition of this manual. He holds a Ph. D. degree from Oregon State University and master's degrees from the University of Washington and the University of California at Berkeley. His background includes successful careers as journalist, teacher, psychotherapist, and more recently, author and publisher. He is the founder and principal of Baskin Publishing Co., Eugene, Oregon, specializing in the preparation and publication of training manuals and how-to books for business, industry and a general audience.

Table of Contents

Successful coffee retailing is about the proper execution of a million little details. Bean Business Basics *has proven an invaluable resource for guiding coffeehouse and espresso bar operators in establishing workable systems and standards for managing their growth and success. I highly recommend it be in everyone's library—as essential and well worn as the Thesaurus is to a writer.*

—Don Holly, Corporate Quality Control Manager, Green Mountain Coffee Roasters

Part II - Getting Open

Part III - Being Successful

Bean Business Basics is *as straightforward, friendly and accessible as its title suggests. It is authoritative and generous with its information and unremitting in its commitment to helping the new entrepreneur succeed.*

    —Kenneth Davids, world renowned coffee expert and writer

IMPORTANT— PLEASE READ!

DISCLAIMER

This is the most important information in this book for the reader to thoroughly understand. If you have any questions, or do not possess a complete understanding of the following statements, you should seek clarification from your attorney, or from the authors and publisher of this book at: Bellissimo Inc., P.O. Box 5182, Eugene, Oregon, U.S.A. 97405 or (541) 683-5373.

This book is intended to provide the reader with *general information* about the retail business opportunities, and many of the possible operational variables, that exist within the specialty coffee industry. The information provided in this book should be used as a general guide, and is not to be considered an absolute authority.

The reader should understand that recommendations made by the authors and the publisher are only suggestions based upon our prior experiences, and upon a limited knowledge of current accepted practices, codes, and laws within the United States, at the date of publishing. The authors and publisher do not claim to: thoroughly understand, to have properly interpreted, or to possess a complete knowledge of, all the municipal, city, county, state, and federal codes, rules, regulations, restrictions, and legal implications that may exist. There are simply too many jurisdictions, each with its own set of rules, for us to speak with authority about every reader's location. The authors do not claim to have any knowledge of these subjects outside of the United States.

All final legal, financial, and business decisions of significant importance are the sole responsibility of the reader. This book is not intended to be, nor should it be expected to provide, a guarantee of business success. Furthermore, the reader should be aware that a retail specialty coffee business is a food-service business, and that retail food service is a very high risk business. The reader should be aware that the failure rate for start-up food service businesses is over 95 percent, within the first 24 months of business operation.

The success of a business is a product of many variables including, but not limited to: sufficient start-up and operating capital; the quality and extent of pre-opening research and planning; proper location selection; establishing and securing a lease with favorable financial terms and conditions; awareness of, and compliance with, all governmental requirements and procedures; approval of appropriate governmental agencies; the consistent production and acquisition of high quality products; the adherence to, and satisfaction of, all agreements regarding the payment of any debts incurred for products and services delivered or provided in good faith; the establishment of successful hiring and training practices; providing consistent excellent customer service; understanding and adhering to all local, state, and federal employee labor practices and regulations; the establishment of an effective and consistent marketing plan; effective in-store merchandising and promotional programs; establishing, maintaining, and achieving realistic, profitable, budgets and cost controls; maintaining current and accurate records; establishing sufficient risk management protection; and, satisfying all tax obligations and liabilities. These topics are addressed in the chapters of this book. We can offer our suggestions, but we can offer no guarantees that you, the individual entrepreneur, will succeed in your business.

In addition to the above mentioned, **the authors and publishers of this book consider the guidance and counseling of other specific professionals to be essential and mandatory for the protection of the reader**. Contractual, financial, and business decisions of significant importance should not be made before obtaining the counsel of attorneys, bankers, accountants, real estate brokers, qualified consultants, government agencies, etc.

Although the authors and publisher have carefully prepared the information set forth herein, we cannot guarantee the accuracy of the information contained within this book, as it may relate to the individual application of a given reader. This book is sold with the understanding that the authors and publisher are not offering, nor are they qualified to offer, legal, accounting, or other professional advice or services. The authors and publisher accept no responsibility or liability to any entity or person with respect to any damage, loss, or injury caused or alleged to be caused directly or indirectly by the information contained in this book.

Acknowledgements

We would like to thank the following individuals and
companiess whose help and encouragement made this book
a reality:

Valle Beverari

Mauro Cipolla

Stefano Del Vanga

Fotografia

Don Holly

Peter Kelsch

Kris Larson

Ted Lingle

Charlie Magee

Bruce Mullins

Julia Schnabel

PREFACE

How to use *Bean Business Basics*

Bean Business Basics is a comprehensive "how-to" manual which has been designed to, hopefully, help you open and operate a successful retail specialty coffee business.

This manual is a "step-by-step" teaching tool. Start at the beginning of the manual, work and read through the book in a progressive sequential order. Every chapter is a building-block, providing you with the information necessary to proceed to the next chapter. Because many of the subjects are interrelated, you may be referred to previous or subsequent chapters as you research a specific subject.

We suggest you read through the entire book one time to gain an overall understanding of the book's content. You will begin to understand how this information interrelates to the overall creation and operation of a prospective coffee business. Carefully study each chapter, take notes, or use a high-lighting pen to distinguish important points specific to your scenario.

As you begin the process of creating your business, the section entitled *Getting Open,* Chapters 15 through 30, should help you prioritize the tasks which will be necessary to move your concept from the idea stage to opening day. We suggest you complete all the details associated with each chapter before moving on to the next.

We have created checklists for some of the chapters to help ensure that the majority of information, details, and functions, have been considered or completed. These checklists are located at the end of the chapter when applicable.

The information in this book has been organized and divided into the three sections, as follows:

I. Your Product

Chapters 1 through 14 will cover information necessary to obtain a basic understanding of coffee. Remember your mission...you are opening a specialty coffee business, and to be successful you will need to understand thoroughly the product you will be selling.

In this section you will learn about the discovery of coffee, and its path and significance throughout history. In addition, we will discuss present trends in coffee purchasing and consumption, so you may better predict the future.

You will gain an understanding of what coffee is, how it is grown, cultivated, and processed. You will learn the important role played by roasting and blending in the development of flavor and aroma within the bean.

You will learn how to taste, judge, select, purchase, handle, and store fine coffees. We will explain how to prepare coffee and its beverages, using a variety of methods, and finally, how to maintain your equipment to preserve optimal flavor characteristics.

Understanding this product, before you make many of the business-related decisions, is essential. Your understanding of coffee and the coffee industry may greatly influence such decisions as location selection, negotiating lease terms, store design, menu planning, purchasing equipment, and selecting vendors.

II. Getting Open

Chapters 15 through 30 will guide you through many of the actions leading to your opening day of business.

You will begin by understanding the relationship between the dollars you have available to invest, and the type of business that capital investiture will enable you to create. We will discuss the importance of creating a detailed, comprehensive business plan, so that you, and others, will have a vivid picture of what you intend to create and what it should achieve.

You will learn about important considerations when selecting a location, and how to negotiate a lease with favorable terms and conditions. We will address how to create your menu, and its significance in determining your store's design. And we will discuss the physical construction of your business, including the selection of your equipment.

You will learn how to find and select vendors of quality food products.

You will understand the importance of creating operational systems, prior to opening your business, to assist you in managing the many details of your day-to-day operation.

We will discuss how to find and hire quality employees, and then how to train and manage them efficiently.

And finally, we will discuss that anxiously awaited event: your opening day.

III. Being Successful

Chapters 31 through 40 will provide you with information which will contribute to the efficient and profitable operation of your business.

You will learn how to market and merchandise your business. You must attract people to your operation—effectively displaying and promoting the products you have available for sale will allow you to maximize your income.

Your employees must provide excellent customer service and produce a superior product, so that those who visit your business will want to return. We will discuss the important fundamentals of good customer service.

You will learn the importance of maintaining accurate records for financial analysis and planning. You will want to pay close attention to this entire section, as it may relate to legal considerations you may have.

We will talk about risk management, and also discuss the importance of timely reporting and payment of taxes.

You will learn how to budget and control your cost of sales and your expenses.

We will discuss the importance of goal setting and planning, and the fundamentals necessary to achieve profitability. Finally, we will look at business expansion.

Some words of caution

Most people who have made the decision to enter this business want to get open as quickly as possible. You need to temper your eagerness.

It will become obvious as you study this manual that there are literally hundreds, if not thousands, of details which must be attended to before you will be ready to open. Attending to all of these details may take months, or even years. If you rush the process, if you ignore the warnings, if you make poor decisions, the results could be emotionally and financially disastrous.

You need to realize that learning how to open and operate a business is an ongoing process and not a destination. It is not unlike studying to be a doctor or a lawyer. You do not make the decision to enter a profession, and then obtain all the knowledge and expertise overnight. It takes years of preparation. If you possess no previous experience in business ownership, or food-service management, it may take you a year or longer to conduct the basic research necessary to embark on your journey towards business ownership.

We believe opportunities will exist for years to come in the specialty coffee business. For those who do their research, plan carefully, and open and operate their businesses properly, the prospects are positive. You may only have one opportunity to open your business, and you need to protect your investment by doing everything right, from the beginning.

Finding your way around

P.S. A few words about finding your way around *Bean Business Basics*:

The table of contents in the front of the book (pages ix-xi) tells you where to find each of the chapters in the three sections. A list of chapters contained in each section also appears at the front of each section. Then, in front of each chapter, you will find a contents page listing the topics to be found in that chapter and their page numbers.

And for speedy reference as you flip through the book, check the black box in the upper right-hand corner of any page for the number and title of the chapter you are looking at. The upper left hand corner of any page lets you know to which section the chapter belongs.

INTRODUCTION

Specialty Coffee

Specialty Coffee is an elevation of the world's most popular and widely consumed beverage to a new level of quality and enjoyment. In terms of dollars traded on the commodities market, coffee is second only to petroleum. Specialty coffees are those coffees that are sourced from the very highest quality coffee beans of the Arabica species. They are typically handcrafted, roasted in small batches, and sold fresh, directly to the retailer or consumer.

Specialty coffees can be enjoyed as single-bean origin coffees or as blends. An origin coffee is a coffee that comes from one country or growing region and possesses a distinctive flavor influenced by the plant's genetics, as well as the soil and climatic conditions of that particular area. Several origin coffees can be artfully combined to formulate a blend. Created by a skilled roaster, blends can produce a full balance of flavors, or new and interesting flavors that cannot be achieved from a single origin coffee.

The global explosion of popularity and demand for specialty coffee is growing every day.

Single-bean origin coffees and blends can both be prepared and enjoyed as brewed coffee. Espresso, which is a special method of preparing coffee, requires a specific blend of typically two to seven different origin coffees to create the desired result. The espresso process releases the coffee oils from the ground coffee. These oils are where the majority of flavor and aroma are contained within the coffee beans. The coffee extracted during the espresso process is usually combined with steamed milk to create the beverages we know as cappuccinos and lattes.

The global explosion of popularity and demand for specialty coffee is growing every day. Opportunity is abundant. Recent estimates

coffee business owners who are not realizing financial success cannot blame the viability of this business

indicate that there may be as many as 15,000 specialty coffee operations in the United States. Italy has over 200,000. The United States has a population of about 260 million people. Italy has a population of about 60 million people. On an annual basis, Americans consume more coffee per capita than Italians. Statistics on the coffee consumption habits of Americans have shown a rapid movement away from institutional canned coffees to high quality specialty coffees. The Specialty Coffee Association of America predicts that this industry will not peak until the year 2015. Any retail specialty coffee business owners who are not realizing financial success cannot blame the viability of this business.

To achieve success in this business, you will first need to have a passion for coffee and a love of people. Next, you will need to understand and embrace these *four principles:*

Educate yourself

1. Educate yourself; obtain knowledge and do extensive research before you start.

2. Plan, thoroughly, every detail of the creation and operation of your business.

Plan thoroughly

3. Execute your plan with professionalism, and be prepared to modify your plan.

4. Possess an attitude that you are responsible for your success, and that you will do whatever it takes to achieve this goal.

If you will keep these four principles embedded in your mind, if you write them down and place them on the wall in your office, if you put them on the mirror of your bathroom or the refrigerator door at home, you will have a constant reminder of the focus it will take to succeed.

Execute your plan

Possess an attitude

We always ask these two questions of those who are considering entering the business: Have you ever owned your own business before? Have you ever managed a food-service business? If your answer is no to both of these questions, you have a much greater challenge ahead of you than someone who already possesses some experience in one or both of these areas.

Education and Research

You must become a student of this business.

Be prepared to spend $500 to $1,500, and six months to a year to learn all you can about opening and operating a coffee business. This will be the wisest investment you will ever make.

Subscribe to every available coffee periodical, and purchase as many of their past issues as possible (see appendix for list of publications).

Buy books about coffee, and especially manuals dealing with opening and operating a coffee business. We believe this manual, *Bean Business Basics,* is the most complete and finest available.

You must become a student of this business

Buy video tapes about this business and its products. This is a quick way to absorb an abundance of information, and best of all, it is visual. Our video, *Spilling the Beans*, will provide you with a complete overview of the specialty coffee industry. You will hear predictions about the future of this industry from highly respected industry professionals, as well as real-life experiences and advice from those on the front lines: baristas and coffee business owners. Our award-winning video, *Espresso 101,* has become the definitive industry standard to teach new entrepreneurs and their employees about the coffee business, and the subtle nuances of preparing superior espresso and espresso beverages. *Espresso 501*, the companion video to *Espresso 101*, provides a detailed understanding of the variables essential to create a superior espresso beverage experience. *Everything BUT Coffee* teaches you how to maximize your business sales by offering a variety of complementary foods and beverages. Learn about origin coffees by viewing *The Passionate Harvest*, which takes a detailed look at the inner workings of the diverse processes involved in coffee production, emphasizing the enormous amount of effort and care required to produce quality coffee, and highlighting some of the issues and decision points that affect final cup quality and character.

Attend coffee trade shows and seminars devoted to teaching you about this business. Those who have extensive hands-on experience in this business can provide you with a wealth of information, and steer you in the right direction (see appendix for list of tradeshows).

It may be wise for you to consider using a coffee industry business consultant. Many times the few thousand dollars spent by our clients on consulting actually saves them money beyond our consulting fees. An experienced, qualified consultant can help prevent you from making serious, or even fatal, business mistakes. Sometimes this help may be difficult to place a true dollar value on. Because hind sight is always 20/20, the potential repercussions of a decision that you may be considering will surely become obvious when you discuss your intentions with someone who has experience and insights about that subject. For more information on Bellissimo consulting, visit www.espresso101.com.

Finally, read books, take classes and attend seminars relating to owning your own business. Most community colleges will offer a course dedicated to this subject. The more you know, the less likely you will be to make fatal mistakes.

Plan Thoroughly

After you have obtained as much information as possible, you will need to plan every detail of your business.

You will need to plan every detail of your business

What type of specialty coffee business will you open?

Where will it be located?

What will your monthly rent be?

What construction work will be necessary at your business location prior to opening, and who will do it?

Who will you buy your equipment from?

What will all of this cost?

Where will the money come from?

Who will be your customers?

What variety of products and menu items will you sell?

What will you charge for those items?

What will the cost of these items be to you?

What will all of the other expenses related to the day-to-day operation of your business be?

What level of sales will you need to achieve on a weekly basis to cover all of your expenses and provide you with a profit?

What level of profit do you want from your business?

Will your business be able achieve the necessary sales?

How long will this take?

How will you pay your expenses until you achieve your sales goals?

If you do not achieve the necessary level of business, what will you do to increase sales?

How will you make all of these sales and expense estimates and cost calculations?

How will you learn about coffee and its proper preparation?

What philosophy will you have about customer service?

How will you train and manage your employees?

How will you manage the thousands of details that will be so critical to the efficient and profitable day-to-day operation of your business?

Unless you have the answers and a plan for every one of these questions (plus the thousand more that will be critical to your success), you should not embark on your business venture.

Fear NOT! Many of the answers, or the information on how to find the answers, are in this book.

Temper your eagerness until all conditions are right

We recently watched a television special on what it takes to launch the Space Shuttle. There were literally millions of details that had to be attended to before a launch could occur. Several times the rocket was wheeled to the launch pad, only to be returned to its hanger because of a minor malfunction. A two dollar part failure caused a multi-million dollar launch to be aborted. It had to be "all green lights" on the control panel before the mission would be risked.

Your business is not unlike a Space Shuttle launch. You need to be looking at "all green lights" before you embark on your mission. You need to temper your eagerness until all conditions are right. The price of not doing so may be the sacrifice of your life savings.

Execute Your Plan

Once all the necessary research and planning has been completed, you can execute your plan.

You must create an appealing physical location to attract the maximum number of customers.

You must carefully manage the build-out of this location to stay within your allocated budget and schedule.

You must source the highest quality products available to sell from your operation.

You must select and hire employees who will provide good customer service, have the ability to promote and sell your products, and be a positive reflection upon your business.

You must instill in your employees an attitude of perfection, and teach them how to produce beverages of uncompromising quality.

You must thoroughly, and consistently, market your business to build your sales volume as quickly as possible.

You must manage all the details of your business to maintain a consistently high standard of operational performance.

This is a "hands-on" business

This is a "hands-on" business. This is not the type of business where you can merely drop by two or three times a week and just pick up deposits. We say, "This business is like an automobile; it will only run by itself downhill." You must manage all the daily, weekly, and monthly expenses of your business to realize the desired profit. Finally, you must manage the profits from your business, protecting them from excessive taxation, and assuring their availability for future expansion, if desired.

Proper Attitude

If you do not possess the proper attitude you will never be able to endure the work, challenges, frustrations, and disappointments you will encounter in achieving the first three principles we have discussed. You need to "humble" yourself and realize that you have much to learn, and be willing to go through the learning process. You will need to be patient and not let your enthusiasm cause you to make poor business decisions. You must have the tenacity to find solutions to whatever problems are put before you. You must be flexible so that you can adjust your plans if there are no apparent solutions to problems. You must remain optimistic. If you do not project a constant positive attitude, not only will your enthusiasm erode, but those around you (who will be playing major roles in the realization of your dreams), will also lose confidence in you.

Realize that you have much to learn

Bellissimo receives phone calls every day from people wanting to open their own specialty coffee businesses. We talk to them about all of the factors that have been discussed in this Introduction. If they become overwhelmed or scared—this can be positive. It is important to find out what you do not know!

Careful consideration needs to be taken before embarking on the journey to open a specialty coffee business. If one is not fully prepared to handle the challenges and work it will take to be successful, it is better that their dreams be crushed now, than for them to waste several years of their lives and their entire savings. It is not desirable, nor beneficial, to the wanna-be entrepreneur or the industry, to have individuals opening specialty coffee businesses if they will not be successful. It is also detrimental to the industry to represent specialty coffee with poor product quality.

After having read this book, if we have scared you out of opening your own coffee business, if you have changed your mind, if you have determined that perhaps this business is not right for you, then this book is the most valuable time and cost-saving purchase you have ever made.

An arsenal of information

But, if you are up for the challenge, if you still have a burning passion and desire to own your own cart, drive-thru, or café, then you will come to realize that the information in this book is worth ten times what you paid for it.

This book is designed to equip you with an arsenal of information. It will provide you with insight and advice, that are products of years of hands-on experience. It will guide you down the road, avoiding the pot holes, to your desired destination. For those who are willing, and able, great rewards should await their efforts!

PART I - Your Product

Contents

CHAPTER 1

A Brief History of Coffee

Legend abounds about the discovery of coffee. Many romantic and colorful tales speak of an Ethiopian goat herder named Kaldi. Noticing his goats acting in a strange and spirited manner after they ate the berries and leaves of a shrub found on a nearby hillside, Kaldi, curious about this phenomenon, ate the berries himself. He found himself motivated with renewed vigor. He told his friends, and the news of this energy-laden fruit spread throughout the region.

...in the seventh century the first true cultivation of coffee began

Monks hearing about these special berries consumed the fruit, which enabled them to have a more "awakened" time for prayer. The monks then dried the berries so they could be transported long distances to other monasteries without spoiling. It is when they reconstituted these berries in water that the first coffee beverage was created.

Coffee grows wild in Ethiopia, where today it can still be gathered from wild trees. It is believed that shortly after its discovery, the coffee seeds were brought to the Arabian peninsula to what is today the country of Yemen. Thus, in the seventh century, the first true cultivation of coffee began.

The Arabs consumed coffee as a fruit, boiled it with water to make a beverage, and also made a wine from the fermented pulp of the ripe berries. Once the coveted coffee seeds were transported to neighboring Turkey, they were roasted for the first time over an open fire, which created a crude version of coffee, similar to what is familiar to us today.

By 1763 there were over 200 coffee bars in Venice alone

Coffee came to the European continent by means of Venetian trade merchants around 1615. By 1763, there were over 200 coffee bars in Venice alone. The clergy of the Church reacted by suggesting to the Pope that this new brew should be banned as the drink of the devil. The Pope, already a coffee drinker, blessed the drink, proclaiming it a truly Christian beverage.

Debate has always raged about the alleged health benefits or ill effects coffee may possess. In 1732, Bach wrote the Coffee Cantata ridiculing the campaign of German physicians to discredit coffee.

As coffeehouses spread across Europe, their political, social, and economic importance became significant. Trade was extensive, and the intellectualizing and conversation in coffee bars was quite different than in pubs. Coffeehouses became intellectual and artistic gathering places. Many great minds of Europe used the beverage throughout the centuries as a tool for a sharper thought process.

Coffee was declared the national drink by the Continental Congress

It was in the early 1700s that a French infantry captain brought the first coffee plant to the New World, which he planted on the French-colonized island of Martinique, in the Caribbean. Only 50 years later, nearly 19 million coffee plants were growing on the island. From here, the coffee plant found its way to the rest of the tropical regions of South and Central America.

Coffee was declared the national drink of the then colonized United States by the Continental Congress in protest of the excessive tax on tea, levied by the British crown.

Espresso, a fairly recent innovation in coffee preparation, appears to have originated with the development of the first crude espresso machine in France in 1822.

The Italians refined and perfected the espresso machine to its present level of development. They were also the first to commercially manufacture these wonderful machines. Italy is considered, by most, to be the true homeland of espresso. It is so essential to daily life that café prices for coffee are regulated by the Italian government. There are over 200,000 coffee bars in Italy today.

...over 200,000 coffee bars in Italy today

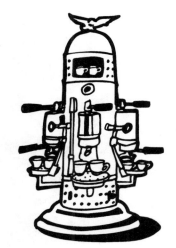

Today, coffee is a giant industry employing over 20 million people globally. This valuable commodity ranks second only to petroleum in terms of dollars traded in the International Marketplace. With over 400 billion cups consumed every year, coffee is the world's most popular beverage. In Brazil alone, over five million people are employed in the cultivation and harvesting of over three billion coffee plants.

...the world's most popular beverage

Gourmet coffee sales in the United States have reached a multi-billion dollar level, and sales are significantly increasing for premium specialty coffees on an annual basis.

For more information on this specific subject, refer to the following video from Bellissimo—800-655-3955.

- **Espresso 101**

CHAPTER 2

Understanding Coffee

Contents

CHAPTER 2

Understanding Coffee

What is coffee?

Coffee is the seed of a berry from a tree that grows around the world in a narrow subtropical belt from sea level to approximately 6,000 feet.

Coffee trees are evergreens and grow to heights of 20 feet. To simplify harvesting, the trees are pruned to eight to ten feet.

Coffee berries ripen at different times, so they are predominantly picked by hand. It takes approximately 2,000 Arabica cherries (about five pounds) to produce just one pound of roasted coffee. Since each berry contains two beans, your one pound of coffee is derived from 4,000 coffee beans.

The average coffee tree only produces one to two pounds of roasted coffee per year and takes four to five years to produce its first crop.

As with all fruits, the coffee plant first produces delicate clusters of white blossoms resembling jasmine in shape and scent. These blossoms last only a few days. Small green coffee berries then begin to appear and ripen to yellow, red, and then almost black, in six to nine months.

Once the coffee berries are picked, they are transported for processing. The fruit is then removed from the seed. This is accomplished by drying the berries and processing them through a mechanical husker, or by a soaking method in which the fruit separates away from the seed. The green beans are then dried, sized, sorted, graded and selected, generally by hand. The green beans are then bagged and ready for shipment to local roasters around the world. Few products we use require so much in terms of human effort.

Coffea Arabica & Coffea Robusta

The two commercially significant species of coffee beans are *Coffea Arabica* (ahRAH-bee-kah) and *Coffea Robusta* (row-BOOST-ah, or row-BUST-ah).

Arabica trees are grown best at altitudes over 3,000 feet. They produce beans of a much higher quality that are more aromatic and have greater flavor. They contain approximately half the caffeine of the Robusta beans.

The Robusta trees grow at lower elevations. They are easier to grow, produce higher yields, and are more disease resistant than the Arabica trees. Robusta beans are much less expensive and are considered inferior to Arabica. They are used when a lower price, or the addition of caffeine, is desired.

Arabica production represents most of the world's coffee trade. However, only the top 10% of this supply is of the quality to meet specialty coffee standards.

Caffeine

Caffeine, the naturally occurring chemical stimulant found in coffee, has been an issue worldwide in the past decade.

A single shot of espresso contains approximately half the caffeine of a cup of institutional, canned, brewed coffee. This is due in part to the shorter period of time that the ground coffee is in contact with the water during the espresso process. The other factor is that most institutional coffees will contain a significant percentage of Robusta.

In order for a coffee to be classified as decaffeinated, at least 97% of the caffeine must be removed from the bean. Some flavor is generally lost in the process which decaffeinates the coffee bean. For this reason, many roasters save their better beans for the decaffeination process. The removal is achieved by one of several methods:

- THE DIRECT METHOD; a chemical process that removes caffeine with methylene chloride.

- THE WATER PROCESS; in which the caffeine is removed with water containing solvents.

- THE SWISS WATER PROCESS ™ ; the best known specific process, removes caffeine without the use of chemicals.

- THE CO_2 METHOD; a process that removes caffeine from the water with carbon dioxide gas.

- GENETICALLY ENGINEERED CAFFEINE-FREE COFFEE; a new coffee varietal that was developed in Hawaii and contains no caffeine. In the coming years, we should begin to see this coffee on the market.

We are told all methods have been proven effective and are safe. We suggest you choose your decaffeinated coffee on the basis of its flavor.

For more information on this specific subject, refer to the following books and videos from Bellissimo—800-655-3955.

- **Achieving Success in Specialty Coffee**

- **Espresso 101**

- **The Passionate Harvest**

CHAPTER 3

Roasting & Blending

Contents

CHAPTER 3

Roasting & Blending

After the roaster obtains high quality coffee beans, the most important phase of the production of gourmet coffee begins—the roasting and the blending.

Roasting

A good roaster must be part artist and part scientist to maintain quality and consistency. It is during the roasting process that the sugars, starches, and fats within the coffee bean are emulsified, caramelized, and released, creating the fragile coffee oil. This substance isn't actually an oil (it is water-soluble), but it is what gives the coffee its flavor and aroma.

oil gives the coffee its flavor and aroma.

Most green coffee is roasted at approximately 400 degrees, usually in large mechanical machines called *cylindrical* or *drum roasters*. The beans tumble in a horizontal rotating drum that is heated by gas, electricity, or wood. When the desired roast is achieved, the beans tumble from the drum into a cooling hopper to keep them from overcooking. The cooling hopper is round in shape, and incorporates a rotating arm with paddles that move and spread the coffee beans. This arm may also provide a spray of cold water or air to facilitate quicker cooling. Air cooling is considered a superior method to water cooling, and most specialty coffee is cooled in this way.

An alternative device to the drum roaster is the hot-air roaster, also known as a fluid-bed roaster. The air roaster, which is heated by gas or electricity, roasts the coffee beans as they tumble on a current of hot air.

The roasting process causes the bean to swell and increase in size by approximately 50%.

A lightly roasted bean may range in color from cinnamon to a light chocolate-tan. Lighter roasts are generally not used for espresso since they produce a sharper, more acidic taste than do darker roasts.

Darker roasts, in contrast, have fuller flavor, approaching a bittersweet tang. The amount of oil drawn to the surface of the bean increases proportionately to the length of roasting time. Dark roasts can range in color from a medium chocolate color with a satin-like luster, to an almost black bean with a slightly oily appearance.

The darker the roast the more you will taste the char, rather than the flavor of the bean. Many extreme dark roasts will tend to have a smokey flavor and are better suited for brewed coffee than espresso. As the roast darkens, caffeine and acidity decrease proportionately.

Many roasters refer to the following terms concerning the degree of roast, light to dark:

Roast	Color	Characteristics
Cinnamon; New England; Light	Light cinnamon brown with a dry surface	Toasted grain taste; distinct acid overtones
Regular; American; Medium-high; Medium; Brown	Medium milk-chocolate brown with a dry surface	No grain taste; sharpness of acid is rich and rounded
Full City; City; High; Viennese*	Darker brown with a slight sheen of oil on the surface	Slight bittersweet tang; less acid with a more rounded flavor
Italian; Espresso; European; French; After-dinner; Continental; Dark	Dark chocolate-brown with patches of visible oil	Definite bittersweet tang; very little acidity
Heavy; Dark Italian; Dark French	Darker brown to black; oily appearance	Definite bittersweet tang; virtually no acid overtones
*Viennese is sometimes referred to as a blend of 1/3 dark roasted beans and 2/3 medium roasted beans.		

On the West Coast of the United States, "French roast" is the term used for the darkest roast. It is important for you to understand that these terms have no relationship to where the coffee is grown or roasted.

Blending

With more than 100 different types of coffee beans, each with its own characteristics, proper blending is essential to the balance of flavors necessary in creating superior coffee and espresso. The experienced roaster, with his knowledge of each bean and its specific characteristics, selects beans from different areas of the world and then artfully combines them to create the desired blend of flavors. The roaster's blending knowledge is a closely guarded secret.

The roaster's blending knowledge is a closely guarded secret

A single coffee bean doesn't usually possess the complexity necessary for good espresso. Some better espresso blends contain three to seven different types of beans. In the U.S., 100% Arabica beans are usually used for gourmet espresso blends. In Italy, some Robusta beans will often be added to the blends for the abundance of crema they will produce in the espresso process. They will also add a different complexity and higher level of caffeine.

Roasters still argue as to which should occur first, the roasting or the blending. The Old World tradition, prior to computerized roasting, is to roast each type of bean individually to achieve the optimal characteristic, then blend. This is our preference, but we have tasted excellent espresso blends created both ways.

Freezing will have a damaging effect on the delicate coffee oils

Freshly roasted beans will release hundreds of chemical substances in the form of vapors. One to three days are generally required for these gases to vent before the beans should be used. Today, many quality roasters are packaging their beans in airtight bags with a one-way valve that allows gases to escape without exposing the beans to the damaging effects of air. Beans packaged in this way will deteriorate at a much slower rate. If beans are not packaged in this way, or if they are exposed to the air after they are packaged, they begin to deteriorate rapidly. Roasts in which oils are exposed on the surface of the bean are much more vulnerable to deterioration.

Once exposed to the air—but if properly stored—beans will stay reasonably fresh for one to two weeks. We recommend storing beans in a clean, dry, airtight container.

For more information on this specific subject, refer to the following books and videos from Bellissimo—800-655-3955.

- **Achieving Success in Specialty Coffee**

- **Espresso 101**

CHAPTER 4

Coffee Trends

Contents

CHAPTER 4

Coffee Trends

A Growth Industry

An industry's overall prospects for the future are important to consider when determining which business to enter. For most industries, this type of analysis can be summarized by determining where an industry lies within its life-cycle.

This lifecycle begins when an industry is young with few competitors and limited barriers to entry.

Next, an industry moves into its growth stage typified by increased competition.

The specialty coffee industry is in a period of rapid growth

In time, most industries approach maturity. Many firms in this stage of development will find it difficult to compete. Entering an industry at this point is difficult and oftentimes not wise. An industry can remain at maturity for many years, or move quickly into decline.

Decline marks the last stage of an industry's life cycle.

Fortunately, the specialty coffee industry is in a period of rapid growth.

The specialty coffee industry has developed in direct response to a growing consumer demand for quality experiences. According to the Specialty Coffee Association of America (SCAA), this industry will continue to grow, and is not expected to peak until the year 2015.

Sales of specialty coffee sold for home consumption are projected to reach $3 billion by 1999.

Retail food service sales of specialty coffee beverages are anticipated to reach $1.5 billion.

The SCAA believes specialty coffee retail business sales will be $6 billion at the century mark.

According to research conducted by the SCAA in January of 1995, the specialty coffee industry employed 70,000 people, including 50,000 in entry-level retail positions. More than half of the jobs were created between the years 1990 and 1995.

Factors Fueling Rapid Growth

According to reports published by the SCAA, coffee cafés (including espresso bars, drive-thrus, kiosks, and carts) are experiencing the fastest rate of growth of any coffee distribution channels. Three factors have fueled this rapid growth:

- High gross profit margins in selling coffee by the cup.

Coffee cafés are experiencing the fastest rate of growth

- Consumers cannot easily duplicate espresso-based beverages at home.

- Existing food service locations will be slow to upgrade their product to the quality level of specialty coffee establishments.

The four major trends which have forged the foundation of the SCAA's "bullish" forecast for the 1990's, and the next century, include:

1. When compared to all other channels of distribution for specialty coffees, coffee cafés will continue to experience the fastest rate of growth. This will be due to the opportunities that exist resulting from strong consumer demands and the modest costs associated with entering the business.

2. Specialty coffees will solidify their niches in all product categories.

3. Retail micro-roasters will become a driving force in the coffee industry—growing in numbers from 385 in 1990, to a projected 1,400 by 1999.

4. Consumers will continue a two-tiered philosophy when shopping. (Two-tiered shopping is the practice of making a portion of one's purchases from large multi-unit discount stores, and the other portion from small specialty retailers.)

Coffee Café Trends

Coffee chain outlets will continue to open new stores in the nation's primary markets because of the abundance of opportunity that exists. Most chains possess the capital and key personnel resources necessary for continued expansion.

Outlets will continue to open because of the abundance of opportunity

Finding good retail locations for coffee cafés will be a challenge as chains compete with expanding franchise groups for the available space. Independent store owners will experience difficulty in finding good locations in primary as well as secondary markets, due to the competition from these two groups.

The SCAA has estimated that by the year 1999, the average annual sales for each of the following retail coffee service venues will be:

Coffee cafés—$300,000;

Espresso bars—$150,000;

Carts—$75,000.

Furthermore, the total retail sales in this distribution channel will reach $1.5 billion annually.

Specialty Coffee Product Trends

Specialty coffee will be in competition for consumer dollars with all other segments of the beverage industry.

The advantages of specialty coffee are the variety of variables and combinations within the category. They include: roasts, single origin coffees, blends, processes, and a wide variety of beverage offerings. These variables make this product category unique.

Major trends within this niche are:

- An increased move towards *"estate"* coffees. These are coffees grown and processed at a district farm or *"finca."*

- Dark roast coffees will remain popular for espresso-based beverages.

The most fundamental change in the industry: the continued increase of micro-roasters

- Local roasters will blend coffees to suit the flavor preferences of their market.

- Decaffeinated coffees will maintain their market share, and consumers will be able to choose from a broader range of products.

- Coffee drinks altered with gourmet flavors will continue to increase in total market share.

- The market for organically grown and fair-trade coffees will increase significantly. The one limiting factor to growth will be a limited availability.

Retail Roaster Trends

According to the SCAA, the most fundamental change in the coffee industry will be the continued increase of *micro-roasters*.

In 1969 there were approximately 20. By 1979 the number had doubled, and in 1989 there were 385 micro-roasteries in operation. Since 1990, the number of micro-roasteries opening annually has increased by increments of 100. This growth rate is projected to continue, with estimated numbers approaching 1,400 by 1999.

Retail roasters will have a major influence on shaping consumer opinion

The SCAA believes that retail roasters will have a major influence on shaping consumer opinion.

Because of their daily face-to-face encounters with the consumer, retail roasters will be the first to discover which product developments will create the greatest demand. These roasters will be able to adjust their product lines rapidly to meet changing consumer desires.

Because the retail roasters will need to differentiate their products from those in the supermarkets (including competitors within the specialty coffee industry), they will need to achieve higher levels of product quality, innovation, offer distinctive *estate* coffees, and raise the standards of freshness through better handling and packaging.

The success of the micro-roaster will reverse a 50-year trend of consolidation in the coffee roasting industry. Smaller roasting firms will take advantage of the expanding niche markets. Large roasters will see their market share erode as consumers change their consumption habits by switching to coffees with unique and distinctive characteristics.

Consumer Purchasing Trends

Supermarkets are the leading distribution channel for coffee purchases of all types. This trend is projected to continue into the immediate future. The SCAA believes that by 1999, one-third of all specialty coffee sales will occur in supermarkets.

Demographically, those areas of the country where the populations typically possess higher levels of education and income represent the greatest potential to consume specialty coffee. Based upon this fact, there are many areas of the country which still have significant potential for specialty coffee retail businesses.

Overall Coffee Market

Globally, the total green coffee traded in 1995 was valued at $14 billion, of which mild Arabica coffees represented approximately $6.7 billion.

Demand for high-quality coffees has motivated many producing nations

Coffee-producing nations are now realizing the potential that exists within the explosive specialty coffee markets. Demand for high-quality coffees has motivated many producing nations to improve their methods, providing a larger supply of high quality coffees.

Green coffee imports of more than 21 million bags are expected for the year 1999, with 3.5 million bags meeting specialty coffee standards.

The SCAA expects that by 1999, specialty coffee will account for approximately 30% of household consumption, and 8% of food service consumption.

(Information in this chapter was obtained from Ted R. Lingle, executive director of the SCAA.)

2002 update from Bruce Milletto

This is a unique chapter… and one of the most difficult to update. We feel there is very little accurate and timely statistical information available. Many reports are produced about specialty coffee, and while they may have value in certain unique areas of the market, they often cost thousands of dollars each to purchase. We also see inaccurate and poorly researched statistics. What follows is my "gut feeling" of the specialty coffee retail market as of January 2002.

We are in a very unique position at Bellissimo…we are often the first company new coffee entrepreneurs contact for information and the one established retailers turn to for answers to specific problems they encounter. As a result, other coffee professionals look to us for information about where specialty coffee is heading. In most cases, what we see and hear is usually very accurate in terms of month-to-month and year-to-year industry conditions.

Bellissimo is very bullish on retail specialty coffee! Each night the news reports that America is in a full-blown recession. Nevertheless, one month after September 11 and the devastation the terrorist attacks caused in an already faltering economy, attendance at the Seattle Coffee Fest trade show increased by 37 percent.

We feel opportunity abounds in this industry and that the individual can compete with large and small chains and prosper. An associate of mine in San Francisco's East Bay owns a café across the street from a Starbucks. I visited her operation recently, and counted over 80 people in her café. I walked across the street to Starbucks, and only six people were inside. You can compete!

Coffee is not going to go away…the second most popular beverage on the planet after water is here to stay. I think the industry will grow a little more slowly than it did in the mid 90s—but this is a good thing. People now know they can succeed IF they get educated and plan their business properly.

The specialty coffee market will continue to grow. Today, everyone knows what a caffe latte is. We are finishing the consumer educational phase of a new industry and are now entering into the quality phase. I am positive this is an industry that is not only fun and rewarding, but has incredible potential for the savvy entrepreneur.

CHAPTER 5

Cupping Coffee

Contents

CHAPTER 5

Cupping Coffee

Cupping coffees help determine the freshness, flavor character- istics, and the overall quality of the coffee

Cupping is a systematic process of tasting coffee to determine its characteristics and quality. The process is used primarily by those who will make decisions when buying green coffee beans. The buyers and roasters of green coffee have to roast and taste a small sample of the coffee being considered before they make decisions related to its purchase. Upon arrival at the warehouse, the green beans will be tested again to verify that the shipment of beans is of the same quality as the sample which was previously tested.

Cupping coffee is not a process reserved for buyers and roasters alone. Specialty coffee retailers can benefit from cupping coffees to help determine the freshness, flavor characteristics, and overall quality of the coffee they will be selling to their customers. Employees should be included in the cupping session so that they can gain an understanding and knowledge about different coffees. Notes should be taken during the session, which will be valuable to your employees when answering your customers' questions about the flavor characteristics of specific origin coffees. Listing these characteristics on your point-of-sales signs will also help to educate your customers.

Your tasting notes will also be helpful as a reference when determining the consistency of your roaster's product, or when comparing it to a product from another roaster.

Interest in specialty coffee has approached a level of sophistication similar to that associated with fine wine. People are becoming actively involved in developing a knowledge and understanding of the nuances of different origins, roasts, and blends. Customers are looking to retail specialty coffee operators and their employees for answers and opinions.

Cupping is one way to develop an educated opinion.

Tools needed for cupping:

To properly cup coffee, you will need the following:

- plate to hold sample of roasted beans

- small grinder (preferably a burr grinder for a more consistent grind)

- tea kettle for hot water (near boiling, temperature of water 192-200 degrees Fahrenheit)

- gram scale* (optional—alternatively you can measure coffee with a tablespoon)

- 8-ounce porcelain cups

- sterling silver spoon

The cupping process

Cupping coffee should be conducted in a quiet, isolated room, where there are no strong fragrances (such as perfume, or baking and cooking odors) which might detract from your senses. Set up your cupping tools and label the coffees you will be tasting, keeping notes on each as you cup. A cup of clean water should be kept on the table so you can rinse your spoon between samples. An empty cup should also be available in which to spit the residual coffee after tasting.

Spread out each sample of coffee beans on its individual plate. You will be visually examining the beans, taking note of the surface texture (smooth is good), color, size, and shape (looking for uniformity), and the presence of oils (which will contribute to the body of the brewed cup). Dependent upon the variety of the coffee, and its intended use, the roast levels and visible oils may vary. In other words, a darker roast is not necessarily better than a lighter roast, and visible oils on the bean do not necessarily indicate a better quality than beans displaying no visible oils on their surface. For your purposes, visual examinations simply provide you with a reference as to how appearance relates to the flavor and aroma of the coffees you will be tasting.

Experienced buyers of green beans will visually examine beans for other deficiencies, such as signs of disease, lack of uniformity in color, shape, and size, bean fragments, and foreign objects such as rocks and sticks which might indicate that a lack of care was taken in their processing and selection.

Following are the procedures to conduct the actual cupping:

1. Grind each coffee to a medium-coarse consistency (similar to a coarse sand, or raw sugar). Do not grind the coffee too fine, or it will become over-extracted, producing bitter characteristics.

2. Fill a cup with 8 to 14 grams of ground coffee (approximately 2 heaping tablespoons).

3. Add six ounces of hot water (200 degrees Fahrenheit).

4. Steep 2 to 3 minutes. The coffee should form a crust or "cap" on the surface. Check the fragrance while the coffee is steeping. If you discern any sour smells, it may be a sign of old, rancid coffee, or that the green beans had begun to ferment before they were dried. Sour smells are not a positive characteristic in coffee.

Aroma is a major component of taste

5. Gently break the cap with your sterling silver spoon. As you gently move the back of the spoon across the crust exposing the liquid, you should notice a fine-celled foam. If no foam is present, the coffee may not be fresh. The grounds should begin to sink to the bottom of the cup as you work the crust with your spoon.

6. Check the fragrance of the coffee as you are breaking the cap. Much of the fragrance of the coffee is trapped under the cap in the form of carbon dioxide gasses. By placing your nose just above the coffee, and inhaling deeply, you will be able to experience the essence of the aroma from these escaping gasses.

Aroma is a major component of taste. Capturing the essence of the aroma will help reinforce the next step in cupping.

7. Tasting the coffee

- Fill your spoon with the brewed coffee, being careful to avoid any floating grounds.

- Slurp the coffee into your mouth with force. Slurping will mix the coffee with oxygen, and will disperse it evenly throughout your entire mouth across the majority of your taste receptors. Roll the coffee around in your mouth to further enhance your ability to taste it.

- Spit the coffee into your disposal cup or a spittoon.

While tasting the coffee, you should try to discern whether the flavor, body, acidity and aroma of the coffee is pleasant, or unpleasant. To understand what the professionals look for during cupping, it is helpful to know how these basic characteristics are evaluated.

Here are the criteria that most tasters use to judge coffee

Here are the criteria that most tasters use to judge coffee:

- *Acidity* is a desirable characteristic in coffee. It is the sensation of dryness that the coffee produces under the edges of your tongue and on the back of your palate. The role acidity plays in coffee is similar to the role it plays in the flavor of wine. It provides a sharp, bright, vibrant quality. With out sufficient acidity, the coffee will tend to taste flat. Acidity should not be confused with *sour*, which is an unpleasant, negative flavor characteristic.

- *Aroma* is a sensation that is difficult to separate from flavor. Without our sense of smell, our only taste sensations would be sweet, sour, salty, and bitter. The aroma contributes to the flavors we discern on our palates. Subtle nuances, such as "floral" or "winy" characteristics, are derived from the aroma of the brewed coffee.

- *Body* is the feeling that the coffee has in your mouth. It is the viscosity, heaviness, thickness, or richness that is perceived on the tongue. A good example of body would be that of the feeling of whole milk in your mouth, as compared to water. Your perception of the body of a coffee is related to the oils and solids extracted during brewing. Typically, Indonesian coffees will possess greater body than South and Central American coffees. If you are unsure of the level of body when comparing several coffees, try adding an equal amount of milk to each.

Coffees with a heavier body will maintain more of their flavor when diluted.

- *Flavor* is the overall perception of the coffee in your mouth. Acidity, aroma, and body are all components of flavor. It is the balance and homogenization of these components that create your overall perception of flavor. The following are typical flavor characteristics:

General flavor characteristics

Richness: refers to body and fullness

Complexity: the perception of multiple flavors

Balance: the satisfying presence of all the basic taste characteristics where no one over-powers another

Typical specific desirable flavor characteristics

Bright, Dry, Sharp, or *Snappy:* (typical of Central American coffees)

Caramelly: candy like or syrupy

Chocolaty: an aftertaste similar to unsweetened chocolate or vanilla

Delicate: a subtle flavor perceived on the tip of the tongue (typical of washed New Guinea arabica)

Earthy: a soily characteristic (typical of Sumatran coffees)

Fragrant: an aromatic characteristic ranging from floral to spicy

Fruity: an aromatic characteristic reminiscent of berries or citrus

Mellow: a round, smooth taste, typically lacking acid

Nutty: an aftertaste similar to roasted nuts

Spicy: a flavor and aroma reminiscent of spices

Sweet: free of harshness

Wildness: a gamey flavor which is not usually considered favorable but is typical of Ethiopian coffees

Winy: an aftertaste reminiscent of matured wine (typical of Kenyan and Yemeni coffees)

Typical specific undesirable flavor characteristics

Bitter: perceived on the back of the tongue, usually a result of over roasting

Bland: neutral in flavor

Carbony: burnt charcoaly overtones

Dead: see "flat"

Dirty: a mustiness reminiscent of eating dirt

Earthy: see "dirty"

Flat: lack of acidity, aroma, and aftertaste

Grassy: an aroma and flavor reminiscent of a freshly cut lawn

Harsh: a caustic, clawing, raspy characteristic

Muddy: thick and dull

Musty: a slight stuffy or moldy smell (not always a negative characteristic when in aged coffees)

Rioy: a starchy texture similar to water which pasta has been cooked in

Rough: a sensation on the tongue reminiscent of eating salt

Rubbery: an aroma and flavor reminiscent of burnt rubber (typically found only in dry-processed robustas)

Soft: see "bland"

Sour: tart flavors reminiscent of unripe fruit

Thin: lacking acidity, typically a result of underbrewing

Turpeny: turpentine-like in flavor

Watery: a lack of body or viscosity in the mouth

Wild: gamey characteristics

The more experience you obtain in cupping, the better you will become at discerning the characteristics of different coffees. Remember to rinse your spoon and take detailed notes before moving on to your next selection.

Cupping is a great way to become familiar with different origin coffees, blends and roasts. It is also an effective means of monitoring the freshness, quality, and consistency of the coffees you purchase from your roaster. If you discern negative characteristics in your coffee(s), you should contact your roaster or distributor and let them know. Cupping will help ensure that you are providing your customers with the highest quality coffees.

Template for *Cupping Notes*

Selection	Coffee #1	Coffee #2	Coffee #3
Coffee Name			
Roaster			
Country			
Region			
Price per pound			
Acidity			
Aroma			
Flavor			
Body			
Aftertaste			
Description			

For more information on this specific subject, refer to the following books and videos from Bellissimo—800-655-3955.

- **Achieving Success in Specialty Coffee**
- **The Passionate Harvest**

CHAPTER 6

Proper Brewing Principles

Contents

CHAPTER 6

Proper Brewing Principles

Brewing coffee is basically a process of flavoring water with roasted, ground coffee beans. There are many methods that will produce a desirable end result. The most common method used for commercial applications is the filter-drip brewing method.

This chapter will cover how to properly, and consistently, brew excellent coffee using the commercial drip machine. The other methods we will cover, which are ideal for one or two cup preparation, are the *infusion method* (often referred to as the *plunger-pot method* or the *French press*) and the *direct pour-over* method.

Proper Brewing Using a Commercial Drip Coffee Brewer

Use fresh, high quality coffee

Always start with fresh, quality, whole bean, Arabica coffees.

Start with fresh, quality, whole-bean, Arabica coffees

Remember, your coffee beans will be at their best if used within one to ten days after roasting. The whole bean is the optimal "natural packaging" to hold and maintain the freshness and flavor of the coffee oil, which is trapped inside of these beans. The Arabica species of coffee beans possess superior flavor and aroma compared to beans of the Robusta species. But less than 10% of Arabica production meets specialty coffee standards, so it is critical that you purchase your beans from a roaster who sources only the highest quality beans.

Grind the proper amount coffee just prior to brewing

Grind only as much as you need for immediate brewing purposes

Grind only as much whole-bean coffee as you will need for immediate brewing purposes. Coffee begins to loose flavor and aroma within one hour after it is ground.

Match the grind to the specifications of the brewing method you will be using.

- For drip brewing, a grind similar to the consistency of granulated sugar will usually achieve a good result.

The goal is to achieve the entire brew cycle within four to six minutes.

- If the brew cycle occurs in less than four minutes, adjust the grind to a finer consistency.

- If the brewing cycle takes longer than six minutes, adjust the grind to a coarser consistency.

The goal: achieve the entire brew cycle in four to six minutes

[We will discuss the proper consistency of grind for the plunger pot and direct pour-over methods (for single cup preparation) when we address those techniques later in this chapter.]

You should use approximately 2 level tablespoons of ground coffee for each 6-ounce cup.

Since most cups designed for brewed coffee hold approximately 8 ounces, you should increase the amount of ground coffee being used to 2 1/2 to 3 level tablespoons for an individual 8-ounce cup.

Use 2 1/2 to 3 level tablespoons for an 8-ounce cup

Brewed coffee that tastes bitter is usually a result of not using enough coffee. The more water that is poured through a portion of ground coffee, the more likely the bitter elements contained within that coffee will be extracted. Increasing the amount of coffee used reduces the chances of over-extraction.

If a less concentrated coffee flavor is desired, hot water should be added to the finished brew.

- Remember, the longer the brew time, the stronger the coffee. Also, the finer the grind, the stronger the coffee.

- *Beware:* brewing too long, or with too fine a grind, may cause the coffee to become bitter.

Water

Always use good quality, **cold** water. Brewed coffee is approximately 99% water...good water quality is essential.

- Charcoal filtering devices will filter out chlorine residues and some chemicals that produce negative taste characteristics.

- Never use softened water for brewing coffee. Using softened water will slow down the extraction/dilution process, resulting in the over-extraction of your coffee.

Temperature

The coffee brewer should produce a brew water temperature of 200° F (+ or - 5°).

- Too low a temperature = under extraction = weak coffee

- Too high a temperature = scalded and/or bitter flavor characteristics

Coffee brewer turbulence

Continuous heating is the principle cause of flavor loss after brewing

Turbulence refers to the amount of agitation the water produces when it comes in contact with the coffee grounds. The force of the water and the pattern of the spray from the brewer's spray head, and how this spray interacts with the shape of the brew basket, creates this turbulence. To make sure your brewer is producing the necessary turbulence, check for the following:

- The spray head is installed in the coffee brewer, and is not clogged or obstructed by coffee or water residues.

- The appropriate brew basket for your particular brewing equipment is being used.

Holding coffee

Brewed coffee will retain optimal freshness for no longer than 20 to 30 minutes

The principle cause of flavor loss after brewing is continuous heating. Once brewed, coffee held in uncovered, heated containers (a glass pot on a warming burner) will retain optimal freshness for no longer than 20 to 30 minutes. Continuous heat will break apart the organic materials, and the coffee will develop a sour or bitter taste with smoky overtones. Heat will evaporate the water, condensing and cooking the flavoring compounds that remain.

Thermal containers are a better way to hold coffee. They are insulated and airtight, preventing evaporation, and will retain the aromatic compounds of the coffee. Because the coffee is not subjected to continuous heating, the coffee can be held for as long as 45 minutes before flavor characteristics will begin to change and dissipate. If your brewing equipment cannot brew directly into a thermal pot, immediately transfer the brewed coffee to a thermal container.

Brewing standards

For a hearty coffee, the minimum brew standards for brewing into a 64-ounce pump pot are: *Ten grams of coffee per six-ounce cup.* This yields approximately 45 six-ounce cups of coffee per pound.

- If you are brewing into a 64-ounce pump pot, use 3.8 ounces of coffee. This makes 10.67 six-ounce cups of brewed coffee.

- If you are brewing into a 72-ounce pump pot, use 4.3 ounces of coffee. This makes 12 six-ounce cups of brewed coffee.

Brewing standards table

Brewing Standard	Coffee per six ounces of water
European Minimum Coffee Standard	10 grams
Coffee Brewing Center Standard	9.07-11.3 grams
Norway Coffee Standard	11.34 -13.46 grams
Specialty Coffee Association of America Standard (recommended)	10.63-12.04 grams

Measurement equivalents: 16 ounces=1 pound=448 grams

28 grams per ounce

Key points for brewing quality coffee (from the SCAA)

- Use a consistent coffee-to-water ratio. These ratios are based on full-capacity brewing, so to attain a balanced brew, use the full capacity of the brewing equipment and;

- Let the brew cycle conclude before removing the pot.

- Do not combine half-empty pots. Mixing old and new coffee produces a less desirable beverage.

- Make sure you differentiate between the decaffeinated and regular coffee pots.

- Discard paper filters after each use.

- Do not hold coffee in a thermal container for more than 45 minutes.

- Do not stack coffee preportioned in filters on top of one another—this hastens staling.

- Remove spent coffee grounds immediately after the brew cycle ends.

- Do not use coffee grounds for more than one brew cycle.

- Do not reheat brewed coffee.

- Keep brewing equipment clean and in good working order.

- Always use freshly ground coffee.

Other Coffee Brewing Methods

Two other methods of brewing coffee are the *infusion* method and the *direct pour-over* method. These are ideal for producing individual cups of coffee.

A new trend we have seen in coffee bars is the fresh preparation of an individual cup. This provides the consumer with the option to enjoy a specific origin or blend, if it is not offered as a house coffee.

The infusion method

The infusion method is commonly referred to as the *French press* or *plunger pot method.* This method produces an excellent, smooth cup of coffee. The French press comes in different sizes, but the most common sizes are two-cup and six-cup.

To make coffee with the plunger pot:

- Hold the lid securely, pull the center knob drawing the filter to the top of the pot, and then remove the entire lid, rod, and filter assembly.

- Next, add the ground coffee. The coffee should be ground to a very coarse consistency (similar to raw sugar or a very coarse sand). Use 2 level tablespoons for every 6 ounces of water.

- Pour the appropriate amount of 200° F brewing water over the coffee.

- Place the filter/lid assembly back on the pot (to help maintain water temperature), but **do not push the filter down into the water yet.**

- Let the coffee steep for 3 to 4 minutes. The coffee grounds should float to the top of the water and form a crust that is referred to as the "cap."

- Now **gently** push the rod forcing the filter to the bottom of the pot. The coffee grounds will be trapped against the bottom of the pot and the coffee is ready to serve. The lid and filter should not be removed until all the coffee as been poured from the pot.

A note on the grind for the infusion method. A coarse grind is used for two basic reasons:

- so that the plunger can be pushed down easily;

- to help ensure that the coffee will not be over-extracted, which would produce bitterness.

Manual pour-over method

The manual pour-over method is based on the same principles as the drip brew method, but requires a few extra steps. You can make one cup of coffee at a time, or use a pot with a cone shaped funnel attached to the lid to brew an entire pot.

To make coffee by this method, grind the beans to the same consistency that you would use for the drip method. If you will only be making an individual cup, you may wish to grind the coffee slightly finer to expose more of the surface area of the bean. This will ensure a full-bodied cup.

You will need to use a cone-shaped filter. Two basic varieties are available; one holds a paper or cloth filter, the other has a permanent screen (usually gold-plated).

- Place the filter directly on top of the cup and scoop in the appropriate portion of coffee. Remember, if you are using an 8-ounce cup, you will need to use 2 1/2 to 3 level tablespoons of ground coffee.

- Slowly pour the water (195-200 °F) over the coffee.

- Wait for all the water to flow through the ground coffee.

- Remove the filter and the coffee is ready to enjoy.

Brewed coffee is still the method of preparation by which most Americans prefer their coffee. Apply all the principles you have learned in this chapter, and you can be assured that you are supplying your customers with the best your product has to offer.

For more information on this specific subject, refer to the following books and videos from Bellissimo—800-655-3955.

- **Achieving Success in Specialty Coffee**

- **Espresso 101**

CHAPTER 7

Extracting Perfect Espresso

Contents

CHAPTER 7

Extracting Perfect Espresso

There are many necessary factors all contributing to the perfect shot of espresso. The first is starting with a quality, fresh blend of coffee beans, specifically blended and roasted for espresso. This information is covered in detail in Chapter 12—*Selecting Your Coffee Roaster.*

The Grind

Of all factors, the consistency of the grind is the most important

We feel that of all factors, the consistency of the grind is the most important. A good benchmark is for your ground coffee to have the consistency of a powder with a slight grittiness, when rubbed between your fingers. The best and most analytical test to ensure the proper grind is trial and error, with test extractions. After the proper dose and tamp, which we will talk about next, your single shot (a 1 to 1 1/2 ounce extraction) should be produced in 22 and 30 seconds, respectively.

If the beans are of good quality, the 25- 30-second extraction should have the consistency of maple syrup, and should be golden in color as it flows out of the portafilter. The extracted shot should have a golden top layer, 1/4 to 1/2 inch thick, called the crema.

Crema is the flavorful and aromatic oils of the coffee

Crema is the flavorful and aromatic oils of the coffee. These oils are released from the ground coffee and frothed into a fine-celled foam during the espresso brewing process. Because oils are lighter than water, this foam (the crema) will float to the top of the shot of espresso, forming a thick layer. Because foam is composed of many tiny bubbles, the crema will begin to dissipate as the bubbles break. Aroma and flavor are lost as the crema collapses. For this reason, espresso should be consumed as quickly as possible after brewing. To check the quality of your extraction, you can test the consistency of your crema by sprinkling a small amount of granulated sugar on top. If the crema is thick and rich, the sugar should float for several seconds.

Many espresso bars have to readjust their grind several times during the course of a day. Factors such as changes in temperature, humidity, and atmospheric pressure, can all affect the rate of extraction. The only way to retain the proper rate of extraction is to adjust the grind.

Too coarse a grind will result in too fast an extraction. The 1 and 1/2 ounce extraction will occur in less than 30 seconds. Because the hot water will not be in contact with the ground coffee for a sufficient period of time, insufficient oils will be extracted from the coffee, resulting in a shot which possesses minimal body and flavor.

If the grind is too fine, the extraction will be too slow. The 1 and 1/2 ounce extraction will occur in more than 30 seconds. Because the hot water will be in contact with the ground coffee for an excessive amount of time, the resulting shot may be scalded and over-extracted, creating very bitter espresso. There is a limited amount of positive flavor components in the 7 to 8 grams of coffee that create a single shot. If the brewing water is in contact with the coffee too long, or if more than 1 and 1/2 ounces of water is driven through the coffee, the bitter and acidic components of the coffee will also be released, resulting in a bitter shot.

Proper extraction is a science

Proper extraction is a science. Espresso that has been over- or under-extracted is not unlike any food product that has been over- or under-cooked—it will not be appealing!

The correct grind will produce the desired volume of espresso in the precise amount of time. As a result, the brewing water will be in contact with the ground coffee for a length of time that is sufficient to extract the aromatic and flavorful oils, yet leaving the bitter elements in the coffee grounds. The result will be a thick, luscious, sweet yet powerful, shot of espresso.

The proper grind is the most important factor contributing to the perfect shot of espresso.

A Hot Portafilter

It is necessary, and actually critical, for the portafilter to remain in the machine at all times (except when dosing, tamping, or cleaning). The reason for this is the heat generated from the machine will keep the portafilter at the necessary temperature for proper extraction. If the portafilter is cold, critical heat will be lost when the hot water comes in contact with the cold metal, resulting in insufficient water temperature to extract the oils from the ground coffee. During slow periods, you should run hot water through your empty portafilter to insure that is at its maximum heat level before you pull a shot of espresso.

The Dose and the Tamp

The *dose* refers to the amount of ground coffee deposited into the portafilter, typically 7 to 8 grams for a single shot, and 14 to 16 grams for a double shot. Most portafilter baskets will have a fill line indicating the proper amount of coffee needed after compaction. It will be necessary to fill the portafilter with ground coffee higher than the level of the fill line, so it will be at the fill line after being compacted by the tamp. We suggest filling the portafilter to a level where the coffee is slightly above the rim. Then brush the excess coffee back into the dosing chamber of the grinder with your finger, leveling off the ground coffee even with the top of the portafilter. This will typically provide the necessary amount of ground coffee to result in the proper level, after compaction.

The compaction of the grounds into the portafilter is known as the *tamp*. Most grinders have a protruding tool that will accomplish this function. We prefer the individual handheld tamp because a firmer, more even compaction can be achieved.

The coffee should be hard-packed

The coffee should be hard-packed, with an even downward twisting motion. This will insure that the pressurized water will be forced evenly through the grounds. If the coffee is not firmly compacted, the pressurized water may displace the coffee grounds, creating a hole, and allowing the water to find the path of least resistance. Because the majority of water will travel through the hole, the coffee surrounding the hole will be over-extracted, and the remaining coffee in the portafilter will be under-extracted. A firm, level compaction is essential to an even extraction.

Always be sure to brush excess coffee grounds from the rim of the portafilter with the palm of your hand before inserting it back into the group head. Doing this will insure a snug fit, and will help avoid damaging the rubber gasket located in the group head.

The pressure one applies when tamping should always remain consistent. If multiple employees are working at the same time, we recommend that only one be designated to dose, tamp, and extract the espresso. It is difficult for multiple operators to all apply the same force when tamping. Multiple operators will usually result in inconsistent espresso extractions. If the rate of extraction changes due to weather conditions, it should be corrected by adjusting the grind, and not by varying the pressure applied while tamping. A consistent tamp is essential to a consistent extraction.

Water Quality

Because coffee is approximately 99% water, water quality is essential

Because coffee is approximately 98 to 99% water, it almost goes without mention that water quality is essential. Depending upon the quality of your water supply, an in-line water filter may be necessary to produce great espresso.

Your local water department should be able to supply you with information about the chemical and mineral content of your water. Supplied with this information, a knowledgeable espresso equipment company, or coffee roaster, should be able to make recommendations as to which water treatment devices might be necessary.

Contrary to what you may think, distilled water and extremely soft water are not advantageous to brewing. Some mineral content is necessary for optimal extraction. If you would like detailed information about optimal water characteristics, we suggest that you contact *Fresh Cup* Magazine, and ask to purchase a copy of the June 1995 issue, which contains a detailed article about water quality.

The Extraction

Now in the normal sequence, let us discuss what it will take to extract the perfect shot of espresso.

Start with quality, fresh coffee beans, roasted and blended for espresso

- First, start with quality, fresh coffee beans, roasted and blended for espresso.

- Be sure your portafilter is hot.

- If no espresso has been brewed within 15 minutes, dispense water from the brew head for 5 seconds. This will purge any water which may have become overheated by the boiler. If this water is not disposed of, it may result in scalded espresso.

- Dispense the proper dose of ground coffee for the desired extraction.

- Hard pack the coffee with a firm and consistent tamp.

This thin stream should be no larger in diameter than a cooked strand of spaghetti

- Place the portafilter back into the group, start the brew cycle, taking note of the extraction time, volume, and the amount and color of the crema produced.

When the brew cycle is first activated, no espresso should pour from the portafilter for the first few seconds. Then, the espresso should begin to drip from the portafilter, transforming into a thin stream within a few more seconds. This thin stream should be no larger in diameter than a cooked strand of spaghetti, be golden in color, and have the appearance of maple syrup in body. Extract the espresso into a clear shot glass which has measured increments printed on its side.

Time the extraction making sure that it produces the 1 and 1/2 ounces in 30 seconds. If the time for the extraction varies by more than 3 seconds in either direction, dispose of the shot and readjust the grind. Adjust the grind finer for a slower extraction, and coarser for a faster extraction.

The crema accumulating on top of the shot should form a thick, deep rust colored layer

There are also several visual indicators that will prove useful in determining the perfect shot. The crema accumulating on top of the shot should form a thick, deep rust colored layer. As the extraction continues, the stream of espresso pouring from the portafilter will begin to lighten in color, forming a light colored dot on the surface of the crema. When this dot is first observed, the shot should be immediately pulled out from under the stream. This light colored dot indicates the beginning of over extraction. At this point, all of the favorable characteristics have been extracted, and only the negative, bitter characteristics will be deposited into the shot should the extraction be allowed to continue.

The perfect shot is the foundation of every espresso beverage

If the layer of crema on the finished shot is light in color, thin, or nonexistent, this will usually be an indication of under extraction. This may be the result of a grind which is too coarse in consistency, insufficient hot water temperature, or machine pressure. Poor crema production can also be related to a lack of freshness or quality of the coffee beans.

If the layer of crema on the finished shot is excessively dark, or is accented with dark splotches or striations, this will usually be an indication that the coffee has been scalded during brewing. This can be caused by too slow of an extraction, which is a result of a grind that is too fine in consistency. It may also be the result of excessive water temperature. Try dispensing some water from the brew head and then repeating the process to see if conditions improve. If not, call a machine service technician to adjust your machine's temperature.

The perfect shot is the foundation of every espresso beverage, and wonderful espresso beverages are the key to your success in the specialty coffee business. Always insist on perfection!

For more information on this specific subject, refer to the following books and videos from Bellissimo—800-655-3955.

- **Achieving Success in Specialty Coffee**

- **Espresso 501**

- **An Evening with the Experts**

CHAPTER 8

Steaming & Foaming Milk

Contents

CHAPTER 8

Steaming & Foaming Milk

The art of steaming and foaming milk for lattes and cappuccinos is achieved with the use of your espresso machine's steaming wand. This wand injects hot steam into the milk.

Technique is critical to produce a fine, velvety, small-celled foam.

Technique is critical to produce a fine, velvety, small-celled foam

To the inexperienced or uneducated operator, foam is often thought of as a tasteless collection of large, dry milk bubbles, spooned on top of coffee.

Foam that has been properly made will have an appearance similar to heavy cream, and can be poured into the coffee. This foam will possess a texture similar to a wet shaving cream, composed of bubbles so small they can barely be discerned with the naked eye.

The taste of correctly made foam will not only enhance the flavor of coffee, but also deliver an almost dessert-like quality to your cappuccino or latte. Heating milk with steam alters its chemical composition, creating a different and wonderful flavor that harmonizes when combined with your shot of espresso.

Generally the lower the fat content of the milk, the easier it will be to create a larger volume of foam. Skim or 2% milk should foam easier than whole milk. However, whole milk and half & half will create a richer, denser foam, with a more velvety texture.

The most critical factor is the temperature of the milk when steaming begins. **Cold milk is essential**. Because of this, we suggest only steaming the amount of milk needed for each order.

Milk will approximately double or triple in volume as it expands during the steaming process

- When estimating the amount of milk needed to prepare a beverage, it is important to remember that the milk will approximately double or triple in volume as it expands during the steaming process.

- If hot milk is left over after preparing drinks for a particular order, always place the pitcher back into the refrigerator.

- New cold milk can be combined with a small amount of leftover warm milk for the next order.

Steaming pitchers

We recommend having several steaming pitchers so that if a significant amount of warm milk is left over after preparing beverages, you will have another pitcher available to facilitate steaming with new cold milk.

Milk steams best in a stainless steel pitcher because of the thermal properties of stainless steel itself. A glass or ceramic pitcher may act as an insulator, and may cause your milk to retain heat. The milk will heat too rapidly, typically reaching the upper limits of acceptable temperature, before the necessary injection of air can be achieved.

The size of the pitcher used should be determined by the volume of the beverage you are preparing. Generally, pitchers will range from 12 to 32 ounces.

A small pitcher is sometimes ideal for a single 8- to 12-ounce drink.

Larger or multiple drinks will require a larger size steaming pitcher.

Proper technique

As we describe the proper method for achieving perfect foam, we will assume that your machine has sufficient power and capacity to steam and foam milk. We have seen numerous techniques for foaming milk. Here is the technique that has proven most successful for us:

- Fill your pitcher one-third but never more than half full of cold milk. If you fill the pitcher beyond half full, there will not be sufficient room for the milk to expand during the steaming process.

- Next, purge the steaming wand on a damp towel or into your machine drip tray. This can be achieved by opening the valve, which releases the steam, for several seconds.

  Be careful not to burn yourself with the hot water that may have condensed inside the wand.

  The purpose of purging the wand is to remove this excess water. You will not want to inject this water into your milk.

- Submerge the wand under the surface of the milk, positioning the wand tip as close as possible to the bottom of the pitcher.

- Quickly turn the steam valve on to full power. Be careful not to allow the tip of the wand to surface above the milk, which will result in the creation of large tasteless bubbles.

- Lower the pitcher until the tip of the wand is just below the surface of the milk, and against the right of the pitcher. The proper alignment of wand to pitcher is necessary to create the proper circulation.

The swirling milk should always remain liquid in appearance

The goal is to achieve a swirling, clock-wise circulation of the milk, similar to that of water spinning down the drain of a bathtub. As the milk expands, you will need to continue to slowly lower the pitcher, so that the nozzle of the steaming wand will maintain the proper position in relationship to the surface of the milk. A slight intermittent hissing sound should occur when the tip is at precisely the right level.

The swirling milk should always remain liquid in appearance. If larger bubbles, or a cap of foam accumulates on the surface of the milk, adjust the position of the wand so that the milk reestablishes a visible swirling motion. This will roll any larger bubbles and dry foam back under the surface of the milk, maintaining the desired velvety texture.

Milk is heated to a temperature of at least 140 degrees, but no more than 160 degrees

- We feel it is important that the milk is heated to a temperature of approximately 140°F.

  It is difficult to heat milk to an exact temperature without the aid of a thermometer. We highly recommend that you incorporate thermometers on each of your steaming pitchers.

  We usually start to shut the steam valve off when the thermometer indicates 130 degrees, because there will usually be a few seconds of lag time between the temperature that the thermometer indicates, and the actual temperature of the milk. Heating the milk beyond 160 degrees may result in scalding, which will create an unpleasant flavor and aroma.

  Make sure the wand tip stays fully submerged until the steam valve is totally closed. Otherwise, once again, perfect foam can be ruined in an instant at the end of the process.

  If some larger bubbles should occur by accident in the steaming process, tapping the bottom of the pitcher on the counter top will help condense the foam and break these larger bubbles.

Creating perfect foam requires hands-on attention

- For wand maintenance and sanitation purposes, it is advisable to once again purge the steaming wand after it has been removed from the milk, and immediately wipe the wand with a clean, damp towel.

The foamed milk will be useable in lattes for a minute or so after the completion of steaming. We advise almost immediate use when preparing a cappuccino.

In the rare case that a customer requests a drink with no foam, steamed milk can be produced by keeping the tip of the wand fully submerged during the entire process.

Creating perfect foam requires careful hands-on attention.

Improper techniques

We have observed numerous incorrect techniques being practiced. Quality foam cannot be created by merely inserting the wand into the pitcher, turning on the flow of steam, and then leaving the pitcher unattended while the operator walks away to attend to other details. This practice, which we call "auto-steaming," almost always results in scalded milk with a total absence of foam.

Other incorrect techniques that we frequently observe are what we have named, the "up-and-down" or "merry-go-round" methods of steaming and foaming. These methods incorporate up and down or gyrating motions with the steaming pitcher.

We are not really sure where these techniques were developed. You will see the up and down technique used a lot...this does not mean it is correct! It only means that there are a lot of people who have no idea of what they are doing, when it comes to preparing proper textured milk foam.

We realize that frothing milk and the creation of perfect foam can be somewhat intimidating. Like any art form, after learning the proper technique essentials, practice will be necessary to feel comfortable and to become proficient.

 For more information on this specific subject, refer to the following video from Bellissimo—800-655-3955.

- **Espresso 101**

CHAPTER 9

Your Basic Espresso Bar Beverages

Contents

CHAPTER 9

Your Basic Espresso Bar Beverages

Let us now discuss how to make the basic espresso beverages. Many specialty drinks that you have heard of, or experienced, are only variations of this basic beverage menu.

The Straight Shot

The straight shot is the foundation of every espresso beverage. It is the most commonly consumed coffee beverage in Italy.

The straight shot is the foundation of every espresso beverage

The straight shot is the only true way to judge the quality and consistency of your blend of espresso coffee.

In the United States, the straight shot will be a very small percentage of your total beverage sales for two reasons: the American palate is not accustomed to the strength and volume of the straight shot, and many coffee roasters produce an over-roasted bean which will leave an undesirable, bitter taste on the palate of the consumer.

A good coffee, when extracted as a straight shot, will produce a smooth yet complex taste, providing a satisfying experience. As we discussed in the section on preparing the perfect shot, the volume, extraction time, and golden crema are the keys to good espresso.

Volume, extraction time, and golden crema are the keys to good espresso

To maintain the maximum amount of crema, the straight shot should always be extracted directly into a warmed demitasse cup, and should be served immediately. Preheating the demitasse cup on top of the espresso machine, or by filling it with hot water, will help keep the straight shot warm and will prolong the crema.

The two variations of the straight shot are the *long shot* or *lungo*, extracted to a volume of one and one-half ounces, and the *short shot* or *ristretto* (which means restricted), extracted to a volume of three-quarters of an ounce. The ristretto is the manner in which a shot of espresso is usually served in Europe, as the short restricted pour magnifies the essence of the coffee. Also, because less water has passed through the coffee grounds, the chance of any bitter elements being extracted is minimized.

The Espresso Macchiato

Start once again with the customer's preferred shot of espresso. Served in a demitasse...the only difference from a straight shot is a small amount of foamed milk spooned over the shot (typically one heaping teaspoon). Macchiato in Italian means "marked," which describes this beverage—espresso marked with foam.

The Espresso Con Panna

This is a variation of the macchiato substituting whipped cream in place of the foamed milk. Translated, con panna means "with cream."

The Caffé Americano

A single or double shot of espresso is extracted and then combined with hot water out of the espresso machine to produce a drink similar to American brewed coffee. This method produces a smoother and fresher cup of coffee than conventional brewing.

WARNING: Because this cup of coffee is served immediately after brewing, it may be much hotter than brewed coffee which has been in a thermal pot or on a warming burner. We feel it is wise to advise your customer of this. Many Americanos served in paper cups are double-cupped for this reason. Your customer should be advised that the coffee is hot when it is served.

The Cappuccino

Most cappuccinos in Italy are consumed primarily in the morning. In the United States, it is a popular drink at all times of the day. Rumor has it that the name cappuccino was derived from the chocolate brown color of the Capuchin monks' robes.

The cappuccino is without a doubt the most difficult drink to prepare properly. Cold milk is essential as is expertise in the foaming process.

Without a doubt the most difficult drink to prepare properly

What is often served in the United States (we term it the "American restaurant cappuccino") is typically thought of as espresso with dry, tasteless foam spooned on top. These misprepared beverages will often look as if they have a column of meringue floating on top.

Properly prepared, authentic cappuccino is produced with a velvety, wet foam, mixed with the coffee upon the pour, to create a harmony of the two flavors. Because of the larger volume of foam, it will be a lighter weight drink than the latte which we will discuss next.

Contrary to many products being marketed presently, there is no such thing as an iced cappuccino. Foam is the essential element of this beverage, and it is impossible to produce iced foam. In reality these drinks are iced lattes.

The Caffé Latte

This is the drink that Seattle made famous.

It is similar to the cappuccino with much less foam and more steamed milk. This can be achieved by holding back the foam with a spoon while pouring the frothed milk from the steaming pitcher. The drink should be topped at the conclusion of the pour with a small amount of foam (approximately 30%)

This drink can be served over ice. It is not necessary to steam the milk first for the preparation of an iced latte. The espresso can be combined with the milk, poured directly from its carton.

Latte in Italian means milk. Caffé latte, of course, refers to the addition of coffee to the milk.

The Caffé Mocha

A variation of the caffé latte is the caffé mocha. This is basically the same drink as the latte with either powdered or chocolate syrup added at the beginning of the drink preparation.

Add the chocolate to the hot shot of espresso, and stir well

It is important to first add the chocolate to the hot shot of espresso, and stir well to thoroughly blend the two flavors together. The procedure should be the same with iced mochas, with the ice added after the coffee and chocolate have been blended. The steamed or cold milk can then be added to the espresso-chocolate mixture to complete the drink. Mochas are generally topped with whipped cream.

Cappuccinos, Lattes, and Mochas can be garnished with shaved chocolate sprinkles, at the customer's request.

Flavor-Based Drinks

The foundation of these beverages is, once again, the caffé latte.

Almost any gourmet flavored syrup can be added. Some of the more popular flavors are vanilla, Irish creme, almond, hazelnut, and caramel. Some fruit flavors such as orange and raspberry also work well. Syrup can also be added to chocolate and the espresso to make a flavored mocha.

Consistency in the amount of flavored syrup added is critical

When adding flavors to the beverage, they should be combined with the hot espresso and stirred. The milk can then be added to the flavored espresso and stirred again.

Consistency in the amount of flavored syrup added is critical. We suggest that you set specified portions to be used for each size of beverage you will be preparing. Portion controlled pour spouts, pumps, or a measured shot glass should be incorporated in the preparation of your drinks by your baristas to ensure cost control and flavor consistency. It is also important to remember that the sweetness of a flavored syrup will intensify when it is added to hot liquids.

All of these drinks work very well over ice. Once again, you will pour the milk straight from its container rather than heating it first.

One important point: when adding milk to the espresso, the taste of the coffee will be diluted proportionately to the amount of milk added. As a rule of thumb, we suggest the following:

• a single shot will work fine in a six- to eight-ounce drink; larger 12- and 16-ounce drinks will require a double shot to retain their appealing coffee characteristics. We personally frown on milk-based drinks larger than 16 ounces. If you do serve a larger size than this, additional espresso shots will be needed to flavor your drink properly.

Hot Chocolate and Steamers

These drinks are made like lattes and mochas without the addition of coffee. You may wish to slightly increase the amount of flavoring added to offset the absence of coffee.

Typically, the chocolate or syrup is added to the milk in the steaming pitcher and is then heated. You will need to exercise caution because some flavors will tend to curdle if overheated when combined with milk. Hot chocolate and steamers can be topped with whipped cream at the customer's request.

Italian Sodas And Creamosas

An Italian soda is merely a combination of a flavored syrup with a good carbonated mineral or soda water, served over ice. A generous portion of syrup is usually required to provide an adequate flavor.

A small amount (an ounce or two) of heavy cream or half & half may be added to create what is known as the creamosa. The cream or half & half is generally added last and only gently stirred to create a swirled appearance in the drink.

The Breve

This term originated in Seattle for an extra rich caffé latte made with half & half instead of milk.

The Cafe Au Lait

Fill the desired cup size half way with drip coffee, add steamed milk and top with a small amount of milk foam.

Granita

Granita is an Italian style granular ice drink similar to a slushy but much more dense in consistency. Granita is typically created from a flavored syrup or powdered or liquid concentrate. The syrup or concentrate is combined with water and poured into a granita machine which freezes the mixture. Granita flavors are generally coffee- or fruit-based.

We talk about granita, and the equipment necessary to prepare it, in chapters 24—*Planning Your Menu,* and 25—*Choosing and Buying Equipment.*

The beverages that you have just read about are the basics common to most specialty coffee operations. You will want to get creative and experiment to create some recipes which are unique to your establishment!

 For more information on this specific subject, refer to the following books and videos from Bellissimo—800-655-3955.

- **Everything BUT Coffee**

- **Espresso 101**

CHAPTER 10

The Magic of Syrups

Contents

CHAPTER 10

The Magic of Syrups

Ann King, advertising executive for a bay area media firm, is a three to four latte a day junkie.

You might say, *What is so unusual about this? A lot of folks drink that many coffee drinks each day.*

What is unusual is the fact that Ms. King, less than one year ago, had never drank coffee in her life. Her college days were filled with memories of her sorority sisters drinking pots of the black brew, especially during finals and midterms. She always had a desire to drink coffee but could never really acquire a taste for it, no matter how much cream and sugar she dumped in.

So what made this woman do a complete 360 degree turnaround?

Three words; *gourmet flavored syrups.*

In the past decade, the specialty coffee industry has been rocked with the uniting of these flavorings to a beverage second only to water in terms of global consumption...*coffee.*

Syrup's Sweet History

Gourmet flavored syrups have been around for a lot longer than the three or four years that consumers have been aware of them.

Most of us know these syrups by the name *Italian syrups*, which is their land of origin. Syrups have been produced in Europe for years, and are still quite popular there, but suggest to any Italian the idea of putting a syrup flavor in their morning cappuccino and you will get a look like, *Are you nuts?* Syrups on the European continent are used primarily for additions to sodas and toppings for deserts.

Most of us know these syrups by the name Italian syrups

So, how is it that America has expanded upon and embraced such a concept?

In the early 80s, a coffee marketer named Brandy Brandenburger working for General Foods, asked the Lucietta family of San Francisco for a few bottles of their Torani Italian syrup. He took them back to his Portland home and experimented with an idea he had for flavoring Italian espresso drinks. The rest of the story we can call "sweet history."

Many feel that syrups are the reason that Seattle became the espresso capital of North America. Cart and café operators understanding the potential of syrup, and its ready availability, became very creative and produced drinks which their customers had never experienced.

Before Mr. Brandenburger's observations and research, one could only find espresso in places like North Beach in San Francisco, Little Italy in New York, or maybe an authentic Italian restaurant. There is little argument that syrups have changed the way Americans think about Italian coffee.

The irony is, of course, that most syrups we have tasted in the States are not Italian at all. Only Monin, a French syrup manufacturer, has made significant impact on the American market, and they, too, have established a manufacturing plant in the United States.

During a recent visit to Italy, the president of a prominent Italian syrup company told us that one of the main reasons that Italian syrups have made little or no impact in the States is because shipping, especially of glass bottles, can be burdensome in a market as price driven as ours. The other major reason lies in the fact that most foreign companies do not understand the American market and mentality, and have difficulty competing with homegrown companies. French-based Monin is the one European exception. Not only do they produce a wonderful product, but they truly understand our American market.

Why The Popularity?

Many consumers are no longer satisfied with the commonplace

Americans have become quite discriminating in the 90s. Many consumers are no longer satisfied with the commonplace. The issue of quality vs. quantity can be seen in the success of Haagen Dazs and Ben & Jerry's. Many of us will welcome one or two flavored lattes a day over pots and pots of brewed, canned coffee.

The acceptance of the café culture in this country has contributed to the significance of the coffee experience. Americans are seeking enlightened social interaction, and are less interested in the numbing and potentially dangerous effects of alcohol. Many of these enlightened consumers, after trying these fancy espresso drinks in their local café, are becoming aware of syrup's possibilities and want to be able to produce similar products in their home kitchens.

Label Choices

How do you go about choosing a good syrup and what makes one better than another?

Car shopping might require you to look for horsepower and anti-lock brakes; a computer purchase, RAM, hard drive size, and processing speed.

In the specialty syrup market, sugar content and flavor concentration are the determining factors.

Sugar content and flavor concentration are the determining factors

Sugar content is rated in *brix*. This rating will tell you a lot, along with an investigation as to which types of sweetener a company uses. Some say all natural juice-based is best, others prefer pure cane sugar. Lesser quality syrups will use beet or corn sugars, which have a lower brix level.

The higher the brix level and concentration of flavor, the less syrup you will need to flavor your recipe.

You will want to determine your intended use for your syrup, and investigate for what applications it was formulated, before making a choice. For example,

> *Was your syrup formulated for hot drinks? cold drinks? baking? dessert preparation?* etc.

We were told by industry experts there are over 50 manufacturers in the market. Of this number most are regional or are private label. The major players are Torani, Monin, DaVinci, Sterns & Lehmans/Dolce, and Sterling. It has been our observation that all of these brands are excellent. If you run a gourmet store or coffee operation you may want to investigate and taste each of these along with any regional brands. Find out what types of marketing support each company offers, compare flavor choices, availability, and shipping costs. Talk to each company and find out why they feel their syrup is the best.

Flavor Choices

The flavors that generally sell best year around are vanilla, hazelnut, Irish cream, and amaretto.

Certain flavors enjoy seasonal popularity, and you should ask your suppliers for their advice and experiences concerning these.

Berry flavors are quite popular and will merchandise best in hot climates and in the summer months.

The flavors that generally sell best year around are, Vanilla, Hazelnut, Irish Cream, and Amaretto

Winter months may find flavors such as butter rum, eggnog and peppermint leading in popularity.

Each company in this intensely competitive market is constantly researching and developing new flavors. Some of the latest entries are: tiramisu, melon, Kiwi, black currant, lemon meringue, cranberry, nordic spice, ginseng, white chocolate mocha and root beer. Many flavor blends are also available.

One of the most novel marketing innovations is the introduction of "co-branding." Torani has partnered its long history with that of an established, renowned confectioner, Brown & Haley, to produce a flavor named after their famous candy; Almond Roca. We should see more flavors with the "co-branded" concept in the future.

Most companies have created lines of 30 to 50 different flavors to choose from.

Your Marketing Of Syrups

As a retailer, there are a multitude of ways you can merchandise this product. Be aware that many brands come in two or three sizes. The smaller sizes will allow your customers to try many different flavors at home, with a minimum investment. Of course, if you have an espresso machine, the best way to introduce your customers to flavors is through your own drink menu.

Other methods of marketing can employ:

- in-store sampling,

- cross merchandising,

- creative signage,

- bottle neck recipe cards, and

- combining the smaller size bottles in coffee-based gift baskets.

Educate yourself and your employees as to the multitude of uses

Specialty syrups on your shelf not only yield high profit margins but make a beautiful display! With proper lighting, the various colored bottles will almost embody a neon sign allure to a product area.

You will need to educate yourself and your employees as to the multitude of uses for this product. You and your staff should experiment, get creative, and you will discover that gourmet flavored syrups are not just for coffee and sodas.

The Many Uses

Bakers love specialty syrups! They have found a multitude of uses in their kitchens and are enamored at how they contribute to the moisture of their creations.

Chefs use them in salad dressings, vinaigrettes, salsas, and find that they work remarkably well for glazes on meats and vegetables.

At a recent trade show, Monin had a renowned smoothie expert blending various fruits, juices, and yogurts with their syrups, and the result was heavenly! Do not overlook syrup's many uses as a dessert topping contributing to both visual and taste appeal.

Tea is the newest frontier for syrup use. Many creative and wonderful beverages can be orchestrated using these flavors. One needs only to look at the success of such brands as Snapple to realize *ice tea ain't ice tea no more.*

Two or more of these flavors can be combined

In coffee serving establishments, the possibilities are endless. Beyond flavored lattes and cappuccinos, steamers, Italian sodas, and granita have given young children, as well as those avoiding caffeine, a wide range of choices. In very young specialty coffee markets, flavored coffee beans are still very popular. By adding syrup to brewed coffee, you can eliminate the problem of contamination to your brewer and grinder from the extracts on the flavored beans, while offering an even greater variety of flavor options to your customers.

It is very important to realize that two or more of these flavors can be combined, and it is a large part of what makes this product so much fun. Differentiate yourself from your competition by creating your own signature drinks using various combinations of these syrups. The only limits are your imagination!

What's New?

Almost every competitive syrup company now produces its own line of sugar-free syrups for weight-conscious Americans. The awareness has been raised to this alternative, and the demand has produced a huge market.

Non-sweetened flavorings like Torani "Fiori" allow you to flavor a drink without introducing any sweeteners—perfect for satisfying the flavored brewed coffee drinker who wants a "hazelnut coffee" but doesn't want it sweet. In addition, you won't have to stock, grind, and brew flavored beans. Simply flavor by the cup, or offer a pot of flavored coffee of the day.

The possibilities seem almost endless in this exciting, highly competitive, young industry. Many of the major players employ staff chefs, culinary directors, and flavor researchers whose major task and mission is to innovate, create new flavors, strive to improve product quality, and find new and artistic uses.

It all adds up to gourmet flavored syrups having arrived as a fun and versatile tool for the specialty coffee retailer.

 For more information on this specific subject, refer to the following books and videos from Bellissimo—800-655-3955.

- **Everything BUT Coffee**

- **Espresso 101**

CHAPTER 11

Espresso Bar Beverages Beyond the Basics

Contents

CHAPTER 11

Espresso Bar Beverages Beyond the Basics

While you are striving to open a specialty coffee business, fine coffees and quality espresso drinks should be your primary focus; however, you would be wise to plan a menu that includes beverage items beyond the standard coffee and espresso drinks.

It is wise to plan a menu that includes beverage items beyond the standard coffee and espresso drinks

There may be locations where you can limit your beverage selections to drip coffee and basic espresso beverages only. An operation such as a cart, kiosk, or even a small in-line space situated in a good location such as a busy airport, college, stadium, performing arts center, or the lobby of a large office building, may be able to realize handsome returns with only basic coffee offerings.

The decision to serve a basic or an expanded beverage menu should be based upon your location's potential volume, and the overhead and available space associated with your location. If there will be a non-stop flow of customers during your business hours, then other innovative beverage offerings may not be necessary. In fact, their preparation may actually slow down your operation. Also, if you are working from a cart or small kiosk, there may not be the physical room necessary to install a blender station or a granita machine. If your rent factor is significant, you may need the extra revenue that an expanded beverage menu can provide.

However, the main reason that the majority of specialty coffee businesses serve a diverse menu of beverages is because they are not in locations like busy international airports. They do not enjoy a level of business where endless consumers are at their counters every minute of every day. They have periods of time when there are few or no consumers in their store. A diversified beverage menu can attract new consumers and create additional reasons for existing customers to visit more often.

Your goal is to have as many people as possible purchasing products from you for each and every hour that you will be open for business

Coffee is primarily a morning beverage, and if you plan to stay open into the afternoon and evening, wouldn't it be wise to have items on your beverage menu that will cater to consumers who don't drink coffee all day long? Don't forget, you will be paying rent on your location for its use—24 hours a day, 7 days a week.

Understandably, you probably will not be open 24/7, but isn't it your goal to have as many people as possible purchasing products from you for each and every hour that you will be open for business? You will be paying staff to service your customers and make beverages whether there are customers in your store or not. It doesn't take any more time—nor is it any more difficult—to make a smoothie than it does to make a cappuccino.

When we at Bellissimo work with consulting clients, we strongly recommend that they think of their future business as a specialty beverage business, and not simply as a coffee business. A diversified beverage menu provides attractions to those who would never think about drinking coffee, or at least traditional hot coffee.

If your morning coffee customers drink less hot coffee drinks during the afternoon, then perhaps a blended white chocolate mocha might be more appealing to them. If a customer is a non-coffee drinker, but would like to accompany her friends on break to your espresso bar, then a hot chai latte or specialty tea might be the perfect beverage solution for her. If someone didn't have time for breakfast but desires a quick nutritional hit, a real fruit smoothie might be just what he or she needs for a lift. And, if a mom is running errands with her kids, and she's craving a latte, then the milkshakes you offer at your coffee bar might be a popular attraction for her young ones and the motivating factor in her stopping at your establishment.

What needs to be understood is that if you are starting your business with anything less than an A+ location (and understand that A+ locations are few and far between), you will usually have to put forth extra effort in attracting customers and maximizing revenue. One of the easiest and most effective ways to create a broad-based appeal is to have a diverse and interesting menu of beverages for consumers to choose from.

New beverage product offerings abound in the specialty coffee industry. Attend any specialty coffee trade show, or flip through the pages of one of the monthly industry periodicals, and you'll find dozens of innovative beverage products. Which ones to choose will be dependent upon a number of factors. First, there is your personal preferences. As you sample different products it will only be natural to want to add those items to your menu that you like. Next, you'll want to take into consideration the clientele you will be serving. If your coffee operation is near a high school or located adjacent to a neighborhood, you should probably consider having things on the menu that children will enjoy, like milkshakes, smoothies, and bubble tea. However, these may be items that you would not choose to have on your menu if your store is located in a professional office building. Finally, you need to take weather and cultural factors into account. In Phoenix, Arizona, because of the hot weather, you would be wise to offer an extensive selection of iced and blended drinks.

So keeping these factors in mind, let's look at some of the commonly offered beverages that have found their way into coffee bars. Understand that new beverage innovations are being created on a regular basis, so the beverages that follow represent both the "accepted" and "cutting edge" at the time this book was published.

Gourmet Hot Tea

Tea is made from selectively picked leaves from the Camellia Sinensis bush

Tea is a popular beverage that can be found at almost every coffee serving establishment. Tea is made from selectively picked leaves from the Camellia Sinensis bush. This bush grows in over 30 tropical countries around the world. The most common tea varieties consumed in North America are: black, green, oolong, flavored, and herbal.

Black teas account for 94% of tea consumption in the United States. Harvested green tea leaves are exposed to oxygen for several hours. As the tea leaves oxidize, they turn from green to almost black. It is this oxidation that gives the tea its hardy flavor.

Green tea is the most widely consumed tea in Asia. The green tea leaves are steamed or fired to prevent oxidation. Green teas contain less caffeine that black teas, and tend to possess a more delicate "grassy" flavor. Green teas have gained widespread media attention for their health-promoting, antioxidant properties.

Oolong teas are considered a cross between black teas and green teas. The green tea leaves are briefly withered in the sun, and then pan fried or fired over charcoal. They typically offer complex flavors with fruity-floral nuances. They are the tea of choice for many tea professionals and enthusiasts.

Teas can be bought in bulk, or in preportioned brew bags

Flavored and scented teas are made with tea leaves that have been exposed to flowers or fruits. The tea leaves absorb these flavors and aromas. Jasmine flowers and orange peel are two popular ingredients used to flavor and scent black teas.

Finally, there are herbal teas, which most often contain no tea leaves at all. They are made from dried flowers, berries, roots, peels and leaves. Peppermint, chamomile, rose pedals, hibiscus, lavender, and ginger are all common ingredients from which herbal teas can be made.

Teas can be bought in bulk, or in preportioned brew bags. Preportioned brew bags are more convenient since the tea does not have to be weighed, and additional small wares such as tea pot and infusers are not required for preparation.

Because brewed tea is 99% water, good water quality is essential. Tea can be made with hot water from your espresso machine or coffee brewer; however, most tea aficionados will cringe at this method. For optimal brewing, fresh, cold water should be heated and then poured over the tea leaves. It is important to use the proper water temperature for the type of tea selected for brewing. Improper temperature will effect the flavor of the finished product.

Generally, two grams of tea should be used for each 5 and 1/2 ounces of water. If served in ceramics, the tea cup or pot should be preheated prior to the addition of the tea and brewing water.

For black teas, water should be heated to 212° Fahrenheit, and the tea should be steeped for 3 to 5 minutes.

For oolongs, heat the water to 195 to 210°, and steep the tea for 4 to 7 minutes.

Green and herbal teas typically require a lower water temperature—about 180°. Greens should only be steeped for 2 to 3 minutes, and herbals for 5 to 7 minutes.

Most tea manufacturers offer a start-up kit with a variety of the types of teas we've discussed, and will also usually have some type of display rack available for merchandising.

Iced Tea

Iced tea is a popular warm weather drink. In the southern U.S. "sweet tea" (brewed tea incorporating dissolved sugar) is a staple at most places that serve food. Many high quality teas have been blended and packaged specifically for iced tea brewing. Ask your tea distributor for brewing recommendations. While automatic tea brewers are a preferred method, if iced tea sales are expected to be an insignificant portion of your total sales, you may want to consider just using you coffee brewer for iced tea preparation. If you use your coffee brewer for tea, be sure to purchase an extra filter basket so the flavor of your coffee and tea do not become cross contaminated. The finished iced tea can be stored in a pitcher in your refrigerator.

Flavored iced tea is a beverage option that is immensely popular with consumers. Sales of bottled flavored iced teas have enjoyed amazing success. You can offer fresh brewed iced tea by the cup, flavored with the customer's choice of a gourmet syrup. Popular flavors include peach, raspberry, and mango.

Chai

Chai is the term used for tea in India

Chai is the term used for tea in India. In America, chai is though of as a sweetened, spiced tea, combined with milk. In India, "masala chai" is the actual term used for this method of preparation.

Chai is a popular beverage in coffee bars, and is often thought of as a spiced tea latte. The sweetened, spiced tea concentrate is usually available in either liquid or powdered form. Each manufacturer will specify the recommended ratio of concentrate to milk to achieve a balanced, desirable flavor. Chai can be served hot, or over ice.

When heating chai with the steam wand of your espresso machine, keep the tip of the wand at the bottom of the steaming pitcher during the entire steaming process. This will help reduce or eliminate the creation of milk foam. Creating foam during the preparation of chai is not desirable. To avoid scalding the milk, the chai-milk mixture should not be heated beyond 160° Fahrenheit.

To create an iced chai, the concentrate and milk can be combined over ice.

With chai being a widely accepted and popular coffee bar menu standard, manufacturers have broadened their offerings by adding more flavor variations to their product line. Chocolate chai, vanilla chai, spice apple chai, Thai chai—the choices seem endless. Choose from the flavors your distributor offers, or consider using the basic chai concentrate and modifying it yourself with the gourmet chocolate or syrups you use in your coffee drinks.

Blended Tea Drinks & Bubble Tea

A number of manufacturers have introduced tea-based products that can be served over ice, or blended into an icy refresher

As long as we are addressing variations on teas, we should talk about the popular new line of iced and blended tea beverages that have emerged on the market. A number of manufacturers have introduced tea-based products that can be served over ice, or blended into an icy refresher. These products range from concentrated fruit purees incorporating tea, to powdered, sweetened, green tea-based beverages flavored with fruits, flowers, or spices. Typically these beverage concentrates and mixes only require the addition of ice, and water, milk, or brewed iced tea.

Bubble tea, a popular beverage in Southeast Asia, has also found its way to the U.S. A sweetened, flavored, green tea base is usually mixed with milk to create an iced beverage. Tapioca balls are deposited in the cup prior to the addition of the ice and liquid. These balls add an interesting dimension to the drink. The consumer sips and chews their way through the beverage experience. You should be aware that the tapioca balls need to be cooked in a steamer or an electric rice cooker prior to use. While bubble teas are certainly interesting beverages, we feel the verdict is still out on whether or not they are here to stay. Only time will tell.

Hot Chocolate

Hot chocolate is a common espresso bar beverage; however, by adding a small amount of gourmet flavored syrup to the milk and chocolate in the steaming pitcher, a variety of wonderful variations can be created. Almond, hazelnut, caramel, cinnamon, and raspberry all work well. For a finishing touch, top the hot chocolate with whipped cream and a drizzle of the customer's desired flavor of syrup.

Some manufacturers have created convenient preflavored hot chocolate mixes. These powders are usually available in both bulk and portioned packages. Simply add water or milk, and steam until hot.

Granita

Of all the frozen beverages, granita is one of the most popular and profitable—and it's also the quickest and easiest to serve. In Italian, the term granita means "little granules." This refers to the tiny bead-like ice crystals that are formed in the freezing process.

Of all the frozen beverages, granita is one of the most popular and profitable, and it's also the quickest and easiest to serve

The beverage is made with a specialized piece of equipment called a granita machine. This machine freezes the liquid as it is kept in constant motion by a rotating auger (or impeller). Granita is not to be confused with the slurpee-like products sold in convenience stores. Unlike slurpees, granita is made with high quality concentrates, and is not expanded with air. Granita is a dense, frozen, gourmet beverage.

The sweetened granita mixes can be fruit- or coffee-flavored. Typically, these concentrates will come in the form of a liquid syrup, or as a dry powder or crystal mix. Fruit-flavored granitas will usually only require the addition of water. Coffee-flavored granitas typically come as a dry mix, and require the addition of water, and/or brewed coffee. Frozen latte and mocha mixes will usually incorporate a non-dairy creamer. This eliminates the need for the addition of fresh dairy products, thus enhancing stability, and reducing any health department sanitation concerns.

The level of sugar in the concentrate (know as the brix level), is critical in obtaining the proper frozen consistency. If too much sugar is present in the mix, it will resist freezing. If not enough sugar is present, the mixture will become too thick and may freeze-up, which will make the product difficult—if not impossible—to dispense, and could potentially damage your granita machine. For this reason, we do not recommend that you attempt to create your own granita mixes from scratch. Manufacturers who have specifically created mixes for use in a granita machine have formulated their products to contain the proper brix level. Be sure to carefully follow the manufacturer's directions when creating a granita mix from a concentrate.

Smoothies

Fruit smoothies are another product that is gaining tremendous popularity. Smoothies differ from granita in that they are usually made from real fruit, (as opposed to a flavored syrup or powder). They will also typically contain less sugar than granita.

Smoothie bars are appearing in cities across the country, offering a healthy meal replacement alternative to busy Americans. A successful smoothie program can be implemented by most coffee bars with a minimal investment. Typically, all that is required is a quality smoothie concentrate, a superior commercial blender, and ice.

A wide variety of mixes are available in the form of purees, frozen concentrates, and even dry crystals, to create smoothies

Smoothies can be made from fresh or whole frozen fruits; however, we do not suggest this option for several reasons. Using fresh fruits presents several challenges. It may be difficult—if not impossible—to find a dependable supply of high quality, ripe, fresh fruits, especially when are not in season. Seasonal fluctuations in price will make it difficult to plan and maintain a consistent margin of profitability. Also, the potential for spoilage with fresh fruit brings another concern. And whether using fresh or whole frozen fruits, creating smoothie recipes, and then training employees to produce a consistent quality product, can present a challenge.

For these reason, we suggest using a fruit mix designed specifically for smoothies. A wide variety of mixes are available in the form of purees, frozen concentrates, and even dry crystals. Purees and concentrates usually only require the addition of ice, while dry crystals will require water or juice, and ice.

Because those seeking smoothies are usually health conscious, it is important to select a smoothie concentrate formulated for nutrition. Be sure to compare the ingredients and nutritional information of the products you are considering.

Another factor to consider when selecting smoothie ingredients is storage. If you have limited freezer and refrigeration space, it would be wise to select one of the smoothie concentrates that is shelf stable, and can be stored at room temperature before being opened.

Nonfat yogurt, or milk can be added to create a creamier smoothie.

Blended Coffee-Based Drinks

If you are not serving granita from your establishment, or not offering a coffee-based beverage in your granita machine, you may wish to offer frozen coffee beverages made with a blender. The same coffee-flavored products that are available for granita machines, can typically also be prepared in a blender. Simply add the manufacturer's specified portion of product to your blender for the size of beverage you desire. Add ice and the recommended liquid, then blend until smooth. A variety of flavored coffee-based mixes are available, or use an unflavored coffee base and add chocolate or gourmet flavored syrup to create your own variations.

Milkshakes

If you plan to incorporate smoothies onto your menu, then you will also have most of the equipment necessary to offer milkshakes. The mere addition of an ice cream freezer and a dipper well can provide you with this option.

The chocolate syrup that is used in your caffe mochas, or the flavored syrups used in lattes and Italian sodas, are ideal for flavoring milkshakes. Simply add one, or a combination of these flavorings, to your blender, along with ice cream, a small amount of milk and ice, and then simply blend. The addition of milkshakes is sure to make your business a popular destination for ice cream lovers, and will be a definite attraction to children.

Fountain Soft Drinks

While offering fountain soft drinks (Coke, 7-up, etc.) may seem to be in conflict with the quality of beverages that you are offering on the rest of your menu, if there is a market to sell these soft drinks you should certainly consider them. Fountain soft drinks are very profitable, and if consumers are already purchasing them from a nearby convenience store or fast-food restaurant, then why wouldn't you want to compete for those sales?

Specialty Bottled Beverages

Here is a large variety of specialty coffee, tea, and fruit-flavored bottled beverages that you may wish to consider stocking. One word of caution: realize that the cost of bottled beverages will usually be much higher than those beverages you produce from scratch. It can certainly be desirable to sell some bottled beverages, but you should choose selections that will complement your beverage menu (as opposed to replacing items on it).

Beer, Wine, & Liqueurs

Finally, depending upon your location and clientele, you may want to consider adding some alcoholic beverages to your menu. If your business location is near large professional office buildings, or if it's located in the suburbs and their is no local "watering hole" near by, you may be able to attract a significant afternoon business with those seeking a libation at the end of their work day.

The proper development of your menu in the present competitive marketplace cannot be underestimated. Your menu is one of the most important parts of planning in your business.

For more information on this specific subject, refer to the following books and videos from Bellissimo—800-655-3955.

- **Achieving Success in Specialty Coffee**

- **Everything BUT Coffee**

CHAPTER 12

Selecting the Right Coffee & Roaster

Contents

CHAPTER 12

Selecting the Right Coffee & Roaster

Choosing your coffee roaster will be one of the most important decisions you will ever make

It goes without mention that, because you are opening a specialty coffee business, choosing your coffee roaster will be one of the most important decisions you will ever make.

If you are a start-up company, begin the selection process well ahead of your opening. Check the reputations of several coffee roasters and ask them to send you samples. Taste their coffee. Taste as many different coffees as you can, and narrow your decisions based on what your palate tells you is best.

Then bring in other people—friends, relatives, neighbors—and have them taste the various coffees. Get a consensus from them as to which coffee they like. Allow your own palate and the palates of others you respect help you make that very important decision. One consideration, which should not be a deciding factor in the selection of the coffee you will be serving, is the price.

Source the finest coffee you can find, regardless of the price

What type of business are you opening?

A gourmet coffee business!

You want to source the finest coffee you can find, regardless of the price. Think of it this way: if you were opening a steak house, would you want to serve the finest steaks you could find, or the cheapest?

I. Your Product

Coffee is your major product.

If one coffee is better than another but it costs more, buy it! You will get approximately 50 single shots of espresso, or 35 8-ounce cups of brewed coffee, from one pound of coffee beans. If a superior coffee costs a few dollars more a pound than what you had intended on spending, simply increase the prices by a nickel or a dime a cup. Ten cents more a cup will offset the price of a coffee which is three to five dollars more a pound.

In our opinion, great coffee will be much more advantageous in developing a significant level of business and customer loyalty than a five or ten cent price advantage.

When choosing a roaster for your coffees, there are several important factors to consider.

1. *Does your roaster source only the highest quality Arabica coffees?*

2. *Do they have an extensive knowledge of their craft?*

> Do they understand how to roast each varietal to the level which best compliments its characteristics?

> Do they understand how to combine coffees to create appealing blends?

> Do they produce a consistently good product?

> Who taught them how to roast and blend?

> What is the background and reputation of the person who taught them?

3. *How often does the roaster roast the coffees you desire?*

> Do they roast every varietal and blend every day, or do some only get roasted once every week or two?

> If you place an order for Ethiopian coffee today, and they only roast Ethiopian every two weeks, the last time being ten days ago, by the time you receive the coffee it will be almost two weeks old.

Remember, coffee is at its best one to ten days after roasting. It only deteriorates in quality after that.

When was it roasted?

Ask the roaster if they "open date" their coffees. This is a practice of indicating on the package the date the coffee was roasted. So, always ask,

If I order my coffee today, when will I receive it, and when was it roasted?

Selecting An Espresso Blend

Following are three essentials of choosing a quality espresso blend.

1. *Taste tests should always be conducted on a commercial espresso machine.*

Most home machines will not provide the proper pressure, heat, etc. that is necessary to allow one to taste a coffee at its best.

It is also important to remember that many espresso blends are created quite differently for use on a home espresso machine vs. a commercial application.

Proper preparation is the most important of all factors

2. *Proper knowledge of correct preparation of the product is essential.*

Proper preparation is the most important of all factors. An excellent coffee can be ruined with the improper grind, dose, or tamp.

It will be critical to secure this knowledge or use the expertise of one who understands the nuances of correct preparation. If you have no experience in preparing espresso, be careful! Many will look for guidance from their equipment salesperson or someone else who claims they know how to make espresso.

Most people have never tasted a properly made espresso beverage

From our travels and experience, we have found only a small percentage of coffee bars in the United States have a good understanding of how to properly prepare this beverage and most people have never tasted a properly made espresso beverage. If you have ever traveled to Italy you know that there, the complete opposite is true—most of the coffee bars understand how to prepare the beverage. (Our video training tool, Espresso 101, can provide you with the detailed information to understand the proper preparation of this beverage, and best of all, it is visual.)

3. *Acquire multiple samples for a tasting, and make sure the coffees you will be tasting were roasted and blended for espresso.*

We feel it is essential that the coffee you use for espresso be a blend of different beans rather than a single-bean varietal.

The roaster must be experienced and knowledgeable in combining beans specifically for the espresso process. A blend that has been formulated for drip coffee will oftentimes not be suitable for an espresso application.

The flavor of an espresso coffee should be derived primarily from its blend

The flavor of an espresso coffee should be derived primarily from its blend, not from the over-roasting of the coffee. The Italians are famous for their multi-bean blends. They frequently add robusta to achieve additional crema and complexity.

How does one find a good variety of coffees to properly taste?

- Look at advertised brands in coffee periodicals.

- Talk to your local roasters.

- Ask other operators/owners for their recommendations.

- Call professionals in the industry.

Taste testing your espresso coffee

Taste testing is a delicate art form that ultimately relies on subjective preferences to flavors, aromas, appearances, and aesthetics. The following conventions and procedures can help you make those subjective responses more reliable and meaningful:

Who should judge the coffee?

- It will be important for you, the owner, to be intimately involved in a tasting if it is to play a large role in the final decision of which coffee you choose to serve.

- If possible, ask others to participate. Choose those who you feel have discriminating palates, and others who may make up a typical cross section of your clientele.

- Rely heavily on your roaster's expertise in choosing blends that possess the characteristics you desire.

Staging the test

- If possible, use more than one commercial grinder so that you can extract all your shots as close in time to one another as possible.

- Use coffee samples of equal freshness.

- Limit the number of coffees you will taste to four or five at any one time to avoid palate burn out. If you want to taste more coffees, consider scheduling several tastings.

- Taste all your coffees blind (without knowing which brand or blend you are sampling) to avoid preconceived ideas, marketing bias, etc.

Taste your coffee three ways

- Keep accurate notes during your tasting, listing both positive and negative characteristics observed.

- Taste your coffee three ways: as a straight shot, as an Americano, and as a latte or cappuccino.

   If you are choosing only one espresso blend for your operation, it will be very important that a coffee that tastes fantastic as a straight shot, will also hold up in flavor when used in a latte or cappuccino.

   We estimate that more than 80% of drinks served in the United states are espresso-based drinks, which means you want to taste the coffee both as a straight shot, which allows you to experience the essence of that coffee, and in milk. Often, the coffee that tastes the best straight, is not the one that tastes best in milk.

   For example, one Seattle roaster has a blend that we like very much as a straight shot. In fact, it is our favorite choice of all coffees for a straight shot—but it would not be a blend we would use if we only had one grinder and were anticipating a menu mix of 80% milk drinks. This is because it is a blend with very delicate and subtle tastes which will not hold up well when combined with milk. So we would choose one of his heartier, darker, more robust roasts if we limited ourselves to only one choice.

- Taste each coffee hot, then warm, and again at room temperature.

  Coffee changes taste at various temperatures—aroma and acidity are more pronounced when the coffee is hot, and flavor and body are more evident at room temperature. Flaws in a particular coffee should become evident by tasting in this manner.

Other considerations in choosing an espresso coffee

- Your area of the country and the overall preference of your area.

  Typically, darker roasts are preferred on the West Coast of the United States, and lighter roasts in the Midwest and on the East Coast.

- The sophistication and age of your market (less complex blends may work better in young markets).

- What drinks will be most in demand? A coffee that works well on Mulberry Street in New York City may not be the best coffee to use in Scottsdale, Arizona.

You may wish to consider using more than one brand or blend

- You may wish to consider using more than one brand or blend of coffee. We have seen the trend of multiple blends and brands working very well in firmly established markets.

  How many pubs serve beer from only one manufacturer?

  Multi-brands and blends allow you to cater to many different taste preferences with a greater variety of different beverages. This may be a wonderful market niche that allows your operation to rise above the competition.

- After you have tasted all your choices, narrow them down, remembering to look at every aspect that may affect your choice.

  Investigate the roasters' customer service, support network, reputation, and training aids.

Choose your coffee and your roaster with as much scrutiny as any decision you make in your operation.

Selecting drip coffees and bulk beans

Besides your espresso blend, you will need to produce quality brewed coffee, and you may wish to sell a variety of bulk coffees for your customers to brew at home. You may wish to purchase all of your coffees from one roaster, but it is not unusual to purchase you espresso blend from one, and all your other coffees from another.

Do not hesitate to buy your coffees from two roasters

Because roasting and combining coffees to produce a superior espresso blend is a fine art, some roasters specialize exclusively in this craft. Others produce wonderful drip coffees and varietals, but their espresso blends may not compare. So do not hesitate to buy your coffees from two roasters if you cannot source one who can meet all your needs.

Another consideration is that some coffee roasters will loan you the use of a brewer and bulk grinder if you use their coffee. This certainly should not be a determining factor in selecting your roaster. But if you find several roasters which produce coffee of equal quality, and one will provide you with brewing equipment, it can save you $500 to $1,000 if you have limited start-up capital and are looking for ways to save money. Make sure that the brewing equipment they will supply you with is of good quality and, if it is used equipment, that it has been well maintained.

The methods for sampling and choosing your brewed coffees should incorporate the same principles that were suggested for selecting your espresso blend:

Involve those whose palates you respect to do the sampling with you

- Use a commercial brewer.

- Use coffees of equal freshness.

- Try four or five similar coffees from different roasters side by side.

- Taste your coffees blind.

- Involve those whose palates you respect to do the sampling with you.

- Taste the coffees at different temperatures; take accurate notes.

One characteristic you may wish to judge in your brewed coffee samples is the rate at which their flavor deteriorates as they are held for a period of time. Hold the coffees by the method you intend on using in your store, whether that be in a thermal pot, or in a glass pot on a warming burner. Then taste the coffees side-by-side in ten-minute increments. You may discover that one coffee loses a significant amount of flavor or develops bitter characteristics in 15 minutes, while another may hold up well for 30 or 40 minutes.

Flavored coffees

Flavored coffees are generally more popular in less mature specialty coffee markets. Because the true characteristics of the beans are masked with a flavor extract, roasters usually use their lower quality beans for flavored coffee. The roaster creates flavored beans by spraying a flavor extract on the freshly roasted beans.

The biggest problem with flavored beans is they will contaminate your storage containers, grinder, brewer, and air pots with the flavor of the extracts.

If you will be selling brewed flavored coffees, or be grinding bulk flavored beans for your customers' home use, you will need some additional equipment. You will need a second bulk grinder, a second brew basket for your drip machine, and some additional air pots.

Also, you will need to realize that once you have stored flavored beans in a container or bulk bin, you should never store any other coffee in that container or bin other than that flavor.

An alternative to flavored beans

We feel a better alternative to carrying flavored beans is flavoring your regular drip blend with a flavored syrup or extract. This will allow you to offer your customers a multitude of flavor options, and you can flavor coffee by the pot or the cup.

Adding flavors by this method will also allow you to tailor the amount of flavoring to the customer's preference. While syrups are the standard way of flavoring coffees, they do contain a substantial amount of sugar. If your customer desires a flavor, but does not want their coffee sweetened, you can use a flavor extract.

Flavor your regular drip blend with flavored syrup or extract

Some of the companies who produce flavorings for coffee roasters and the syrup companies also offer unsweetened flavor extracts. These are usually available in small plastic bottles, and because they are highly concentrated extracts, a few drops will easily flavor a cup of coffee.

The manufacturers of these extracts often have tiny sample bottles available. These can be perfect for resale or inclusion with a bulk coffee if your customers want to purchase flavored coffee for home use.

Convincing your customers to flavor their own coffee at home may require a little promotion and education, but it is a convenient alternative to stocking flavored coffees and, ultimately, your customers will be enjoying a better product.

Whole beans

Most specialty coffee shops offer a variety of whole beans which their customers can purchase to prepare at home. We strongly recommend that you limit your selection to no more than 12 varietals, maybe 16 if you are planning on offering flavored coffees as well.

We strongly recommend that you limit your selection

Our experience has been that if you offer more varieties than this, your customers will become overwhelmed. Also, you will experience a higher level of waste because your coffees will not sell at a rate to maintain acceptable freshness, especially with those varietals which are more obscure and unknown.

An important thing to consider if you sell whole beans, is the size of your storage bins. We highly recommend that you select small capacity bins (three- to five-pound capacity). In this way, you can have the eye appeal of full bins without exposing an excessive number of beans to the damaging air. Nothing looks worse than a bin that is only 10% full, and nothing hurts more than throwing away five pounds of stale beans.

You should probably offer a number of varietals encompassing the different characteristics peculiar to their specific area of the world, as well as some popular blends and roast levels. When considering single-bean varietals, we recommend that you choose some coffees from the following areas: Central America, South America, Africa, Indonesia, and the Caribbean and Hawaiian Islands.

Here is a selection of bulk beans that are typical, and enjoy strong customer acceptance:

- Espresso Blend
- Gourmet Drip Blend
- French Roast
- Decaf
- Guatemalan
- Costa Rican
- Colombian
- Kenyan
- Ethiopian or Yemen (Moka Java)
- Hawaiian
- Sumatran

A good drip coffee program will help promote your bulk coffee sales.

Select one coffee to be your "house drip brew" (we suggest a drip blend), and then also offer a different brewed varietal each day. This will help to rotate your bulk stock, and will allow your customers to explore the many different flavors and characteristics of these coffees from around the world.

Do not be hasty in your decision when choosing coffee.

Take your time and learn this product well.

Ask many questions of the coffee roasters you are considering; their knowledge and opinions will help you narrow the pack.

From there...let your palate be the judge.

A good drip coffee program will help promote your bulk coffee sales

For more information on this specific subject, refer to the following book from Bellissimo—800-655-3955.

- **Achieving Success in Specialty Coffee**

Chapter 12 Check List

Considerations in Selecting a Coffee Roaster:

_____ Do they use only hard bean Arabica coffees?

_____ Do they offer espresso blends and varietals?

_____ How often do they roast each varietal and blend?

_____ Where did they attain their roasting knowledge?

_____ If they ship, is the shipping charge included in the price per pound or is it an additional charge?

_____ Will they provide you with samples for evaluation?

_____ Do they practice open dating? (Do they indicate on the package when the coffee was roasted)?

_____ Do they nitrogen flush their roasted beans and immediately heat seal them in foil packaging incorporating one way valves?

_____ How long after you have placed your order will it take for your coffee to be shipped? How long will it take for you to receive it?

Coffee Selection Process:

_____ Conduct research by examining industry periodicals, and by talking with individuals within the industry who are knowledgeable, as to which roasters possess reputations for producing excellent products.

_____ Obtain samples of like coffees from multiple roasters.

_____ Conduct blind taste tests on commercial brewing equipment.

_____ Involve others in your tasting.

_____ Taste the espresso blends in multiple beverages.

_____ Taste all coffees at different temperatures.

_____ Take accurate notes and carefully score each coffee.

_____ Select a roaster(s).

Other Considerations:

_____ What terms of payment does the roaster require?

_____ If two roasters produce coffees of equal quality, does one offer a price advantage?

_____ Will the roaster provide you with any brewing equipment?

_____ Can you purchase all your desired coffees from one roaster, or will you have to buy from more than one?

_____ Will the roaster provide you with customer references?

CHAPTER 13

Ordering, Handling & Storing Coffee

Contents

CHAPTER 13

Ordering, Handling & Storing Coffee

You have now researched various coffee roasters, asked all the important questions, obtained samples, conducted taste tests, and selected your coffee roaster(s). Now we will discuss the mechanics of ordering and handling your coffees.

Ordering Coffee

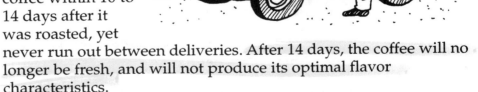

Order your coffees on a weekly basis & use all of that coffee within 10 to 14 days

Your objective when ordering coffee should be to order your coffees on a weekly basis, use all of that coffee within 10 to 14 days after it was roasted, yet never run out between deliveries. After 14 days, the coffee will no longer be fresh, and will not produce its optimal flavor characteristics.

Determining your opening order

Initially, when you first open, ordering will be a hit-and-miss proposition.

By conducting weekly inventories, and carefully determining your usage, you should be able to project your needs in a fairly accurate manner after several weeks. But when you place your first orders, it will be important to remember that you will yield approximately 50 single shots of espresso, or 30 eight-ounce cups of brewed coffee (40 six-ounce cups) from one pound of roasted beans.

If you have formulated some estimates of your initial anticipated transactions per day, you can create an opening order with the assistance of this information.

Unless you are located in a densely populated area, with numerous potential customers anxiously waiting for you to open, we have found that the following quantities will usually work well for the average opening week or two of business:

- espresso blend—20 lbs.

- drip blend—20 lbs.

- whole bean varietals and blends—5 to 10 lbs. of each.

Let us examine how these quantities will break down over one week, and two weeks of estimated business:

- *Espresso blend—20 lbs. = approximately 1,000 single shots.*

   If half of your espresso beverages incorporate a single shot, and half will require a double shot, then this represents 333 beverages using doubles, and 334 using singles, or **667 beverages total.** [333 x 2 (doubles) = 666 shots + 334 (singles) = 1,000 total shots].

   667 total beverages divided by 7 days = 95 espresso beverages per day.

   667 total beverages divided by 14 days = 47 espresso beverages per day.

Your 20 lbs. of espresso beans should be a sufficient quantity to last 7 days if you are selling 95 espresso beverages a day, and they should last for 14 days if you are selling 47 espresso beverages a day.

- *Drip coffee—20 lbs. = approximately 600 eight-ounce cups.*

   600 cups divided by 7 days = 86 cups per day.

   600 cups divided by 14 days = 43 cups per day.

Your 20 pounds of drip coffee beans should be a sufficient quantity to last 7 days if you are selling 86 cups per day, and they should last for 14 days if you are selling 43 cups per day.

> • *Bulk beans (each variety)—*
>
> **5 lbs. = 5 one-pound bags or 10 half-pound bags**
>
> **10 lbs. = 10 one-pound bags or 20 half-pound bags**

Avoid the situation where you run out of coffee

You will want to review your daily detailed beverage sales report from your cash register to help you determine your rate of usage in the early stages of your business.

You should also physically check your inventory level on a daily basis to assess if any of your coffees are running low in supply. If you are running low, you want to take into account the lead time that may be required for roasting and delivery. You want to avoid the situation where you run out of coffee, and have to scramble to attain some back-up beans, especially if they will be of a lesser quality. It is vital that your customers have confidence that your product will always be consistently good.

Establishing a par system for ordering

Once three or four weeks of business have passed, you will be able to observe some patterns and trends related to the amount of product you are using. Using a *par system* for the weekly inventorying and ordering of your coffees will simplify this task.

By examining several weeks of usage information you may determine how much you must have on hand

A par system is a procedure where you record the amount of product on hand and the quantity that you are ordering. Then, the following week when you take your next inventory, you can assess how much you have used since your last inventory by using the following formula:

> *First week's inventory, plus amount purchased, minus the second week's inventory, equals the amount which was used.*

Example:

> *2 bags of coffee (first week's inventory), plus 3 bags of coffee (order), minus 1 bag of coffee (second week's inventory), equals 4 bags used the first week.*

An important feature of the par system ordering sheet (see form in back of book) is a column devoted to recording the weekly usage. It is by examining several weeks of usage information that you may determine how much you must have on hand, and if that amount appears to be increasing or decreasing.

So if we are looking at 5 weeks of usage (an average month), and observe that our weekly usage in bags of coffee was 4,5,5,5,6, we can instantly make the following two assumptions:

1. Since we used 6 bags of coffee in one week, it is possible we could use 6 bags in any given week next month, therefore our par (the supply we should always have on hand after our order arrives) should be 6 bags.

2. The amount of coffee we have been using appears to be consistently increasing. If we do use 6 bags the first week of the new month, we will want to keep a close eye on our supply, and we may need to increase our par.

When you are taking inventory and determining the usage of a given product, always record your inventory and usage in the units that are used when ordering that product.

In other words, if you order your espresso coffee beans in 5 pound bags, count 5 pound bags and not pounds. It will only complicate matters if you try to inventory and analyze usage in units of measurement that are different than those used for ordering.

For example: If you purchase your coffee in 5 pound bags, why would you want to know that you have 23 pounds on hand? You cannot order 2 pounds to bring your inventory to the needed 30 pound level (6 bags). You will still need to order one 5 pound bag. If you do not use the ordering units for your inventory and usage analysis, you will be complicating the system needlessly, and increasing your chances for mistakes, for no apparent benefit.

A note on coffee roasters and terms

Terms, or method of payment for your coffee, will vary widely from roaster to roaster.

Given the volatility of retail business, it is quite common for a coffee roaster to insist on guaranteed payment (C.O.D.—cash on delivery; credit cards, or prepayment by check) before they will ship you your coffee.

Some will offer terms after a credit check, providing you with 15 to 30 days from the date on the invoice to pay the bill (net 15, or net 30 respectively).

If you are given a line of credit, and the roaster or distributor offers a percentage discount for early payment, and if your cash flow allows, we highly recommend taking advantage of this discount. No matter what terms you and your roaster agree upon, and regardless of how tight your cash flow may be, **paying your roaster needs to take a high priority.**

You are in the business of selling coffee, so a good relationship with your roaster is extremely important. If you do get into a financial crunch, talk to your roaster and work together on a payment schedule you can both live with.

A good relationship with your roaster is extremely important

Storing Coffees

Keeping it fresh

The flavor essence of the roasted bean is very vulnerable to destruction. Whole-bean roasted coffee begins to lose its flavor after one week, ground coffee within an hour after grinding, and brewed coffee within minutes. Correctly ordering and handling coffee will minimize its vulnerability to deterioration.

Your roasted coffee may be packaged in a variety of ways.

Better roasters package in foil or plastic film bags which are flushed with nitrogen and immediately heat sealed. Many times these bags incorporate a one-way valve called a "valve lock" which will permit the gasses emitted by the freshly roasted beans to escape without allowing air to re-enter the bag. Valve locks are helpful in keeping the potentially damaging air away from the beans. They will retard the deterioration of the coffee beans, but are not a substitute for freshness.

Some smaller roasters may package their coffees in plastic bags or wax-lined paper bags. These packages do not offer as much protection, but can still be acceptable if you receive the coffee immediately after roasting and transfer it to an air-tight container.

Cans without one-way valve locks are unacceptable forms of packaging.

Store your coffee in the bags it came in if they are heat sealed film or foil. Once these bags have been opened, you can either transfer the coffee to a clean, dry, air-tight container, or simply roll the top of the bag closed, forcing out as much air as possible, and seal the bag with a piece of tape or a rubber band.

Enemies of coffee are extreme temperatures, air, light, moisture, and strong odors

The enemies of coffee are extreme temperatures (hot or cold), air, light, moisture, and strong odors. We recommend that you store coffee in a dry, air-tight container, in a dark place, at room temperature.

We do not recommend refrigerating or freezing coffee. We think cold storage is **not advisable** for several good reasons:

First, after coffee is roasted, it needs to de-gas and age naturally. While freezing and refrigeration will make the coffees last longer, this type of storage will alter the natural aging of the coffee and change its chemistry.

Second, refrigerators tend to be damp and filled with odors. Moisture is one of coffee's enemies, because the flavor "oils" in roasted coffee are delicate and water soluble. Moisture immediately dilutes the coffee. Odors will taint coffee. You do not want your coffee to absorb the faint aromas of other items in your refrigerator.

Additionally, when coffee is stored under natural conditions, the beans grind more easily, respond better to water pressure, temperature, and to the brewing process in general.

Bottom line on storing roasted coffee:

It is best to buy fresh-roasted coffee in quantities that you will use within seven to ten days. Be careful with this product, as it is one that is volatile and most important to your business success.

For more information on this specific subject, refer to the following video from Bellissimo—800-655-3955.

- **Espresso 101**

Chapter 13 Check List

Ordering Coffee:

_____ Estimate your opening volume for your first one to two weeks of business.

_____ By conducting some research with the public and some other local coffee service establishments, try to determine what percentage of your daily sales will be for brewed coffee and for espresso beverages.

_____ Create an opening order for your first week or two of anticipated sales.

_____ Place your order with your coffee roaster. Be sure to allow sufficient time for your delivery. Be sure your coffee will arrive no later than two days before your grand opening. (You may wish to order 5 or 10 pounds of espresso blend before that time if you will be conducting training sessions with your employees.)

_____ Set-up a *Vendor Ordering Guide* for your coffee roaster so that you can log your purchases and begin to track your usage.

_____ Determine how and where you will store your coffee.

_____ Determine and set an ordering "par", after you have analyzed the usage from your first three to four orders.

CHAPTER 14

Equipment Maintenance

Contents

CHAPTER 14

Equipment Maintenance

Cleaning, maintenance, and safe operation of all your equipment is vital for the productive and efficient functioning of your specialty coffee operation.

Like any good tools, your coffee brewing equipment, grinders, storage containers, serving vessels, and ceramic cups will require periodic maintenance to continue to perform at, and maintain, optimum levels of flavor.

Roasted coffees contain oils that are extracted from the coffee grounds during brewing, and will create residual build-ups on everything they come in contact with.

If these residues are not removed, they will create bitter overtones that will detract from the true characteristic of the coffee.

Periodic cleaning of all your equipment will be essential.

To maximize the flavor of your coffee beverages, develop a daily, weekly, and periodic maintenance check list. Your customers will appreciate your efforts.

Espresso Equipment and Accessories

Espresso machine daily maintenance

On a daily basis, back-flush your machine at the end of each day of use.

This is done, as follows:

Back-flush your machine at the end of each day of use

- Replace the perforated filter basket in the portafilter, with the basket that has no holes.

    (Most machine manufacturers will provide a solid basket with your machine.)

- We advise adding the manufacturer's recommended amount of an espresso machine detergent into the basket.

- Place the portafilter back into the machine, and activate the brew cycle, allowing the machine to run for about 10 seconds.

- Remove the portafilter and dispose of the soapy water that has collected in the basket.

- Without adding additional detergent, repeat the backflushing process multiple times until the water appears clear. A few additional back-flushes will then be necessary to ensure that all the detergent residues have been rinsed away.

This backflushing procedure will push water and cleaning solutions back through the group screen and a portion of your water lines, removing residues from those areas of the machine.

In addition:

- Inspect the water daily for off tastes or odors.

- Check the water pressure gauge to make sure your machine's water pump is delivering 120 to 130 psi.

- Check the water temperature at the group head to assure that your machine is producing a temperature between 192° and 198° F.

Portafilter

The portafilter is another part of the machine in which cleanliness is critical.

Because the extracted coffee pours through this part of the machine, residues can be built up rather quickly, creating a bitter flavor in your extracted shot. We recommend:

- Daily cleaning of your portafilters with a small amount of espresso machine detergent and a soft scouring pad and small brush.

- Avoid any metal or highly abrasive pads as these may wear away the plating and expose the soft brass under-metal.

Drain grate

It is important to remove the drain grate each day to remove the build up of coffee sediments in the drip pan underneath.

Steam wand

Your steam wand should be wiped clean after each drink is prepared, then thoroughly cleaned at the end of each day. Open the steam valve and let it vent-off steam for several seconds to remove any milk residues that may have collected inside the wand.

Periodic machine maintenance

You should at least institute a bi-weekly cleaning of the *group head screen* and *shower head*. The screen and showerhead are located up in the *group head*, and will be held in place by a center screw. The screen and shower head should be soaked in water overnight with a small amount of machine detergent, then scrubbed with a soft brush. **Rinse well before replacing**.

The *rubber gasket* located in the group head will also need to be brushed clean. This gasket may become worn over a period of time, and will need to be replaced.

A good indication that this gasket needs replacement is when the portafilter returns **beyond** its normal position, or additional water leaks out around the group head during the brewing process, even though the portafilter is properly installed and snug. Helpful Hint: During slow times and at night, put your portafilters loosely back in the machine. This will insure longer gasket life.

Your *steaming wand tip* should also be removed and cleaned thoroughly on a weekly basis.

Your espresso machine will probably require a semi-annual tune-up

- Soak the wand tip in hot water and wipe clean with a dry towel.

- A Q-tip can be useful in cleaning the inside of the tip, and a needle or straight pin can be used to make sure that the steam holes in the tip are open and free of residues.

Beyond weekly maintenance, your espresso machine will probably require a quarterly or semi-annual tune-up by a qualified service technician. He can replace the gaskets in your group heads, calibrate your machine's brewing temperature and pump pressure, replace in-line water filters, and conduct a general check of all the other components in your machine.

- If you are in an area where the water contains a high mineral content, you may want to ask about having your machine's boiler de-limed.

- Your machine's gasket, which is contained in the valve that controls the flow of steam to the wand, will also become worn over time. If your machine's wand drips water, or leaks steam, your technician will need to install a new one.

Grinder maintenance

Daily maintenance of the grinder merely requires:

- A thorough external cleaning with a damp towel. It is important to dispose of any unused ground coffee that is left in the doser. This coffee will be unacceptable for your next day's use.

On a weekly basis you should:

- Remove all the coffee from your grinder, and brush clean any grounds remaining in the doser and the grinding chamber.

- Be sure to brush the burrs clean.

- Wipe the dosing and grinding chambers with a clean damp towel and then dry thoroughly.

- Remove the whole bean hopper and **wash in hot soapy water**. Rinse thoroughly and dry with a clean towel. Built up oils may become rancid if not periodically cleaned.

On a monthly basis we suggest that you remove the burrs from your grinder and scrub them with a brush in hot soapy water. Once again, rinse clean and dry thoroughly before reassembling.

Grinder burrs will become dull after extended use. Even though your naked eye may not be able to discern any difference in the ground coffee, the granules of ground coffee will not be consistent in size and shape. This will have a very negative effect upon the flavor of the finished shot of espresso. Depending on your business volume, you will want to replace your burrs once or twice a year.

General maintenance and sanitation

All utensils, thermometers, and steaming pitchers should be cleaned with hot soapy water, and rinsed thoroughly, on a daily basis or more often if necessary.

Drip Coffee Equipment and Accessory Maintenance

The same principles which are important to espresso equipment maintenance also apply to drip coffee equipment.

Drip brewers

On a daily basis:

- Clean your machine's brew basket to remove any coffee or flavor extract residues.

- You will also need to wipe clean any grounds and coffee splatters that have accumulated up around the brew head.

On a weekly basis:

- You may wish to soak this basket in water with the addition of an urn cleaner to remove any stubborn build-ups. Be sure to rinse thoroughly before using.

Periodically:

- You will want to check the showerhead to be sure that all the water holes are free of residues, and that it produces an even and unobstructed spray of water.

We suggest a *quarterly or semi-annual* visit from a qualified technician to check the brew temperature, water dispensing time, water diversion ratio, and the condition of your water filters.

Bulk bean grinders

The bean hopper and grinding components should be brushed and wiped clean *on a daily basis.*

Your grinder's burrs and the grinding chamber should be cleaned thoroughly on a weekly basis

Your grinder's burrs and the grinding chamber should be cleaned thoroughly *on a weekly basis.* Because your bulk grinder will typically process a large volume of coffee on a weekly basis, these components must be kept free of residues to maintain optimal coffee characteristics.

We suggest a thorough *daily* cleaning of the grinder you will use for processing flavored coffees. The extracts that have been sprayed on the beans will present an extra challenge in maintaining cleanliness.

As we emphasize in other chapters, always use a separate grinder or brew basket when processing flavored coffees. If you do not do this, these extracts will **contaminate** your unflavored coffees.

As with your espresso grinder, the burrs on your bulk grinders will need to be replaced *once or twice a year.*

Bulk bins, coffee pots, and cups

The oils from your roasted coffee beans will leave deposits inside your bulk bins. Your bulk bins should be emptied, washed with hot, soapy water, and thoroughly dried *at least once a month.* These oils are not only visually unattractive, but will become rancid, producing a negative effect on the flavor of the coffee beans.

Coffee pots need to be thoroughly washed at the end of each day

Glass coffee pots and thermal pots need to be emptied and thoroughly washed *at the end of each day.*

These pots, and their components, should be soaked in water containing an urn cleaner *once a week.* The internal parts of your thermal pump pots should be disassembled and scrubbed, inside and out, with brushes designed for their cleaning.

Ceramic coffee cups will tend to develop a film of residue after a period of time. Soaking these cups in a water-urn cleaner solution *over night* should remove these residues.

Always thoroughly rinse all equipment and accessories that have been cleaned with an urn cleaner or detergent.

Safety precautions

It is always important to remember that your espresso machine is a powerful piece of equipment that produces extreme temperatures under significant pressure.

Your drip brewer will produce temperatures of approximately 200° F.

Great care should be taken when extracting coffee, dispensing hot water and steaming milk, so as to avoid serious burn injuries.

Your grinders incorporate moving parts which are very sharp. Caution should be exercised to keep fingers, hair, clothing, and jewelry away from these moving components.

Be sure to ask a lot of questions regarding safety from the person selling you your equipment. Do additional research if necessary and pass along to your employees all the required instructions about how to operate each individual piece of equipment with maximum safety.

For more information on this specific subject, refer to the following books and videos from Bellissimo—800-655-3955.

- **Achieving Success in Specialty Coffee**
- **Espresso 101**

PART II- Getting Open

Contents

CHAPTER 15

Your Financial Resources

Contents

Chapter 15 Contents - Page 2

CHAPTER 15

Your Financial Resources

Your resources will determine your concept

Many times when someone is considering opening a coffee business, they overlook a key factor in the realization of their vision. They tell us about how they are going to open a large coffee bar, about how they are going to have entertainment, serve pastries, lunches, and sell home-brew accessories. They talk about the aggressive expansion plans they have for opening multi-units and then franchising their concept. More than anything else, what really determines *What kind?* and *How large?* and *How many?* is: *What financial resources do you have to work with?*

What financial resources do you have to work with?

People often start out with grandiose expectations. They do not focus sufficiently on establishing sound financial plans for their businesses.

So, rather than starting out by investing a lot of energy into pre-planning your business concept, the first thing you need to do is to determine—*How much money can I pull together?* —whether it be from your own bank account, leveraging against your home, getting it from family members who are willing to invest in your dream, or going to a lending institution and borrowing. You need to plan in accordance with the total amount of money you will have available to work with.

Another factor we will be discussing later in this chapter is that you cannot spend your entire budget on the initial opening. Once you open your doors, you will also need operating capital. If it turns out that your dreams are bigger than your pocketbook, do not give up and do not get discouraged.

...plan in accordance with the total amount of money you will have available to work with

If your ultimate goal is to own a nice sit-down coffee bar, but you do not have enough money to achieve that goal initially, it does not mean that you cannot go into the business. What it does mean is that you may have to start with a more modest plan; perhaps with a cart or kiosk operation. This will give you an opportunity to find out if you like the business. If you learn about the business, and can turn a profit, it will then be easier to go back to a bank and say, *"This is what I've done! Look at how successful I've been! Now I would like to borrow money because I want to open a beautiful, sit-down coffee bar!"*

Typical start-up costs for various concepts

Cart operation

Espresso carts are self-contained, stand-alone, coffee operations. Typically, they will include the espresso machine, a burr grinder, refrigeration, self-contained fresh water and waste water reservoirs, a hand-wash sink, and all the necessary water pumps, filters, heaters, electrical converters, circuitry and outlets to facilitate this equipment. In most cases, all that will be required for operation is a 220-volt power source, an approved source for fresh water, and a means for disposing of waste water.

Espresso carts are self-contained, stand-alone, coffee operations

Local health, fire, electrical, and plumbing codes are becoming increasingly critical of the components and specifications required for cart approval. For this reason, **we do not suggest that you consider fabricating your own cart.**

A cart operation may be composed of a single cart unit, or several units arranged in a configuration to provide additional space for a more extensive product offering. Brewed coffee, teas, juices, Italian sodas, baked goods and granitas are common items that might be sold from an espresso cart business. (See *Planning Your Menu—* Chapter 24)

Carts are available in a variety of sizes and materials. Like most things in life, you get what you pay for. Beware of those advertisements in magazines and various media offering: *"Special cart, with machine, at a ridiculously low price."*

Like most things in life, you get what you pay for

Start-up costs for a nice cart operation will probably approach $15,000 to $25,000. It is important to realize that it is going to take more than equipment to go into business. You will have to stock your shelves with inventory, secure permits, and establish workman's compensation and liability insurance.

If you are putting your cart in a location where there is no 220-volt electrical outlet, and the landlord is not willing to address this issue, you are going to have to pay for an electrician. Also, you will probably have some expenses for advertising, and as we mentioned, until you generate sufficient sales to break even, you will need operating capital to pay your bills.

Our own experience is probably typical. When we started our first cart operation, we had spent almost $20,000 by the time we opened for business, and the business was debt-servicing itself.

About bargain basement prices

If you purchase a bargain basement cart, and it will have to be moved daily for security purposes, make sure the cart will be strong enough to endure the punishment. Many carts are not designed for daily transport; they are made to stay in one place.

Do not buy a cart until you look at your venue and see how you are going to be using that cart. If the possibility of a permanent cart location exists, you may be able to have the cart designed so that it is lockable and never has to be moved. Everything will be dependent upon your particular venue and location.

The same caution should be exercised with the advertised "bargain-basement" espresso machine that will accompany your cart. Perhaps you had considered buying a $7,000 machine, and they say they will sell you a comparable one for $3,500. Pay attention! It may have two groups and a steam wand, but that may be where the similarities end. What is the size of the boiler? What is the recovery rate of the boiler to bring the water back up to temperature? What about a service network and the availability of parts?

If you are going to be at a fairly low-to-moderate location—say 75 to 100 cups a day—the bargain machine may be fine. But if you anticipate being in a location where you expect to do 200 to 400 cups a day, the bargain basement-machine may not keep up with your volume demands. In this case, you may be dissatisfied with the machine within a few months, and you may have to trade it in on a more expensive machine. You will probably "take a beating" on the trade-in.

Kiosk operation

In terms of start-up costs, a kiosk operation is usually the next step up from a cart operation.

A kiosk is a small to medium-sized coffee operation which is, or appears to be, more permanent than a cart. Kiosks can be open air or enclosed, and are usually multisided.

There are a variety of ways in which a kiosk can be configured to meet the desired need. It can be two- three- or four-sided, circular, with or without a roof, or soffited; the possibilities seem endless. The two

The obvious advantages to a kiosk are that it looks more permanent than a cart, and its appearance is more upscale

obvious advantages to a kiosk are that it looks more permanent than a cart, and its appearance is more upscale. A kiosk will also allow you to offer a much broader menu (granita, blender drinks, etc.).

If you are planning to be located in a mall, a performing arts center, or an airport, your operation may require a more professional and permanent appearance than a cart. You are probably looking at a minimum $25,000 to $60,000 price tag for a kiosk operation with the basic equipment. The price can go well beyond that, depending upon options such as choice of materials, lighting, security features, counter surfaces, type of finishes, food-service equipment (additional refrigeration, pastry cases, granita machines), and signage. All of these items are at additional cost.

Drive-thru operation

Drive-thru espresso operations are becoming increasingly popular, and good opportunities exist in many parts of the country for this venue. We are a busy society and fast-food chains have proven the viability of a quick service drive-thru operation. Many people do not have the time to brew coffee at home in the morning, so the option of purchasing a quality cup on their way to work is appealing.

A drive-thru operation can be free-standing, or a drive-thru window can be incorporated into an in-line espresso store, if conditions allow.

...fast-food chains have proven the viability of a quick service drive-thru operation

We see drive-thrus with equipment being advertised for as low as $25,000—but you are probably going to be getting something that is basically a prefabricated shed with a cart operation inside. Once again, you will get what you pay for. More realistically, there are some very beautiful drive-thru operations that are totally self-contained and equipped for about $50,000. It is not unusual for someone to invest $100,000 to $200,000 in a drive-thru operation.

...most of the manu-facturers of these units understand the specifi-cations typically required by health departments

Self-contained units have some advantages. Because they are prefabricated, a location can be established quickly, and if the location does not prove to be viable, the unit can be moved. Also, most of the manufacturers of these units understand the specifications typically required by health departments and other government agencies. (By *totally self-contained*, we mean a system that has both the fresh water tanks and the waste water tanks built into the unit.) You will still have to hand carry fresh water to fill the supply tanks, and the waste water will have to be drained into containers and dumped at an authorized commissary, or pumped into a truck that empties septic tanks.

It will cost significantly more if you want to hard plumb the unit with a water supply and a drain line connected to public utilities. Site development (the pouring of a concrete pad to place the unit on) and utility connections, can cost as much as $10,000, or more.

Another option in drive-thru structures is to custom build a permanent unit. The construction trade refers to this type of structure as "stick-built." It offers a permanent physical unit, built on a solid foundation, and connected to public utilities, that suits your exact purpose. Construction of this type of unit can range from $50,000 to $200,000, depending upon size, materials, location, equipment, and options (restrooms, outside seating areas, signs, etc.). If you choose this option, be sure your contractor is familiar with the requirements for a food-service facility.

...be sure your contractor is familiar with the requirements for a food-service facility

One option that should not be over looked are drive-thru units on wheels. These generally are nothing more than the self-contained units built on a trailer bed. The wheels can be skirted so they are not visible and it looks like a permanent drive-thru. What you often eliminate with this unit are certain building code considerations that permanent structures have to contend with. Different sets of codes typically apply to a unit that is mobile versus one that is stick-built and attached to a foundation. There can be huge advantages to this.

For example:

- If it is stick-built and permanent, the codes may require you to have a bathroom attached for your employees. You will have to factor in the cost of constructing a bathroom, not to mention the extra square feet that will be required, and the impact that may have on your lease rate or space limitations.

- The largest advantage is the ability to move the unit easily if you desire to change locations, or if you wish to move it for a day or a weekend to do a special event. With a unit on wheels, you have this flexibility.

If you are planning to open a drive-thru coffee operation, we highly recommend you purchase Bellissimo's *Opening a Specialty Coffee Drive-Thru*. Written as a companion piece to *Bean Business Basics*, this manual covers aspects of concept planning, location selection, drive-thru construction, bureaucratic considerations, and day-to-day operations. Includes estimated start-up costs. Like all other Bellissimo publications, *Opening a Specialty Coffee Drive-Thru* is teeming with valuable business insight.

Mobile operation

Since we were just talking about the advantage of having a concept on wheels, another concept to consider is the mobile espresso operation. This is a business where you take the product to your customers, rather than having your customers come to you for the product.

...ask for an exclusive contract

Mobile operations are self-contained operations built in, or towed behind, a vehicle. A number of companies build these. The prices usually start around that of a lower-end drive-thru; probably in the $30,000-$80,000 range.

We have seen some trucks outfitted similarly to a catering truck, where the sides roll up and the espresso machines are serviced by an operator standing outside. Another option is an outfitted truck or trailer where the operator remains inside the vehicle (and protected from the elements).

Business parks, factories, construction sites, schools, and special events are all prime locations for a mobile espresso unit. Be aware that many times mobile catering businesses may sign an exclusive contract to provide services to these locations, so check with the appropriate authorities to see if your services are welcome, and if they are, ask for an exclusive contract yourself.

In-line (storefront) coffee café

The term In-line refers to an espresso coffee café

The term *In-line* refers to a specialty coffee café.

...we tell our clients that in this business, small is beautiful!

Typically, we tell our clients that in this business, small is beautiful!

Even in a café situation, a good percentage of your clientele are going to walk in, buy a beverage and be on their way back to the office, or wherever they are going. So it is not necessary—except perhaps in some venues—to have a shop that is several thousand square feet. Remember, the larger your space, the larger your rent payment. The extra $2,000 a month that you are not paying in rent will go directly to the bottom line.

We typically tell people: *Look for a space that is 1,000 to 1,500 square feet—even as little as 600 to 800 square feet could work if the population mass is present and the conditions are right.*

A wide variety to choose from

When it comes to in-line cafés, there is a lot of variety to choose from. There are specialty coffee shops that strictly sell coffee, and perhaps some bagels and scones on the side. Other venues serve light lunches and/or light breakfasts and add specialty drinks and foods to their menu.

As we discuss in detail in later chapters, you will likely want to avoid a concept and menu items that will require the incorporation of a full-blown kitchen—unless you have deep pockets and a lot of food-service experience. When you start adding in kitchen exhaust systems, with built-in fire suppression, you are looking at a significant expense. You can estimate that for each linear foot of exhaust hood length, it is going to cost you $1,000. So if you will need a 10-foot hood system over your kitchen equipment, you are looking at a minimum additional investment of $10,000.

There are many different food items that you can serve without a full-blown kitchen—and we will be talking about some of them in the section on "Planning Your Menu."

$75,000 and up

We usually tell people not to consider an in-line espresso bar of any size with sit-down seating for less than $75,000 to $100,000. It can possibly be done for less, but it will be a challenge, especially from the respect of aesthetic appeal. It is not unusual to spend to $250,000 on a very high-end operation.

Perhaps you can put a small espresso bar together for $50,000-$60,000, but only if the space that you are moving into is in pristine condition and you are not going to have to pay for a lot of tenant improvements. If you need to replace wall surfaces, floors, build partitions, and add a restroom, your costs will be much higher. In addition, if the landlord is unwilling to provide any leasehold improvements—new flooring, new walls, plumbing, electricity—your costs will increase exponentially.

You will find that every situation is different, and you need to have realistic ideas of what each of these different venues is going to cost, right from the very beginning. Do your homework and price-out building and equipment costs carefully!

Opening & operating capital

As we touched on earlier, when you are putting together a food-service operation, the one thing that you have to allow for is your need for operating capital.

You have to realize that it will likely take you 60, 90, or 180 days to turn the corner to where you are actually making a profit. Probably the biggest single mistake that people going into the food-service industry make, is: *They spend all their money getting the doors open, and then do not have any left to pay for their operating expenses during the first few months of operation.*

Take about one-third of the money you are planning to spend on your investment and set that aside for operating capital

Our rule of thumb:

- Take about one-third of the money you are planning to spend on your investment and set that aside for operating capital. Typically, $25,000 to $50,000 will provide a sufficient buffer.

And, perhaps more importantly, you should be able to:

- Project your estimated expenses on a monthly basis, and what you think your income is going to be.

- Set aside enough money so that if you have to buy all your food items and pay the rent with no outside financial help, you will be covered for your first three or four months, minimum.

Keep in mind that all of your costs are going to be at their highest in the very beginning of your operation; especially your marketing and advertising costs. That is because you have to get people through your door for the first time. So, where normally in your second and third year you may plan on an advertising budget of 5% of your total sales, your advertising expenditure may be 10% to 20% during the first six months.

arrive at a bottom line figure of what you think it will cost to get open, then multiply that figure by about 150 percent

Just getting your doors open involves many hidden and unexpected costs. We always tell people that in planning your operation, you need to *estimate carefully.* When you plan out everything meticulously, and you arrive at a bottom line figure of what you think it will cost to get open, then multiply that figure by about 150 percent and you are probably going to be pretty close. You may think this is an exaggeration, but keep track of what you actually spend versus what you thought you might spend, and you will be happy that you took this statement seriously.

You will be amazed at how many incidental expenses are going to sprout up in the opening process that you had never thought of. Altogether, they will consume a sizeable amount of money.

Where & how to find money

First of all, you obviously have to see how much money you can put together yourself. Typically, if you are not willing to invest any of your own dollars, you will have difficulty raising capital. We can not imagine anybody wanting to contribute to your project if you do not have the confidence to risk any of your own hard-raised capital. So, obviously, there is your own money first. As for the rest, you have several options.

You will need a business plan

No matter which option you choose to resource your start-up capital, you will need to prepare and present a well-thought-out business plan to potential lenders. (See Chapter 19 for detailed information and instructions.)

In brief, there are basically two types of business plans that we create for our clients:

The first is a *Conceptual Presentation Plan.* It is usually 10-30 pages in length and basically describes the business concept, the products, the principals (owners & key management), the target market, etc. It contains no financial projections or statements, and is primarily used to convince landlords and property managers that you have an appealing, positive, business concept, and that you are interested in negotiating a lease for available space.

The second type of business plan is a *Full Financial Business Plan.* This is what you will need to borrow money from a lending institution, or

Everyone who opens a retail business should have a Full Financial Business Plan

to entice investors to lend you money. This type of plan can consist of 15 to 20 pages of information. The *Full Financial Business Plan* can contain all of the elements of the *Conceptual Presentation Plan*, but typically goes into depth on what the total cost of the project will be, when the business will turn a profit, and what level of return can be expected.

Everyone who opens a retail business should have a *Full Financial Business Plan* completed before they open. The extensive research necessary to project all expenses, and to estimate sales and profitability, is essential to gaining a basic understanding of the financial operation of your business. Setting menu prices, establishing cost of sales and expense budgets, creating sales goals—the importance of each of these management functions can only be appreciated when understood individually, and how each relates to the overall financial statement.

Banks and Savings & Loans

There are lending institutions like banks or savings & loans that you might want to investigate. You will need to test the water early before you count on your banker to lend you the money.

Over 95% of all new food service operations will go out of business before 24 months

If you go to a bank with no previous business experience, and no food-service experience, and you are hoping to borrow money, you could be in for a rude awakening. Even with experience in both of those areas, but without substantial collateral to secure the loan, you may find an uphill battle. Oftentimes, lending institutions are not eager to lend money for the creation of a food-service operation. This is probably due to the grim statistic: 95%+ of all new food-service operations will go out of business before 24 months! This statistic is based primarily on full-service restaurants.

Specialty coffee businesses are typically easier to operate and have more generous margins. However, all the details that need to be attended to and controlled for a full-service restaurant, also exist in the most simple coffee operation. That is why we have created this manual; to help you beat the odds!

Finding your personal banker

Even if your bank will not lend you money for your business start-up, you should plan on finding your own personal banker to assist you as a financial resource and advisor. Perhaps you already know someone in your bank—a loan officer, a customer-service rep, a branch manager—who you trust and feel comfortable with. If not, then check around, ask for recommendations, do some interviewing.

Look for a banker who:

- is someone in whom you feel confidence and have a rapport;

- takes the time to understand your business plans and needs; and

- is willing to work with you and your business on an ongoing basis.

There are many advantages to selecting your own personal banker, and developing a shared understanding of where your business is headed. Some advantages, are:

- having a single point-of-contact for all of your banking needs, including: business accounts, loans, personal accounts, and credit lines;

- having ready access to financial advice and counsel from an expert who already has all the information she or he needs about you and your business; and

- getting valuable assistance in making connections with other small business owners.

Developing rapport and exchanging ideas with your own personal banker, who is on board as a member of your management team, can benefit your business in many ways, both in the short and long-term.

Other lending institutions

Check out the Small Business Administration

In addition to your bank and savings and loan, check out the Small Business Administration. The SBA will not typically lend you money, but they can guarantee loans made to you by a private institution.

Also, there are lending programs available to select categories of borrowers. If you are a military veteran, a woman and/or a member of a select minority, there may be government programs that you can look to for financial backing.

Your family

Finally, we come to family, which has both up and down sides.

One word of caution when it comes to family. If they tell you they will help you with a financial investment, make sure they are committed to keeping that promise. Did they discuss it with their spouse? Are they taking you seriously, or do they believe you will never get far enough with your project to actually ask them for the money?

A Case in Point

Let us relate to you a sad story.

A while back, we provided consulting services for a man and his wife who were determined to open a small espresso café on the East Coast. They were about the nicest and most dedicated people you would ever meet.

After months of searching, they found a beautiful little café at a major crossroad in their community that was available for lease. They remodeled the building, doing everything right, and opened their doors for business.

Several months after they had opened, we called to see how things were going, confident that they would be enjoying tremendous success. To our surprise there was no answer at their café, and, in fact, a recording said: "The number you have called has been disconnected, or is no longer in service." We called their home phone number to see what had happened. They related to us what had gone wrong.

It seems that our client's brother had, from the beginning, promised to invest $30,000 in the business, and work as a partner once the café was open. When the doors were finally opened for business, he backed out on his word, leaving our clients with no operating capital and short one key manager. Our clients found themselves working 70-hour weeks, with no days off, and without sufficient capital to market their business, or to cover their bills until they could turn the corner to profitability.

Leasing, partnering and creative financing

Leasing companies

There are leasing companies that will loan on espresso equipment, food-service equipment and furnishings. You want a lease with a buy-out at the end. This will allow you to get into the business with a smaller amount of up-front capital. Typically, the leasing company will require a down payment of approximately 20% of the value of the equipment. Unfortunately, lease interest rates have climbed significantly over the past several years, so you will want to weigh the lease option against traditional bank financing. Frequently, the buy-out is only a penny (or at most, a very nominal amount). Leasing companies, typically, do not want to take their equipment back at the end of the lease. In a leasing arrangement, you will have a monthly lease payment that will come out of your operational revenue, but at least you will not be spending all of your investment capital up front.

There are leasing companies that will loan on espresso equipment

Remember that leasing companies—and banks for that matter—will generally loan only on equipment that has some residual value, *i.e.*, equipment that, should you default, can be seized and auctioned off. In this situation, the leasing company stands a good chance of getting some of its money back.

If you do not have substantial collateral, a leasing company will not lease on—and a bank will not lend money on—inventory or capital improvements that you are investing into the landlord's building. If you are replacing floors and ceilings, the leasing company or lending institution know they cannot get any money back from the sale of those items because they have become fixtures of the building.

If you have a small amount of your own capital to work with, and you are looking to borrow money through a lease or a bank loan, plan on the lease money or bank loan going for the hard equipment. Save your own money for the build-out, inventory, and operating capital.

Partnering

If you are borrowing money from another individual, you will generally have two options:

1. You may have to promise a fairly healthy rate of interest and provide the security that you are going to make the payments; or

2. You can involve someone as a partner.

If you choose to involve your lender as a partner, you will have to make the decision up front as to, what kind of partner?

- If you do not want your lender to be on-site, sharing the workload with you, and "dabbling" his fingers in your operation, then you want him to be *a silent partner.*

- If he is working the business with you, obviously you want him to be *a working partner.*

- If your financial backer is a rich attorney or doctor, and feels that coffee is a viable business, and is willing to put up some of their hard-earned money to help you with your business, then they likely will be a silent partner.

You will have to decide: *What percentage of the business are you willing to give to these people?* If it is a 50-50 partnership, and you are the one who understands the industry and have done all the research, are you going to retain the control necessary to make the decisions that will determine the success of the business?

In our opinion: *If it is your concept, you always need to have the controlling interest in your future.*

If it is your concept, you always need to have the controlling interest in your future.

If it is a venture on which you have done the research and your partner knows nothing about the business, then you want to make it very clear that you are going to make the operational decisions and they are not going to be involved in the day-to-day operation. The last thing you want is somebody who has no idea of how a coffee business is run, telling you how to run your business.

It is a good idea to sit down with your partners and listen to their ideas! Obviously, they have invested money and have a vital interest. The state of the business and of their investment may well create some stress in their minds. Sharing information by honest communication can alleviate their concerns about the viability of the business, or about whether they are going to get their money back. As partners, they need to know exactly what you are doing, so they can feel confident that everything possible is being done to build the business and make it prosper. Put your arrangement on paper and get your attorney involved.

In addition, you have to decide: *What percent of the profit is your partner going to be paid?* And you have to decide: *For how long?* Is it for the life of the business? Is it for a period of time until the loan is paid off, plus x-amount after that? All of these are important issues that need to be decided up front.

A final caution

It is a good idea to sit down with your partners and listen to their ideas

When you are considering giving somebody a percentage, you should always be offering *a percentage of the net profit,* and not *a percentage of the gross sales.*

You want to make sure that if your business is operating below a break-even point, you are not having to make up the additional dollars out of your pocket every month. This will mean a little more work on your part because you will have to generate profit and loss statements, and have your books open so your partners can examine the numbers whenever they want. But at the same time, it is going to assure you that if you are not making any money, you are not going to have to pay out additional money to your partner.

For more information on this specific subject, refer to the following books from Bellissimo—800-655-3955.

- **Achieving Success in Specialty Coffee**
- **Opening a Specialty Coffee Drive-thru**

Start-up Cost Estimates

Seminars/Trade Shows/Educational Materials	$	
Legal and Professional Services		
Accountant	$	
Attorney	$	
Consultant	$	
Commercial Realtor	$	
Utilities	$	
Pre-opening Lease Payments and Deposits	$	
Remodeling		
Architect	$	
General Contractor	$	
Carpentry	$	
Plumbing	$	
Electrical	$	
Cabinetry	$	
Floor/Wall Coverings	$	
Painting	$	
Signage	$	
Licenses and Permits	$	
Insurance	$	
Food Service Equipment	$	
Small Wares	$	
Opening Advertising	$	
Beginning Inventory	$	
Unanticipated Expenses (30%)	$	
TOTAL ESTIMATED COSTS	$	

Chapter 15 Check List

Financial Resources (potential sources for capital)

Personal	$_____
Family/Friends	_____
Investors/Partners	_____
Lending Institutions	_____
S.B.A. Guarantee	_____
TOTAL	$_____

Total X .33 = Operating Reserve	$_____
Total X .67 = Start-up Capital	$_____

Concept Selection (as determined by available start-up capital)

_____ $15,000 to $25,000 Cart operation

_____ $25,000 to $60,000 Kiosk operation

_____ $40,000 to $100,000 Drive-thru or Mobile operation

_____ $100,000 to $200,000+ Espresso bar/Specialty coffee store

Preparation for securing finances

_____ Prepare Full Financial Business plan (see chapter 19 & 37)

Estimate start-up costs:

_____ Remodel (see chapter 23)

_____ Equipment (see chapter 25)

_____ Inventory (see chapters 24 & 26)

_____ Permits (see chapter 21)

_____ Investigate possibility of bank/lending institution financing

_____ Investigate possibility of leasing equipment

CHAPTER 16

To Franchise Or Not To Franchise

Contents

CHAPTER 16

To Franchise Or Not To Franchise

What is franchising?

Franchising is basically buying, lock stock and barrel, a concept that someone else has created rather than creating your own concept.

It is purchasing someone else's business idea, their operational expertise, and the use of their name.

In this chapter we are going to talk about the advantages and disadvantages of franchising.

Advantages Of Franchising

We can think of at least seven possible advantages of buying a franchise, as opposed to going it alone. These are:

- Name recognition

- Proven record of success

- Buying power

- Established products, menus and operational systems

- Ongoing Corporate support

- Networking with other franchisees, and

- Benefiting from corporate-based advertising

• *Name recognition*

The first advantage you are buying with your franchise is name recognition.

Especially outside the coffee world, if you have the money to buy a McDonald's, Subway or Domino's—or any other franchise that has an established name nationwide—your chances of success are usually greater than opening your own fast-food hamburger, sub, or pizza store.

Be sure to find out if the franchise you are considering has good name recognition.

• *Proven record of success*

Some companies that offer franchises have successfully opened and operated multiple units. In some cases you may be reassured that at least their concept has worked consistently in numerous markets, and that the systems they have developed created profitability. You are not buying an unknown quantity.

• *Buying power*

Another advantage can be buying power.

Generally, franchises have established national contracts with distributors of equipment, coffees, groceries, paper goods, etc. Because all the franchisees combined purchase a significant quantity of product, their collective buying power allows the parent company to negotiate prices based upon volume discounts. Compare the prices you would pay for products bought from the chain with what you would pay for them on your own.

• *Established products, menus, and operational systems*

Set menu prices and specified products or recipes that have proven to be successful have been developed and properly tested. Operational controls and systems that are necessary for the profitable day-to-day operation of the business may be part of your package.

• *Ongoing corporate support*

Ongoing corporate support might start with the franchiser assisting you with a number of the pre-opening activities, such as:

- *finding a good location,*

- *helping with negotiations of your lease,*

- *assisting you with your store design,*

- *making your equipment purchases painless (from a time standpoint),*

- *providing initial employee training,*

- *showing you proper merchandising methods, and*

- *teaching your managers various operational systems.*

If the chain is established and has a successful track record, these services could be very advantageous to someone who has never been involved in a start-up before, or who has no previous experience in the specialty coffee business.

Some level of ongoing support will usually be available after you have opened for business. If you are challenged with problems, there may be someone you can call who has dealt with similar problems themselves. They may be able to suggest solutions to help solve these problems.

•*Networking with other franchisees*

Having your own franchise often allows you to network with other like franchisees with whom you can share ideas. You might find out how they have overcome particular operational challenges, what promotions they have run that have worked well for them, and so forth.

Fellow franchisees are usually more willing to share information because you are not competing with them as an independent operator. It is often to their advantage for you to do well, inasmuch as you are part of the same team.

•*Benefiting from corporate-based advertising*

Part of the corporate support they may be offering you will be advertising.

In certain situations or locations, the corporate headquarters may be able to buy large blocks of advertising, using co-op money to purchase ads that you would never be able to afford as an independent operator of a single store.

They might have their own graphic artists produce print-ready ads that can be inserted into your local papers, so you do not have to be involved in the formatting and graphic production.

They might also have 15- or 30-second radio or television spots for special or seasonal promotions. If you go into a McDonald's or Subway you will see point-of-sales advertising reinforcing their current media promotions. A good franchiser should provide you with these types of ongoing support materials. Please note that only a few truly national franchises can assist in the aforementioned programs.

Disadvantages Of Franchising

Numerically, we can count as many disadvantages to franchising as we can count advantages. The major disadvantages that we see, are:

• *Up-front costs PLUS a monthly percentage of your income*

Up-front costs can be quite large

The first disadvantage of franchising is the up-front costs. The up-front costs can be quite large— and you will usually pay a percentage of your gross profit on a monthly basis.

Generally, the average purchase price for many of the franchise packages we have looked at is in the $25,000 to $50,000 range, but this will usually only include the use of their name, access to their vendors, operational systems, and usually some form of ongoing support.

If your net profit averages 15% to 20%, and you are paying 6% right off the top, you may be giving away 1/3 to 1/2 of what you have earned

Twenty-five thousand dollars to $50,000 is certainly not the turnkey price for these types of operations. You may still have to locate a space, pay for the remodel, buy the equipment, purchase the inventory, make your monthly lease payment, and pay a percentage of your monthly gross sales as a franchise fee.

When you are giving away a significant portion of your gross income, as opposed to a portion of your net profit, you are facing a situation which you must evaluate very carefully.

You need to consider that your franchiser may not care if you are making money or not. If your net profit averages 15% to 20%, and you are paying 6% right off the top, you may be giving away almost a third to a half of what you have earned. So you really have to ask,

What kind of support am I really getting on a monthly basis that justifies paying this monthly franchise fee, PLUS a significant amount of money up front to get my doors open?

•*Name recognition is not always a plus*

We talked about name recognition (if it exists) being the strength of a franchise, but it can also be a disadvantage. Consider your dilemma if other franchisees are not doing well or are not giving the corporate name a good image; name recognition can be a big disadvantage. The disadvantage can be monumental if your particular franchise gets a bad name should something major happen.

A good example of something major happening was the E-coli outbreak experienced by a well-known hamburger chain a couple of years ago. If the food is mishandled in a store in California, and people get sick or die as a result, your business will surely be affected, even if your business is 3,000 miles away.

Another key point about name recognition: When we look at the coffee industry we can only think of one company that has what we would consider *excellent national name recognition*, and of course, *they do not franchise!*

By *excellent national name recognition* we mean that if you go out on the street and ask 100 people, *Have you ever heard of XYZ Coffee Co.?* a large percentage will tell you *Yes.* If a large percentage tell you *No*...then what are you paying for?

You may be paying a lot of money for something that is not going to give you the name recognition you might attain with a franchise from some of the well-known fast-food chains or national franchises of other industries.

•*Beware of questionable franchisers*

We have come across a lot of franchises we do not feel good about.

There are a lot of people out there in the franchise world who are taking advantage of the growing specialty coffee industry. They have seen the fastest way to create money in the coffee business is to put other people into the business and make money from their efforts. In many cases, we have seen that these franchisers are not as reputable as you may think they are. The value of what they have to offer may be quite questionable. So, you have to ask a lot of intelligent questions, do your homework and investigate any offering carefully.

You have to ask a lot of intelligent questions and do your homework

We know of one fast-food chain that, in the name of profitability, would sell a franchise to almost anybody. They sold a franchise three blocks away from one of their existing franchises. The two franchisees were in direct competition with one another.

Another question:

> *What if this corporate franchise falls on hard financial times, and they are just trying to survive themselves?*

The support might diminish. They might start making some poor short-term decisions. If you are locked into buying coffee from them, they may go to a lower grade of coffee and still charge you the same price per pound. Suddenly, you do not have the quality of product you once had.

These are all things to be concerned about in buying a franchise.

• *Lack of flexibility and no freedom to make decisions*

We were recently at a coffee trade show in California when two women came into our booth and asked questions about our consulting services. At the end of 20 minutes or so, one woman turned to the other and said, *Helen, why couldn't we have met this company three years ago?*

We asked, *What does that mean? Are you already in the coffee business?*

She answered, *Yes we are. We bought an XYZ franchise.*

XYZ (not the real name) happens to be a franchise we know well, and is one that we considered to be one of the better franchises.

We asked, *You haven't been happy with that decision? Was it the size of the up-front fee?*

Her response was that the up-front fee was not the problem (although they thought it was high) but a number of other issues were.

> *We went into a mall and there were two size shops that were available. One was around a 1,000 square feet, and one was about 1,800 square feet. The franchiser convinced us that we needed 1,800 square feet for our shop. We now know that the smaller space would have been much better.*

Secondly, the franchiser insisted that they carry a large line of the franchiser's retail items. She told us,

> *Many of those retail items don't sell well, but we're locked in and we have to stock them. We've wanted to cut back on this retail space and put in more seating,...but they wouldn't allow us to do that. We really don't feel that we have any control over our lives with this franchise.*

On top of everything else, the franchise takes 6% off her bottom line.

> *That's our paychecks! We're not very happy that we went the franchise route. We know now it was a huge mistake.*

We are not suggesting that everyone who buys a coffee franchise is unhappy. There are certainly other people who can give you success stories and will tell you how happy they are with their franchise situations. However, we believe it is important to relate what these women experienced, and reinforce the importance of doing thorough research and investigation before you make a very expensive decision.

The Alternative to Franchising

We could never own a franchise.

We want the freedom and creativity to run our own business, and to make all our own decisions.

We have more confidence in our abilities to determine our destiny, than we have in someone sitting in a corporate office a 1,000 miles away.

But there are a lot of people who do not have the entrepreneurial spirit or self-confidence to feel this way...and perhaps you are one of them.

However, if you have some confidence that you can run your own business, if you are a quick learner, then a great alternative to franchising is to find a qualified consultant.

As consultants, we believe that we offer many of the advantages of franchising without the disadvantages. We cannot offer the name recognition, or the buying power of a franchise, but we, and other competent consultants, offer a wide range of valuable help, such as:

- assisting in development of a sound concept, determining start-up costs and viability of the proposed business

- developing a business plan for presentation to landlords and lending institutions

- assisting with site selection

- creating an ergonomic space design

- sourcing quality equipment

- choosing coffee and food vendors

- setting up your operating systems

- hiring and training your employees

- developing a marketing plan

A good consultant can also provide you with ongoing support.

We have many clients who have been open for many years and who still call us for advice when they need it.

Regardless of whether you decide to franchise, open a business on your own, or use a consultant for help, the important point is that you need to carefully investigate and consider all the advantages and disadvantages of each—before you make your decision.

Chapter 16 Check List

Franchise Cost Considerations:

Cost for franchise $_____

Monthly franchise fee   _____%

Other estimated expenses:

       Remodel $_____

       Equipment purchases   _____

       Inventory purchases   _____

       Operating capital reserve   _____

TOTAL up-front capital needed $_____

Franchise Support Considerations:

_____ Will they help you find a location?

_____ Will they be flexible in regards to the square feet they will require you to lease?

_____ Will they help you negotiate a lease?

_____ Will they help you assess the realistic sales potential of your proposed location, and estimate accurate operating costs, so that you may evaluate the location's potential before you enter into the lease agreement?

_____ Will they provide you with design services or assistance for the remodel of your space?

_____ Will they help you source reputable contractors who will perform the needed services in a timely fashion at a competitive price?

_____ Will they help you purchase your fixtures, equipment, and furnishings, and will they guarantee you a better price than you could achieve on your own?

_____ Will they help you select vendors of quality products and assist you in placing your opening orders?

_____ Will someone help you with equipment installation and product merchandising?

_____ Will they help you with staff hiring?

_____ Will they help you with staff training?

_____ Will they provide you with all the necessary operating forms and systems, and will they teach you how to use them?

_____ Will they help you to produce a full set of financials at the end of your first month of business?

_____ If you are not producing a sufficient level of sales and/or profitability after 60 to 90 days, will they send someone out to evaluate your operation and lend assistance?

_____ Will they provide you with marketing support? If yes, what kind?

_____

_____

_____ Do they provide ongoing phone support?

_____ Do they provide semi-annual or annual business development training or educational seminars?

Franchiser Flexibility and Stability Considerations:

_____ Will they let you sell your franchise operation should you desire?

_____ Will they let you bring in additional products?

_____ Will they let you eliminate products if they do not sell?

_____ Can you modify your menu selections?

_____ Can you add more seating?

_____ Can you change vendors if the quality of products are equal or better?

_____ Will they provide you with a detailed corporate financial performa?

_____ Will they provide you with actual financial performas of their franchisees in similar markets? (If you are in rural America it will not be useful to compare your market potential to a cumulative franchisee performa if it includes franchises in Manhattan, N.Y., and downtown Chicago.)

_____ How many franchises have they sold to date, and how many are still in operation?

_____ How many franchises did they sell last year?

_____ Are they a member of the Better Business Bureau, and what does the Bureau say about them?

_____ Are there any complaints filed against this company with the Attorney General's Office of the state where their corporate offices are located?

_____ Has this company been written about by any national business periodicals, and what have they said about them?

_____ Does this company offer stock, and what has the history of their stock's performance been?

CHAPTER 17

Creating a Paper Trail

Contents

CHAPTER 17

Creating a Paper Trail

The importance of early record keeping

From our experience, what has really become evident when creating a new business is that when you first start writing down your ideas, making phone calls, and conducting your basic research, you must keep good records.

You must keep good records

We will get into the details of record keeping in Chapter 34, but the point that needs to be made is that you must begin your record-keeping process early, at the very beginning stages of your planning.

Your initial records do not have to be complex. Use a spiral notebook to keep **all** your notes in one place, so when you need to go back and look for something, you will know where to find it.

Keep all your notes in one place

If you make notes on multiple legal pads, sticky notes, the backs of envelopes, or on anything else that is handy to write on, the information will get lost, or be harder to retrieve. That important name or phone number of the person you talked to six months ago will be somewhere other than where you are looking for it. You will waste vast amounts of time and become extremely frustrated in the process.

Writing down and preserving your early notes and memos in an organized fashion is very important.

Keeping accurate records is also very important from an accounting standpoint. Obviously, there are going to be initial costs in setting up your business, and some costs may begin in the very early planning stages—phones calls for information about equipment, about available training seminars, or calls to various people in the industry.

Your accountant will probably tell you that many of those initial costs are tax deductions and you will want to keep an accurate record of them. You do not want to be paying avoidable taxes on money you spend for the research that was necessary to launch your business. If the IRS should ever conduct an audit, your record of all those early expenses will support you.

Getting organized

Do not mix your personal finance with your business

The first and most important rule is: *Do not mix your personal finance with your business.* We suggest that you open a separate bank account reserved strictly for business related expenses. You do not need to deposit a large amount of money into this account initially, but as needed, you should transfer the necessary funds from your personal account into this business account. This will minimize the chances of intermingling and confusing your personal finances with your business finances.

It is important, right from the very beginning, that you make an investment for a file cabinet for your business records or, at the very least, for a box which will hold hanging files.

The paper trail involves more than just keeping notes. It also requires that you do the following:

- Hold on to all those early invoices, receipts, and paid bills.

- Set up file folders for categories like *Receipts, Phone Contacts, Initial Plans, Resources* (such as equipment dealers).

- Develop the habit of filing and storing all of this information on a regular basis, so you can find it when you need it. If you cannot find the notes and information from your previous research, you will incur extra work and phone calls to obtain the information a second time.

- Take notes when people are quoting you prices on equipment, or lease rates for potential locations. Log the name of the person you are speaking with, and take detailed notes of your conversation.

- Note taking is especially important if you are talking to city or county employees. Once again, take names and write down what they tell you over the phone. It is a good idea to take your tape recorder with you if you are talking with someone from one of these agencies in person.

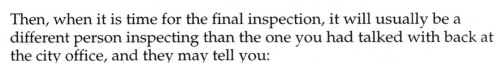

As we will be discussing in detail in Chapter 21, we have often found that when dealing with city and county officials, no one wants to take responsibility. It is difficult to find the person who has the authority to give you the permission you request. It has been our experience that many government employees love to talk in generalities. If you are not careful, your interactions could result in a conversation like this:

> *Well, I don't really see a problem with what you are proposing, I think you can do that.*

Then, when it is time for the final inspection, it will usually be a different person inspecting than the one you had talked with back at the city office, and they may tell you:

> *You can't do that.*

And, when you say:

> *Wait a minute! They told me at the office that I could!*

They will say:

> *Who told you that?*

At this point, you are going to have problems if you find yourself in the position of having to say:

Oh! ...well, I don't remember his name. I don't think I wrote it down.

You want to protect yourself by being organized and keeping accurate records of all your business contacts, from the very beginning.

Computer bookkeeping systems

In this day and age, there are many excellent computer bookkeeping systems available to choose from. Any one of the more popular software programs will do the job. A few of the better ones are: *Quick Books Pro, Mind Your Own Business (M.Y.O.B.)* , and *Peach Tree.*

If you already have a computer and know how to operate it, go down and talk to your computer software salesman for some advice and a demonstration. (If you are still somewhat out of the loop computer-wise, you will have to start further back to obtain some initial training.)

The real advantage of computer bookkeeping is the instant access to information

It will be helpful if you can find a salesperson who has some accounting software experience. Tell them what accounting functions you will need to perform in your business (recording and tracking sales data by category, day, week and month; logging invoices; tracking payables, etc.), and they should be able to direct you to the program/s that will be right for you.

The time to start becoming familiar with your accounting program is at the very beginning. Take a class at your local community college or a computer store that will teach you how to use your accounting software program. Then, before you open your doors for business, you can do a dry-run on your anticipated business with your computer. Practice recording expenses and deposits, and generate a sample profit and loss statement of your initial preopening financial activities. With some practice, you should become familiar with your accounting program before you open for business.

We cannot over emphasize the importance of learning to use your software accounting prior to opening. Once you are operating, your time will be consumed with the details of running your business. You will be overwhelmed if you try to learn how to run a computerized accounting system simultaneously.

The real advantage of computer bookkeeping is the instant access to information. Also, when you get to the end of the year, you can accumulate and print out all your financial data for that year. You will not have to spend countless hours trying to calculate data and reconcile balances. Computer bookkeeping will simplify that end of-the-year nightmare of preparing materials for taxes.

Most of these accounting software programs will offer versions with *Payroll* capabilities. Once you have entered the pertinent information for each employee (wage rate, exemptions, etc.), you simply need to enter the hours they have worked for a specific period, and the program calculates all the deductions and provides a net payment amount. Payroll can be very time consuming without such a program.

When it comes to producing financial reports on a monthly basis, timeliness is a major advantage in controlling costs. You should strive to assess your business performance for a particular month within 24 to 48 hours after the conclusion of that month. If it takes three weeks to obtain this information, it will be of little use for impacting problems and improving the financial performance of your present month.

You need to be able to react quickly if you are to make timely corrections in performance. Having the necessary information on computer will certainly quicken the financial analysis process.

Chapter 17 Check List

Setting Up Your Office

____ Purchase one spiral notebook for all your notes

____ Purchase a file cabinet or a box with hanging file folders

Set-up files for:

____ Receipts and paid bills

____ Product brochures for equipment and furnishings

____ Product brochures for food items

____ Recipes and menus

____ Product and services price quotes

____ Start-up cost calculations, and business performance estimates

____ Resources and phone contacts

____ Seminar and trade show information

____ County and city information—codes, permits, traffic counts, etc.

____ Coffee bar designs, sketches of ideas, etc.

____ Project check lists

Checking Account

____ Open a separate checking account for your pre-opening business activities.

Selecting a Computer Accounting Program

____ Conduct research with your computer software store's professional or a
computer accounting consultant as to which program might be best for you.

____ Determine if your present computer will have sufficient capacity and features
to operate the desired program.

____ Purchase an accounting program and begin to work with it by entering your
pre-opening financial activities.

CHAPTER 18

Getting Help From Professionals

Contents

CHAPTER 18

Getting Help From Professionals

Professionals can help you achieve your business dreams and goals

No matter who you are, and how much experience you possess, it is highly unlikely that you will succeed or maximize your level of success in the specialty coffee industry without the help of some very important professionals. You need to have a strong partnership between yourself and all the professionals on your team. Everyone needs to work together to formulate the strongest possible program for your business. In this chapter we look at how professionals can help you achieve your business dreams and goals.

Consultants to the specialty coffee industry

Consultants to the specialty coffee business, like ourselves at Bellissimo, provide you with an opportunity to learn from our mistakes, successes, and real-life experiences with hundreds of clients. Good consultants can provide you with valuable information. For example, they often know who in our industry is honest, and

179

who is not. Who is proficient and professional at what they do, and who is not. Which manufacturers have good reputations for producing dependable equipment, and providing excellent service, and those that do not. A good consultant can also help you find those companies that produce the highest quality food products, with proven consumer acceptance.

If you are a newcomer to this business, your lack of information may cause you to make some very bad business decisions. Consultants, with their knowledge and expertise, can guide you through the building, learning, and growth processes of your new business.

Using professionals offers another important benefit: They can provide you with objective advice.

Your emotions will tend to sway your best judgment

You have a passionate vision in your mind of your desired business. You can imagine your coffee bar in vivid detail, the multitudes of customers you will be serving, the smells of the fresh baked pastries and coffee brewing, the music that you will have playing—you are emotionally involved with your dream. Your emotions may tend to sway your best judgment.

The professionals do not really care about all of these factors except for how they might relate to the success of your business. Your consultant will help you look at projected numbers, working designs, operational systems, equipment and vendor selections, etc. Hopefully they will use their experience to look after your best interests. A good consultant can prevent you from making those critical, costly, emotionally-based mistakes.

Saving on equipment costs

Consultants can often save you money by allowing you, through their contacts, to purchase equipment at a better price than you might be able to negotiating on your own. Consultants often have business relationships with equipment companies who will give the consultant's clients a good price, primarily because they want the consultants to bring them additional business.

Some companies are the direct importers of the equipment. Because they make high-volume purchases and, because they are purchasing the equipment directly from the manufacturer, they will usually be able to provide you with the best price. When you purchase equipment from someone who is two or three middlemen down the line from the manufacturer, you will undoubtedly pay thousands more than if you were to buy that equipment from the importer.

Navigating the potholes

When we talk to our consulting clients, we always ask two questions. The first is:

Have you ever been in business for yourself before?

If the client says *No,* we get a bit worried. The next question we always ask is,

Have you ever managed a food-service business before?

And if the answer is again, *No,* we tell them that unless they are extremely astute, and do a lot of homework, there is a high probability they may fail in this business.

We always tell people:

*The coffee business is **food service!** This business is very complex...not unlike a juggler with 50 balls...if you drop any one of them, it can affect the performance of your entire business.*

If you are about to embark into the world of specialty coffee, you will benefit from the experience of someone who has traveled the same path hundreds of times.

Help in site selection

An obvious example of how you can benefit from the help of an experienced consultant is in the matter of site selection.

A few thousand dollars spent on a consultant could be the wisest money you will ever spend

Imagine what happens if you pick the wrong location...spend $150,000 on your dream espresso café, and then find it will not produce the income you need to pay yourself a liveable wage. Then, to add insult to injury, your business will not even generate enough revenue to debt-service itself! It goes almost without saying that a mistake made in choosing your location can be very costly.

The few thousand dollars you spend on a consultant to keep you from losing a few hundred thousand could be the wisest money you will ever spend.

We highly recommend to people who have not had prior business experience, or food-service management experience, that they use a reputable consultant to help them make these types of critical decisions. Even those who own businesses can benefit with good advice about the coffee industry.

Realtors

Work with someone who deals strictly with commercial property

It may be wise to solicit the help of a commercial real estate agent or broker who works in the area you are planning to open your business.

We emphasize the word *Commercial*.

Avoid dealing with someone who dabbles in commercial properties, or who has had only a small amount of commercial experience. You want to work with someone who deals strictly with commercial property; someone who really understands the commercial real estate market.

Who pays them

Generally, real estate agents will tell you that they represent you, but be careful. Be aware of who will be paying the realtor. Typically they will collect a small percentage of what the owner will receive from you in monthly rent. The real estate agent is actually being paid by the building owner or the property manager. So, you have to ask these questions:

> *Is this person really trying to negotiate the most advantageous lease for me?*

Or,

> *Would they actually like to see the rent factor be a little bit higher?*

How realtors can help you

Once you feel comfortable that the commercial real estate professional you have chosen will be looking after your best interests, here are some advantages in using their services:

- Commercial realtors are the people who thoroughly understand the market.

- They know where the potentially "hot" properties are in town. In many cases they may know of a property which will become available before the "For Lease" sign goes up on the window.

- They have connections with the relevant owners and landlords.

- They can tell you about typical maintenance charges, taxes, etc.

• They can be very helpful in finding the situation that is right for your specific needs.

• They know what the fair market rate should be for a specific property.

Do not ever totally rely on a real estate broker or agent to find your location for you. You need to lay the groundwork yourself. Unless you are indicating that you will be opening multiple units, there will be insufficient commissions to motivate the realtor to invest the time necessary to do a thorough job. The realtor may just happen to know of something, or have a relationship with someone, that presents an opportunity which will make it easy for them to find you a location. But if this is not the case, they are not likely to put in the hard work which will be required to find a property.

Once you find the great location, and you are dealing with a realtor who knows the property manager, *then* you have an advantage. For example, if you want to put an espresso kiosk or cart in the lobby of an office building, your plan will have an advantage if the realtor has previously supplied the owner of the building with multiple tenants. Because the broker and the building owner or property manager already have a business relationship, you have a better chance of getting the location than if you were to make the initial contact on your own. In this case, the realtor is in a better position of selling *you,* than you are.

You want to be the one who presents your business idea

Do not, however, depend on the broker to pitch *your idea* to the property manager for you. You want to be there. You want to be the one who passionately presents your business idea. The broker will not have the same vision, understanding or excitement that you do about your business.

Think of this professional as a *facilitator,* someone who can make the connection between the property manager and you, and someone who is capable of getting you an appointment and can provide you with a little credibility by virtue of the fact they are associated with you. But never forget that the responsibility of promoting your business is up to you. No one else will have the passion or the understanding that you will have.

Accountants

The tax laws have become so complicated that you could probably spend 10 hours a week just studying current codes. You will not have time to do this if you are running a business. It is well worth the money to hire a professional to help you. Someone who can handle your taxes, payroll, payroll deductions, quarterlies reports, etc. If you can have an accountant handle these details for you, then you will not have to worry about them.

If there is a problem...if the IRS or the state writes you a letter claiming that you did not pay this tax, or file that report, you have a third party to represent you.

And because your third party is a professional, there is a better chance they have processed your documentation correctly and have a better idea of what is going on than you do. They can deal with the agencies for you and eliminate that worry from your mind.

Another important consideration is the help your accountant can provide in setting up your business. For example:

- They can provide you with information as to what might be advantageous in your tax situation, and perhaps in your liability situation.

- They can help you decide if you will be better off structuring your business as a sole proprietorship, partnership, S-corporation, or as a C-corporation.

- When you start to accumulate significant profits, they can advise you on how to shelter some of that income.

- If you are trying to pull some money out of your business, they can advise you as to whether it should be taken as wages, a loan from your business, or a stock dividend distribution, thus reducing your tax liability.

Attorneys

Most everything that you do in your business can have legal implications. Because of this, you will always want to establish a personal relationship with a good law firm or firms.

More specifically, your attorney is extremely important when you are presented with a lease, or any other legally binding contract.

Find an attorney that specializes in real estate and business law

It would be wise to find an attorney who specializes in the real estate laws of the specific area and state where you will be operating. With regard to the lease you are considering, red flags may come up in your attorney's mind that you may never think of.

For example, a few years ago we were negotiating a lease in an older building that was being remodeled. One of the lease provisions said that we would pay any increases in property taxes over the base year. We were not really concerned about this provision, knowing that property taxes normally went up a minimal amount annually, and we were prepared for that.

But our attorney looked at that provision and asked,

> *What is the base year?*

You do not ever want to sign anything that is a legal contract without having your attorney review it first

And we responded,

> *Well, we don't know.*

And she told us:

> *You'd better find out. If it's this year, you should be concerned because this is a very old, run down building. When the owner is done remodeling this building, the appraiser is going to come out and reappraise the building and it may go up in value significantly.*

So the lawyer told us to go to the county and check the tax records to see what the value of the building was assessed at. She told us that if the building was assessed at a fair market value, that amount should be around $90 or $95 per square foot.

But the property owner, being very shrewd, had been down complaining to the local tax officials about how dilapidated his building was, and how excessive the taxes were that he was being charged. As a result, he had beaten down the value of the building on the tax rolls to $17 per square foot! After his improvements were made, he was well aware that the value would increase to around $95 per square foot! We, of course, would have had to pay the taxes for the increase in value from $17 to $95, on each square foot of our space—a giant difference in taxes.

If your attorney discovers one little point like this, it could save you tens of thousands of dollars over the term of a lease.

Remember...you do not ever want to sign anything that is a legal contract without having your attorney review it first.

Facilitators

Getting official approval for your new project may entangle you in a maze of various governmental jurisdictions, each with its own rules and regulations. This process can be confusing and frustrating. In most states, the city and county planning laws are so incredibly complicated, that it may be necessary to retain the services of a facilitator.

A facilitator usually has a background in architecture or city planning. He may have the experience to clearly understand the rules and laws involved. He should understand how to get around the roadblocks and proceed through the various steps involved in the approval-seeking process.

An example from our own experience was a drive-thru that we proposed to build in Portland a few years ago:

We walked into the City Planning Department to find out what permits we needed to file, and the employee behind the counter laughed at us.

> *You mean, you're going to attempt to do this yourself?* he asked.

> *Well, yes,* we answered naively.

> *Well,* he replied, *I can tell you right now, this process is **so complex**, I would think the chances of you working through all this paper work by yourself is almost impossible.*

He told us if we were to try, it could take us well over a year!

We were pretty outraged by this. We learned very quickly that our best option was to retain a facilitator who understood exactly what the city was looking for, and who could move the application through the system with the least difficulty.

The bottom line is that cities and other local jurisdictions can become so complex that the average person needs some specialized assistance to deal with the bureaucracy.

Different rules for different places

Obviously some areas of the country can be much worse than others. We had a client in California who was told:

You aren't expected to understand the rules and the laws. They weren't written for the common person to be able to understand.

For our small drive-thru in Portland, they wanted to know things like:

- What kind of shadows would our structure produce? They asked for a shadow study that would show where the shadows would fall on the parking lot at different hours of the day.

- They wanted to know how the rainwater would roll off the roof of our 8 x 12 foot building and how it would drain across the paved lot.

- We were asked to get surveys from the local schools, police and fire departments as to their opinions on an establishment of our type, and what impact it would have on them.

- They wanted light stanchions on the corner! We said,

Why? It's only going to be open during the day, and they said,

That doesn't matter, we still want light stanchions, wired underground in 5' deep trenches, and located exactly where we want them, and they must, of course, be code-approved.

- And the curb cuts for car-access—which were good enough for the gas station that had been there a year before—probably did not meet the current standards and we would have to provide and pay for all new curb cuts.

We initially went into our project thinking that for $50,000 or $60,000, we could put a little drive-thru on this location in a matter of two to three months. But a little investigation made us realize that because of entire project.

We have had clients in states where there are few regulations, nothing to compare to the examples we have cited above. But if you are in one of the states that is bureaucracy-heavy, a couple thousand dollars spent on a facilitator to help you through the maze, may save you both time and money.

Architects, Builders & Designers

Perhaps not as important with a kiosk or cart location, but if you are considering a location for an in-line, stand-alone coffee bar, you would be wise to bring in an architect or builder who is familiar with current building codes.

You may think, *Gee, this is a great location,* but when you bring a builder in to look at it, he may tell you:

This was a dress shop before, but with all the additional equipment that you intend on adding, the circuit breaker box will not be sufficient. We will need to run a significant amount of new wiring. And what about bathrooms? You only have one bathroom, and you'll need two, and they'll both have to be handicapped accessible. I don't think this water heater is going to meet your needs....etc., etc.

The remodel that you thought was going to cost $15,000 to $20,000—to build a couple of counters and change a few plugs, just turned into a $50,000 to $75,000 project within a five-minute inspection. These are all facts that you will want to be aware of before you enter into lease negotiations.

Change of use requirements

Getting help from your builder or architect is valuable, especially in situations where there is a "change of use."

The term "change of use" refers to a structure or space that is being converted into a different type of business than it was previously. If the space had previously been a café or food-service establishment, a change of use permit would usually not be required. But in our analogy above, converting a dress shop to a coffee bar would constitute a change of use.

Very often, filing a change of use permit will require you to bring everything up to code

Very often, filing a change of use permit will require you to bring *everything* up to code before you open your doors. This may include new regulations for parking (number of spaces required per square foot of retail area), plumbing, electrical, or any other changes in the laws and codes. When a change of use filing is made, you are no longer protected by the "grandfather clause." The grandfather clause states that if a space is used for the same type of business, you typically will not have to bring everything up to the new standards.

So for example, even though your shop may already have two bathrooms, if you are applying for a change of use, there may be questions you will have to ask, like:

- Are the bathrooms handicapped-accessible?

- Are the doors big enough for a wheelchair?

- Can you run a wheelchair under the sink basins?

- Are there handrails in the bathroom stalls?

And so forth.

If you have to totally remodel the two bathrooms, and perhaps remove walls and enlarge hallways to make them the proper size, you may have a big problem and a significant financial expense.

We will be talking more about the implications of *Change of Use* in chapters 20, 21, and 22.

Note: Most coffee bars we have seen that were designed by local architects are laid out improperly. Why? Because they do not understand the business, product requirements, ergonomic flow, storage needs, etc. We highly recommend you use a business that specializes in designing coffee operations.

 For more information on this specific subject, refer to the following book from Bellissimo—800-655-3955.

- **Achieving Success in Specialty Coffee**

Chapter 18 Check List

Professional Relationships

_____ Will you need, and have you established a relationship with, a good industry consultant?

_____ Talk with several commercial real estate professionals and determine who may best help you with your search for a good location.

_____ Talk with a certified public accountant about handling your monthly and annual tax calculations, and discuss which form of business might be most advantageous for your situation.

_____ Establish a relationship with a good real estate and general law attorney.

_____ Talk with the city/county and find out if the use of a facilitator is recommended. If so, ask if they could recommend one, and establish a relationship.

_____ Investigate some architectural firms and general contractors that you might use during your design and construction phase.

Note: as when establishing any important professional relationship, obtain the following information:

_____ Rates for services

_____ Inquire as to how many years they have been in business

_____ Ask for references and check them

_____ Inquire with the Better Business Bureau, the State Attorney General's Office, and their professional organization to determine if they are in good standing.

CHAPTER 19

Developing a Business Plan

Contents

Chapter 19 Contents - Page 2

CHAPTER 19

Developing a Business Plan

Your business plan becomes your calling card

A business plan is simply a resume for your proposed business. Its primary importance is that your business plan becomes your calling card. Anytime you are going in to talk to a property manager about leasing space for your business, or you are meeting with a potential lender or investor, your business plan will announce/outline who you are and what your purpose is.

In most cases, a business plan is created to explain and illustrate the vision you have for your business, and to persuade others to help you achieve that vision. To accomplish this, your plan will need to demonstrate on paper that you have a firm visualization of what your business is going to be. It needs to convince others that your business concept can be successful, and that you possess the expertise—alone or collectively—to assure that it will be both successful and profitable.

While it is obviously important to be able to present your business concept in a way that allows others to understand quickly and precisely what you hope to be doing, you also need to develop a business plan for your own use. The process of developing your business plan will require you to focus on exactly what you are trying to achieve, precisely where you want to be going, and exactly how you plan to get there. It will force you to detail the many expenses involved to open your business, the projected sales and monthly expenses of actual operation, and the volume of business you will need to generate to meet your obligations.

All of this information will greatly influence your many choices, including the kind of location you will be looking for.

Two Types of Business Plans

Its primary purpose is to convince landlords and property managers that you have a sound and appealing business concept

There are basically two types of business plans that we create for clients who are looking to open their own retail espresso operation. Both business plans are designed to help you develop your new business from conceptualization to opening day.

Once you are actively operating on a daily basis, both of these business plans will have achieved their purpose. From that point on, you will be gathering and measuring the actual performance data of your operation as the basis for planning your future.

The first type of business plan you will need is a *Concept Presentation Plan.*

Concept Presentation Plans are typically 10- to 24-pages long, and basically describe your business concept, products, principals (owners and key management), target market, trends in the industry, etc. This type of plan contains no financial projections or financial statements. Its primary purpose is to convince landlords and property managers that you have a sound and appealing business concept, and that you are interested in negotiating for the lease of an available space.

The second type of business plan is a *Full Financial Business Plan.*

You will need a Full Financial Business Plan to borrow money

Typically, you will need a Full Financial Business Plan to borrow money from a bank, or to entice investors to lend you money. Depending upon the contents, it can consist of anywhere from 25 to 100 pages of information. It can contain all the elements of the concept presentation plan, but primarily it examines in-depth what the total costs of your project will be, when the project will turn a profit, and what level of return you can expect.

Everyone who opens a retail business should have a full financial business plan completed before they open. It is probably more important for you, than anyone else, to be able to see the potential profit and loss for your proposed business. The extensive research which will be necessary to project expenses, sales, and profitability is essential to your understanding of the financial operation of your business. The importance of each of your management functions— setting menu prices, establishing cost of sales and expense budgets, creating sales goals—can only be appreciated when understood individually, and as they relate to the overall financial statement.

It is also very important for you to identify the people who do not need to see your financials

It is also very important for you to identify the people who *do not* need to see your financials. In fact, it is to your advantage that they do not. Realtors and property managers fall into this category. It is not to your advantage for a property manager to see what level of financial performance and profit you are expecting from your proposed business. Your future landlord might be justifiably concerned that you have enough capital to pay your rent each month. He may legitimately wish to see a personal financial statement to be reassured that you own some equity in your house, have some funds in your bank account, and are running your household on a positive cash-flow basis. But these concerns can be addressed with your personal financial statement.

You want to avoid putting your landlord in the position of saying to himself:

> *Wow, this guy's going to be doing 500 cups a day and netting $120,000 a year. I'm certainly not going to rent him this kiosk space for $500 a month! I am going to hold firm at $1,000 a month!*

Concept Presentation Plan

Your *Concept Presentation Plan*—the nonfinancial business plan—should include the following elements:

- Cover Page
- Mission Statement
- The Principals
- Products
- Service Philosophy
- Market Trend Analysis
- Target Market
- Marketing Techniques
- Target Market Locations
- Sample Menu

Each of these elements is described in detail in the sections that follow.

Cover Page

The first page of your business plan, the cover page is not unlike the cover of a book and should be professional in appearance, enticing the reader to explore the rest of your proposal. This page should feature:

- a large image of your logo,

- the name, address, phone number, and fax number of the contact person for your organization, and

- a confidentiality statement or warning.

Mission Statement

Typically the first page after the cover sheet, your mission statement is your conception, your vision of the business you want to create. It need not go into specific details, but your mission statement should provide a clear picture to your vendors, financial backers, prospective landlords, employees, clientele, and, most importantly, *you* , of what your company is going to do, who you plan to serve, and how you want to be perceived.

If the readers of your business plan go no further than this page, they should be able to understand your basic business concept.

The content of your mission statement is more important than its length, and yours can begin with: *The mission of (The XYZ Coffee Company) is to provide....*

As an example: The mission statement for one of our own retail locations states:

> *Bellissimo Espresso is a young aggressive company dedicated to opening multiple gourmet retail coffee outlets to serve an already coffee conscious Oregon market.*

It goes on to touch briefly on our commitment to quality products and service, talks about who will benefit from our service, and why we will be different and better than similar businesses.

Your mission statement should establish:

- What your physical business will be (café, cart, drive-through, etc.).

- Why you are creating it.

- Who will benefit from it.

- Who your customers will be.

- What products and services you will be providing.

- What you plan to obtain from it.

If the readers of your business plan go no further than this page, they should be able to understand your basic business concept.

The Principals

In this section you provide information about key personnel (owners and managers) of your company. This should consist of a brief resume for each member of your management team that includes:

- Education

- Work experience

- Special skills or experiences which lend credibility to their abilities as related to your project.

If you team with consultants, you can add their expertise to your Principals page

Many of the clients we work with have no prior business or food service experience. In such cases, teaming with a qualified consultant can be very helpful. As we mentioned in Chapter 18—*Getting Help From Professionals*, that is one of the advantages of using a consultant. If you are going to a property manager and you have never owned a coffee operation or a small business before, you may have difficulty convincing them that you can run a successful and thriving operation. If you team with consultants, you can add their expertise to your *Principals* page, which will lend a lot more credibility to your operation...and to your landlord's perception that you will be able to succeed in this business.

In our consulting business, with our own client's permission, we add ourselves to our client's resume. We do this by stating that our client will be partnering with Bellissimo, and then we talk about our own backgrounds, as well as the backgrounds of the other people in our company. Even though we will not be entitled to a percentage of the profits, or be involved in the day-to-day operation of their business, the fact that we are assisting with the crucial start-up phase and will remain an expert resource to the operator, will help to strengthen their overall business plan.

Products

If I told you, *I'm going to open a store,* the first question you would probably ask is, *What are you going to sell?*

Your *Products* section will give the property manager a good idea of the array of products that you will be selling from your store.

Use laudatory and colorful adjectives to describe your products

Talk in specific terms about the products you will be offering, including:

- Types of coffee and other beverages

- Types of food items

- Other items you may intend on selling

In this section you want to talk in-depth about your business's philosophy of product quality. And you want to use laudatory and colorful adjectives to describe your products, such as:

- *Award winning,*

- *The finest, freshly roasted, gourmet coffee,*

- *Daily-fresh baked homemade goods and pastries,*

- *Imported candies,*

- *Decadent delights tempting the most discriminating of palates.*

The idea is to establish in the *Products* section that you are not going to be serving soft drinks and candy bars. By using bright descriptive language you can keep your products section fairly brief but still drive home to a property manager some of your more distinctive ideas. Remember, he or she is probably going to be skimming over your 12-page business plan and not reading it word for word. They are seeking to know quickly whether yours is going to be a makeshift or an upscale operation.

Keep in mind that you may want to adjust your product section to accommodate different possible locations. For example, if you are going to be putting a drive-thru in a shopping center that may already have an established deli and bagel operation, there may be a no-compete clause in your lease to prevent you from serving sandwiches or bagels. You will have to adjust your business plan to reassure your property owner that you will not be conflicting with the existing rights of other businesses (who are also his tenants).

On the other hand, you may already know from your realtor that an ice cream store just went out of business at that location, and that the property manager is looking for someone to fill that particular void. In this case you may want to adjust your menu to include ice cream or Italian gelato. Your menu adjustment then becomes a selling point in your favor.

So have your basic business plan ready—but be ready to adjust it to suit each specific location.

Service Philosophy

Your *Service Philosophy* is a statement of your values and beliefs as they relate to your firm's attitudes and behaviors toward its clientele. In operational terms, it consists of specific service beliefs, policies, and practices of your firm and its employees. It should address such aspects of service, as:

Specific service beliefs, policies, and practices

- Courtesy

- Responsiveness to customer needs expressed through good listening and problem solving skills

- Dedication to quality preparation of the product on a consistent basis

- Timeliness of service

- Cleanliness

In your statement of service philosophy you should also make clear that it is your intention to only hire employees who are—or are committed to becoming—dedicated professionals.

This is also an appropriate place to address the importance of your initial selection of key personnel, as well as the training programs and standards you will be implementing.

Market Trend Analysis

This section talks about what is happening in the specialty coffee industry in general throughout the United States. In your business plan be sure to emphasize that the recent spread of the specialty coffee business is part of a long-term trend, rather than a short-term fad.

Unless you are in the Pacific Northwest, it is possible that your prospective property managers might think that the espresso wave is just a fad, or a regional phenomenon peculiar to Seattle and the West Coast. So, in this section we talk about the overall marketability of this product nationally and globally.

Talk about the overall market-ability of this product

To substantiate the long-term validity and marketability of specialty coffee, you will need to do some research to find statistics and predictions by experts within our industry. Good source information is available from the Specialty Coffee Association of America (SCAA), and in our industry's trade periodicals (phone numbers for these are located in the back of this book). You should have little difficulty substantiating that this explosive-growth industry is part of a national long-term trend which is rapidly becoming firmly entrenched in our national culture.

What is happening in specialty coffee is not unlike what happened to gourmet ice cream. When Ben & Jerry's and Haagen Dazs first came on the market, these were products that could only be found in specialty stores. Now, if you run a convenience store and you do not carry one or both of these ice creams, you can expect your customers to be outraged. High quality, high end ice cream is no longer thought of as a passing fancy; it has become a trend within the ice cream industry.

The same holds true in the coffee industry. America has been drinking pre-ground canned national brands for years, but gourmet coffee has now grown to be the accepted coffee experience.

So, if you are in an area where the gourmet coffee trend has not made a large impact, this section will help your potential landlord understand how viable your business venture is. He or she may not know what is happening in this industry. When you mention "gourmet coffee" the response is likely to be:

Oh, you mean flavored coffee.

That is the first thing people think of. You need to explain to them:

No, we're not talking about flavored coffee, we are talking about high quality varietals, and specific artistic blends of these varietals which are brewed through an espresso machine.

And again:

No, espresso is not a small amount of dark, pungent, bitter coffee. It is a concentration of the best flavor characteristics from the coffee, which can be enjoyed straight, or combined with steamed milk, chocolate, and gourmet flavored syrups to create an array of wonderful beverages!

Target Market

This is the section of your business plan that should describe exactly who your customers will be, and where they will come from. It should explain why these people will use your business and what benefits your business offers to these individuals.

Describe exactly who your customers will be

You will want to conduct a demographic survey of the immediate area around your proposed location to identify your target market. Things you can do:

- Conduct a count of anything that moves by your potential location—foot traffic, cars, bicycles, etc.

- Take notes of how many pass your location per hour, and at what times of the day.

- Get a map of the city or neighborhood and draw a circle around your location within a one-half mile radius. Drive around that neighborhood and become familiar with it. Analyze where your potential customers may come from.

- Talk to people—shopkeepers, policemen, city officials, and the folks at the post office. Get to know the people who live and work in your area and let them begin to know you. Be free to share your plans with them and note their responses and the suggestions they offer. These are the people who are your prospective customers, and their input will help you develop your marketing plans.

Naturally, your customer base will vary depending upon location. For example:

- If you are planning to open an espresso cart in a shopping mall, your customer base will include shoppers, tourists, students, and employees of other retail establishments.

- If you are in a downtown office situation, your primary target market will be executives, professionals, office workers, and these business's clientele.

- If you are near a University, you are probably targeting students and faculty.

- If you are at an airport, they will be business travelers and tourists.

Regardless of location, your targeted customers are generally a little more up-scale with more discriminating palates. Your business will afford them a cup of delicious coffee to start their day, or serve as a break from the activities of an already hectic day.

Marketing Techniques

This section looks at how you plan to market your products, and how you are going to give your business some pizzazz.

Keep in mind that your specific marketing strategies will vary according to your type of operation and location.

How you plan to market your products

For example:

- If you are located in a book store, you and the bookstore owner may decide on a coupon program which entitles the purchaser of a $25 book sale to a 50% discount coupon for a latté.

- If you are located in a music center, you can choose to name your different drinks after composers or musical works.

- If you are a drive-thru, you might think about buying billboard space two or three blocks away to advertise your business to oncoming traffic.

- If you are on a college campus, you might opt for print ads in the college paper. We always choose Fridays to advertise, because this paper will be distributed for three days.

Details about your marketing plans can be an assurance to your property manager that you have given thought to both who your customers are going to be and what incentives you are planning to offer to attract them. Specific information on how to market your business can be found in Chapter 31—*Marketing Your Business.*

Target Market Locations

This section is designed to help your realtor find the right location for you by explaining exactly what you are looking for.

For example, if you are planning to open a drive-thru, you might specify:

Parameters of what you are looking for in a location

- Streets where the traffic count is more than 25,000 cars a day.

- A location on the inbound morning commute side of the street (where the majority of cars are taking folks to work in the morning).

- A minimum of 150 yards of oncoming visibility from the street.

- A certain amount of lane width or approach length to your facility.

If you are planning a cart operation you might tell your realtor that you are looking for a university campus location with heavy foot traffic, or for hospitals with a certain amount of employees, or for office buildings with a certain number of occupants.

This section will specify the parameters of what you are looking for in a location.

Sample Menu

Your *Sample Menu* informs your landlord of the products you will be selling.

Your Sample Menu can really create interest and appeal

Keep in mind that a picture is worth a thousand words and a menu is much like a picture. As we have said, your business plan is likely to be skimmed over by property managers. Your *Sample Menu* is one section of your business plan that can really create interest and appeal.

A generic sample menu includes basic espresso beverages that you will find in any coffee operation—straight espressos, cappuccinos, lattés, mochas, and so forth.

In addition, we usually develop a *Signature Drink Menu* for our clients that is specific to their operation. This menu includes drinks that have been uniquely formulated and named to affirm and enhance the unique theme that our client wants to project. Signature drink menus attach an identity to your drinks and help set your operation apart from your competition. For example, if your operation is located in a ski resort, the names of your drinks might be those of the ski runs or surrounding mountains.

See Chapter 24—*Planning Your Menu,* for detailed information and sample menus.

Full Financial Business Plan

A full financial business plan will generally be needed when you are seeking capital for the creation or ongoing operation of your business.

Typical information needed for this type of plan is as follows:

Statement of Required Capital

You need to request a specific amount of funds that you will need *after* your personal investment in the business. This will usually cover the expense of the lease space build-out, costs of equipment and small wares, inventory, and an operating capital reserve.

Determine the amount of funds you will require

One advantage to raising capital for your specialty coffee business is that many people are passionate about coffee. It makes sense to these individuals to invest in something they love.

Most lending institutions will only lend on long-term assets, so if you will be investing some of your own money, be prepared to make your personal investment in capital improvements, inventory, or retained as operating capital. Generally you will need specific cost estimates, provided by professionals (carpenters, plumbers, electricians, equipment purveyors, etc.), to determine the amount of funds you will require for your proposed build-out and equipment package.

Personal Financial Statement

Your personal financial statement should list the typical information you need to apply for a bank loan including:

- Monthly income and expenses

- Assets and liabilities

- Equity in properties

- Past tax returns

Typically, it is very difficult to persuade others to invest in your business if you have no personal financial risk. So, in addition to your financial statement, this section should also declare how much you will personally invest or secure towards your business.

Projected Income Statements

You will need to create *estimated income statements* for each month of business for a minimum of your first two years of operation. You should be prepared to:

You will need to create estimated income statements for each month of business for a minimum of your first two years

- Conduct sidewalk surveys in front of your proposed locations and in adjacent areas to determine the coffee consumption habits of your potential clientele.

- Along with the results of your sidewalk surveys, analyze your potential customer base in the immediate area of your proposed business to estimate possible daily and monthly sales volume.

- Cost out your menu fully. Estimate a *sales product mix* to gain an understanding of what your *total products cost* might be.

- Create a *master employee schedule* to determine your *expected labor expenses,* including employee taxes and insurance.

- Estimate your *fixed expenses* by contacting services you intend to use, such as utility companies, phone company, bookkeeping services, etc.

- Prepare a **realistic and believable** *income statement* that reflects minimal returns (or even losses) in the early months of operation, and shows increasing sales and profitability as time goes on.

Projected Balance Sheets

Balance sheets are different from income statements in that they provide a snapshot of the total value of the business at a particular point in time.

Typically, for a business plan, you should project *year-end balance sheets* for your business covering the first five years of your operation. The balance sheets should show:

- your retained earnings at the end of the year

- the value of long-term assets after depreciation

- accounts receivable, petty cash, capital stock, and any other areas of equity not stated on a monthly income statement.

Overall Appearance, Logos and Graphics

Regardless of which type of business plan you are going to prepare, it should look neat and professional.

It should look neat and professional

Remember that if your looking at a great location, a dozen other people might also be looking at that location and the property manager may have six similar business proposals on his or her desk. Your business proposal is not unlike a resume. It needs to make an impression sufficient to induce the property manager to want to talk with you. If you are ruled out immediately because of the poor quality or appearance of your business plan, you have lost the opportunity.

Following are some of the elements to pay close attention to, which may bring your proposal to the top of the stack for consideration:

Overall Appearance

To achieve a finished professional look we suggest that you:

- Generate your plan on a computer using software that provides different fonts and typographical styles.

- Make sure your finished plan is free of typographical errors (your spell-check program comes in handy), and is grammatically correct and consistent.

- Take advantage of the resources available to you at your local copy shop.

- Laser print your report copies on high quality paper.

- Have your copy shop put your presentation in a nice binder. A spiral binder with clear plastic front and cardboard back usually works well.

Logos

A $1,000 or more invested in the production of a professionally prepared logo may prove to be the wisest money you will ever spend. A phenomenal logo will set the right tone and create the desired perception of your business, even though you might still be in the planning stage.

The first thing many people will see is your logo

Your logo, along with your business cards and stationery letterhead, establishes your identity. The first thing many people will see is your logo. And the first question that will come to their mind is, *Does it look professional?* And if your logo does not look professional, how can anything else in your operation be?

We have worked with a few clients who insisted upon designing their own logos and more often than not, the results were not good. We periodically go back and look through the business plans we have prepared. Even though the content of those proposals are equal, those with logos designed by professional artists stand well above those with home-drawn ones. It is very difficult to impress a property manager with a business plan that has a poorly produced logo on its cover.

Graphics

In addition to the logo, you should consider embellishing your business plan with graphics. We offer our clients our clip-art programs featuring hundreds of easy-to-use coffee business graphics. When you talk about the pastries and various different food items, there are a variety of graphics available to give your plan that extra touch of pizzazz. If you are preparing your own business plan, and desire to add some graphics, our clip-art programs, *Sip Art Vol.1, 2 and 3,* are available from our offices.

It will do you no good to find that great location and then lose it...because your business plan failed the appearance test

Another thing you can do without incurring a lot of expense, is to have an artist prepare a rendering of your concept—perhaps the interior of your coffee bar, or the exterior of your cart, kiosk or drive-thru.

The picture that you have in your mind of your operation, may not be the same one that property manager will perceive from your written description. A professionally-prepared drawing of your proposal will help convey that picture, and clear up any misunderstandings over what it is you are trying to achieve.

You can usually have a rendering done for a few hundred dollars. It may make a difference in helping you obtain the lease for a prime retail space.

Finding that great location for your business is, as we discuss in Chapter 20, absolutely vital for your success. But it will do you no good to find that great location and then lose it to your competition because your business plan failed the appearance test.

A Case In Point

Shortly after we signed on as consultants to represent a particular client, we discovered that numerous other folks were also attempting to lease the same location—including a national chain with high-powered emissaries who were flown out to woo the management of this particular development.

Knowing what we were up against, all of us in our office put on our gloves (so to speak) and prepared a business plan that was, quite honestly, a knockout. We came up with a great name, a great logo and, in this case, we even went the extra step of preparing a computer CAD-designed walk-through of the completed coffee bar on screen.

In most cases we do not advise clients to go to these extremes because of the expense involved, but in this case we were convinced it was necessary.

It took months (not unusual) for the developers to make their final decision. When our client finally called us with the good and unlikely news that he was offered the location over this very stiff competition, the developer confided to him that,

It was the business plan that blew them away!

Never underestimate the POWER of a great business plan.

Disclaimer

Please understand that the following eight pages of financial projections are "best-guess" estimates. Bellissimo, Inc. cannot guarantee that the following financial estimates, can or will be achieved, if or when you open for business. These financial estimates do not, and are not intended to, guarantee your business success.

These financial estimates are based upon our personal experiences gained as a result of owning and/or operating food service related businesses during the past 25 years. The estimates provided represent industry typicals, and should be used only as a model to assist with financial planing.

If you do not fully understand the following eight pages of financial statements, or have any questions, call Bellissimo at (1-800) 655-3955, or contact your attorney and/or accountant.

Projected Income Statement — *Fictitious Coffee House*
(Sales based on 30–Day Business Month)

	Month 1	Month 2	Month 3	
	(75 cust. per day)	(100 cust. per day)	(125 cust. per day)	

(Average sale estimated at: coffee $1.80 per cup; other bev. $1.95 ea.; 66% of beverage sales coffee/ 33% other beverage; food- every 5th customer at $2.00 ea.; bulk beans every 25th customer at $9 per lb.)

	Month 1	Month 2	Month 3	(% mth. 3)
Gross Sales				
Food	900.	1,200.	1,500.	
Coffee Beverages	2,673.	3,564.	4,455.	
Other Beverages	1,447.	1,930.	2,413.	
Bulk Coffee	810.	1,080.	1,350.	
Hard Goods	514.	685.	856.	
Sales Tax Collected (X%)	X.	X.	X.	
Net Sales	6,344.	8,459.	10,574.	100.0%
Cost of Sales				
Food	450.	600.	750.	50.0%
Coffee Beverages	535.	713.	891.	20.0
Other Beverages	362.	482.	603.	25.0
Bulk Coffee	535.	712.	891.	66.0
Hard Goods	339.	452.	565.	66.0
Total Cost of Sales	2,221.	2,959.	3,700.	35.0
Gross Profit from Sales	4,123.	5,500.	6,874.	65.0%
Expenses				
Wages				
Employee	4,505.	4,505.	4,505.	
Owner/Manager	1,500.	1,500.	1,500.	
Payroll Taxes/ Benefits				
Payroll Taxes	841.	841.	841.	
Employee Meals	100.	100.	100.	
Total Labor Costs	6,946.	6,946.	6,946.	65.7%
Smallwares	150.	50.	50.	
Laundry/ Uniform	50.	50.	50.	
Office Supplies	50.	50.	50.	
Printing	200.	100.	100.	
Repairs & Maintenance	25.	25.	25.	
Paper & Chemical	250.	331.	414.	
Phone	100.	100.	100.	
Utilities	400.	400.	400.	
Garbage Service	50.	50.	50.	
Janitorial Service	500.	500.	500.	
Sales Tax Payable (8%)	X.	X.	X.	
Cash over/ short	30.	30.	30.	
Advertising	500.	500.	500.	
Rent/ Payment	1,250.	1,250.	1,250.	
Loan Payments	0.	0.	0.	
Interest	___	___	___	
Business Insurance	75.	75.	75.	
Bank Charges/ Discounts	59.	84.	99.	
Licenses & Permits	21.	21.	21.	
Professional Fees	80.	80.	80.	
Total Expenses	10,736.	10,642.	10,740.	101.6%
PROFIT / LOSS	$<6,613.>	$<5,142.>	$<3,866.>	-36.6%

Projected Income Statement — *Fictitious Coffee House*
(Sales based on 30-Day Business Month)

	Month 4	Month 5	Month 6	
	(150 cust. per day)	(175 cust. per day)	(200 cust. per day)	

(Average sale estimated at: coffee $1.80 per cup; other bev. $1.95 ea.; 66% of beverage sales coffee/ 33% other beverage; food- every 5th customer at $2.00 ea.; bulk beans every 25th customer at $9 per lb.)

	Month 4	Month 5	Month 6	(% mth. 6)
Gross Sales				
Food	1,800.	2,100.	2,400.	
Coffee Beverages	5,346.	6,237.	7,128.	
Other Beverages	2,896.	3,378.	3,861.	
Bulk Coffee	1,620.	1,890.	2,160.	
Hard Goods	1,027.	1,198.	1,370.	
Sales Tax Collected (X%)	X.	X.	X.	
Net Sales	**12,869.**	**14,803.**	**16,919.**	**100.0%**
Cost of Sales				
Food	900.	1,050.	1,200.	50.0%
Coffee Beverages	1,069.	1,247.	1,425.	20.0
Other Beverages	724.	844.	965.	25.0
Bulk Coffee	1,069.	1,247.	1,425.	66.0
Hard Goods	678.	791.	904.	66.0
Total Cost of Sales	**4,440.**	**5,179.**	**5,919.**	**35.0**
Gross Profit from Sales	**8,249.**	**9,624.**	**11,000.**	**65.0%**
Expenses				
Wages				
Employee	4,505.	4,505.	4,505.	
Owner/Manager	1,500.	1,500.	1,500.	
Payroll Taxes/ Benefits				
Payroll Taxes	841.	841.	841.	
Employee Meals	100.	100.	100.	
Total Labor Costs	**6,946.**	**6,946.**	**6,946.**	**41.1%**
Smallwares	50.	50.	50.	
Laundry/ Uniform	50.	50.	50.	
Office Supplies	50.	50.	50.	
Printing	100.	100.	100.	
Repairs & Maintenance	25.	25.	25.	
Paper & Chemical	494.	577.	660.	
Phone	100.	100.	100.	
Utilities	400.	400.	400.	
Garbage Service	50.	50.	50.	
Janitorial Service	500.	500.	500.	
Sales Tax Payable (8%)	X.	X.	X.	
Cash over/ short	30.	30.	30.	
Advertising	500.	500.	500.	
Rent/ Payment	1,250.	1,250.	1,250.	
Loan Payments	0.	0.	0.	
Interest	————	————	————	
Business Insurance	75.	75.	75.	
Bank Charges/ Discounts	126.	147.	167.	
Licenses & Permits	21.	21.	21.	
Professional Fees	80.	80.	80.	
Total Expenses	**10,847.**	**10,951.**	**11,054.**	**65.3%**
PROFIT / LOSS	**$<2,598.>**	**$<1,327.>**	**$<54.>**	**-3%**

Projected Income Statement — *Fictitious Coffee House*
(Sales based on 30-Day Business Month)

	Month 9	Month 12	Month 15	
	(260 cust. per day)	(290 cust. per day)	(300 cust. per day)	

(Average sale estimated at: coffee $1.80 per cup; other bev. $1.95 ea.; 66% of beverage sales coffee/ 33% other beverage; food- every 5th customer at $2.00 ea.; bulk beans every 25th customer at $9 per lb.)

	Month 9	Month 12	Month 15	(% mth. 15)
Gross Sales				
Food	3,210.	3,480.	3,600.	
Coffee Beverages	9,266.	10,355.	10,691.	
Other Beverages	5,020.	5,599.	5,792.	
Bulk Coffee	2,808.	3,132.	3,240.	
Hard Goods	1,780.	1,985.	2,053.	
Sales Tax Collected (X%)	X.	X.	X.	
Net Sales	**21,994.**	**24,531.**	**25,376.**	**100.0%**
Cost of Sales				
Food	1,560.	1,740.	1,800.	50.0%
Coffee Beverages	1,853.	2,067.	2,138.	20.0
Other Beverages	1,255.	1,400.	1,448.	25.0
Bulk Coffee	1,853.	2,067.	2,138.	66.0
Hard Goods	1,175.	1,310.	1,355.	66.0
Total Cost of Sales	**7,696.**	**8,584.**	**8,879.**	**35.0**
Gross Profit from Sales	**14,298.**	**15,947.**	**16,497.**	**65.0%**
Expenses				
Wages				
Employee	4,505.	4,505.	4,505.	
Owner/Manager	1,500.	1,500.	1,500.	
Payroll Taxes/ Benefits				
Payroll Taxes	841.	841.	841.	
Employee Meals	100.	100.	100.	
Total Labor Costs	**6,946.**	**6,946.**	**6,946.**	**27.4%**
Smallwares	50.	50.	50.	
Laundry/ Uniform	50.	50.	50.	
Office Supplies	50.	50.	50.	
Printing	100.	100.	100.	
Repairs & Maintenance	25.	25.	25.	
Paper & Chemical	858.	957.	990.	
Phone	100.	100.	100.	
Utilities	400.	400.	400.	
Garbage Service	50.	50.	50.	
Janitorial Service	500.	500.	500.	
Sales Tax Payable (8%)	X.	X.	X.	
Cash over/ short	30.	30.	30.	
Advertising	500.	500.	500.	
Rent/ Payment	1,250.	1,250.	1,250.	
Loan Payments	0.	0.	0.	
Interest	—	—	—	
Business Insurance	75.	75.	75.	
Bank Charges/ Discounts	188.	243.	251.	
Licenses & Permits	21.	21.	21.	
Professional Fees	80.	80.	80.	
Total Expenses	**11,273.**	**11,427.**	**11,468.**	**45.2%**
PROFIT / LOSS	**$3,205.**	**$4,520.**	**$5,029.**	**19.8%**

Projected Income Statement — *Fictitious Coffee House*

(Sales based on 30-Day Business Month)

	Month 18	Month 21	Month 24	
	(310 cust. per day)	(320 cust. per day)	(330 cust. per day)	

(Average sale estimated at: coffee $1.80 per cup; other bev. $1.95 ea.; 66% of beverage sales coffee/ 33% other beverage; food- every 5th customer at $2.00 ea.; bulk beans every 25th customer at $9 per lb.)

Gross Sales				(% mth. 24)
Food	3,720.	3,840.	3,960.	
Coffee Beverages	11,047.	11,403.	11,759.	
Other Beverages	5,985.	6,178.	6,371.	
Bulk Coffee	3,348.	3,456.	3,564.	
Hard Goods	2,121.	2,190.	2,258.	
Sales Tax Collected (X%)	X.	X.	X.	
Net Sales	**26,221.**	**27,067.**	**27,912.**	**100.0%**
Cost of Sales				
Food	1,860.	1,920.	1,980.	50.0%
Coffee Beverages	2,209.	2,281.	2,352.	20.0
Other Beverages	1,496.	1,544.	1,593.	25.0
Bulk Coffee	2,210.	2,281.	2,352.	66.0
Hard Goods	1,400.	1,445.	1,490.	66.0
Total Cost of Sales	**9,175.**	**9,471.**	**9,767.**	**35.0**
Gross Profit from Sales	**17,046.**	**17,596.**	**18,148.**	**65.0%**
Expenses				
Wages				
Employee	4,505.	4,505.	4,505.	
Owner/Manager	1,500.	1,500.	1,500.	
Payroll Taxes/ Benefits				
Payroll Taxes	841.	841.	841.	
Employee Meals	100.	100.	100.	
Total Labor Costs	**6,946.**	**6,946.**	**6,946.**	**24.9%**
Smallwares	50.	50.	50.	
Laundry/ Uniform	50.	50.	50.	
Office Supplies	50.	50.	50.	
Printing	100.	100.	100.	
Repairs & Maintenance	25.	25.	25.	
Paper & Chemical	1,023.	1,056.	1,122.	
Phone	100.	100.	100.	
Utilities	400.	400.	400.	
Garbage Service	50.	50.	50.	
Janitorial Service	500.	500.	500.	
Sales Tax Payable (8%)	X.	X.	X.	
Cash over/ short	30.	30.	30.	
Advertising	500.	500.	500.	
Rent/ Payment	1,250.	1,250.	1,250.	
Loan Payments	0.	0.	0.	
Interest	——	——	——	
Business Insurance	75.	75.	75.	
Bank Charges/ Discounts	260.	268.	276.	
Licenses & Permits	21.	21.	21.	
Professional Fees	80.	80.	80.	
Total Expenses	**11,510.**	**11,551.**	**11,625.**	**41.7%**
PROFIT / LOSS	**$5,536.**	**$6,045.**	**$6,523.**	**23.4%**

(handwritten annotations: 25% near Payroll Taxes/Benefits; 4% near Paper & Chemical; 1.4% near Utilities; 1.8% near Janitorial Service; 4.5% near Rent/Payment)

Projected Income Statement — *Fictitious Cart Operation*
(Sales based on 30-Day Business Month)

	Month 1	Month 2	Month 3	
	(50 cust. per day)	(75 cust. per day)	(100 cust. per day)	

(Average sale estimated at: coffee $1.80 per cup; other bev. $1.95 ea.; 80% of beverage sales coffee/ 20% other beverage; food- every 10th customer at $1.00 ea.)

	Month 1	Month 2	Month 3	(% mth. 3)
Gross Sales				
Food	150.	225.	300.	
Coffee Beverages	2,160.	3,240.	4,320.	
Other Beverages	585.	878.	1,171.	
Sales Tax Collected (X%)	X.	X.	X.	
Net Sales	**2,895.**	**4,343.**	**5,791.**	**100.0%**
Cost of Sales				
Food	75.	112.	150.	50.0%
Coffee Beverages	432.	648.	864.	20.0
Other Beverages	146.	220.	293.	25.0
Total Cost of Sales	**653.**	**980.**	**1,307.**	**22.6**
Gross Profit from Sales	**2,242.**	**3,363.**	**4,484.**	**77.4%**
Expenses				
Wages				
Employee	2,500.	2,500.	2,500.	
Owner/Manager	1,500.	1,500.	1,500.	
Payroll Taxes/ Benefits				
Payroll Taxes	560.	560.	560.	
Employee Meals	100.	100.	100.	
Total Labor Costs	**4,660.**	**4,660.**	**4,660.**	**80.5%**
Smallwares	25.	25.	25.	
Laundry/ Uniform	35.	35.	35.	
Office Supplies	25.	25.	25.	
Printing	100.	100.	100.	
Repairs & Maintenance	25.	25.	25.	
Paper & Chemical	112.	169.	226.	
Phone	100.	100.	100.	
Utilities	175.	175.	175.	
Garbage Service	0.	0.	0.	
Janitorial Service	0.	0.	0.	
Sales Tax Payable (8%)	X.	X.	X.	
Cash over/ short	30.	30.	30.	
Advertising	0.	0.	0.	
Rent/ Payment	400.	400.	400.	
Loan Payments	0.	0.	0.	
Interest				
Business Insurance	75.	75.	75.	
Bank Charges/ Discounts	30.	30.	30.	
Licenses & Permits	21.	21.	21.	
Professional Fees	80.	80.	80.	
Total Expenses	**5,893.**	**5,950.**	**6,007.**	**103.7%**
PROFIT / LOSS	**$<3,651.>**	**$<2,587.>**	**$<1,523.>**	**-26.3%**

Projected Income Statement — *Fictitious Cart Operation*
(Sales based on 30-Day Business Month)

(Average sale estimated at: coffee $1.80 per cup; other bev. $1.95 ea.; 80% of beverage sales coffee/ 20% other beverage; food- every 10th customer at $1.00 ea.)

	Month 4 (125 cust. per day)	Month 5 (150 cust. per day)	Month 6 (175 cust. per day)	(% mth. 6)
Gross Sales				
Food	375.	450.	525.	
Coffee Beverages	5,400.	6,480.	7,560.	
Other Beverages	1,464.	1,757.	2,050.	
Sales Tax Collected (X%)	X.	X.	X.	
Net Sales	7,239.	8,687.	10,135.	100.0%
Cost of Sales				
Food	188.	225.	263.	50.0%
Coffee Beverages	1,080.	1,296.	1,512.	20.0
Other Beverages	366.	439.	513.	25.0
Total Cost of Sales	1,634.	1,960.	2,288.	22.6
Gross Profit from Sales	5,605.	6,727.	7,847.	77.4%
Expenses				
Wages				
Employee	2,500.	2,500.	2,500.	
Owner/Manager	1,500.	1,500.	1,500.	
Payroll Taxes/ Benefits				
Payroll Taxes	560.	560.	560.	
Employee Meals	100.	100.	100.	
Total Labor Costs	4,660.	4,660.	4,660.	46.0%
Smallwares	25.	25.	25.	
Laundry/ Uniform	35.	35.	35.	
Office Supplies	25.	25.	25.	
Printing	100.	100.	100.	
Repairs & Maintenance	25.	25.	25.	
Paper & Chemical	282.	339.	395.	
Phone	100.	100.	100.	
Utilities	175.	175.	175.	
Garbage Service	0.	0.	0.	
Janitorial Service	0.	0.	0.	
Sales Tax Payable (8%)	X.	X.	X.	
Cash over/ short	30.	30.	30.	
Advertising	0.	0.	0.	
Rent/ Payment	400.	400.	400.	
Loan Payments	0.	0.	0.	
Interest	——	——	——	
Business Insurance	75.	75.	75.	
Bank Charges/ Discounts	30.	30.	30.	
Licenses & Permits	21.	21.	21.	
Professional Fees	80.	80.	80.	
Total Expenses	6,063.	6,120.	6,176.	61.0%
PROFIT / LOSS	$<458.>	$607.	$1,671.	16.5%

Projected Income Statement — *Fictitious Cart Operation*
(Sales based on 30-Day Business Month)

	Month 9 (190 cust. per day)	Month 12 (205 cust. per day)	Month 15 (220 cust. per day)	(% mth. 15)

(Average sale estimated at: coffee $1.80 per cup; other bev. $1.95 ea.; 80% of beverage sales coffee / 20% other beverage; food- every 10th customer at $1.00 ea.)

	Month 9	Month 12	Month 15	(% mth. 15)
Gross Sales				
Food	570.	615.	660.	
Coffee Beverages	8,208.	8,856.	9,504.	
Other Beverages	2,226.	2,402.	2,578.	
Sales Tax Collected (X%)	X.	X.	X.	
Net Sales	**11,004.**	**11,873.**	**12,742.**	**100.0%**
Cost of Sales				
Food	285.	308.	330.	50.0%
Coffee Beverages	1,642.	1,771.	1,901.	20.0
Other Beverages	557.	601.	645.	25.0
Total Cost of Sales	**2,484.**	**2,680.**	**2,876.**	**22.6**
Gross Profit from Sales	**8,520.**	**9,193.**	**9,866.**	**77.4%**
Expenses				
Wages				
Employee	2,500.	2,500.	2,500.	
Owner/Manager	1,500.	1,500.	1,500.	
Payroll Taxes/Benefits				
Payroll Taxes	560.	560.	560.	
Employee Meals	100.	100.	100.	
Total Labor Costs	**4,660.**	**4,660.**	**4,660.**	**36.1%**
Smallwares	25.	25.	25.	
Laundry/Uniform	35.	35.	35.	
Office Supplies	25.	25.	25.	
Printing	100.	100.	100.	
Repairs & Maintenance	25.	25.	25.	
Paper & Chemical	429.	463.	497.	
Phone	100.	100.	100.	
Utilities	175.	175.	175.	
Garbage Service	0.	0.	0.	
Janitorial Service	0.	0.	0.	
Sales Tax Payable (8%)	X.	X.	X.	
Cash over/short	30.	30.	30.	
Advertising	0.	0.	0.	
Rent/Payment	400.	400.	400.	
Loan Payments	0.	0.	0.	
Interest	——	——	——	
Business Insurance	75.	75.	75.	
Bank Charges/Discounts	30.	30.	30.	
Licenses & Permits	21.	21.	21.	
Professional Fees	80.	80.	80.	
Total Expenses	**6,210.**	**6,244.**	**6,278.**	**49.3%**
PROFIT / LOSS	**$2,310.**	**$2,949.**	**$3,588.**	**28.2%**

Projected Income Statement — *Fictitious Cart Operation*
(Sales based on 30-Day Business Month)

	Month 18	Month 21	Month 24	
	(235 cust. per day)	(250 cust. per day)	(265 cust. per day)	

(Average sale estimated at: coffee $1.80 per cup; other bev. $1.95 ea.; 80% of beverage sales coffee / 20% other beverage; food- every 10th customer at $1.00 ea.)

	Month 18	Month 21	Month 24	(% mth. 24)
Gross Sales				
Food	705.	750.	795.	
Coffee Beverages	10,152.	10,800.	11,448.	
Other Beverages	2,754.	2,930.	3,106.	
Sales Tax Collected (X%)	X.	X.	X.	
Net Sales	**13,611.**	**14,480.**	**15,349.**	**100.0%**
Cost of Sales				
Food	353.	375.	398.	50.0%
Coffee Beverages	2,030.	2,160.	2,290.	20.0
Other Beverages	689.	732.	777.	25.0
Total Cost of Sales	**3,072.**	**3,267.**	**3,465.**	**22.6**
Gross Profit from Sales	**10,539.**	**11,213.**	**11,884.**	**77.4%**
Expenses				
Wages				
Employee	2,500.	2,500.	2,500.	
Owner/Manager	1,500.	1,500.	1,500.	
Payroll Taxes/ Benefits				
Payroll Taxes	560.	560.	560.	
Employee Meals	100.	100.	100.	
Total Labor Costs	**4,660.**	**4,660.**	**4,660.**	**30.4%**
Smallwares	25.	25.	25.	
Laundry/ Uniform	35.	35.	35.	
Office Supplies	25.	25.	25.	
Printing	100.	100.	100.	
Repairs & Maintenance	25.	25.	25.	
Paper & Chemical	531.	565.	599.	
Phone	100.	100.	100.	
Utilities	175.	175.	175.	
Garbage Service	0.	0.	0.	
Janitorial Service	0.	0.	0.	
Sales Tax Payable (8%)	X.	X.	X.	
Cash over/ short	30.	30.	30.	
Advertising	0.	0.	0.	
Rent/ Payment	400.	400.	400.	
Loan Payments	0.	0.	0.	
Interest	—	—	—	
Business Insurance	75.	75.	75.	
Bank Charges/ Discounts	30.	30.	30.	
Licenses & Permits	21.	21.	21.	
Professional Fees	80.	80.	80.	
Total Expenses	**6,312.**	**6,346.**	**6,380.**	**41.6%**
PROFIT / LOSS	**$4,227.**	**$4,867.**	**$5,504.**	**35.9%**

Chapter 19 Check List

Creating a Business Plan

_____	Develop a business name and a professional logo
_____	Cover page
_____	Mission statement
_____	Principals
_____	Products
_____	Service philosophy
_____	Market trend analysis
_____	Target market
_____	Marketing techniques
_____	Target market locations
_____	Sample menu
_____	Personal financial statement
_____	Estimated start-up capital needs
_____	Projected monthly income statements (24 months)
_____	Year end balance sheet projections (5 years)
_____	Business plan is neat and professional in appearance?
_____	Graphics inserted to enhance appearance and maintain interest?
_____	Printed on quality paper and bound with cover and back?

Other Considerations

_____ Have you created two versions of your plan, one for presentation to landlords, and another for your financial consideration and for soliciting financial investors?

_____ Have you modified your plan for the specific needs or conditions of a particular location?

CHAPTER 20

Finding a Great Location

Contents

Chapter 20 Contents - Page 2

CHAPTER 20

Finding a Great Location

Four Essentials

Finding the great location is absolutely vital

The three words most frequently associated with success in any retail business are: *Location, Location, Location.* The coffee business is no different!

Finding the great location that is going to work for you is absolutely vital to the success of your entrepreneurial dream. There are specific steps you can take to give your dream a fighting chance. Following are four steps you can take that we regard as essential in the process of finding a good location:

Step 1: Look good

Your business plan is only part of your package. By itself, the plan is not likely to win for you that great location; you need to make it work. Among the ingredients in the total package you will be presenting is...*Yourself.*

Your physical appearance is a part of the package you are marketing, so pay attention to your dress and appearance when making your business contacts.

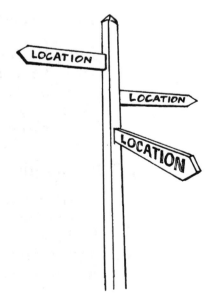

Step 2: Do your homework

You have to be knowledgeable to qualify for the great location. You cannot depend on your business plan selling itself. You have to be able to sell it the same way you sell yourself in a job interview.

One thing we might suggest is that you rehearse your presentation a few times in front of the mirror, or to your spouse, or a friend. Be honest with yourself, and ask those to whom you are presenting, to be critical of your performance. It is better that you work the bugs out of your presentation and gain some confidence before you have an actual opportunity.

The great locations go to those who have done their homework

The great locations go to those who have done their homework. Not only do you have to look good, you also have to understand your product. You must have a firm grip and understanding of the specialty coffee industry. You have to be able to communicate your understanding clearly to others. You may be new to the industry and you may have no hands-on experience in coffee...but you can read everything you can get your hands on about coffee. Watch videotapes, talk to people in the business, learn from others.

Doing your homework puts you in position to answer questions that may come up, with the knowledge to take away objections. When the property manager says to you,

> *I think the whole coffee business is a fad that will blow over in a few years,*

you have the knowledge and confidence to come back and say,

> *No, I do not think that's the case. Specialty coffee has been the hottest trend in the food industry since drive-up windows and fast food. This is actually a global trend. It's the same thing we've seen happen with wine , micro-beers and gourmet ice creams. People want quality in the products they purchase.*

Step 3: Is it a right fit for you?

The right location for your business also has to be the right location for you personally. You want a good fit between the location of your business, your personality, and the strengths and interests that you bring to your business. You want to be able to examine a prospective location and ask the more deeply personal questions, such as:

> • *What feeling responses am I having to this location? Will I enjoy spending 40-60 hours a week here?*
>
> • *What do I like most about this location? What do I like least? How important is that to me?*
>
> • *How do I feel about the people who dwell and work in this neighborhood? Are they the sorts of people I want to be around and doing business with on a daily basis for the next several years? Are there enough of my kind of people in this neighborhood to comprise a good customer base?*
>
> • *Will this location allow me to capitalize on what I see as my strengths and interests? Will this location allow me to grow and develop in ways that are important to me?*

Make sure your location is right for both you and the business you want to create

Remember, for your success story to have a happy ending, you will have to achieve happy outcomes in both your business and your personal life. Making money but being dissatisfied with how you are doing it, compromises your success story. You want to be able to have both. You want to make sure your location is right for both you and the business you want to create.

Step 4: What is in it for them?

Take time to put yourself in the shoes of the property manager and landlord. Consider a situation where you walk into a location and you are thinking,

> *There are thousands of people walking by here, this would be a great spot, we could be incredibly successful here.*

What's in it for the property manager

• Always put yourself in their situation and ask yourself, *What's in it for the property manager and the building's owner?*

• As you talk to them, try to work the conversation around to why your business will be good for them.

• By being observant while you are talking to them, you can usually see what catches their attention and interest and then you can stress these points.

When we wanted to set up an espresso cart in an office building, we told the landlord:

> *We cannot pay you more than a couple hundred bucks a month to be down here in your lobby, but look at it this way:*

This is dead space that's generating no income for you now and with our operation you will at least generate some income. More importantly, it's going to add some sophistication and class to your office building. It's going to provide a service that will help keep your existing tenants happy; and, when you have vacancies, it's going to attract new tenants. And if the landlord of that building across the street doesn't have a coffee bar in his lobby, it's going to give you a competitive leasing advantage.

In this way, we appeal to the property owner's needs and interests rather than just our own. So, appeal to his sensibilities. Appeal to his wants and needs.

A case in point

In a similar vein:

A client of ours in Central California was interested in setting up an espresso cart in a large hospital. When we arrived on the scene, the first thing we did was to look around and do a little research. We talked to the food-service people there and we found out that food service inside the hospital was basically a non-profit operation staffed with all-volunteer help. At that point we realized that, since the hospital was not sub-letting to people for profitable ventures, it might be difficult to convince the hospital administrator to allow us to rent space for a **for-profit** espresso cart.

The angle we decided to take was to approach the hospital administrator and, instead of saying:

We can offer you $400 a month rent to operate an espresso cart in your lobby,

we would say:

In lieu of rent, we would be willing to give you five percent (or ten percent) of our gross proceeds and donate it to a mutually agreed-upon charity. What department within your hospital could use some funding?

That kind of solution is great marketing for your business. You can advertise:

Five per cent of all proceeds goes to the Children's Wing of XYZ Hospital.

We know of a cart entrepreneur in Seattle who has done that with a number of businesses. She has negotiated arrangements allowing her to put an espresso cart in front of various businesses in exchange for her donating a percentage of her receipts to mutually agreed-upon charities. It can be a win-win situation for all.

What to Look For in Great Locations

Finding a good location requires a lot of effort, persistence, and patience

One compelling reason why location is critical in this business is that research in the Seattle area indicates that while people love coffee, they will rarely go more than a block and a half for it. You have to put your business "where the action is," so to speak.

Finding a good location generally requires a lot of effort, persistence, and patience. Your location considerations will, of course, depend upon your concept. One may consider very different types of locations for an upscale, sit-down coffee bar than for a cart or drive-thru operation. One factor common to all desirable locations, however, is the proximity of a large population of potential coffee drinkers. Finding such locations can often prove difficult, but the net result if you do, is profit.

High visibility

You have to count on high visibility and high numbers of people passing by your location on a daily basis

Because coffee is primarily a convenience product and is often an impulse buy, your customers are not likely to go far out of their way to find you. You have to count on high visibility and high numbers of people passing by your location on a daily basis.

High visibility is more important in some business than others.

If you are going into business for yourself as an accountant and you want to find an office in which to locate your accounting business, it is probably not important that you have a location with high visibility. An accountant's office is a type of business known as *Destination Business* where location is not a critical factor. So is a dry-cleaning establishment. People will drive four or five blocks out of their way because you are the only dry cleaner in the area and they like your work.

Gourmet coffee businesses, on the other hand, are *Convenience Businesses.* Most of your customers come to your espresso cart or kiosk because it is convenient for them to do so.

Do not expect your customers to drive around on one-way streets and go three blocks out of their way to find you. Your business needs to be in a convenient location—on their way to work in the morning, around the corner from their place of work, in the mall where they shop.

But even a mall location may or may not be a great one for you. If you have a kiosk in the center of the mall or at an intersection in the mall with high traffic, you are probably going to do great business. But if you are in a kiosk or a cart clear at one far end of the mall outside the dollar store, chances are it is not going to be a great location. You want to locate yourself in an area where your customers can see you and get to you as easily as possible.

Exercise patience

Probably one of the hardest things for people to realize is how important location is, remembering the right one is worth waiting for.

It will be worth waiting for the right location

Typically what happens is, we get excited about starting a business, we prepare a business plan, we taste the coffee, we visualize the store, and we just want to swing the doors open and get going. Many times a person will grow impatient and frustrated, compromising their values regarding the type of location they initially set out to look for. That can be a decision you will regret; a decision that can cost you your business and your savings.

In our work, we frequently have clients who have been looking for the right location for six months to a year, and we always try to temper their eagerness and encourage them to be patient. It will be worth waiting for the right location. It really will make a difference.

A case in point

A client who had been looking for the right location for quite a while called us to announce,

Eureka, I found it! It's beautiful!

When we arrived on the spot, she took us to see the shop she was thinking of renting; and it *was* absolutely beautiful. But after we looked around, we had to ask,

It's beautiful all right, but where are you going to draw your business from?

It was not in a heavily saturated business area. It was on the outskirts of a shopping area. There was virtually no foot traffic. There was not a lot of parking. There was little residential located nearby. So although the building was beautiful, paying customers have to be coming through the door for the business to survive.

Call a pro

It is important to keep in mind that you can call on professionals to help you find and evaluate the right location for your business, and we highly recommend that you do so. If you have to spend a thousand dollars to get a professional opinion from someone who has been in the coffee business, someone who has been through all this a number of times before, do it. The reason:

Newcomers cannot see what the professional sees

> *There's a natural tendency to think that the differences between a good location and a bad location are very obvious.*

Working with many clients over the years has allowed us to realize that is *not* always the case! The factors that add up to a great location for people who have been in the business a while may not be visible to people who do not yet have retail in their blood. Newcomers at times cannot see what the professional sees; they do not understand the subtle nature of the business.

We have been taken by clients to eight locations they have picked out in a given town and all eight locations were absolutely disastrous. To us, they were *obviously* disastrous locations...but not to them. The message:

> *If you do not have the retail experience, hire a professional to help you.*

At the very least, talk to other people who are successful in retail and ask for their opinions.

Working with your broker

As we mentioned earlier in the section on working with professionals, working with a commercial real estate broker can be very helpful. It is important that you come to your broker with at least a visual idea of what you are looking for. He or she is likely to ask:

231

If you could have any location, what would your ideal location be? It doesn't matter if there is a business there now, just tell me what your ideal location would be.

When you can point out two or three locations to your broker and can say:

If I could have this corner right here, or that location over there, that would be perfect,

the broker can then start to formulate a vision of the type of location you are seeking for your business.

Brokers often have vital information that you would never have. They may know of a great location coming for rent or lease before a *For Lease* sign ever hits the window.

Some tips regarding a commercial real-estate broker:

- Shop for someone who seems interested in, and understands you and your concept. Once you have found a broker you feel comfortable with, meet with him or her and spend some time explaining your entrepreneurial vision.

- Touch base with your broker at least weekly to ensure he or she is pursuing your interests.

- If your broker finds a potential location, consider enlisting them to help you present your concept to the landlord. You can explain the details specific to coffee operations and the broker can help you discuss the specifics of leasing.

- Make sure your broker is working for you and not for the landlord.

Two Types of Locations to Look For

There are basically two types of locations that we look for: The first is what we call a *High-Volume Migratory Clientele Location*, and the second a *Captive-Audience Location*.

High-volume migratory clientele locations

Typical high-volume migratory clientele locations include:

- airports

- shopping centers and malls

- sports arenas and performing arts centers

- amusement parks

- tourist attractions

High-migratory locations charge a higher rent

Large numbers of people—not necessarily the same people—pass by high-migratory locations on a daily basis and comprise the customer base for your coffee operation. In an airport, for example, most of the folks coming through may never pass your location again. But there are enough bodies flowing through on a daily basis so you can pull the percentage of business you need to become profitable.

Typically, high-migratory locations charge a higher rent. A mall manager will tell you,

> *We have this huge mall, a wonderful environment, we do all this advertising, our anchors are XY & Z. Sure I'll let you put your cart here but I want $2,500 dollars a month for the location.*

Rent factors can create a significant business challenge

Those kind of rent factors can create a significant business challenge. You have to sell a lot of coffee to cover this type of rent and still be able to drag dollars to your bottom line.

The scary part of marketing and servicing your customers in high-migratory locations, particularly airports, is that you do not have repeat business to support you. Even though the bodies are flowing by, you do not see the same people more than once in most cases. You have to market in a different way than in a captive-audience location where repeat business accounts for a large part of your intake and you rely on drawing the same people back, day after day.

It is always important to provide the highest quality product and service regardless of location. But, particularly in high-migratory locations, *Visibility* and *Appearance* are of critical importance. You need to have your customers *see* you. You need to catch them the first time they go by. You will not get a second chance.

Captive-audience locations

We think of captive-audience locations as:

- large office buildings

- business and industrial parks

- hospitals and medical centers

- college and university campuses

- core downtown sites

- military bases

- densely populated neighborhoods

Captive-audience locations have more appeal because many of the same people will be coming back five to seven days a week

Of these locations, colleges, hospitals, and large office buildings provide three excellent options, given the unusually high numbers of coffee drinkers, as revealed in most demographic profiles.

Many university-based operations do their best business during finals and midterms. But, unless a school has a well-attended summer program, business could drop off by 50% or more during vacations. Hospitals, on the other hand, usually supply a steady flow of customers year round.

Large office buildings with a couple of thousand occupants or more are ideal. One factor that is particularly appealing about office buildings is their hours of operation. When do people typically work in offices? Monday thru Friday from 7 a.m. to 5 p.m. This means that your business can operate around those hours and you should be able to have most your evenings and weekends off.

Yes, you can have a normal life and own a food-service operation!

Captive-audience locations have more appeal for most of us because many of the same people will be coming back five to seven days a week and you can keep building your business on a solid customer base. On your first day of business in a captive-audience location, you may do 35 cups of coffee; but if you produce a good quality product and deliver good customer service, there is a good chance you will get 25 to 30 of those 35 people back the next day, and half of them may have told their friends. If you constantly build on the same captive audience, you should do well.

The other good feature about captive audience locations is that you not only see the same customers every day, but most of them will be in the area of your business 8 hours a day. You will find that a certain percentage of your customers will purchase product from you several times a day.

Some of the following information has already been discussed, or will be discussed again in future chapters, but since location is such a key factor to the success of your business, we will touch on it here also.

Looking For Good Cart Locations

Major points to look for in a cart location are:

- high visibility

- high traffic counts

- ability to have your commissary nearby so you can access it easily

- a location that is safe.

Security is always a factor

Security is always a factor. You want a location where your cart can either be locked up and stabilized in place, or can be pushed to a safe close-by location each evening. Carts can often be made permanent by locking them with anchor bolts embedded in the ground, making it difficult for someone to steal the operation at night.

In addition, if you are planning an outside operation, survey each location under consideration on a typical working day, through the 8- or 10-hour period when you would be open. Check on:

- how the sun will hit you at various times of the day

- what kind of protection you might have at one location compared to another, given driving rain, prevailing winds, etc.

- How much it will cost to run electricity and utilities to the location

Make sure you talk to folks passing by and neighboring shop keepers. Find out what they think about having a cart in the location you are considering.

Looking For Kiosk Locations

The functional advantage of a kiosk over a cart is the extra room it provides

With regard to your kiosk location, remember that a kiosk is often thought of as a larger cart location. Kiosks come in a variety of shapes, usually multiple-sided and can be either circular, rectangular, six-sided, fully-enclosed or horseshoe shaped. Kiosks look more permanent than carts and are usually situated in a secure permanent location. But they are usually assembled from modular components and can be taken apart and easily reassembled in a different location. Once electricity is in place, a kiosk can be brought in and usually be assembled in a day or two.

The functional advantage of a kiosk over a cart is the extra room it provides, allowing you the ability to offer a wider array of products. With a cart, you may have to choose between a granita machine and a pastry case. And you may find yourself saying,

Gee, I wish I had room to serve ice cream also.

Typically, a kiosk provides enough space to offer a wider variety of products.

The same factors that dictate the location of a cart should apply also to a kiosk operation.

Check out the type of security the location provides. You want a situation where someone is watching over your cart or kiosk when you are not there. You may want to have your cart or kiosk designed with panels that go up at night so no one can get into your operation when you are not around. If you are in a mall location where round-the-clock security is provided, a simple canvas wrap may suffice.

Room for seating

Another thing you want to consider seriously in locating either a cart or a kiosk is:

Will I have room in this specific location to be able to put some table seating?

Seating will really enhance your business. Even if it is only two tables with six or eight chairs next to your coffee cart , people will come out, buy a cup of coffee, and oftentimes sit down. In addition to table seating at a kiosk, there may be a space on one side for two or three bar stools. The opportunity to have some seating is an advantage.

Looking For Drive-Thru Locations

Heavy automobile traffic for a drive-thru location is an absolute must.

To find out about streets that may qualify, you can go to your city or county planning departments and ask for traffic flow maps. Those black rubber cords lying in the street that you drive over are counting the numbers of cars traveling that stretch of road at various times of day. Those numbers typically appear on maps that are produced on an annual basis. The maps are public information and you should certainly request one.

Heavy automobile traffic for a drive-thru location is an absolute must

And pay attention to the following:

- You will want to locate on the A.M. inbound commute side of the street. (You are going to do most of your coffee business in the morning.)

- Visibility of your drive-thru from the street is essential. If you are located on a parking lot adjacent to a street, there is a big difference between being right on the curb where you can be seen from a block-and-a-half away, and being set back 75 yards from the street where you cannot be seen by oncoming traffic until it is immediately in front of you.

- Utilities are a factor that will enter into your decision. Check on what types of utilities are available, how you are going to hook your drive-thru up to them, and get estimates on what that is going to cost.

And be sure to talk to your city or county planner and find out about:

- The feasibility of putting in a drive-thru at the location.

- What they will want in terms of curb cuts.

- Accessibility of traffic to the location you are considering.

- The length of the lane leading up to and away from the drive-thru. If you need 150 feet of driveway for your approach and egress and the site does not have this, you need to rule it out immediately.

Looking For In-line Coffee Bar Locations

In-line coffee bars generally require a much larger investment

In-line coffee bars (also known as coffee cafés or espresso bars) generally require a much larger investment than a cart, kiosk, or most drive-thrus. For this reason choosing the right location is much more critical because of the greater potential capital loss, should you make a bad choice. You will not have the advantage of being able to relocate to a better spot because your place of business is not mobile. You will not recover the money you invested in flooring, electricity, plumbing, lighting, built-in counters, and so forth.

(When we talk about negotiating your lease in Chapter 22, we will suggest ideas you can use to give yourself some protection.)

So, what should you look for in a location?

- High traffic numbers and high visibility.

- An area that is demographically rich in the types of customers you wish to attract.

- Near other businesses that sell up-scale products and draw a similar clientele to yours.

- Avoid being next to low profile, low end business.

- A maximum amount of store front. A space 80 feet deep and 10 feet wide requires more ingenuity to be visible, and will be harder for you to make an impact.

Small is beautiful

One of the biggest mistakes we see being made in site selection for in-lines is people investing in more space than they really need.

We cannot over emphasize that too much space is much worse than too little. When it is time to pay the rent, this number will come right off the bottom line for the entire term of your lease. If you have 300 or 400 square feet that you really do not need, it is going to be burdensome and what it will cost you is part of your profit. That unnecessary space will eat up more than just rent: you must heat it, pay taxes on it, and you are going to have to fill it with something.

Keep in mind:

Too much space is much worse than too little

- You always want to hold to a minimum the amount of space allocated for beverage preparation—the operations part of your business—and allocate as much space as you can for seating. This is the portion of your space that is going to maximize your income potential.

- Unless you are planning to have a pretty elaborate food operation, or a significant amount of retail merchandise, you probably do not need a lot of space. We tell most people that probably 800 to 1,200 square feet is a nice workable size for a small in-line operation.

- Try to look for a space where you can have some outside seating. When the weather is nice, people love to sit outside and enjoy a cup of coffee in the ambiance of an outdoor café.

- More than likely, you will want your coffee bar to offer a non-smoking environment, and the outdoor seating will be especially attractive to smokers.

- Keep in mind that you do not need the large amount of seating required for a restaurant because much of your business may be "to go."

Check out those hidden costs for improvements

Get detailed answers to the question:

What kind of modifications am I going to have to make to the building itself before I can actually start operating?

Obviously, you will likely have to build in your own counters and you are going to have to buy a certain amount of equipment. But there may be additional costs that you will need to be aware of. If you discover that you are going to have to re-sheetrock walls, re-do the ceiling, put in new lighting, put in new flooring, re-do bathrooms, *and the landlord may not give you any assistance,* you will have to evaluate if this really is the best location.

Perhaps you could open the store for $75,000 if the space was perfect and all you had to add were your furnishings, counters and equipment and modify electrical and plumbing. But it may now cost you $125,000 if you add the costs for floors, ceilings, bathrooms, and so forth.

Will a change of use be involved?

We discussed *Change of Use* in Chapter 17, an important factor to consider when selecting a location. We will also be talking more about this issue in chapters 21 and 22 dealing with *Red Tape* and *Negotiating a Lease.*

Looking For Mobile Espresso Locations

We see the mobile espresso as an up-and-coming phenomenon with possible potential. But unless you are pretty astute at marketing, it presents a lot of unique challenges. You need to know what you are doing from a marketing standpoint to promote your operation to your potential customers.

An up-and-coming phenomenon with possible potential

In considering location, you need to be concerned about:

- The location of your commissary.

- Where you plan to sell these products. Are you going to be doing county fairs, art shows, and ball games? Or, are you going to be working a circuit where you service different business and industrial parks?

Before you buy a truck or van outfitted with an espresso machine, it would be wise—particularly if you are planning on serving industrial complexes—to secure contracts in advance to:

- Assure your customers that you are going to be there daily for service.

- Assure you that you are not competing with every coffee truck in town.

- Assure that you have the client base to generate substantial income before you invest in equipment.

We are always distressed when we hear somebody say,

I've bought the machine and the cart and all I need now is a location.

They have literally put the cart before the horse (in this case, the equipment before the location). Location should always come first.

And Keep In Mind...

And, finally, there are additional location issues to be aware of that we discuss in detail in other chapters, such as:

- *Target market*: Is there a steady supply of your ideal customers at this location?

- *Competition*: Is there existing competition established near this location that will make it almost impossible to compete?

- *Neighborhood image*: Are the images projected by neighboring businesses compatible with the image you wish to project?

- *Neighborhood safety*: What is the neighborhood's reputation regarding public safety?

- *Labor pool*: What is the availability of quality, affordable employees?

- *Services*: Is there an adequate local supplier of milk and pastries?

- *Landlord and tenant history*: If others have failed in a particular location, why will you be successful?

- *Expandability*: Is there room to grow if your business booms?

- *Overall Saturation*: How many other operations in your city serve specialty coffee?

 For more information on this specific subject, refer to the following books and videos from Bellissimo—800-655-3955.

- **Achieving Success in Specialty Coffee**

- **Spilling the Beans**

- **Opening a Specialty Coffee Drive-thru**

Chapter 20 Check List

General Requirements of a Good Location:

_____ Is there a substantial population mass to draw clientele from? (2,000 to 5,000 people **minimum** within 1/2 mile)

_____ Are the demographics of the potential clientele advantageous to your type of business?

_____ Is the location highly visible?

_____ Is the location easily accessible, and is there sufficient parking available if needed?

_____ Is there any substantial competition in the general area?

_____ Is the total proposed lease rate advantageous to making a profit? (Remember, multiply the monthly rent by 10 and that figure will usually represent the monthly sales volume required to turn a profit.)

_____ Will the location require substantial capital improvements?

_____ Have multiple businesses failed in this location before? Why? Will a history of failing businesses in this location carry a stigma which will make it more difficult for you to be successful there?

Specific Venue Considerations:

In-Line

_____ Will a change of use permit be required, and if so what will the implications of that be?

_____ What will the legal occupancy capacity be, and is it sufficient?

_____ Will you need two handicapped accessible bathrooms?

_____ Will the electrical service be sufficient for your required equipment, or will a larger circuit breaker box and additional wiring be needed?

_____ Will the water heater have sufficient capacity for your needs?

_____ What additional plumbing provisions will be necessary, and can they be easily facilitated, including indirect plumbing?

_____ Will you need a 3-compartment sink and a mop bucket dump sink?

_____ Are wall surfaces, floors, ceilings, and lighting acceptable?

_____ Is sufficient space available to incorporate an office space, storage, and a prep area?

_____ How much (if any) is the landlord willing to provide for the above mentioned modifications?

_____ What will your expense be for the above mentioned?

Cart / Kiosk

_____ Will your equipment need to be moved on a daily basis? Will there be some place secure to move it to?

_____ Will your equipment be secure if it is not moved on a daily basis?

_____ Will an approved commissary be conveniently located nearby?

_____ Will you have sufficient storage at, or close to, your location?

_____ Will you be protected from the elements?

_____ Will you be able to access 220-volt electricity, and what will the expense be to establish that service?

_____ Will the local bureaucracies approve your operation and the equipment you are considering?

_____ Will the surrounding merchants welcome your presence?

Drive-thru

_____ Do at least 15,000 to 20,000 automobiles pass your location on a daily basis?

_____ Is the location on the proper side of the street to take advantage of the morning inbound commute?

_____ Does the oncoming traffic have an unobstructed view of your location for at least 100 yards?

_____ Is the location situated close to the street?

_____ Is there easy access to your location from the street?

_____ Will you have easy access to city utilities (power, water and sewer)?

_____ What might the cost of site development be?

_____ Will you be required to use a commissary?

_____ Will the local bureaucracies approve your operation and the equipment you are considering?

_____ Will the location provide the necessary required lane widths, and approach lengths?

_____ Will the surrounding merchants welcome your presence?

Miscellaneous Concerns:

_____ Will there be any restrictions placed upon what you intend to sell because of existing landlord-tenant agreements?

_____ Will the terms of the lease justify the capital investment you will be making? (Will the landlord provide you with an option to renew your lease, will they protect you with a non-compete clause so that another coffee operation will not be established in the same facility?)

CHAPTER 21

Codes, Permits & Red Tape

Contents

CHAPTER 21

Codes, Permits & Red Tape

It's a Jungle Out There!

Navigating your way to official approval of your coffee enterprise in the real world of agency bureaucracy and red tape can run the gamut from *Hey, no problem,* to any of a thousand scenarios from hell. To give you an idea of what you can expect, let us consider some real life examples.

Case in Point #1

The launching of one of our coffee operations in a midsize Oregon city started with finding a building that was about half completed with a *For Lease* sign out front. We went in and approached the building owner who luckily, happened to be on site. The building boasted a large foyer-type entrance, so we asked the owner what he was planning for the foyer and if there was a possibility of doing a coffee operation there. The idea excited him a lot. He had planned to put a bank machine in the foyer but now he said,

> *You know, I think a coffee operation would work better and it would be a bigger draw for the building.*

So, we continued talking and, within weeks, we negotiated a lease.

We set to work with the full cooperation of his architect and all the relevant city agencies. The government agencies had us adhere to many small details in our design and build-out process and, of course, we cooperated fully. For example, they wanted us to put in a special drainage system with grease traps that would have cost us thousands of dollars, but we were successful in petitioning our way around those (as if coffee produces lots of grease?), working with the officials every step of the way. The point to be made is:

We worked closely with the city and they were fully informed and fully approved of our operation in every detail.

We opened our small coffee operation in the foyer one fall, and it was quite successful.

We owned the operation almost two years to the day when one of us went in one evening to pick up a bank deposit and there was a note left by the fire marshal who was conducting an annual routine check on the building.

The note asked us to call him. We did.

To our amazement, he announced that our operation was in violation of the fire code and that we needed to move our coffee operation, and to be out by the end of the month!

The fire marshal was saying that our coffee operation was a fire hazard. He cited to us the possibility of a blind person coming down the stairway from the second floor, into the foyer, and somehow getting lost behind our coffee bar where they could burn to death.

Believe us.

As absurd as it sounds, **this nightmare is a true story.**

We fought city hall for three months. We hired two city code analysts, two attorneys, worked with the building's original architect and hired another architect.

When all was said and done...we lost. Despite the fact that both architects, both attorneys, and both code analysts said this operation was not a fire hazard, *and* everyone agreed the business was *not* in violation of **any** code!

The fire marshal reigned supreme.

So, we had to close down our entire operation. Luckily there was a vacant space in the back of the building that had housed an unsuccessful in-line skate store, and we were able to move into the vacant space. But we were never as happy with the new location and a year or so later, we sold the operation.

The irony in this story is that about 18 months after we sold the operation, the new owner, who was not aware of our history with the city, called up to say:

> *You know, I think this operation would work better in the foyer and I hear that you used to be out there.*

We said, *Yes, we were.* And she said,

> *Well, I talked to the city and fire department and they are allowing me to move back into the foyer again.*

So, what lay behind this absurd turn of events?

We learned later that the fire marshal who had thrown us out was responding to pressure being put on him by a large and influential establishment across the street from us that wanted to put in its own coffee operation and wanted less competition. We are not sure if this was true or not...but the turn of events were so strange and predetermined we suspect it may have been the case.

Welcome to the wonderful world of business politics!

You have to know that this sort of thing can and does happen. You want to take whatever steps you can to prevent it from happening to you. But even your best efforts—though they improve your chances of success—will not always protect you.

Case in point #2

A restaurant we owned was doing quite well until several food carts suddenly appeared in the park behind us.

They had never been allowed to operate in the park before.

It turned out that the food cart operators were issued permits only because the person in charge of permits decided that he would love to be able to buy food quickly in the park during the summer months and have a pleasant outdoor location to eat.

Effectively, what he managed to do—since the carts offered the same cuisine that we offered in our restaurant at a fraction of the cost because they had no overhead—was to put us out of business.

Regional and Local Differences

From a national perspective, state and local codes and ordinances vary widely in the hoops they require you to jump through.

In one state in the Midwest we were called in to consult with a woman who was half-way through developing an extremely complex coffee operation. When we came on the scene to help her, we just about had a heart attack when we realized she had not checked with any government authorities...on anything! We went down and checked with each one of them—health department, city planner, fire marshal—and every one of them said,

Local codes and ordinances vary widely

Fine! No problem! You don't need anything!

In other states—California, Oregon, and Washington, for example— the picture can be much more complicated.

- In California, we ran into a situation where a health department would not allow a drive-thru unit with windows on both sides on grounds that dirt might blow through. And even though this was an 8' x 12' unit, the fire code required a ladder and an escape hatch through the roof in case of fire. Being able to exit out the door or pass-through window was not considered safe enough.

- Some areas in California require two separate water systems— one for hand washing and one for espresso making. Some also require nonremovable tanks for the water source intake which can only be filled up from a licensed commissary, or an approved water supply truck.

- In Texas, some areas and counties may require four-compartment sinks: pre-soak, wash, rinse, and hand.

- In parts of Minnesota, outdoor carts must have stainless steel counters while indoor carts may use laminated counters.

- California's Alameda County (Oakland) requires a Plexiglas shield to cover the espresso machine.

•Reno, Nevada requires eight inches of clearance under your espresso cart, whereas most carts only have four or five inches.

You definitely want to find out what the requirements are for your locality before you purchase your equipment and sign the lease.

Case in Point #3

When we contemplated putting together a drive-thru in Portland, Oregon, we found an ideal corner that had previously been home to a gas station and had since gone through a partial environmental cleanup. The owners decided to shut the gas station down because it would have taken another million dollars worth of cleanup to finish the job and the lot just was not worth that much. When we saw it, the lot was newly black-topped and there were no structures standing on the lot.

To us, it looked like a prime corner with heavy traffic flows and an ideal location for a drive-thru. But when we contacted the agencies whose approval would be required, it became evident there were going to be major problems. In the end, we concluded that the problems were so major and so complex that it would cost us $10,000 *just to find out if it was even feasible* to put a $45,000 drive-thru unit on the lot. Obviously, we did not pursue it.

Get Involved!

Get information— up front, before you make the commitment to actually take a location

You need to know that things like this can, and do, happen. You need to prepare for all manner of eventualities. It is very important that you do all the necessary leg work, find out as much as possible ahead of time— and document everything.

The minute that you start to conceptualize your business and begin planning your operation:

- Visit your agency offices and talk to your zoning and planning people, the building department, the health department, the fire marshal, and whoever else says that they have the power to stand in your way.

- Tell them in clear language: *This is what I am proposing. This is what I want to open up. This is what I want to do.*

- And ask them: *What do I need to know?*

- Get information—up front, before you make the commitment to actually take a location—about codes, specifications, and anything else local and state agencies might foresee as a problem.

And document everything!

It is incredibly important that you document everything.

The problem you may be up against is: You will talk to one person who tells you it is okay and six months later somebody else tells you that it is not okay.

- Take a tape recorder with you. On important matters have the tapes transcribed and put a hard copy in your files.

- Take down the names of the people you talk to, with dates of when you spoke.

Avoid the kind of situation where you find yourself saying to the official behind the counter,

> *But somebody else who was here before told me it was okay.*

> *Who was that?*

> *I don't remember his name, I don't see him here today...*

At that point, you are in big trouble.

How to Work With Agencies

If you think you are going to convince your local health department folks to deviate from their codes, or if you think you are going to be able to appeal to their common sense, forget it! Basically, you have to accept that you are dealing with a government. You have to look at your situation from the health department's point of view:

> *These rules have been adopted over years and years to protect the public's safety.*

If you are to have any success in negotiating with your health department, you must first understand what the agency is trying to achieve with its codes and regulations. Without an understanding of the health department's goals, its rules and regulations will not make sense to you.

The place to start is with a copy of the local health code. Pick one up and read it carefully.

Many times—especially if you are in a part of the country where coffee is not very popular yet—agency folks do not understand this whole coffee business. Perhaps there is not an espresso drive-thru in your town. Maybe they have never seen one or had to deal with one, so to protect their job, they may just say, *No, we won't allow it.*

The secret to getting a permit in an area that is new to carts, drive-thrus etc., is *Education.* You have to learn from your health department as much as you can about the state and local codes and practices. You have to educate your health inspector about the specialty coffee business and how you propose to engage in it.

Involve your equipment supplier

Be sure to talk with your health department before making your decisions on equipment. But once you do decide, get your equipment manufacturer to help you talk to your health department.

Be sure to talk with your health department before making your decisions on equipment

Reputable and experienced equipment suppliers may become involved in working with your health department if you ask for their help. Some drive-thru manufacturers have been around many years. They have worked in many states, and have a lot of experience in working with local officials. They can answer all the technical questions posed from your local health inspector. They can tell him specifically what they have done in other states and what is acceptable to other health departments. This may put the fears and concerns of your local officials at rest.

Some cart manufacturers are taking an aggressive pro-active approach. After calling the health department and asking what they are looking for, they will ship blueprints to various officials for their approval.

Some guidelines

Some guidelines you can use in working with the health department and other agencies, are:

- Never accept as a final answer, *No, you can't do that.*

- Always come back with, *What do we need to do to make this work?*

- Make them state and clarify what it will take to make this workable.

- And get the folks from whom you are going to buy the equipment involved involved in the process.

Always remember the importance of working closely with your local, county, and state officials in every aspect of your operation.

 For more information on this specific subject, refer to the following book from Bellissimo—800-655-3955.

- **Achieving Success in Specialty Coffee**

Chapter 21 Check List

Typical Agency Bureaucracy Concerns:

Health Department

_____ How many hand wash sinks will we need?

_____ Do we need a 3-compartment sink?

_____ Do we need a 3-compartment sink if we have an automatic glass washer that sanitizes in the rinse cycle?

_____ Do we need a mop bucket dump sink?

_____ What specific pieces of equipment will require indirect plumbing?

_____ Do we need thermometers in all our refrigerators?

_____ What is the minimum clearance required between our equipment and the floor?

_____ What are acceptable materials for counters, shelving, walls, and floor surfaces?

_____ Are we, and/or our employees, required to pass or obtain any type of food handling class or certification?

_____ Are we, and/or our employees, required to be C.P.R. and/or first aid certified?

_____ Can we incorporate the following without an exhaust system: Panini press (like an electric waffle iron); electric convection oven; jacketed electric soup kettle?

_____ Do we need a commissary, and what fixtures and features does a commissary require to be approved? (carts, kiosks, drive-thrus, and mobile operations only)

_____ What other requirements should we be aware of for carts, kiosks, drive-thrus, or mobile food service operations?

_____ Are there any other specific requirements we should know about which are related to food service equipment, handling or display?

State, County, or City Departments

_____ Do we need to file a change of use permit, and if so, what are our responsibilities in respect to updating the facility?

Do we need permits, and what are the codes regarding:

_____ Changes to load-bearing walls?

_____ Changes to cosmetic partitions?

_____ Plumbing modifications?

_____ Electrical modifications?

_____ Installation of food service equipment?

_____ Installation of counters?

_____ Installation of floor covering?

_____ Addition of insulation?
_____ Signs?
_____ Outdoor seating?

Other Questions:
_____ Do we need a local business license?
_____ Do we have to provide or fulfill any parking requirements for the establishment of our business?
_____ If we have a supervised burglar or fire alarm system, do we need a permit?
_____ What about bathroom requirements?
_____ What are the handicap requirements regarding counter heights, door and hallway widths, bathroom sizes and equipment, etc.?
_____ Which of the preceding modifications would we be exempt from because of the "grandfather clause"?
_____ Do any special provisions exist in regards to the following operations: food vending carts, kiosks, drive-thrus, or mobile units?
_____ Are there any other areas or items, licenses or permits we should be concerned about?

Fire Marshal or Fire Department
_____ What is our approved occupancy allowance?
_____ Do we need an overhead sprinkler system?
_____ How many emergency exits do we need?
_____ Do we need lighted exit signs?
_____ Do we need battery operated emergency evacuation lights?
_____ Do we need smoke detectors? How many? Where should they be located? Can they be battery operated?
_____ Do we need fire extinguishers? How many? Which type? Where should they be located? How often should they be serviced?
_____ Are there any other requirements we should be aware of for this type of operation?

O.S.H.A. (Occupational Safety & Health Administration)
_____ Do we need a first aid kit, and what is its required contents?
_____ What other factors should we be concerned about regarding our employee's health and safety?

CHAPTER 22

Negotiating a Lease

Contents

CHAPTER 22

Negotiating a Lease

Once you have determined the space or location that is the proper fit for your proposed business—you have checked with the departments and officials about all the things we have mentioned in the previous chapters—what typically happens is:

- You determine that the space is indeed available.

- You find out who the property manager is.

- You phone for an appointment to meet and discuss the details of the location, and then if you are still interested in the space...

- You write a letter to the property manager expressing your intent to lease.

An intent to lease letter

Find out if an Intent to Lease Letter is binding in your area

First, check with your local and state authorities to find out if an *Intent to Lease Letter* is binding in your area. In those states where we have operated, we found that an intent to lease letter is usually *not* binding; but you need to verify that it will not be in your particular scenario.

The basic function of an intent to lease letter is to officially get the lease negotiation process rolling. It is your way of telling the landlord that you are very interested and serious in entering into lease negotiations with him. Your letter will also give him a time frame for the negotiating process so that he knows negotiations will not be dragging on interminably. Your letter might state:

I am interested in leasing [identify the location] *and I would like to begin negotiations within 30 days and complete them within 30 days thereafter* [or whatever time frame you wish].

Setting a time frame for negotiations is important to you. You want to make sure that if you are interested in leasing the space, the landlord is going to negotiate seriously with you and not be sidetracked into thinking,

> *I do not think this guy is really serious about my location, I better find someone who is...*

Also you do not want him putting you off for 90 days or 120 days while he is looking around for someone who is willing to pay him more money. By setting parameters, a letter of intent to lease will usually make both parties feel more comfortable in the beginning of your negotiations.

Do hire an attorney

When you enter into lease negotiations with your potential landlord, accept that you will be starting out at a strong disadvantage.

You will be starting out at a strong disadvantage

Your landlord is in the business of leasing space and his buildings are probably his major asset and interest, which means he is highly motivated and skilled at writing leases that maximize the return on his investment.

Unless you take care to protect your interests, the lease you negotiate may do you great harm. So, again, we stress how important it is—especially when you are negotiating a lease—to hire an attorney. Develop a relationship with him from the beginning, before you are even looking for space to lease. Keep him apprised each and every step of the way and ask his advice.

By all means, find an attorney who specializes in the practice of business law.

Better yet, if you are in a large enough city, you might find an attorney who does nothing but real estate law. Look at the cost of his services as an insurance policy. We already cited one case [Chapter 18—*Getting Help From Professionals*] where our lawyer alerted us to the fact that the lease as written by the landlord would have increased our tax bill for the space from an appraised $17 per square foot to $95 per square foot after the first year—a considerable amount of money.

A good real estate lawyer can help protect your leasing interests

But remember that while a good real estate lawyer can help protect your leasing interests, you must still think for yourself. For example:

> *A client of ours in Ohio had already taken a proposed lease to an attorney who was advising her to sign a five-year lease with no option to renew. From a business standpoint, a one-year lease with 2 two-year options would have been much more advantageous and would not have locked her into a potentially negative (worst case scenario) five-year situation. Worse yet, it was a five-year lease with no option to renew!*

We told her to go back to her attorney and get his opinion on her asking for a 1-2-2- plus 5. She did; he agreed it was better, and ultimately the landlord was happy to write the lease this way.

Beware of leases with no option to renew!

Beware of leases with no option to renew! With a one-year lease and no option to renew, you can find yourself building up a healthy clientele and then be vulnerable to someone else coming in and offering the landlord more money for your space, or to the landlord taking over and putting a bar in himself once you have plowed and seeded the ground. At very least, you can be assured that he will raise your lease rate significantly.

This is a common scenario. It is not unusual for a landlord to see the revenue your coffee operation is generating as a revenue stream of his own. But there are steps your lawyer can take to protect you, such as:

There are steps your lawyer can take to protect you

- *A non-competition clause.* This is an agreement between you and the landlord that prevents him from replacing your operation with one of his own, or allowing competition to move in.

- *A just-reason clause.* This prevents the landlord from terminating your lease without sufficient reason, such as your repeated failure to pay rent in a timely manner, or allowing the premises to degenerate to a specified level of unacceptable repair and appearance.

These are the types of provisions a good real estate attorney should be able to incorporate into your lease to protect you.

A short list of things you want your lease to say and do

Be aware that most leases are primarily written to protect landlords. For your own welfare, you need to be thinking about the specific kinds of protection you may want the lease to provide for you.

Here are **just a few** of the things you might want to think about:

- *Make sure you are paying for real space.*

    If you are renting 1,000 square feet, do not take the landlord's word for it that the space is 1,000 square feet. Tell him you want a blue print of the building and use a scale to measure it out. Or go into the building with a tape measure. You would be amazed how often that 1,000 square feet measures out to be 925 square feet. At $1 per square foot, that is $75/month or $900/year that you are giving away from your bottom line.

- *Pay for usable space only.*

    If you are leasing an alcove on the ground floor of a large office building adjacent to common utility ducts, or corridors, or ventilation vents, or elevator shafts, make sure you are not being charged for that space as part of the square footage you are leasing.

- *Include a release clause.*

    As ridiculous as it may sound, you may want to make sure that there is a provision in the lease that says, if for some reason the building becomes uninhabitable, you are released from the lease.

    We know of situations where a building burned down, and there was no provision in the lease to terminate the obligations of the lease if the building was destroyed...the tenants were legally obligated to continue paying the rent, even though there was no building left standing.

- *Check out the operating expense clause.*

  The operating expense clause may allow the landlord to recover his normal out-of-pocket costs of running the building. It can also be a blank check that provides your landlord with a profit center—and you with bills for charges that have nothing to do with your operation. You need to insist on concise definitions of both the items to be included and the items to be excluded as operating expenses for which you will be billed.

- *Who pays for electricity?*

  Typically, leases provide for paying the power bill in one of three ways: *direct metering, sub-metering,* or *rent inclusion.* If you have a coffee bar operation, *direct metering* is the most straightforward and probably the fairest option because you pay the actual charge for what you use. If that is not an option, be aware that the electricity clause in your lease could work as a profit center for your landlord.

- *Rent increases.*

  Your lease probably will hold you responsible for increases in building expenses and real estate taxes. This means that your rent will go up as these expenses exceed either those in a base year or an expense stop.

  It is important for you to be alert to how these base-points are defined. Generally, a *base year* is defined as the first 12 months of your occupying the space, and the *expense stop* is the landlord's average per-square-foot operating expense during the same period. If your lease specifies something different, you want to become informed and check it out.

- *Real estate taxes.*

  The real estate tax clause, like the operating expense clause, can be used by the landlord as a catchall to cover additional charges from which you derive no benefit.

  Make sure your lease limits your obligation to real estate taxes and protects you from having to pay any of the long list of other taxes imposed on your landlord by various taxing authorities.

- *Alterations and improvements*

  Negotiate for the right to make alterations and improvements inside your space without your landlord's permission, so long as you are not disturbing the building's structural elements or utility systems.

  Make sure the lease limits its definition of structural elements to building components, such as bearing walls, roofs and columns. You do not want elements like lighting fixtures included. And do not rely on your landlord's good will or promise to be "reasonable."

- *Maintenance and repairs*

  Typically, you are responsible for maintaining and repairing everything in your space and your landlord is responsible for taking care of everything else. Make sure that the maintenance and repairs clause of the lease specifies and limits your responsibilities appropriately.

- *Wear and tear*

  Do not agree to a lease clause that requires you to repair normal wear and tear and restore the space to its original condition when you leave. Doing so is pouring your money down a rat hole with little benefit to the landlord, since the next tenant will no doubt require his own modifications.

- *Dispute resolution*

We recommend that your lease includes a dispute resolution clause

  We recommend that your lease includes a dispute resolution clause that calls for mediation or arbitration of landlord-tenant disputes that cannot be settled amicably.

  Do not agree to a clause that requires you to pay now and sue later for costs in dispute, such as operating costs, electric bills, and real estate taxes. Under this arrangement, you get to do all the time-and-money-consuming work and suffer all the agony while the landlord gets to use your money and is under no pressure to settle.

The above items are, unhappily, only a partial listing of items and concerns that you want to pay attention to before you sign that lease. For a more detailed analysis—and particularly if you insist on not hiring a real estate lawyer—we suggest you check with your nearest librarian for a copy of the *Harvard Business Review* of May-June 1988 containing Marisa Manley's article, "Before you sign that lease..."

(Volume 66, pp. 142-44 & 153-56). We did, and it saved us a lot of headaches.

Protect your rights

Usually, if you do not state your protective right in an addendum to the lease, the lease will probably state that you do not have that protective right. For example:

> *Most leases state that you have to leave intact everything that is attached in the leased space, if and when you vacate the premises.*

You might want to build your counter system in modules so that you can pull them out. And even though one end may actually be attached to a wall, you want to have an addendum in the lease stating that you can take those counters out when you vacate. If that leased space does not work out, you want to be able to take with you all of your signage, all your counters, absolutely everything, so you can install your existing coffee concept in a new location.

So always look at worst-case scenarios when it comes to signing a lease and always add the necessary addenda. Remember:

> *If you do not ask for it, you probably won't get it.*

Definitely negotiate

Many new construction for-lease spaces that you look at will be bare space with exposed steel studs for walls, and a concrete floor. The landlord or owner may not be offering anything else up front, so you will have to negotiate. You may negotiate that he provides all the electrical wiring, all the wall coverings, and all the floor coverings.

If you do not ask for it, it may never become a point of contention

Often, a landlord is prepared to offer all that up front, but if you do not ask for it, it may never become a point of contention. If you want the space badly enough so that you will pay for it all yourself, it may be fine with him. Maybe the landlord put in these improvements for the guy next door, but he asked for them and you did not.

Example: We helped negotiate a lease for a client in a coffee bar situation in Phoenix, Arizona, whereby:

- The landlord was required to pull everything out of the space that was previously occupied by a copy shop.

- We would design the counters.

> • The landlord would build the counters to our design, put in all the new floor covering, and cover the cost of new lighting.

Basically, the coffee bar was 80% built out when the client took over the lease.

On the other hand, you will not normally get it both ways. It would be difficult for you to negotiate this type of a deal in a one-year lease with a four-year option. You have to realize that if the property owner is going to spend that kind of money up front, you are probably going to have to sign a five-year lease, minimum. He is putting out a lot of money and he needs some sort of guarantee that he is going to get that money back.

You must realize however, that in the event that in your desired area retail space is in short supply and high demand, you may not have any negotiating power. In this case you must consider carefully the amount you will have to invest to make the space workable, and if it is worth the risk.

Playing your poker hand

One thing you might find frustrating in the lease process is that, quite often, you may never have the opportunity to talk to the person who has the final say on negotiating points and who makes the ultimate decision. Owners often use an agent or a property manager and this makes it very hard when you want to go back and try to appeal to them.

For example: If you want to renegotiate for a better rent factor and you say,

> *Look, I'm going to be putting in new flooring, lighting, and plumbing...can't we do better in light of this major outlay of expenses facing me?*

But you find yourself talking to an agent who is sympathetic but who keeps replying that the landlord is inflexible in his position. The upshot is that by not meeting face to face with the decision maker, it is much more difficult to appeal to their more charitable natures and sense of reason.

It may be helpful for you to go into a negotiation with **the proper attitude**. You have to think of your situation as not unlike going to an automobile dealer to buy a car. You might like the car a lot, it might be perfect, but you want to send the message,

Coming up with a few objections gives you a little power for some negotiation

> *Gee, I really didn't want a white car. I was hoping for red. I do not really like those wheels, you mean the base model does not have power windows, like the Nissan does...hmmm....*

Coming up with a few objections gives you definite room for some negotiations. The car salesman will know that you are not mentally prepared to sign on the dotted line.

It is no different with your lease.

Even though you may be absolutely wild about this space, a great location that is absolutely perfect, you cannot go into the lease negotiation enamored and spouting,

> *I absolutely love this space, I have been looking for over a year and I never thought I would find anything this perfect!*

At that point, you have lost all your negotiating power.

Let them know that you are looking at other spaces

It is like playing poker. You must put on your best poker face.

Even though you love the space, you need to be somewhat nonchalant about it.

Especially in the beginning of negotiations, you need to let them know that you are looking at other spaces, this one is of intense interest to you, but to make a deal you will have to see the right terms fall in place.

And always remember:

> *YOU ARE THE BUYER* and *THEY ARE THE SELLER!*

Even if the space is absolutely perfect, never communicate that.

We advise you to let them know you may have some reservations.

Check your emotions

To the best of your ability, **take your emotions out of the decision-making process.**

Make sure that the person you are dealing with knows, right from the start, that this is a 100% business decision and there is little emotion involved in it.

We realize, of course, that when you are opening your coffee bar operation, in all likelihood your emotions are very much involved. If you have finally found what you consider to be the right space, the perfect space, you may be so excited at that point that you are going to show that emotion to the realtor. And that is okay, up to a point. It is important to let him know that you are very, very interested. You do not want to play it so cool that he thinks,

This guy isn't serious or committed...

Tell him,

*I'm **really** interested in this spot. BUT, I do have a few reservations, and there are some things I am concerned about...*

You need to shift the discussion from the emotional plane.

The generic lease

It would not be unheard of to be looking at a 40- to 60-page lease, for even a tiny location in a very small shopping center.

Owners of these small centers will often procure what is known as "a standard shopping center lease" rather than spend a huge amount of money for an attorney to produce a customized lease for their center. This generic lease may contain many items that will not pertain or are applicable to you.

Check with your attorney. He may advise you if there is anything that does not pertain to you. Make sure that it is crossed out from one edge of the page to the other and make sure that all cross-outs are initialed by you and either the property manager or the owner.

Percentage lease arrangements

Our advice to you is rarely agree to any sort of a percentage arrangement in a lease covering a food-service operation.

Frequently, a property owner will want to take a percentage of your gross sales. If the percentage is in lieu of a portion of the rent you pay under your lease—say, 5% of the gross instead of X dollars per month rent—the arrangement might work out if you push the numbers around on paper and determine that dollar wise the two figures may be similar.

The last thing you want to do is give away the profitability of your business

But even in that situation, we recommend a percentage of the *net* instead of the *gross*; because, while you are always going to have a gross income, you might not be making any money. Particularly in the early months of your business you may be losing money. So why should you be giving additional money away?

In most cases, we recommend that you let the property manager know up front you are not in favor of any percentage rent. Let them know that if they are going to be inflexible on this issue, the lease negotiations may not go very far.

Keep in mind that this is a very tough business and you may very well find that it is difficult to show a profit, especially in the early stages of your business. The last thing you want to do is give away the profitability of your business.

How much rent should you agree to?

In the food-service industry, typically, your lease rental factor should be about 3% to 7% of what your gross sales are going to be. In the coffee bar situation, because there is a little more profitability, you might consider this percentage reaching 10%.

Your lease rental factor should be about 3% to 7% of gross sales

A $1,000 a month in rent means you have to gross $10,000 a month in sales. Three thousand dollars a month rent means $30,000 a month in sales. There is a big difference between those two sales figures. No matter how great the location is you need to be aware of this up front when you are looking at the lease. You cannot afford to allow your emotions to tell you impulsively

I am sure somehow I will make it work...

without figuring out where those sales are going to come from and how these dollars will be generated. Taking the time to do your homework and planning carefully, may be the difference between success and failure for your operation.

Keep those negotiations going

Try to avoid making final decisions that close down negotiations while you are still at the negotiating table.

Maybe you are sitting across the table from a property manager discussing various points, and he is saying,

> *Well, maybe we could do XYZ, if you are willing to pay for it in the lease.*

At that point rarely say:

> *No problem, I can do that...*

What you always want to say is,

> *Well that's certainly something to think about.*

Let them know that there have been some good points made for consideration. You might even want to say,

> *I think we've made some progress. These are certainly things I'm going to have to review and run by my attorney.*

It gives you a chance to walk away from that situation and really think things out and bounce them off others, including your attorney. And then come back.

Once you have stated at the negotiating table,

> *Yes, I can do that,*

Negotiate your best deal, walk away from it, and think about it overnight

it will be very difficult to come back and negotiate the point. The lesson:

Never make a major purchase *quickly* at the negotiating table.

Always negotiate your best deal, walk away from it, and at least think about it overnight. This is one of those important situations in your life where you will want time to think about each and every aspect in the proper time frame.

Once again, call on the professionals and consultants on your team to help you. Their knowledge and expertise will make it a lot easier for you to sleep at night knowing you are making good decisions.

Chapter 22 Check List

Pre-negotiation Activities

_____ Establish a relationship with a business or real estate attorney.
_____ Check with your attorney to verify that an "intent to lease" letter is not binding in your area.
_____ Write an intent to lease letter and submit it to the property manager.
_____ Make sure that you have checked with the agency bureaucracies and your general contractor to assess the needed modifications and the related expense to adjust the space for your use.

Dos and Don'ts of Negotiation

_____ Play it cool, do not be overly excited about the space. Express some reservations and concerns, let the property manager know that you are looking at other spaces.
_____ Never agree to, or reject, any provision at the negotiating table. Always express: *I will have to consider it, and run it by my attorney.*
_____ **Never, never**, sign a lease without having your attorney review it first.

Lease Provision Considerations

_____ Beware of a lease which requires you to pay a percentage of your revenue. We suggest you do not agree to this provision unless it is in place of a monthly lease amount.
_____ Does the lease restrict any of the items or activities that you plan to offer?
_____ Try to structure the lease term as a 1-2-2-5.
_____ Be sure that any lease rate increases, whether scheduled over the term of your lease or upon exercising your option to renew, are defined. Try to tie increases to the C.P.I. (consumer price index), which means your lease rate will not increase above the annual rate of inflation.
_____ Ask the lessor to absorb some or all of the financial burden for capital improvements to their space.
_____ Ask for a grace period during the build-out phase of your start-up. Request 60, 90, or 120 days rent free, or at a reduced rate.
_____ Does the lease provide you with an exclusive or a non-compete clause? You do not want another espresso bar to open next door to you!

_____ Try to have your attorney work an "escape clause" into the lease. This will give you the option of terminating the lease at will should you decide not to continue with the business. Landlords will usually not approve of this clause, but its worth a try.

_____ Can you assign your lease or sublease with the landlord's approval?

_____ Are there any required deposits and are they refundable at the conclusion of the lease?

_____ Check all the lease provisions discussed in the chapter under the "Do hire an attorney" section.

_____ Have your attorney review the lease.

CHAPTER 23

Design & Construction Of Your Coffee Bar

Contents

CHAPTER 23

Design & Construction Of Your Coffee Bar

Build-out and design is not a major consideration if you want to set up a cart, kiosk or drive-thru operation. A wide variety of configurations exist, or you can allow a cart and kiosk manufacturer to design one specifically for you. With the help of computer-aided design (CAD) software, vendors can easily tailor customized kiosks and drive-thrus to suit particular tastes and requirements. Of course, you want to make sure the kiosk or drive-thru looks good and will be constructed of sturdy, lightweight components that will stand up to rough treatment over time.

On the other hand, if you are planning an in-line or storefront coffee bar, build-out and design is of critical importance.

The place to start

The place to start is with a preliminary picture of your operation in your mind

The most important thing to know about build-out and design is that you should have a definite theme as well as a concept of your operation in mind before you ever start your design and layout. Whether you are spending a lot of money or a little, you want your operation to look clean, crisp, neat, well organized, and to have a theme that works.

The place to start is with a preliminary picture of your operation in your mind.

This brings up an important consideration. You must determine the variety of items you will be selling before you begin the design for your coffee bar. Think about:

What food items will you want to offer?

If you plan to sell sandwiches, where will you store the ingredients so they will be readily accessible for assembly?

How and where will you slice the meats and cheeses?

Where will you wash the lettuce?

Where will you store the case of lettuce and the lug of tomatoes?

If you plan on selling coffee brewers, T-shirts, hats, and books about coffee, where will they be displayed?

Will your retail items be in a location that is in the line of sight of your cashier, so they do not mysteriously walk out the door?

If you have not already given these issues consideration, you should proceed to the next chapter *Planning Your Menu,* and then return here to continue your considerations about your coffee bar design.

Look at operations that are successful

The next step is to go out and look at operations that are successful in both the coffee and food-service industry. It does not matter if you are looking at a successful coffee bar or a fine restaurant; you want to be able to see and feel how operations flow that are well-put-together, decorated, and designed.

Here are some suggestions of what to look for:

- Visit businesses that are busy and obviously successful.

- Look at multiple operations, especially coffee operations.

- Go inside, buy a cup of coffee, and sit down with a note pad. List features and ideas that you like. Take note of which features seem to be popular or catch the consumer's attention.

- Watch how the customer flow is patterned, and how the staff services their customers.

Your preliminary vision and concept may change totally when you experience operations that are successful and, in particular, those operations which fit the demographics of your own situation.

Some design notes

There are many components involved in a well-designed and unique coffee establishment. A few to keep in mind are:

- Soothing and relaxing comfortable effects can be achieved with natural finishes, soft earthy colors and sensually-pleasing textures.

- Lighting is a very important element of your ambiance.

- Traffic patterns for customer foot-traffic should be clearly marked with definite beginnings and endings.

- Strive for originality. As much as possible, differentiate yourself from your competition with your own unique design features. Avoid copying your competition's design theme.

Think about the overall feel of your operation:

- There may be operations, such as a high traffic in-and-out downtown coffee bars, where you do not wish to have seating.

- You may have a situation where you want to have your coffee bar open in the evenings. You may prefer to have couches, Internet access, or a piano with a small stage area where you can have entertainment.

All of these options are considerations in your design.

Lighting and lighting fixtures, stereo systems, the kind of music you are going to be playing, other factors that contribute to the atmosphere you want to create—must all be considered.

- Be aware that bright fluorescent light fixtures, neon, and shiny laminates tend to assault your customer's senses. A space might have fluorescent lights in it now, but if you want a warmer environment you will want to consider incandescent lighting with colored bulbs, or mini halogen track lighting.

All these decisions need to be made when you are considering your store design and layout.

And make sure you think these things through in the very beginning. For example: If you must put in a stereo system, you must have the wiring installed before the sheetrock and wall covering go up.

Ergonomics

Service and customer flow are of vital concern to coffee operations and come under the heading of *ergonomics*, also called *human engineering*.

Webster defines ergonomics as,

Service and customer flow are of vital concern

> *An applied science that coordinates the design of devices, systems, and physical working conditions with the capacities and requirements of the worker.*

So take notes on the ergonomics of the places you visit. Hours spent looking at ergonomic weak spots—such as interrupted customer flow—will pay off dollar-wise later.

But do not pay attention only to customer flow. Be sure to pay attention to how efficient the employees' environment is.

Do the employees' work areas seem efficient, or do they have to take excessive steps, or make awkward movements to perform their job function?

Do working paths cross, creating a potential hazard for a collision between employees?

When you finally have your own concept complete and refined—when you know what the dimensions of your space will be, then sit down with a sketch pad and make some rough sketches of your operation as you are visualizing it. After you do this, it is time to bring in some professionals.

Use your professional resources

Hiring an architect may or may not be within your budget but, at the very least, talk and work with another coffee professional. Consulting firms, such as ours, deal with the ergonomics of coffee bars on a daily basis, and generate basic blueprints for our clients to take to their architects or contractors.

If you have not worked in coffee bars or food-service establishments, it may be difficult to understand the importance of flow and work triangles involving key pieces of equipment and the people who operate them. It takes a certain amount of space for three people to efficiently operate several pieces of equipment without bumping into each other. Too small a space may not work; oversizing the area can waste valuable and costly space.

This becomes the challenge when working with many architects. While talented in building design, if they haven't worked in a food-service operation, and specifically a coffee bar, it may be almost impossible for them to understand all of the nuances of design that contribute to an efficient operation.

Make sure that you take into account the possible expansion of your operation

Companies like Bellissimo understand and specialize in the ergonomic design of coffee operations. We understand customer flow, mechanics of drink preparation, proper equipment placement, and efficient employee work spaces.

A good designer not only understands exactly where to place equipment on the counter tops, but also knows where to leave open spaces for drink ingredients, work areas, and to define places where interaction with customers can easily take place.

By virtue of our experience in this coffee bar environment, consultants help people (who may or may not be working with an architect) improve the customer and work flows of their coffee operations.

Generally we get involved with clients in the beginning of their operation. We are usually contacted at the point where clients are still doing their design work and making sketches.

Once in a while we get called in by a client who already has an ongoing operation which is not working properly. They have done their own design work with inadequate foresight and understanding. Corrective measures are difficult and costly at this point, because everything is already built and in place.

In one situation, a client in the Midwest had already designed and built a beautiful coffee bar in a large downtown metropolitan area when we were called in. He had a one-group machine and **already** needed a two-group machine, even though he had only been open but a few weeks. He had done a poor job of designing his work area and had not allowed enough room to expand to a two-group machine, let alone a three- or four-group.

In addition, the work flow patterns were horrendous, at best. If we had designed that coffee bar from scratch, we would have definitely done hundreds of things differently.

Better to spend a few dollars up front than thousands later to go back and retrofit and redesign

This is the kind of situation you can avoid by hiring professionals to help you. Those with experience can solve problems on paper before they materialize in the real world as costly mistakes.

It is much better to spend a few dollars up front, rather than thousands later to go back and retrofit and redesign your coffee bar.

And remember, even if you are working with an architect, you should get a coffee professional involved to review the architect's plans. Your architect may not be knowledgeable about the operational requirements—the importance of equipment layout, work and customer flows—in coffee and food-service establishments.

Modular coffee bars

Since coffee bars in Italy have been around a lot longer than in the United States, there are numerous companies in Italy (and in Europe) that do nothing but build coffee bars. When you look at these coffee bars in their finished state (in Milan or Rome, for example), they look as though they were built in place and have been there for a hundred years.

In truth, in most cases they were built in modular sections in factories and assembled on site. These bar sections can accommodate a variety of corners, frontages, different back bars and so forth.

You can have the same thing done for you here. You can build your coffee bar in modular sections, and there are several reasons for you to do so:

- You have the option of moving or rearranging them.

- They can be built by a cabinet maker in his shop, brought over in sections in the back of his pickup truck and then assembled in place—which can oftentimes save you money.

- If you ever decided to move from your present location to a new one, you would have the option of moving the bar system with you.

- It allows you to easily expand your operation (if space allows) if you want to add products such as gelato, fine candies, a deli case, etc.

An office for you or your manager

If you can put a small office space for yourself into your design, do so.

It is almost essential that you have an office space, especially if you are counting money or assembling bank deposits. An office comes in handy at slow points in your day when you want to do some paper work but you also want to be available to help out your baristas should a big rush occur. In addition, an office allows you to work somewhere other than at a table in your customer's seating area.

It is almost essential that you have an office space

There is a tendency to design the office in the back of your overall space, where it does not offer a view of the service area.

We think it is important that your office provide you with access and a view of the service counter. You need to be supervising your operation while you are there, and be readily accessible and available when needed.

If possible, design an office incorporating a window or a one-way mirror or glass mounted on the wall, so you can sit in your office and view what is going on while doing your administrative work.

If your office must be in the back of the house, then at least install an inexpensive observation camera and monitor so you can keep an eye on your business.

Selecting your materials

The materials you choose for your bar and other surfaces—along with your bar's *motif,* color scheme, lighting, background music, and assorted visuals—help establish the ambiance you wish to create in your coffee establishment.

Before making your selection, look at numerous options.

Check out the various materials you can use for your counter tops, such as laminates, which are the least expensive; mid-range surfaces, such as molded finishes or tile; and, the most expensive surfaces, such as marble or granite. The differences between them in cost, appearance, and durability can be enormous.

If you choose to use laminates, see if you can have your builder surface your table tops and the front of your counter with the same laminate. This will tie your entire bar together in appearance. Sometimes one laminate can be placed inside or bordered with another to provide an expensive accent look.

Choosing your colors

If you do not have a background in the visual or decorative arts, talk to somebody who does about a color scheme.

Color is very important.

If you do not know anyone with an appropriate background, there are color consultants and design companies that specialize in this sort of thing.

Check around.

Ask the industrial or fine arts department of your local college for help.

Look at other successful operations that appeal to you; take notes.

It is important to come up with a good color scheme and then design everything around that. The overall impact of your business has a lot to do with the materials that you select and the colors you choose.

We have seen a few espresso drive-thrus that are bright blue, and, for some reason they do not work well for us—perhaps because the Italian colors are red, green and white and most espresso operations are associated with those colors. We are not saying that these are the only colors to use, but there are colors that you may want to stay away from.

A bright purple drive-thru with light purple trim that opened in our town in a fairly good location was not successful, and we feel that a major reason was its color scheme. It looked like a place you might want to buy flowers from, but not coffee.

Research done in food-service establishments has proven that warm colors—reds and ambers—are conducive to eating. Other colors—blues for example—generate very negative responses, appetite-wise. And because your coffee bar is also a food-service establishment, the findings of research done in restaurants also applies to you.

So simple things, like colored floodlights or spotlights, can affect the overall appeal of your operation.

Getting bids

Once you have some rough drawings done with all the dimensions and materials listed, ask for bids from a number of subcontractors such as carpenters, electricians, plumbers, painters, flooring specialists and cabinet makers.

It might be wise to consider using a general contractor

It might be wise to consider using a general contractor who will coordinate the work of all these individuals for you. If you have ever tried to work with a number of construction subcontractors, then you know how frustrating it is to coordinate their schedules and interactions to achieve the desired result in a cost-effective manner. General contractors specialize in this function and can save you from unnecessary expense and frustration.

The range in bid estimates can be enormous

The range in bid estimates often can be enormous. Cabinet makers A and B may produce the same work at a similar price if their workloads are the same. But if cabinet maker A does not have many jobs right now and he is hungrier than cabinet maker B who is swamped with jobs at the moment, you can be assured B is going to give you a higher bid than A—simply because B does not need your job and probably does not want it at this time (unless there is an unprecedented amount of profit potential involved).

It is also important to know if your general contractor or his subcontractors will be going through the required permit processes. Be clear about whether you or your contractor will be procuring the necessary permits. By all means, make sure all the necessary permits are acquired!

Make sure the permits are acquired!

If you are having any questions about the permit process at this stage, we suggest you go back and review Chapter 21—*Dealing With Codes, Permits & Red Tape.*

The drawings on the following four pages are for reference purposes only. We cannot guarantee they will meet the needs of your proposed concept or the requirements of your local bureaucracies. If you intend to build your own coffee bar, we highly recommend you use a qualified designer, architect, and/or engineer to insure that your design will meet all applicable codes and requirements.

Espresso Bar
1000 square feet

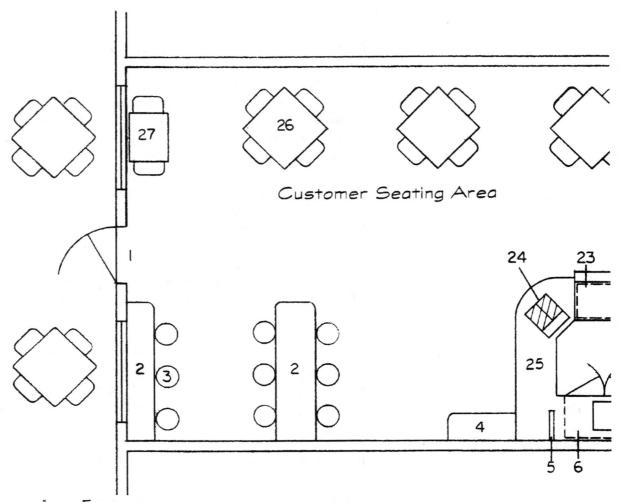

Customer Seating Area

1.	Front entrance	14.	Water heater
2.	Stand-up bar	15.	Ice maker
3.	Stool (typical)	16.	Storage shelves (floor to ceiling)
4.	Condiment counter	17.	Desk
5.	Glass block partition (24" high)	18.	File cabinet
6.	Refrigerator (under counter)	19.	3-compartment sink
7.	Espresso machine (2 group)	20.	Cash register
8.	Espresso grinder	21.	Customer order counter
9.	Knock box	22.	Refrigerated pastry case (under)
10.	Hand wash sink	23.	Dry pastry case (on top)
11.	Thermal pots	24.	Granita machine (2 barrel)
12.	Air pot coffee/tea brewer	25.	Drink pick-up counter
13.	Bulk bean grinder	26.	4 top table w/ chairs (typical)
		27.	2 top table w/ chairs

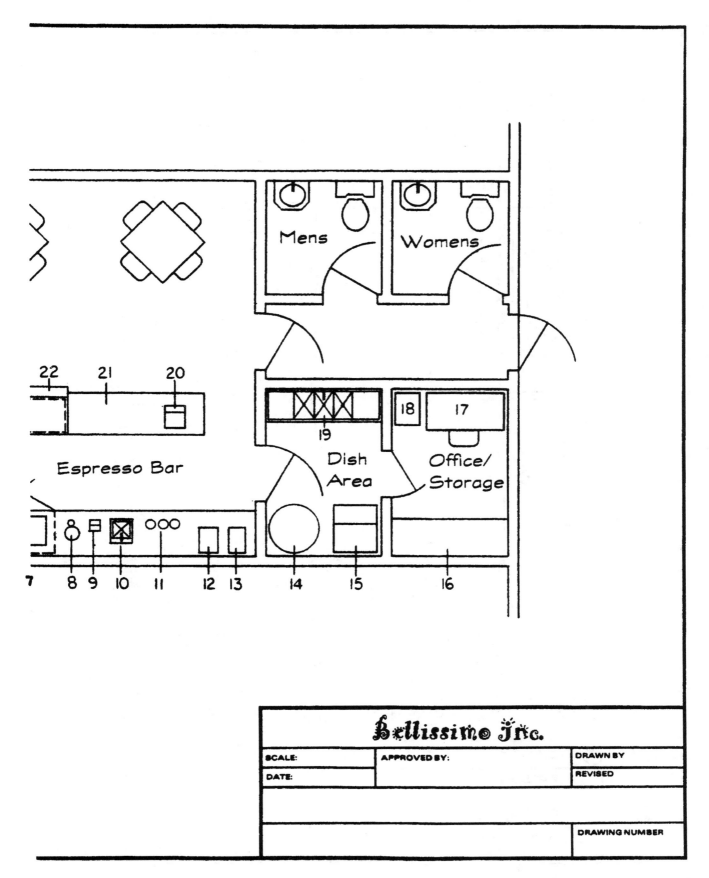

Mens

Womens

22   21   20

Espresso Bar

19

Dish Area

Office/ Storage

18   17

7   8 9 10   11   12 13   14   15   16

Bellissimo Inc.

SCALE:	APPROVED BY:	DRAWN BY
DATE:		REVISED
		DRAWING NUMBER

1. Entry
2. Stand-up bar
3. Stool (typ.)
4. Stand-up bar
5. Table 42" high
6. Stool chair
7. Table (typ.)
8. Chair (typ.)
9. Computers
10. Padded seats
11. Table – round
12. Planter
13. Book shelves
14. Sectional Sofas
15. Coffee table
16. Padded chair
17. Retail shelves
18. Condiment bar
19. Glass block partition
20. Bulk bean bins
21. Granita Mchn.
22. Cash Register
23. Dry Pastry case
24. Refrigerated pastry case
25. Cutting board

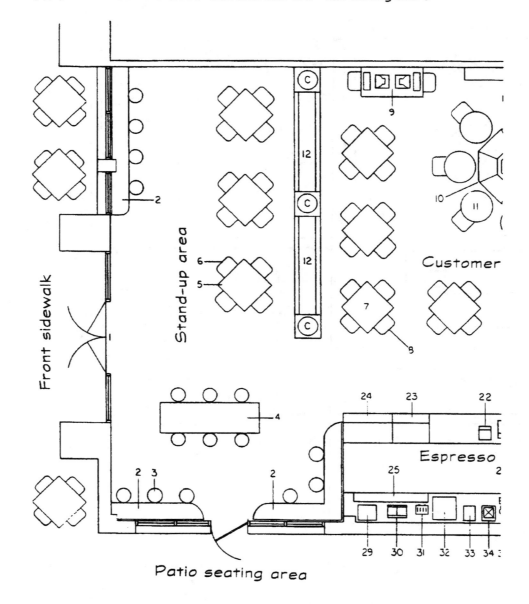

"COFFEE CAFE"
2,425 Square feet

This drawing / design is the exclusive property of
Renee Johnson DBA "Coffee Cafe" – any unauthorized
duplication or use is prohibited

26. Knock box
27. Digital scale
28. Bean grinder
29. Microwave
30. Panini Press
31. Toaster
32. Soft drink dispenser
33. Coffee / Tea Brewer
34. Hand sink
35. Esp. grinder
36. Refrigerator
37. Esp. Mchn.
38. Ice bin
39. Soft Serve
40. Refrig. table
41. Blender
42. Glass washer
43. Ice maker
44. Refrigerator
45. Drive-up window
46. 3-compt. sink
47. Prep table
48. Mop sink
49. Shelves
50. Freezer
51. Refrigerator
52. Desk
53. File cabinet

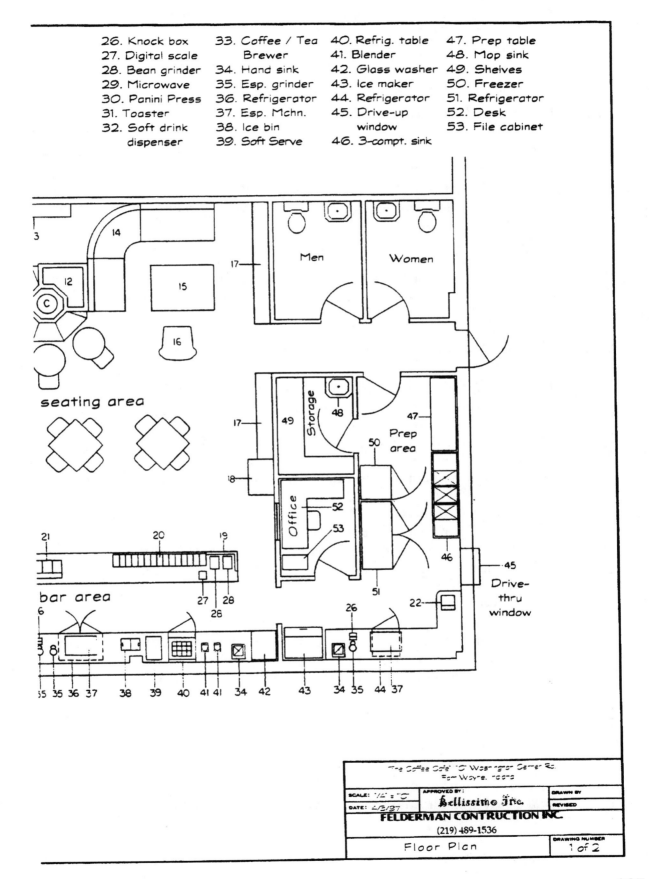

The Coffee Cafe, 110 Washington Center Rd. Fort Wayne, Indiana

SCALE: 1/4 = 1'0"
DATE: 4/3/97
APPROVED BY: Bellissimo, Inc.
DRAWN BY
REVISED

FELDERMAN CONTRUCTION INC
(219) 489-1536

Floor Plan

DRAWING NUMBER
1 of 2

Chapter 23 Check List

Some Predesign Considerations:

_____ Establish a menu and determine what products you intend to sell. Consider every aspect of the production of your menu and take into account special equipment needs, prep areas, storage, etc.

_____ Visit multiple specialty coffee operations, take notes and make sketches of desirable features.

_____ Create or obtain a detailed scale drawing of your lease space.

_____ Create a rough sketch of your proposed space layout and design ideas.

_____ Take into account customer traffic flow, placement of displays to maximize impulse purchases, and ergonomic design of employee work areas.

Working with the Professionals:

_____ Use an architect or draftsman to create a design. At the minimum, they will need to create a floor plan, interior elevations, cabinet details, an electrical plan, and a plumbing plan.

_____ Have a coffee industry or food-service design consultant review your architect's design to assure proper placement of equipment.

_____ Have your local agency bureaucracies review your plans for preliminary approval.

_____ Decide whether you will use a general contractor, or if you will coordinate all the subcontractors yourself. Put your plans out to bid with multiple contractors, check references, and make your selections.

_____ Determine who will be responsible for obtaining all the necessary building permits and inspections.

_____ Choose your equipment (makes and models) and obtain the technical specifications for each piece (dimensions, electrical and plumbing requirements, etc.). This information will be essential for your cabinet maker, plumber, and electrician.

_____ Work with a design consultant to coordinate colors, materials, furnishings, etc.

_____ Select a sign maker to facilitate your signage needs (business sign, menu boards, point of sales signs, etc.).

_____ Create a calendar of scheduled work and estimated completion dates. Be sure to coordinate the ordering of materials, fixtures, equipment and furnishings to allow sufficient lead time for delivery.

_____ Make sure that all final inspections have been performed.

For more information on this specific subject, refer to the following book from Bellissimo—800-655-3955.

- **Achieving Success in Specialty Coffee**

CHAPTER 24

Planning Your Menu

Contents

Chapter 24 Contents - Page 2

CHAPTER 24

Planning Your Menu

Menu Planning Basics

If you are planning a particularly small operation, or have very limited capital, then you may not have the option of providing any type of food service.

But, increasingly, owners of gourmet coffee operations are finding it difficult to ignore a rising consumer demand for a special menu to go along with the beverages they sell.

A case in point

A retired psychologist from Connecticut knew that he and his wife wanted to move to Colorado, and the two of them spent 10 weeks traveling around the state looking at prospective cities in which to open a coffee operation. They had narrowed their list down to eight towns when they hired us to spend a week with them to assist in their decision-making process.

Before we set off to join them, we talked quite a bit by phone and they told us pointedly that they only wanted to do coffee and some pastries. They made it clear they absolutely did not want to get involved in a food-service operation.

So we went looking at various locations, with that in mind. But, in every town we went to, we kept hearing the same message from coffee bar owners:

*Yes, that was exactly our experience also. When we got into this, we were planning on only coffee and pastries, but we have since decided that we also **had to serve** some light lunches.*

By the end of the week, our clients said to us:

You know, we keep hearing the same thing over and over—so we think we ought to incorporate some light food into our operation also.

More and more food product companies are expanding the variety of products they produce specifically designed for gourmet coffee drinkers. Both retailers and suppliers are responding to the booming specialty coffee market.

Advantages of food service

Three important features of incorporating food service into your operation are:

- it gives you more flexibility in how you use your people and time resources,

- it broadens your appeal to consumers, and

- it creates additional revenue.

You always want to take into account that you are paying rent on your space for 24-hours a day...and you want to try to generate sales during as many hours of the day as possible.

If you are serving only coffee and pastries, then basically what you have is a morning operation.

Add some light food and additional beverage offerings to fill in dead or slow times

If you add desserts, then perhaps you have an appeal which will create an after dinner clientele. You can serve ice cream or gelato and it will not take your barista any longer to scoop out an ice cream than it does to make an espresso, so you have another product to offer. We have seen coffee bars that pour fine bottled wine by-the-glass, or have available some nice micro-brewed or imported beer.

If you add some light food and some additional beverage offerings, you can fill in those dead or slow times in which you are already paying rent, without having to make a big investment in equipment or significantly increasing your labor costs.

294

In Italy, 95% of the coffee bars have always served both coffee and liquor products. Perhaps for this reason, if for no other, coffee bars in Italy are just called *Bars.* Traditionally, it is where you go to get something to drink.

Bruce's father tells of the days when he was growing up in Abruzzo/ Molise, that these bars were frequented only by men; that you would never find a woman in a bar. The bars served as social clubs for the men who would go in to drink coffee, wine or other liquors, and meet with friends to talk, catch up on gossip and play cards.

What happened to the coffee bars in Italy about 20 years ago is not unlike what is happening today in the United States. They discovered that more money can be made in the same space by serving additional products and attracting a wider clientele. They started serving panini, pastries, gelato (Italian ice cream), and they increased their customer base by creating an atmosphere that was also comfortable to women. Today, it is common to see children in bars because they serve gelato, Italian sodas and various bottled drinks which kids love.

Since they were already paying rent and hiring people to be on hand to serve their customers, they found ways to generate additional income with the same amount of bottom-line expenses. When you can increase your sales without increasing your bottom-line expenses, you increase your profit.

Keeping your costs down

The most advantageous way to offer food-service products is to do so without taking on significant extra amounts of labor.

Buying your muffins, bagels, and croissants from a bakery saves you the money you would be spending if you were to hire a baker and invest in baking equipment and supplies. If you come to the specialty coffee business with a baking background, you may be thinking,

> *Gee, if I baked my own muffins they'd only cost me 20 cents; otherwise I have to buy them for 50 cents! And I could bake my own Biscotti and save money there, also!*

But you have to ask:

> *How many hours will it take me to do that?*

> *And, What's the investment in ovens, proofing cabinets, a mixer and so forth.*

Your time is valuable.

Your profit margin, obviously, is in your coffee drinks and your beverages—your biggest volume items where your per-drink cost is maybe 12 to 18%.

Your time is valuable

If you buy muffins at 50 cents and sell them for $1, you are running a 50% food cost; so you are probably thinking,

> *Boy, if I bake these muffins myself, I could save a lot of money.*

But, by buying them from a baker, you are avoiding the extra labor and equipment costs.

Unless you want to run a full-scale bakery operation, the extra investment is not warranted by muffin sales. Muffins are not a mainstay item for you. Only rarely will a customer walk in and make the decision to buy a cup of coffee contingent on having a home-baked muffin to go with it. And seldom will they be making a decision between either a muffin, or a cup of coffee. Baked goods are intended to be add-on items to the coffee beverage sale and are simply a way of increasing your per customer sale average, and in turn, your net profit dollars.

Wonderful panini!

If you are going to serve a light lunch in your establishment, perhaps you want a prep cook to come in for an hour or two in the morning who can pre-prep items that will not actually require a lot of assembly time during business hours. And therein lies one of the wonders of the panini (Italian for sandwich).

For people who are not familiar with panini, they typically are made on a crusty roll or a rustic European-style bread, and are filled with a minimal amount of gourmet ingredients. The filling ingredients might be prosciutto and brie cheese, or fresh tomatoes and fresh mozzarella with basil, and generally small amounts of these.

If it is prosciutto, it is one single layer of very thinly sliced prosciutto.

The Italian panini is as different from the American submarine sandwich—where the sliced ingredients are piled high in thick layers on a long split roll—as a Ferrari is from a Mack truck.

A miracle piece of equipment—the panini press

When you first encounter a panini, you may say to yourself,

How can this taste good with such a small amount of filling?

The answer is in the quality of the ingredients and a miracle piece of equipment—the panini press.

Once you put the ingredients in the press, the combination of heat and pressure causes all of these beautiful flavors to permeate the bread. Of course, the spices that you use are very important.

We find that the panini taste experience is much more rich and exciting than your six-inch American submarine. Compared to the panini we experienced in Italy, a submarine sandwich seems to have little or no flavor.

Panini's marketing edge

Panini can also set you apart from a marketing standpoint. For example:

- Because few people are offering panini at this point in time, you may be the only coffee bar in your entire city that has them. You may gain a reputation as a place to come and enjoy a different type of lunch.

- Panini are very cost-friendly.

- Panini can be made in advance, put in your refrigerated pastry case with a sign that tells what is in them. When the customer orders one, all the barista has to do is reach in, grab one and put it into the panini press. A couple of minutes later, the customer is enjoying a wonderful warm gourmet grilled sandwich!

The panini press and other equipment cost cutters

Tips and suggestions:

- Check with your local health authorities and permit departments to be sure that the equipment we are suggesting below can be used without an exhaust system. In most cases they should not require one.

- The panini press is similar to a waffle iron and allows you to prepare a hot sandwich—AND it is one of several valuable pieces of equipment that should not require a costly ventilation system over them. This marketing advantage is very important when you are planning a menu.

- Soups, pasta, or potatoes, for pasta and potato salads, can be prepared with equipment that may not require a ventilation system. Try a jacketed soup kettle if you need something to heat or boil liquids in. It is a commercial version of a crock pot with a thermostatically controlled electric element built in.

- If you do want to do some baking, ask about an electric convection oven.

- When you are planning your menu, take all of these equipment systems into consideration to provide the maximum amount of menu offerings with a minimum amount of food product. Always ask yourself,

  How can I use this food product in four or five different menu items?

  Avoid, wherever possible, bringing in a food product for just one item on your menu.

- Stay away from gas ovens, fryers, grills and broilers—equipment that requires an expensive exhaust system. You may spend tens of thousands of dollars to install this type of equipment.

Choosing food products

Choosing the fabulous foods for your menu that will both please your customers and enhance your bottom line is a tough and challenging task. It involves making decisions that take into account your creative talents and personal preferences, the tastes and demands of your customers, and the resources you have to work with.

But regardless of your resulting menu, never forget the basic lesson:

If you don't bring good-quality products in the back door, you can't serve fantastic products out the front!

There are a lot of wonderful pre-prepared products out there

Within your menu concept, it is important to determine the quality of products you are going to be using.

If you can buy a product that is as good or better than you can make from scratch, why make it from scratch?

There are a lot of wonderful pre-prepared products to select from. Chain wholesale stores offer wonderful salad dressings, continental salad mixes, sliced meats and cheeses, fantastic frozen desserts—some imported from Europe.

So do a lot of research to determine exactly which high quality products you can provide on your menu, at a reasonable cost.

Some do's and don'ts in choosing products

- Do stay away from products that are going to require a lot of preparation during business hours.

- Do not get involved in a deli-type operation where the customer selects types of breads, meats, cheeses and toppings which will require a full-time sandwich maker.

Stay away from products that require a lot of preparation during business hours

- Research an array of gourmet magazines for great menu ideas.

- Do talk to your food-service professionals. Share your concept with the grocery companies that distribute to restaurants and food-service establishments. Your food-service professionals can steer you to the appropriate products, if you can describe your clientele and what you are trying to achieve with your menu.

- Shape your cuisine and menu to fit your customer profile. If you are planning an espresso cart in a high school, your food offerings will be very different from those in a white-collar office building. If you are in an up-scale area with a lot of income and sophistication, your menu offerings will be different than if you are in a blue-collar area.

Take advantage of the resources available in your area

- Explore adding to your menu a selection of tapas—Spanish-style dishes in appetizer-sized portions. This is an old tradition in Spain that has gained some popularity in the United States. Tapas offer a variety of foods for a variety of palates, and range from simple bread dippers to more elaborate recipes.

- Take advantage of the resources available in your area that provide fresh, high-quality products. Buy your pastries and bagels from a bakery or bagel shop rather than from a supermarket.

- There are a lot of coffee-related items available that will work well in your coffee operation, such as biscotti, cookies, candies, etc. There are companies that specialize in items which have a history of working well in coffee bars.

Creating Your Physical Menu

Physical menu—the delivery system that informs and entices your customers

Once you have decided on the items that you want to serve, it is time to create the physical menu—the delivery system that informs and entices your customers.

You should never forget that your menu is not just a menu.

It is one of the most important factors in marketing your business. It is a critical element in the execution of your overall marketing concept.

And there are steps you can take to help your menu do its job effectively.

Wording, writing style, and message

Think about the wording and writing style of your menu.

Simple descriptions help

You want your menu to speak in a language that reflects the identity and flavor of your establishment, and also speaks to your clientele in terms they can understand. When you see menu items like *Machiato, Con Panna,* and *Breve,* you may not know what any of these beverages are unless you have been introduced to them.

In areas of the country where espresso beverages are fairly new, many people have no idea what they are ordering. Simple descriptions of your coffee items can help your customers understand the language your menu speaks so they can make informed choices.

Physical form and placement

How are people going to know what you have to offer when they walk in the door?

Are they going to look at a large board on the wall with your menu offerings on it?

Will you have a menu right on the counter where they order?

Are you going to have a handout copy of the menu they can take back to their offices?

What will the physical appearance of these menus be?

You will have to choose:

Computer-generated vinyl letters allow you ultimate flexibility

- what color lettering, and on what color background

- fonts and types of lettering

- wording that describes your menu items sufficiently without overwhelming the reader

- the grouping of related menu items in appropriate categories

- whether to have your wall menu items hand-lettered, or to opt for computer-generated vinyl letters that will allow you the ultimate flexibility when it comes to making changes.

These are all factors to consider in planning your physical menu.

Your operational theme

You want your menu to reinforce and express the operational theme of your store. You want your menu playing **your** theme music.

In addition to your basic coffee items, consider including signature drinks for those unique recipe creations you have invented that are specific to your operation. And be mindful of how other non-coffee items might blend themselves into your operational theme.

For example, in one of our coffee operations that emphasized an Italian theme, we offered Italian candies that were difficult to find outside of Italy, except in certain Italian specialty stores in larger cities. We procured and offered these candies to further the marketing concept of our particular business.

We also named all of our drinks after cities in Italy so that people could come in and order a *Milano* or a *Verona*.

A *Verona,* for example, was a hazelnut caramel latté. Instead of coming in and saying,

> *I'll have your Hazelnut Caramel Latté,*

the customer would say,

> *I'll have a Verona.*

If they like the drink, it will be easy for them to remember on their next visit. *It is all marketing!* It is no different than going into the country's major fast-food hamburger retailer; you do not have to say,

> *I'll have two all-beef patties on a sesame seed bun with special sauce.*

That particular menu item has been given a signature name, and we all know what that is.

Your signature name identifies the item and announces that it is specific to your operation

Your signature name identifies the item and announces that it is specific to your operation. And it is the fun part of menu planning. Get creative! And keep in mind that you can often tailor your specialty drinks to the tastes of the region you are living in.

A client of ours in Hawaii offers *Coconut Cappuccino, Mango & Papaya Muffins,* and *Sliced Ahi with Bagels and Cream Cheese.*

It works in Hawaii but may not on Madison Avenue.

A signature drink menu that we prepared for a client who wanted his coffee bar to project a galactic theme named the various drinks after constellations, planets, stars, rocket ships, and so forth.

For another coffee bar in the Rocky Mountains, the drinks were named after various ski runs, mountain peaks, and rivers in the area.

Don't let your menu down!

Be sure your operation delivers what your menu says you are selling.

We have a local restaurant in our town whose menu makes the food sound wonderful—smoked duck with capers and goat cheese...but on the plate, smoked duck with capers and goat cheese looks like one big mix of goulash, and it is hard to discern any of those flavors.

The owners have done a superior marketing job and their restaurant is one of the most successful in town...we feel, it is because their marketing and menus are so fabulous.

Just imagine how much more successful they might be if their food quality was of the same high caliber.

Pricing

Another consideration in menu planning—which we will be discussing in Chapter 37, *Budgets & Cost Controls*—is determining the prices on your menu.

Pricing is something you have to calculate and consider.

If you are going to be putting smoked salmon, brie, and prosciutto in your panini, you need to know, in advance, if this will be profitable. Where you are located will influence this decision; it may work in some areas but not in others.

When you go forward to the food-cost calculation section, you will be able to determine if a particular menu item will work, given the food costs and menu popularity of various items in your area.

Be sure to do this before you send your menu to the printer or post your prices on the wall; they will be hard to change.

Add-On Sales—The Frosting On Your Cake

Every coffee operation faces the challenge of how to bring more dollars to the bottom line. Typically, many operators think only of increasing customer counts or reducing overhead. Both of these are valid options, but what many operators do not understand is they have the potential to increase sales without attracting additional customers or without incurring additional labor costs—through *Add-On Sales*.

Add-on sales are items that can be sold over and above the products that your customers initially came in to buy.

The restaurant industry has been well aware of this philosophy for years.

Increase sales without attracting additional customers through Add-On Sales.

When you go out to dinner you may only be thinking of the entree. A good server will offer many other tempting additions to your meal such as: appetizers, mixed drinks, desserts and after-dinner coffee or liqueurs. What might have been only a $20 meal may have doubled, with the addition of these suggestions.

We are not suggesting that increased customer counts are not important, for this should of course remain a major goal for the success of your business. However, the ability to maximize and increase the amount of each transaction will allow you to realize an immediate increase in dollars while developing your customer base.

What is the frosting we are referring to?

The products that will allow an increase in overall sales volume. The addition of food items, confections, apparel, and hard goods can be appealing impulse buys for the customers already patronizing your operation.

Add On Items To Consider:

- Baked goods, pastries and desserts

- Candies and confections

- Granita

- Italian sodas, teas, chai, mineral waters, juices

- Simple food items

- Whole-bean bulk coffee and tea

- Hard goods

• *Baked goods, pastries and desserts*

These are obvious compliments to coffee. If you are not selling a wide range of these items presently, you are missing a golden opportunity in add-on sales.

We recommend contracting with local bakers for such items as scones, muffins, cinnamon rolls, croissants, bagels, cookies, Danish, and brownies. One of our clients has contracted with a retired woman in her small Midwestern town who brings her two or three fresh baked pies daily.

Start off conservatively until you establish your demand and find out which products will sell at your particular location. If you have excess product at day's end, you can discount those items the next day, and market them in a basket next to your cash register. By doing this, you may at least recover your food cost.

Start off conservatively until you establish your demand

In a larger in-line espresso bar, a wide variety of desserts will create popular appeal to an afternoon and evening crowd.

Specialty items such as biscotti, Italian shortbreads, wafer rolls, or baklava, can be purchased from any number of regional or national companies. These items can be delivered by UPS directly to your location, or found at a local wholesale food outlet.

• *Candies and confections*

These items are excellent impulse buys. Chocolate covered espresso beans, truffles, coffee candies, gourmet chocolate bars, mints, and other items like these are typically great sellers.

There are candy companies listed in coffee trade journals which specialize in a large variety of candies tailored for the coffee industry.

• *Granita*

A long time popular cold beverage in Italy, granita can be found at many coffee bars—and even drive-thrus—in the United States.

Granita translated means "little granules." It is similar to a slushy drink, but is much more dense in consistency, and is made from higher quality ingredients. The rolling action of the paddle in the refrigerated cylinder forms the ice granules into tiny balls, so granita has a velvety texture in your mouth.

Some cart operators have designed portable side bars to accommodate this extra piece of equipment.

This beverage, whether fruit-flavored or coffee-based, is ideal for hot climates. The fruit flavors are very popular with non-coffee drinkers and children. There are many granita pre-mixes to sample, or one can develop their own coffee-flavored granita recipes.

One should exercise extreme caution, however, when considering creating their own granita mixture from scratch. The sugar level in the liquid mixture (called the *brix* level) is critical. If the mixture is not perfect, the product will either **not freeze**, or worse yet, freeze-up in the machine causing costly damage.

Whether fruit-flavored or coffee-based, this beverage is ideal for hot climates

Fruit-flavored granita can also be made by simply combining a good flavored syrup formulated for use in a granita machine with water. This cold beverage also provides a handsome profit margin.

• *Italian sodas, teas, chai, mineral waters and juices*

Popular beverage alternatives to coffee-based drinks.

Italian sodas—the most typical item sold from coffee operations—are made by simply combining a gourmet syrup with a good mineral or soda water. Variations on this theme are cremosas and Amalfi's, which are Italian sodas with the addition of half and half or heavy cream.

Tea is seeing a tremendous resurgence in popularity. Tea can, of course, be served hot or cold, flavored with syrup or left plain. There are many varietals to choose from, some with caffeine and many without.

Chai is a variation of a tea-flavored beverage that is brewed tea with the addition of honey and spices. This concentrate is then normally added to milk and steamed with the espresso machine creating in essence a sweetened, spiced tea latte. The drink is now gaining unheralded popularity in many locations in the Northwest.

A variety of *mineral waters and bottled fruit juices* can be served chilled to offer even a wider beverage selection.

- ## *Simple Food Items*

  Simple food items can expand business by creating a demand for lunch and increase afternoon and evening customers.

  Focaccia bread is a popular item and can be topped with many gourmet toppings such as sun-dried tomatoes, kalamata olives, cheese, etc. And do not forget panini—those gourmet Italian sandwiches grilled with a panini press that we talked about earlier—that typically contain small amounts of fillings providing a favorable food cost.

  A creative **enclosed** cart operator in our office park has added a food warmer to his coffee operation and sells soups, chilies, pre-made sandwiches and chips in a very limited space. He has doubled his daily volume with the addition of these items.

  Larger espresso bars may wish to consider other food items such as Caesar or pasta salad.

- ## *Whole-bean bulk coffee and tea*

  Developing a display of bulk beans in bins or a pre-packaged coffee will help you develop a demand for your particular blend and brand. This should also benefit your retail beverage sales.

- ## *Hard Goods*

  Home coffee brewers, French presses, stovetop espresso makers, grinders, filters, ceramic cups, are obvious retail items one is used to seeing in coffee bars.

  There are many other items that will also allow a full keystone markup (selling a product at double the cost) such as greeting cards, T-shirts and sweat shirts, books, coffee jewelry, etc.

  And there are many items—such as travel mugs and clothing items—that can be embellished with your logo. Even if your logo items are sold at little or no profit, they will provide continuing and valuable promotion of your business.

You should, of course, check your lease and your local government agencies to make sure you will not create any conflicts of interest with neighboring tenants or local ordinances.

Putting additional revenue into your cash register

Do not be concerned if your profit margins on add-on items are not as great as the margin on your coffee beverages. The important thing to remember is, _You are putting additional revenue into your cash register._

And, in most cases, the suggestions we have made will require little or no additional labor or extended hours of operation.

Be sure to analyze your specific market and your operation to determine which items might be appropriate for you. Then:

- Start with a very limited number of items and track your sales to determine which items and which types of items there is a demand for.

- Display of any additional items must be aesthetically pleasing and in plain view of the customer.

- You will need to educate and train your employees to suggest and sell these items if you are to realize the maximum benefit from these additional products.

As in any business, your coffee business needs to be constantly adapting and innovating to stay ahead of your competition. We feel that implementing a program based on ad-on sales will result in an immediate and significant sales growth.

Sample Menus

The menus on the following pages are typical for different levels of operation, ranging from the more simple to the more complex:

Menu #1—Basic Espresso Menu

Menu #2—Signature Espresso Beverage (House Specialties)

Menu #3—Pastries & Baked Goods / Panini

Consider these sample menus as prototypes or models in planning your own menu. You should find them useful. If you expand beyond this, you are, then basically designing a restaurant.

For more information on this specific subject, refer to the following books and videos from Bellissimo—800-655-3955.

- **Achieving Success in Specialty Coffee**

- **Everything BUT Coffee**

ESPRESSO BEVERAGES

Espresso
The essence of coffee extracted into a concentrated one-ounce beverage

Caffé Americano
Espresso combined with hot water, creating a gourmet brewed coffee.

Cappuccino
Espresso combined with a velvety milk foam.

Caffe Latté
Espresso combined with steamed milk, topped with a small amount of a velvety milk foam.

Flavored Latté
The Caffe Latté with the addition of a gourmet flavored syrup. Try one or combine several! Choose from: vanilla, almond, hazelnut, macadamia nut, caramel, Irish cream, raspberry, orange, etc.

Caffé Mocha
The Caffé Latté with the addition of gourmet chocolate, topped with whipped cream and chocolate sprinkles.

Caffé Olé
Espresso combined with brewed coffee and steamed milk, topped with whipped cream.

Espresso Macchiato
The straight shot of Espresso topped with a spoon of velvety milk foam.

Espresso Con Panna
The straight shot of Espresso topped with whipped cream.

Brevé
An extra rich version of the Caffé Latté made with half & half.

CAFFE SIGNATURE DRINKS

Nutty Raspberry

Espresso coffee combined with gourmet raspberry and almond syrups, steamed milk, topped with whipped cream. (Iced upon request)

Caffé Milano

Visit Milan with Espresso coffee, gourmet caramel and hazelnut syrups, combined with steamed milk, topped with whipped cream. (Iced upon request)

White Mocha Sunset

Espresso coffee, gourmet white chocolate and orange syrup, combined with steamed milk, topped with whipped cream. (Iced upon request)

Chocolate Macadamia Nut

Espresso coffee, gourmet chocolate and macadamia nut syrups, combined with steamed milk, topped with whipped cream. (Iced upon request)

Vanilla Cappuccino

Cappuccino made with a velvety gourmet vanilla milk foam.

Rockin' Java

Espresso coffee combined with gourmet brewed coffee. Guaranteed to get you rollin' !

PASTRIES AND BAKED GOODS

Bagels
> *with cream cheese*
> *with cream cheese & lox*

Stuffed Croissants
> *(almond, ham & cheese, or spinach & feta)*

Scones

Muffins

Cinnamon Rolls

Toast or English Muffin

Cake

Brownies

Cookies

PANINI

(Italian-style grilled sandwiches made on fresh focaccia bread)

Turkey Cranberry Cream Cheese

Roast Beef Cheddar Melt
> *Lean roast beef, grilled onions, cheddar cheese*
> *and a special horseradish sauce*

Southwest Chicken
> *Mesquite broiled chicken breast with Monterey*
> *jack cheese & mild Ortega chilies*

Prosciutto & Brie
> *Italian style Prosciutto ham & creamy Brie cheese*

Fresh Tomato & Mozzarella
> *Ripe garden tomatoes, mozzarella cheese & basil*

Add a small mixed green salad, a scoop of potato or pasta salad, or potato chips for an additional...

Chapter 24 Check List

Menu Planning:

Establish a menu for each of the following:

_____ Basic espresso beverage menu

_____ Other beverage menu (juices, teas, sodas, mineral waters, granitas, smoothies, shakes, chai, etc.)

_____ Signature drink menu (recipes unique to your operation)

_____ Baked goods menu (morning pastries and desserts)

_____ Other food items (panini, sandwiches, salads, etc.)

_____ Impulse or prepackaged items (biscotti, cookies, candies, bulk beans, etc.)

_____ Determine the availability of all these products, or the components which will create these items.

_____ Determine your cost for purchasing these products and ingredients.

_____ Determine if ingredients will be used for multiple menu items.

_____ Analyze the consumer demand and acceptance of these menu items. Who is your target market and what do they want?

_____ Determine what equipment will be necessary to store, prepare, and display these products. Analyze the cost associated with this equipment, and the space requirements.

_____ Analyze any additional labor hours/dollars which will be required to prepare your menu.

_____ Take into consideration any additional training which will be required to teach your employees how to make these items.

_____ Determine your actual cost for each menu item.

_____ Create a projected menu mix.

_____ Determine a selling price for each menu item, and create an estimated cost of sales based upon your projected menu mix. Adjust your pricing until your estimated cost of sales meets your financial goals.

_____ Create item descriptions for your physical menu.

_____ Work with your sign maker to create your physical menus.

CHAPTER 25

Choosing & Buying Equipment

Contents

Chapter 25 Contents - Page 2

CHAPTER 25

Choosing & Buying Equipment

Getting To Know Your Equipment Dealers

Once you have determined your menu and bar design, you can then start selecting and purchasing your equipment. A good place to start learning about your various equipment options is by talking to numerous equipment dealers. Keep your eyes and ears open and remember, everyone will tell you their equipment is the best.

Remember, everyone will tell you their equipment is the best

Anytime you can purchase your entire equipment package through one source, you can generally work a package deal and get a better price than if you are putting items together piecemeal.

Of course, it may not be possible to purchase everything from one company, especially if you are planning a sit-down coffee bar with ice machines and jacketed soup kettles. You most likely will be purchasing some items from a restaurant supply company and others from an espresso equipment company. But whether you are buying from a company that sells restaurant supplies or only espresso equipment, you need to ask:

• *Who is selling me this equipment?*

> • *How long have they been in business?*

> • *Do they belong to the Better Business Bureau (BBB)?*

Do they belong to the Better Business Bureau

Of course, not all companies may join a local BBB for any number of valid reasons, but if they do belong, you can call the bureau for a rating of the company. Then ask yourself:

> • *Do they deal with me in a professional manner?*

> • *How long have they been selling espresso/food-service equipment?*

> • *Is their equipment N.S.F. and U.L. approved?*

> • *What are the conditions of the machine warranty and will the company selling the machine be the warranty agents?*

If the manufacturer or importer is the warranty agent rather than the company who sold you the machine, you will probably have to pay for the initial repair and then seek reimbursement from them.

> • *Do they have an authorized factory-trained service technician? If not, who will repair your machine?*

A lot of espresso equipment companies will tell you they have a nationwide service network but, in many cases, they merely subcontract their servicing to local appliance repair people who may have no actual hands-on experience with your equipment. They may only have a manual that tells them about your machine but no actual experience in fixing it.

Do their service technicians carry a large inventory of parts in their trucks?

> • *Do they have a complete inventory of parts and a service department available 365 days a year, 18 to 24 hours a day?*

Here again, if the company that sold you the machine does not have a substantial supply and variety of parts, will you be able to get your equipment repaired in a timely fashion or will you have to start hunting for parts around the country; or worse yet, wait for them to be sent from Italy? So, ask this question:

> • *Do their service technicians carry a large inventory of parts in their warehouse or trucks?*

If your machine breaks down at 9 a.m. on a Saturday morning, will you be able to expect a service technician to facilitate a repair then, or will it have to wait until Monday? Will your customers just stop drinking coffee for two days until you are up and running again? We think not.

Try to work with those companies that can provide the services you may need beyond the initial sale.

Get and check references

Everybody is going to tell you that they will provide you with wonderful service! So, it is important to:

- Get some references from the dealer or the equipment company under consideration.

- Call the references and find out what their experience has been with the machine and the company. If there were problems with equipment, was the company there to help their clients? If you will be looking to this company for your training, are they or their staff qualified to teach you the nuances of correct espresso preparation?

- If the company does not provide you with numerous references that check out, **be very cautious about buying anything from them.**

Check other sources

Obviously, companies will provide references who they feel are happy with their product and service—in other words, somebody who has never called them with a problem. So be sure to check around in your own area and identify people using the same type of machine. Go in and ask the owner questions. Find out what kind of reputation this equipment company has.

Find out what kind of reputation this equipment company has

Before making a substantial cash investment in an espresso machine, do your best to get unbiased information from as many sources as possible about the manufacturer's history and reputation for the particular brand you are considering. Shop and compare at least three brands of machines. Make a checklist and compare and evaluate their features. As each dealer points out the superior features of their machine, you will begin to understand how espresso machines work and what features are important to producing a quality product. Remember to:

- Take your time

- Do good research

- Focus on quality and reliability

Get it in writing

And, finally, when you buy the equipment of your choice,

Get everything in writing!

If they tell you the warranty guarantees your espresso machine totally for 24 months, you want that in writing. If they tell you they will come out on a Sunday to fix a problem with the machine, make sure you have that in writing. Then, when you call them on a Sunday and they say,

No, no, no, I never said that,

you have something to fall back on.

Remember, your espresso machine is the heart of your specialty coffee business and one of the most important business decisions you will make.

The espresso machine's strange path to America

Before we get into the specifics of how an espresso machine works, we thought you may enjoy hearing about its evolutionary path to America.

The majority of espresso machines on the market are from Europe, and in particular, Italy. The Italian culture of coffee consumption is quite different than ours, in that most of the coffee in Italy is consumed as espresso, and most espresso is enjoyed as a straight shot, or occasionally as a cappuccino. Large 12- and

The majority of espresso machines on the market are from Europe

16-ounce espresso beverages are unheard of in Italy. The demand upon an espresso machine in Italy is primarily for the extraction of the coffee, and not for the seemingly endless production of steamed milk.

Another factor worthy of mention is that electricity is very expensive in Europe. Because of this, many European merchants desired espresso machines with boilers that could be heated by less expensive natural gas. Here lies the root of the problem:

Surface area is advantageous when heating with flames, so these gas heated espresso machines were designed with very large boilers. When these machines were brought to the United States (where electricity is economical), many of these machines continued to use the same size boilers which were now fitted with an internal electric heating element.

A huge boiler is not an advantage when heating is achieved with an electric element, unless the element has significant watts of power flowing through it. So, many of these machines were introduced to the United State's market with powerful heating elements. Unfortunately, the wiring and switches did not meet U.L. (Underwriter's Laboratories) approval for the amount of volts and watts that were traveling through these components.

Solution? *Use a much less powerful heating element.* Less watts traveling through all the components, and U.L. was happy. Unfortunately, the majority of these machines were now grossly underpowered, incapable of obtaining or maintaining the temperature necessary for proper extraction and prolonged steaming.

Because many of the business owners in the United States who were preparing espresso did not understand the characteristics of a good shot, they were not concerned about tepid espresso with the total absence of crema.

However, they were concerned that their machines could not produce sufficient steam to meet the demand for large quantities of steamed milk...the major component of the espresso beverages enjoyed by the American public.

Solution? *Install steaming valves that restrict the flow of steam, and equip the wands with tips which have tiny holes.* By greatly restricting the flow of steam, the pressure and longevity of steaming power seemed improved to the operator. Unfortunately it now took a lot longer to steam a pitcher of milk, and the steam was extremely wet, producing minimal froth.

The point of this history lesson is to make you aware that some companies brought machines to this country that were a patchwork of alterations and modifications.

There are good reasons why one machine costs thousands more than another

This was the case five years ago or more, but since then most, if not all, manufacturers have adjusted their design to meet the demands of the American beverage market. Past concerns such as temperature stability and sufficient steaming capacity are no longer problems. We tend to make decisions on machine selection based upon design features related to ergonomics and ease of use. Two features we look for in a machine are sufficient distance between the portafilter and drain grate so that larger cups (16 and 24 ounce.) can be placed directly under the portafilter, and a long steam wand length so that larger volume steaming pitchers can be used.

Price does not necessarily dictate quality, but it is often a good indicator. Obviously, there are a few brands that will cost more. You will need to decide if your operation can afford the BMW, or if one of the medium-priced machines will do the job and fit within your budget better. This is a decision you will need to make.

You would be wise to educate yourself to which factors are important in an espresso machine, and the reputations of the companies that manufacture them.

What Makes An Espresso Machine Tick?

Learn as much as you can from several different manu-facturers

Whether you are buying a machine for the first time or not, it is undoubtedly helpful to know as much about this piece of equipment as you can. Each manufacturer and their sales reps will tout the advantages of their features and the disadvantages of the other brands. Take all this with a grain or two of salt.

However, retain as much information as possible and take notes. Ask other companies about their machine's features, and the features which were emphasized as important by the previous company.

As you gain more and more information, you will be able to sort out what is truly considered important. Learn as much as you can from several different manufacturers, find the best machine for your situation, and then ask their customers a lot of questions—the folks who are out there acquiring the hands-on experience that turns amateurs into professionals.

And the place to start is with some basic knowledge of what an espresso machine is and what it does.

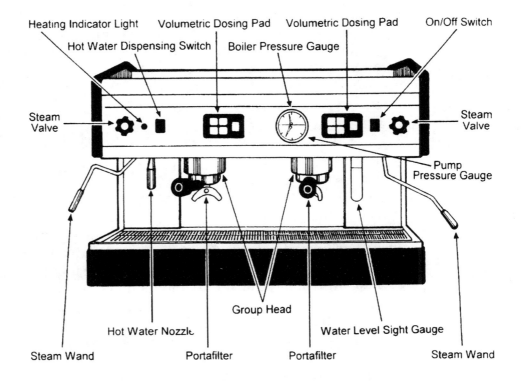

Heating Indicator Light Volumetric Dosing Pad Volumetric Dosing Pad On/Off Switch
Hot Water Dispensing Switch Boiler Pressure Gauge
Steam Valve
Steam Valve
Pump Pressure Gauge
Group Head
Hot Water Nozzle Portafilter Portafilter Water Level Sight Gauge
Steam Wand Steam Wand

There are five basic components to every espresso machine:

- *Boiler*

- *Heat exchanger*

- *Pump*

- *Group (consisting of the portafilter and the group head)*

- *Steam wand*

The basic function of the first four components is to force water at the proper temperature and pressure through properly ground coffee beans to deliver the perfect shot of espresso.

The ground coffee comes to the espresso machine by falling out of your gravity-fed grinder into a doser (with a pull of a lever), into the portafilter, where it is firmly compacted, placed back into the machine, and hot water is forced through it. (The grinder is not a part of your espresso machine—unless you have a fully-automatic one—and we will talk more about the grinder further along in this chapter.)

Boiler

The water is heated for brewing and steaming by the boiler—a sturdy metal tank inside the espresso machine, heated by an enclosed electric heating element which heats the water.

The boiler is used in two ways:

- It vents out steam from the machine's steam wand(s) for foaming milk.

- It heats the brewing water via a heat exchanger.

Boilers are made of either copper, nickel-plated copper, or stainless steel. Each metal has its advantages and disadvantages. Many will swear that a copper boiler is best, but several highly qualified machine technicians we have talked to told us they can see very little or no difference. Some concerns have been expressed about the lead content of copper boilers and the effects it may have on health. For this reason, many of the copper boilers today have been nickel-plated.

Most boilers are equipped with a pressure sensor that automatically signals the pump, or opens a valve, to send more water to the boiler when the water level drops below a certain point due to steam escaping from the steam wand. The refilling of the boiler is accomplished by either a pump, or the normal pressure of your local water system.

Some machines are built with two boilers, one for the steam wand and the second for heating the brewing water.

The advantage of a two-boiler system is that there is a separate heat supply for the brewing water and for the steaming wands, and the excessive use of one will not affect the performance of the other. Also, each boiler can be maintained at a temperature that is best suited to its purpose: the brew-water boiler can be set for an optimal extraction temperature (around 195° Fahrenheit), while the steam-wand boiler can be maintained at 212° Fahrenheit, the temperature at which water turns to steam.

The disadvantage to a two-boiler machine is there is the potential for double the trouble: two heating elements, two fill valves, two temperature sensors, etc.

Two-boiler machines were the standard years ago, but most newer machines accomplish all functions with one boiler.

A more powerful element is better

Much debate exists over the importance of the capacity (size) of the boiler. Perhaps more important than the actual capacity is the relationship of the boiler's capacity to the heat produced by the electrical heating element. A small boiler with a stronger element may actually have a faster recovery time and less temperature fluctuation than a large boiler with a smaller heating element. The one fact that does seem to hold true is, a more powerful element is better.

The heating element inside the boilers varies according to its manufacturer's specifications but, in general, heating elements in quality machines will remain functioning and trouble free for a very long time.

Heat exchanger

The heat exchanger is a copper or stainless steel tube or coil which runs through the boiler and heats the brewing water as it travels through the tube. The water used for brewing does not come directly from the boiler. This water would be too hot and would scald the ground coffee.

Important features for multiple group machines

The overall length of the heat exchanger in the boiler is important; the longer the heat exchanger, the more consistent the brewing temperature.

Important features for multiple-group machines (machines with 2 or more groups) are the number of heat exchangers and the relative length of the supply tubes to each group.

For example:

If you are considering a machine with three groups, it is advantageous that the boiler contains three heat exchangers, and that the length of the tubes from each exchanger to their respective group is similar in length.

If you are considering a three-group machine with only one exchanger, typically the brew water feed tube will travel from the exchanger to the first group, then from the first group to the second group, and finally to the third group. Valuable water temperature will be lost along each leg of this journey. The result will be an inconsistent and different brewing temperature at each group.

A similar inconsistency can exist if the feed tubes from multiple heat exchangers to their respective groups are of significantly different lengths.

Pump

Your pump must produce 130 pounds of pressure for a proper extraction

The pump is a mechanical device that pushes water through the portafilter for extracting the espresso, and it may pump water into the boiler for steaming.

There are two types of pumps used in espresso machines: vibrating pumps (primarily used in home espresso machines) and rotary pumps, which are typically used in commercial machines.

Having an adequate pump is essential. Your pump must produce 130 pounds of pressure for a proper extraction.

The Group

The group is composed of two major sets of components: the *portafilter* and the *group head*.

The *portafilter* is the "metal cup with the handle" that holds the coffee grounds.

Inside the portafilter is the *filter basket*, a stainless steel perforated basket into which the ground coffee is actually dispensed and compacted. During brewing, the hot water passes through the coffee, and the holes in the filter basket, and finally out the spigot(s) extending from the bottom of the cup.

Typically your machine will come with two different size filter baskets. A large one (double shot) which holds 14 to 16 grams of ground coffee, and a smaller one (single shot) which holds 7 to 8 grams of ground coffee.

The *group head* is the round metal housing attached to the espresso machine into which the portafilter is inserted.

The brewing water is dispensed from the group head into the portafilter. The group head contains the shower head, which disperses the brewing water, the group screen, which prevents grounds from migrating into the holes of the shower head, and the rubber gasket, which ensures a tight fit when the portafilter is inserted.

The group head provides another important function beyond holding the portafilter. The group head transfers heat, which it has accumulated from the heat of the boiler, to the brew water.

The group head's ability to retain heat is essential in producing the proper water temperature at the point of brewing.

Typically, the group heads will either be attached directly to the boiler, achieving a transfer of heat from *direct contact*, or they will be located above the boiler and are heated by the *convection* of heat radiating off of the boiler.

The group head transfers heat to the brew water

Group heads in *direct contact* with the boiler can over heat the water if a substantial amount of time passes without brewing. This may result in scalding the coffee during the brewing process.

Group heads heated by *convection* can have problems in recovering heat if multiple extractions occur in a very short period of time.

Steam wand

The *steam wand* is a small tube coming off the espresso machine that sprays steam and is used to foam milk.

On the end of the wand will be a *screw-on tip* which should have three to five small holes from which the steam will escape.

Some wands have been outfitted with what we call "carnival devices." They are attachments which may look something like large chrome cylinders, or flat plastic discs. These devices are "innovations" that have been created to help the unskilled operator produce an inferior simulation of proper foam.

Foaming milk is not difficult if you understand how (see our video *Espresso 101*), but foaming milk properly with these devices is almost impossible. We do not recommend them.

Other important features you should look for in a good steaming wand are its length, and its ability to swivel to multiple angles away from the machine.

If the wand is too short and will not reach the bottom of larger steaming pitchers (32-ounce size or larger), it will be impossible to properly steam a small volume of milk (enough for only one drink) without having to use a smaller pitcher. The wand tip must remain under the surface of the milk in your pitcher for the entire steaming process. If the wand only reaches half way down into the pitcher, you will have to fill the pitcher at least that full to steam properly, and you will end up with substantial leftover milk after you have poured your beverage.

The wand should swing out or swivel away from the machine to achieve a variety of positions and angles. A wand which can travel from a vertical position, out to an angle of about 45 degrees, will provide you with the flexibility to achieve the proper position to create the needed circulation of the milk in the pitcher.

Important features in a good steaming wand are its length, and ability to swivel

Steam wands are usually chrome-plated or stainless steel. We recommend stainless steel because the chrome plating can flake away after an extended period of use.

One other consideration is the control that releases the flow of steam to your wand. There are basically two types: *levers,* which operate a cam, and *augers,* which are controlled by turning a knob.

Levers are quick and easy to activate, but opponents of these controls point out that they do wear faster and tend to leak.

Augers offer more variation in control, but require greater effort and more time to open fully.

How To Pick An Espresso Machine

There are many fine, high quality espresso machines on the market, and many with very similar features, which means that your choices are abundant. Although most machines appear to be similar, and some of their components are similar or identical, there can be dramatic differences in engineering, design, prices, sizes, and features.

We tell our clients, they all are beautiful red shiny boxes on the outside! We suggest that you narrow your selection of a machine based on the following considerations:

• ***The role espresso will play in your business***

What role will espresso play in your business? Will espresso drinks be your primary product, or will espresso merely be an addition to an existing product line, menu, or service?

Your machine will need to be able to meet the demands of your predicted volume. An operation that may serve 200-500 cups a day will certainly require a different machine than a business serving only 25 cups a day. Your machine's ability to handle peak loads is even more important than the daily totals, if you are to avoid losing customers because of inadequate performance by your equipment. Matching the machine to your business is critical.

•*Determining your potential volume*

Do some research to find a similar operation to the one you are considering.

For example:

- If you are planning on opening a coffee cart in a mall, travel to malls in other areas and observe the types of equipment other operations are using. It will be necessary to take into consideration the comparable variables such as customer counts, demographics, competition, and so forth.

- If you are not in direct competition, do not hesitate to ask other owners or employees for information. In many cases they will be happy to talk about their operation and share their machine buying and usage experiences with you.

Using this information, try to estimate your daily volume and type of beverages you will be primarily selling.

Finding the machine that fits your needs

Espresso machines come in all shapes and sizes with many different equipment options. Estimated volume will be your key consideration.

We recommend two-group, automatic machines with a 12-liter boiler and 3500-watt heating element

Typically, an operation serving 50 drinks or less per day may find that a one-group machine is sufficient. But we recommend two-group, semi-automatic or automatic machines with a 12-liter boiler and 3500-watt heating element for most start-up operations where coffee will be your predominant product. A machine with two groups will meet the needs of most medium- to high-volume operations.

Businesses producing upwards of 300 beverages a day may certainly wish to consider a three- or four-group machine.

Your volume will determine how critical the need will be regarding boiler size and recovery time for water and steam temperature.

Make sure the machine you are considering has gauges or indicators to let you monitor critical functions. Remember that the majority of drinks consumed in North America are combined with steamed or foamed milk, so we usually recommend a machine with two steaming wands and a sufficient boiler temperature recovery rate to keep up with your anticipated demand.

And, make sure your espresso machine will not only meet your present needs but will be sufficient for your first two years of anticipated growth. You want to choose a well-built machine that will function efficiently as your business grows.

A well-built machine of any size is expensive, but it is an investment that can continue to pay off for you with satisfying years of generating revenue.

Which type of machine should you select?

There are four types of espresso machines to choose from:

1. *Manual or piston machines* are manually operated by pulling a lever which forces the water through the coffee. This lever action creates pressure with the assistance of a piston which replaces the function of the electric pump. The operator controls water flow and length of extraction time.

Automatic machines are the most commonly used machines today

Ideal for owner/operator situations where sufficient electricity is not available (such as at special events like outdoor fairs or weddings). Many times these machines are available with boilers which can be heated from a propane supply. These traditional old-style machines can also add an element of theatrics if this is something you desire.

2. *Semi-automatic machines,* with an on/off push button control, requires the operator to turn the machine off upon completion of the desired extraction. These machines drive the water through the ground coffee with an electric pump and were for years the most common type of machine used.

3. *Automatic machines,* with push button water-dosage control and auto shut-off, are the most commonly used machines today. They are a variation of the semiautomatic machine which reduces mistakes during the extraction process with precalibrated water dosage and automatic shut-off features.

4. *Fully or Super Automatic machines*, grind, dose, tamp, and extract the coffee, as well as froth milk, dispensing the proper portion of each into your cup, all automatically. Push button computerization controls all functions before it serves the completed beverages.

Fully automatic machines are rapidly finding their place in businesses where multiple employees with minimal experience or interest may be required to prepare beverages, or in self-service applications. Fully automatics are making possible the delivery of fast-food style espresso drinks in places other than the hands-on specialty coffee venues, which are the focus of this book.

Manufacturers of these types of machines usually identify their target markets as restaurants, hotels, fast-food eateries, airports, theme parks, and convenience stores.

The well-built and expensive fully automatic machines are an appropriate solution to the problem of maintaining drink consistency when you do not have skilled baristas. It is certainly a better solution than serving a third-rate product. But if you are committed to a hands-on delivery service of specialty coffee drinks, the more appropriate solution is in the direction of training your baristas to deliver the unique products you feature on your menu.

Well-trained baristas are more than a match for fully automatics in any coffee bar situation. We always say,

a super automatic machine is better than a bad barista, but a good barista will always prepare a better drink than a super automatic.

And keep in mind...

- If your machine will be in view of the customer or is a centerpiece in your business, then you want it to look good, in addition to its being an efficient workhorse. In this case, you may want to consider cosmetic features such as brass domed cupolas and special decorative metal finishes.

- To assure drink consistency, larger operations with several employees minimally require a semi-automatic machine with electronic control of water flow and output.

- Control buttons or pads should operate independently of each other on semiautomatic or automatic machines so you can use the remaining pads or buttons if repairs have to be made.

- All machines should have a system to let the operator know when the water supply is low. A sight glass or warning light in clear view to alert the operator is a must.

- We recommend stainless steel steaming wands rather than chrome-coated ones to avoid the possibility of the chrome flaking off into a customer's latté.

Espresso Grinders

Second in importance to your espresso machine is your *espresso burr grinder*. A consistent, controllable grind is essential to create superior espresso.

A consistent, controllable grind is essential to create superior espresso

The type of grinder you may use at home to grind beans for your brewed coffee will not work for espresso. These types of grinders are called *blade grinders* and they facilitate grinding by battering your coffee beans with a spinning blade. This method will not produce a consistent granule size which is essential for proper espresso extraction.

A commercial espresso burr grinder grinds the coffee beans between two spinning wheels which have surfaces equipped with sharpened ridges (called *burrs*) for cutting. These two wheels can be adjusted closer to each other to create a fine grind, or further apart to create a coarse grind. There are two different types of burr assemblies available, *flat burrs,* and *conical burrs.*

Think of flat burrs being like two hockey pucks, one on top of the other. Conical burrs are like two-pointed ice cream cones, one inside the other. The grinding action occurs between the contact surfaces of both types.

Conical grinders are reputed to produce a better result. The disadvantage of conical grinders is because of the high price of the burrs, they cost more. Another consideration is that burrs need to be replaced periodically, in high volume situations, perhaps as often as every three to six months.

An important feature of a flat burr grinder is the diameter of the burr wheel. Larger diameter burrs can grind more coffee in a shorter period of time.

An important feature of a flat burr grinder is the diameter of the burr wheel

- We suggest that you look for a grinder which incorporates 64 to 88 millimeter burrs. A grinder with 54 millimeter burrs may only grind the coffee at one-half the speed of a larger grinder.

- Also, consider a "step-down" grinder. This is a grinder where the motor drives a belt that turns the burr. The difference in size between the drive shaft of the motor and the larger wheel of the burr reduces the burr speed. If your burrs spin too fast, and you grind for an extended period of time, your burrs will become hot and will burn your coffee as it grinds.

- Be sure that the grinder you select has a grind adjustment control which moves easily and is embellished with some reference numbers. It is advisable to choose a grinder that has "infinite adjustments" vs. "notch adjustments." This will allow you to make very fine adjustments to the consistency of your grind. Notch adjustment provides you with less flexibility when fine-tuning your grind. It is helpful if the grind adjustment control indicates which direction will create a coarser and finer grind. It should lock into place after an adjustment has been made.

The grinder will have a container called the *hopper* which will hold the whole coffee beans. The beans will flow by gravity into the grinding chamber.

- It is advisable to look for a grinder where the hopper has a gate to stop the flow of beans out of the hopper. This will allow you to remove the hopper, should you desire, without the beans spilling everywhere.

The ground coffee will fall from the grinding chamber into a dispensing unit called the *doser*. By pulling a lever on the side of the doser, coffee will be dispensed out of the bottom into your awaiting portafilter.

Choose a grinder that has "infinite adjustments" vs. "notch adjustments"

Some newer grinders will not permit the grinder to operate when the lid is off the doser. This is unfortunate, because an open doser cylinder provides you with a place to brush the excess coffee from your portafilter. You do not want to waste good coffee, so you may need a bowl or other container nearby so you can save it to put it back into your doser. This stop-operation feature is meant as a safety precaution.

Another option you will encounter when looking at grinders is an *automatic activation* feature. This feature will activate grinding automatically when the level of ground coffee in the doser falls below a certain level (usually half way full). In Italy, where a barista may be serving 100 shots per hour, this can be a valuable time saver. But in most instances you will not be experiencing this level of volume, and will not want this feature for two reasons:

First, grinders with this feature cost more and it is just one more component that has the potential to fail.

Second, but more importantly, since coffee starts to loose flavor and aroma almost immediately after being ground, you do not want to have a significant amount of ground coffee in your doser waiting to be used.

Make sure the grinder you choose is built for abuse. We recommend the grinder's dosing chamber and pull levers are made of metal and not of plastic. This piece of equipment will see a lot of use in your operation and must be a quality product.

Drip Coffee Brewers

A number of reputable companies manufacture quality drip coffee brewers. We will discuss three different types.

1. *Conventional drip brewers* are those which dispense hot water over the ground coffee in a filter basket, which then streams into a glass pot, that sits on a warming burner below. These can be hard plumbed to your building's water supply.

Another common model is called a *pour-over* in which the operator obtains a pot of water from another source and then manually pours it into a port on the top of the machine where it is heated before brewing occurs.

Holding coffee in a glass pot on a warming burner is acceptable provided the pot is used up within 20 minutes. Longer than 20 minutes will result in a less than desirable, bitter cup of coffee. Any remaining coffee left in the pot after 20 minutes should be disposed of, and a fresh pot brewed. One option is to brew coffee into the glass pot and then immediately transfer it to a thermal pot. This will extend the life of the coffee to about 45 minutes to one hour.

Whichever type of coffee brewer, look for one with a large brew basket

2. *Thermal pot drip brewers* or *Air pot drip brewers* function in a manner identical to conventional brewers. The difference between the two is that the thermal pot brewer does not have a warming burner, and the brewing head and filter basket are much higher in relationship to the base so that a thermal coffee pot will fit directly below the brew basket. The thermal pot brewer brews the coffee directly into the thermal pot.

3. *Drip Coffee/Tea Brewers* are a new innovation in the marketplace. They should have a different brewing cycle for tea than they do for coffee. For tea, only a portion of the hot brewing water passes through the tea leaves; the balance of the water bypassing the tea to fill the remainder of the pot. This is the optimal method for creating quality tea. Ask your equipment dealer for more information.

Whichever type of coffee brewer you may decide to purchase, look for one with a *large brew basket*.

Some of the air pot brewers we have seen are basically stretch versions of conventional brewers, but still incorporate the smaller eight-cup brew basket. The problem is that you are passing 72 ounces of water through a brew basket which was designed and sized to hold the proper amount of ground coffee for brewing 48 ounces. Of course you measure out extra coffee for the 72 ounce pot, but because the brew basket was not specifically designed for this quantity of ground coffee, the characteristics of the finished beverage can be less than optimal, or the brew basket can overflow during brewing.

Look for adjustable water diversion in a good coffee brewer

Another feature to look for in a good coffee brewer is *adjustable water diversion*. This is a feature which sprays the majority of the brewing water over the ground coffee, and pours the rest down the inside edge of the brew basket in a small stream, combining with the coffee as it pours from the brew basket into the pot.

The brew basket for this type of machine will have a wire basket inside which holds the coffee filter away from the sides of the basket, thus providing the space for the flow of the diverted water. The reduced amount of water which pours over the coffee creates a more concentrated extraction and the remaining water is then added to create the proper balance of flavor. This feature is advantageous because it lessens the chance of over extraction which can result in bitter tasting coffee.

Bulk Coffee Grinders

You will need at least one bulk coffee grinder for your operation to grind coffee for your brewed coffee preparation.

If you plan on serving or selling ground flavored coffee beans, you will definitely need more than one grinder

You may need a second if you will be selling bulk beans, but at very least, you need the capability to adjust the grind consistency if you only plan to use one.

If you plan on serving or selling ground flavored coffee beans, you will definitely need more than one grinder.

Creating various grind consistencies for different home uses can be accomplished with a "grocery grinder." The grocery grinder has been the standard for years.

But if you are a real aficionado, and closely examine the consistency of the size of the granules, you may not be satisfied with the results the grocery grinder produces.

If you desire a more precision grind, we suggest that you explore some of the high-quality adjustable grinders.

Granita Machines

About eight years ago we asked a highly respected equipment technician about his thoughts and experiences with granita machines, he answered with great passion —*I hate all of them!* Granita machines had a reputation for problems.

We feel a good granita machine is a huge plus to an operation because of the profit potential and desirability of the product, especially with children, and in warm weather climates. In the past few years, granita machines have dramatically improved in terms of cleaning, service and dependability.

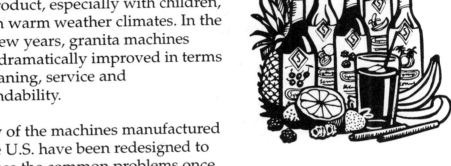

The biggest problem with granita machines is "freeze-up."

Many of the machines manufactured in the U.S. have been redesigned to address the common problems once associated with the machine. We have personally experienced fewer problems with granita machines that have horizontally mounted chambers as opposed to those that are vertically mounted.

The biggest problem that occurred with granita machines in the past was "freeze-up." If freeze-up occurs the resulting damage can be costly. This is a problem that is usually more the fault of the granita mix than the machine. [This subject is addressed in Chapter 24, *Planning Your Menu*.] The key factor is that the mix must be formulated exactly to prevent freeze-up. The proper ratio of water to mix must be exact.

Most new machines incorporate a tore sensor that will shut off the freeze cycle if the mix becomes too thick. This feature has helped eliminate most of the "freeze up" problems that these machines once experienced.

Mixes made from syrups or properly prepared dry mixes alleviate most problems because leading syrup and powder manufacturers now have products with the proper brix content to be used as a granita mix.

- If using a syrup as a base, be sure to look at the label to see if it is recommended for granita or ask the manufacturer, and be sure to use exact measurements.

Selecting The Basics For Your Venue

We have talked about the various types of equipment that you would purchase given different types of coffee venues. Following are minimal lists of basic equipment you might choose given your particular venue.

Cart venue

• *Espresso Carts*

- There are dozens of equipment companies from which you can buy a cart. Some are manufacturers, and some are resellers. To acquire the best price you would be wise to deal with the manufacturers.

- If you explain to your equipment dealer what you wish to sell from your cart, and where you are located, they will probably be able to direct you to a model which will fit your needs.

- Be sure to ask if the cart incorporates components which are N.S.F. (National Sanitation Foundation) and U.L. (Underwriter's Laboratories) approved. These two stamps of approval may be important to your local bureaucracies.

- Ask each manufacturer about their specific features and construction methods and why they are superior to their competitors. Each dealer will be more than happy to give you an earful. Take notes and make your own determinations. They may tell you things like:

- *Plywood Carts* were the standard for years and are still a viable option. The plywood must be covered inside and out with a water impervious material like a plastic laminate.

  Typically these carts are very strong and stable. Be sure that the cart sits on wheels that are attached to a metal frame.

  The downside to these carts is they tend to be heavy, so if you have to move it every day you probably will not enjoy it unless you are a body builder.

  Another point of concern is if you ram it into something while moving it, you might crack or damage the plastic laminate. If the laminate is damaged or comes unglued, either by impact or failure of the contact cement which holds it in place, moisture can make its way into the plywood causing further release of the cement, wood rot, and bacteria growth.

- *Welded Steel Frame Carts* are strong and sturdy and can be sided with any number of materials including painted sheet metal, stainless steel, diamond plate, laminate-covered foam core, laminate-covered plywood, or laminate-covered press board.

  The advantage to these carts is their strength as compared to a plywood cart. Opponents of this construction cite that you still have the problem of damaged laminate if you ram something, and they also tend to be very heavy.

- *Extruded Aluminum Channel Carts* are carts where the frame is assembled from extruded aluminum channels that slide and lock together. These carts are strong and extremely light weight.

  Supporters of this construction method point out that if a panel or component is ever damaged, it can be replaced. Also, one has the flexibility of changing color schemes or design of the panels because they can be replaced with new ones.

  If you wish to expand your operation by adding a second cart, or a couple of side carts to form an L or U-shaped configuration, the additional units can be easily attached to the original cart.

  Opponents will point out that these carts are not very stable, or if they start out stable, they may not stay that way over an extended period of use. Many are now welded or screwed together to address this problem.

Whichever type of cart you may choose to purchase, be sure that it has: sink(s), water tanks, waste tank, water pump, water filtration system, water heater, and hoses between these different plumbing features, all N.S.F. approved.

In addition, the cart must have a 220V power cord, circuit breaker box, voltage converter, and convenience outlets for your grinder and refrigerator, all U.L. approved. Be sure to check with your local agencies for their particular requirements concerning cart operations.

- *A refrigeration unit.* This usually comes with the cart and may be included in the price.

  If you do purchase refrigeration equipment separately, or are evaluating the refrigeration included with a cart, be sure that it is a "front drafting" refrigerator. The fan which cools the refrigeration coils blows out the back in some units, and out the front in others. If the refrigeration vents from the back, and the refrigerator is enclosed in the cart, there will not be sufficient breathing space to optimize cooling performance.

  You should insist upon a front venting refrigerator because it will cool more efficiently, and create less stress on the unit's compressor.

- *An espresso machine*— discussed earlier in this chapter.

- *An espresso grinder*—perhaps two, one for your espresso blend and one for decaf.

- *Possibly a granita machine*—if you have room on your cart or sidebar.

- *A cash register*—We suggest you purchase one with pre-set keys that allows you to program in specific beverages and provides you with valuable information on the items you have actually sold. This data will be essential to calculate ideal beverage and food costs.

Kiosk or Coffee Bar venue (in addition to all items listed for a cart)

- *An ice machine*—for iced beverages.

  In a kiosk, you may want a small under-counter ice maker if you have access to city water and sewer.

  For a large sit-down coffee bar, consider a full-size stand-up machine in the back of the house. The ice can be transported to a built-in counter top ice bin, which should be situated near the location where drinks will be prepared.

- *A brewer*—for brewed coffee.

- *An adjustable bulk bean grinder*—for grinding beans for your brewed coffee, as well as grinding bulk coffee beans which have been purchased by customers.

- *Additional espresso grinders*—to offer a second or several additional espresso blends or brands of coffees.

  A new trend in this business is to offer different espresso blends. Some espresso blends have been created to be consumed as straight shots, and others to be blended with milk. Offering an espresso blend from several different major roasters will provide a variety of styles and flavors.

- *Pastry cases*—come in refrigerated and unrefrigerated forms:

  Refrigerated display cases—provide a higher humidity environment with less air flow than deli cases. This will allow the storage and display of desserts and pastries without having to cover them with plastic wrap. A refrigerated pastry case will typically cost more than a deli case.

  Unrefrigerated dry pastry cases—Some styles can be piggy-backed or stacked on top of a refrigerated pastry case. Dry pastry cases are glass cases for holding bagels, croissants, scones, and other baked products that do not really need to be refrigerated. **We recommend a dual zone case** that allows for both dry pastries such as scones and muffins, but also desserts such as cheese cakes and mousses.

- *Panini presses, soup kettles, and convection ovens*—as required by your menu offerings.

- *An under-counter commercial glass washer*—may be necessary or desired if you are planning to serve coffee in ceramic cups. A commercial glass washer is much more quiet and efficient than your dishwasher at home, and can wash and rinse a rack of cups in about a minute or two.

- *Sinks*—qualify as fixtures, but you will still probably have to buy yours. Make sure you have done your homework with the health department regarding sink requirements.

  A *hand wash sink* will most certainly be required. A hand wash sink is usually not considered acceptable for food preparation or dish washing.

  Do they require a *three-compartment sink*? If you do not have an automatic dishwasher (or even if you do), your health department may require a three-compartment sink. A three-compartment sink provides separate basins for rinsing, washing, and sanitizing. Be aware that your bureaucracy's standard for this sink will probably require that drain boards be part of the design.

In many cases, if your dishwasher will achieve a sterile temperature in the rinse cycle, you may not be required to have a three-compartment sink. The determining factor will be whether or not the largest piece of washable equipment will fit in the dishwasher, and if your bureaucracy will allow its use without a three-compartment sink.

If food preparation will be required to facilitate you menu (such as scratch baking, cutting salad greens, etc.) you may be required to have a separate sink dedicated to food prep.

Some times one of the basins in your three-compartment will be acceptable for this task. The needed feature will be a drain which incorporates indirect plumbing. This is a drain which is not hard-plumbed into the sewer line, but instead terminates a foot above a porcelain basin, which is in your floor, and is plumbed to the sewer system.

This method of plumbing makes it impossible for any bacteria in the sewer lines to infiltrate your prep sink because they are not physically connected.

Finally, you may be required to have a *mop sink*. This is a sink into which buckets of mop water and other cleaning chemicals should be disposed of. Many times these can be installed under your three-compartment sink.

- The following equipment in your bar may also be required to have drains which incorporate indirect plumbing:

    espresso machines, ice bins, ice makers, soda dispensers, granita machines (if drain is hard-plumbed), *tap water dispensers for drinking water*, and *dipper wells for ice cream scoops.*

Beyond the basics

• *A coffee roaster*

Some coffee bar owners roast their own coffee in-store with a small batch roaster.

This can add an appealing ambiance to your store if effectively ventilated.

If done properly, in-store roasting can be very profitable, while providing you with total control and the freshest possible product.

One needs to understand however, that roasting coffee is an art unto itself. Blending coffee, as would be necessary for espresso, is extremely difficult and requires the skill and knowledge which is only acquired through years of experience.

Sourcing the finest quality green coffee beans is another challenge faced by the small retail roaster. It is likely that larger, well-established roasters with established business relationships with green bean brokers will have command of the best supply of beans.

In-store roasting may be an area that you will want to explore after you already have a well-established successful retail operation, but we generally recommend against considering it at the inception of your business.

Buying Your Equipment

Following are additional considerations to be aware of when you are finally at the point of making your equipment purchases:

Negotiating price

Like any other major purchase you make, the equipment dealer's markup may provide a margin for you to negotiate the price. Negotiate with your equipment dealer in the same way you negotiated your lease:

Tell your *potential* supplier,

> *I'm looking at your company but I'm looking at several other companies too, and I'm going to buy wherever I get the best value for my dollar.*

Then ask,

> *What can you do for me?*

The equipment dealer's markup may provide a margin for you to negotiate the price

Again, it is very important that you start out by looking at everything on the market that you can possibly find. Then at some point in time, narrow your choices down to two or three selections.

If you are looking at more than three of anything—whether it be a car or an espresso machine—you are only going to be confused. Pick three makes of equipment and then compare them: A against B, B against C, then go back to the A dealer again and tell them that B said his was better because of such-and-such, and play one against the other.

Compare the products! Do your homework! Negotiate!

It is a great way to educate yourself, too. When you ask your equipment dealer,

> *Why would I want to buy your machine over XYZ machine?*

He will be more than happy to give you dozens of reasons, and describe all the features which make his machine better.

Then bounce that information off of the XYZ supplier and see what their responses are.

As you talk to all the people that you are considering buying equipment from, you will learn a lot about equipment. And you can use all of that knowledge to your best advantage.

Will your supplier be there for you?

Your equipment purchases constitute one of your largest expenses in opening your coffee bar, so make sure you are not just dealing with a good salesman. Make sure you are dealing with a reputable firm with a proven track record.

There are many reputable equipment companies and sales people out there. *But be careful! Do your homework!*

You may have no one to turn to if the company is no longer in business

There have been a lot of equipment companies that came and went very quickly. And once you purchase your equipment—regardless of what the warranty says—you may have no one to turn to if the company is no longer in business.

If you are not quite sure about a firm's track record, you can check with the state to see if they have ever had law suits filed against them for fraud.

You want to find companies that want to partner with you, that want to help you to be successful, not those that are just interested in closing an equipment sale.

Check out used equipment options

Depending upon what part of the country you are in, there is usually used equipment on the market that you might want to at least check out. Remember though, this is the heart of your coffee business, sometimes a penny saved might not equal a dollar earned.

There are espresso machine suppliers who sell reconditioned espresso machines with a warranty —but be sure to find out what the warranty covers, and get it in writing.

Many restaurant equipment suppliers will have an inventory of used equipment. There may be a business in your city that deals in only used equipment. The mortality rate of restaurants is high, and many times you will be able to find equipment that has had minimal use.

To source used equipment, you can start by checking newspaper want-ads, trade journals, bulletin boards, auction houses, restaurateurs, used equipment supply houses, and, of course, the Internet.

Keep in mind that buying a used espresso machine is not unlike buying a used car. You are either getting a good deal, or buying somebody else's headaches. If you have done your homework the machine you desire could exist used...but be careful!

Buying vs. leasing equipment

You can either buy your equipment outright, or lease it.

Before considering a lease, you should definitely check with a few leasing companies to see what interest rates and terms they offer and with another professional member of your management team about this issue—your accountant. Find out if your accountant feels that leasing is right for you.

You can either buy your equipment outright, or lease it

We have found over the years that leasing can be very advantageous in particular situations. For example, We opened a coffee cart where we wrapped the entire cart operation into our equipment lease—espresso machines, grinders, refrigeration, cart, awning, the whole nine yards, even the cash register. Our lease term was for three years, on which we made monthly payments, with a buy-out cost at the end of the three years of one penny.

Generally, the more responsible equipment companies are not interested in taking the equipment back. They would much rather have you be successful and sell you upgrades from your original equipment than see you fail and have to deal with your used equipment.

You want to deal with leasing companies that your equipment sales person would recommend, that have experience in this industry, companies not afraid to lease on this type of equipment and that understand the viability of the specialty coffee business.

In the early '90s, we looked at leasing some equipment in Eugene, Oregon, but ended up going with a leasing company in Tacoma, Washington, because they had experience and good success with these leases. They were more than happy to make a deal because they had enough successful experience in this industry to know that they would probably not have to take the equipment back.

The leasing company here in Eugene had not dealt with espresso equipment before and were more cautious about this new industry.

Another thing that we like about leasing is that it allows you to see what your total investment in the operation equates to on a daily, weekly, monthly, and annual basis. It brings home in clear terms the reality that your equipment costs are a tangible part of your operational costs every month. It is part of what your income has to be financing.

The disadvantage to buying your equipment outright is that you have taken $50,000 out of your bank account that could be earning you money, or that you could be doing other things with.

It is really costing you a fair amount of money that you can easily lose sight of. If you are just breaking even every month, you may be misled into thinking you are doing okay. But you are really *not* breaking even if you have poured your $50,000 into your equipment, and you are forgetting to factor that into your calculations.

Obviously you are paying interest on an equipment lease, so it does cost you more when you lease your equipment than if you pay cash. But the big advantage to a lease is that you do not tie up all your capital.

So often the people who come to us wanting to open up coffee businesses have a limited amount of capital to work with. They might have enough money to buy all their equipment and the inventory outright—but these outright purchases would leave them no operating capital.

But beware! Recently, interest rates and terms have become less desirable. A client of ours who checked into the lease option was quoted a 21% interest rate, and the leasing company would only extend payment over 24 months. in this case, he was better off wrapping his equipment purchase in his bank loan.

You *must* have operating capital.

You *must* have a healthy amount of reserve cash in your bank account to cover your expenses until you turn the corner to profitability.

The big advantage to a lease: you do not tie up all your capital

It is very unlikely that you are going to open your coffee bar and make a profit your first month. It is much more likely that you are going to struggle for three months, six months, a year, before you turn that corner. Especially if you are paying yourself a wage.

By leasing equipment—while you create an extra monthly expense and are paying a little bit more for the equipment—you have allowed yourself working capital in the beginning stages of your business.

And do not forget that one essential up-front cost you must afford will be for marketing.

Additional advantages of leasing:

- A lease sometimes can be structured for up to 60 months and with as little as first and last payments in advance.

- The equipment may pay for itself from the profits it generates.

- Lease payments may be partially or entirely tax deductible.

- Your line of credit is preserved for future business needs.

And keep in mind...

- *On-time delivery.* Make sure the delivery date of the package of equipment you are ordering fits your game plan for the opening day of your business. You will want to order your equipment at least two months prior to opening day.

- *Equipment installation.* Most reputable equipment suppliers will come to your site and install the equipment they sell. In considering the purchase, take into account whether or not your supplier will install the equipment he is selling to you. We highly recommend that you make sure yours does.

  You want to have your espresso machine installed and plumbed with the proper water filters. Ask your dealers about their recommendations on this.

  Avoid a situation where the delivery truck dumps a pallet of boxes on your door step and you have to break them open and figure out what goes where. Get all the information about the installation of your equipment up-front. Ask the relevant questions. Keep in mind that every company will do things a little differently, so never assume anything.

- *Advice from equipment dealers.* Limit the advice you seek from your equipment dealer to what he knows best—equipment. In most cases, he is a specialist and an expert in his field. Do not look to him for expertise in the other business concerns of yours, such as the right location for your coffee bar.

  An equipment dealer's response to your request for business advice beyond his area of expertise could be motivated by his business needs rather than yours.

  Espresso is a gourmet product. Equipment sales people should be able to give you information about equipment, but in some cases may not be capable of teaching you how to prepare this product properly.

The dangerous part is that nobody wants to admit that they do not know. So if you say to them, *How do I prepare this?*, they may be more than happy to make an attempt to show you how to prepare espresso. But you have to question,

> *Do they have the expertise? Do they understand all the nuances of this product?*

Remember our grill analogy: If you are opening a restaurant, do not expect the person who sold you your grill to come in and teach you how to become a master chef. Do expect him to teach you about the grill, how to turn it on and off, and how to service and clean it.

- *Deal with companies that are coffee-specific.* Our experience in working with numerous clients is that they have often been given misinformation by equipment suppliers. **(Try to buy your machine from a company that deals primarily within the coffee industry.)**

  Restaurant equipment companies that handle espresso machines may also be selling soft-serve ice cream machines and chicken broasters. The espresso machine may be only one of a thousand products they sell. And although you may be able to get good equipment from those companies, you need to question how knowledgeable they are about the espresso coffee industry.

Espresso is not a product that can be prepared with the ease of French fries. Espresso coffee takes exacting preparation. Very small particulars can create tremendous differences in the end product that you serve to your customers. Generally, you want to deal with companies that fully understand all of the particulars involved in making great espresso beverages

 For more information on this specific subject, refer to the following books and videos from Bellissimo—800-655-3955.

- **Achieving Success in Specialty Coffee**

- **Espresso 101**

- **Espresso 501**

Coffee Bar Equipment

Item description	Typical price range		

Essentials

• Espresso machine—2 group; automatic	$5,500.	to	$10,000.
• Water filtration system	650.	to	1,200.
• Espresso grinder—burr	650.	to	850.
• Refrigerator—under counter; 2 door	1,450.	to	1,800.
• Air-pot drip brewer—automatic	700.	to	1,000.
• Bulk coffee grinder—adjustable; burr	700.	to	1,200.
• Cash Register with Preset Keys	350.	to	1,500.

Basics

• Pastry Case—60"; refrigerated	4,800.	to	7,500.
• Pastry Case—60"; dry	2,900.	to	4,000.
• Glass Washer; under counter	3,300.	to	4,500.
• Ice Bin; Counter top drop-in	330.	to	650.
• Ice Cube Maker—400 lb capacity	2,400.	to	3,000.
• Toaster—commercial	450.	to	1,200.
• Microwave Oven	199.	to	650.
• Bulk Coffee Bins	150.	to	250.
• Scale—Electronic Digital 2lb Capacity	250.	to	850.
• 3 Compartment Sink with Faucet	648.	to	950.
• Mop Bucket Dump Sink	250.	to	500.
• Hand Sink with Faucet; drop-in	200.	to	350.
• Granita Machine—3-barrel	3,200.	to	3,600.
• Storage Shelves—wire metal shelve with poles 42" x 15"	252.	to	370.

Extras

• Blenders	305.	to	1,000.
• Soft Serve Ice Cream Makers	4,300.	to	6,500.
• Ice Cream Dipping Cabinet	1,400.	to	3,800.
• Panini Press	1,475.	to	2,500.
• Condiment Table; refrigerated	980.	to	1,650.
• Prep Table—Stainless Steel	260.	to	450.
• Refrigerator—commercial 2-door upright	2,500.	to	3,500.
• Freezer—commercial 1-door upright	1,800.	to	2,800.
• Deli Slicer	840.	to	1,850.
• Jacketed Soup Kettle	2,450.	to	4,500.
• Soup Warmer—holding kettle	199.	to	300.

Coffee Bar Equipment

Item description

Small Wares

- Espresso hand tamp
- Can Opener: 1 rotary; 1 can punch
- Small Tool Kit
- First Aid Kit (OSHA approved)
- Mixing Spoons (long handle)
- Glass Merchandising Jars
- Steam Pitchers: 3—48- to 56-oz pitchers; 1—24 oz
- Steam Pitcher Thermometers
- Refrigerator Thermometer
- Shot Glasses with measured increments
- Salt and Pepper Shakers for Condiments (cinnamon, chocolate powder, nutmeg)
- Containers for Sugar/Sweetner Packets
- Straw Dispenser
- Dessert Spatula
- Pastry Tongs
- Paring Knife
- Ice Scoop
- Syrup Pour Spouts
- Pump (chocolate, syrup dispenser)

Cleaning Products

- Window/Glass Cleaner
- Bleach
- Bar Towels
- Paper Towels
- Anti-Bacterial Hand Soap
- Espresso Machine Cleaner
- Coffee Pot/Urn Cleaner
- Bleach bucket
- Diswashing Soap

Chapter 25 Check List

Equipment Considerations:

_____ What equipment will the production of your menu require? Make a list of all your equipment needs.

_____ Attend trade shows, read articles, and call professionals within the industry to secure as much information as possible about what features are important, and which manufacturers have good or bad reputations.

_____ Identify your local suppliers of espresso and food service equipment.

_____ How long have these companies been in business?

_____ Check the reputations of these companies with: The Better Business Bureau; the Attorney General's Office of the state their business is headquartered in; their past customers.

_____ Give them a list of your equipment to obtain a price quotation.

_____ Ask about their warranties, service and repair policies, availability of parts, and if they will do the initial installation. Get all this information in writing!

_____ Obtain this same information from at least two additional companies in your area.

_____ Determine if they work with a leasing company and what terms are available to lease this equipment with a buy-out at the end of the lease.

_____ How long will it take to have your equipment on site from the date of your order?

Suggested Equipment Specifics:

Espresso Machines:

_____ Two group, automatic

_____ 12-liter boiler with 3,500-watt heating element

_____ A separate heat exchanger for each group

_____ Control pads that operate independently from each other

_____ Two steaming wands; stainless steel preferred

Espresso Grinders:

_____ Burr grinder with 64 to 88 millimeter burrs

_____ "Infinite grind adjustment" (vs. notch adjustments)

_____ Manual on/off control

_____ Parts constructed from durable metal

Drip Coffee Brewers:

_____ Large filter basket designed specifically for the number of cups that will be typically brewed

_____ Adjustable water diversion feature

Granita Machines:

_____ Horizontal cylinders preferred to vertical cylinders

_____ Belt drives preferred to direct drive motors

Refrigeration (under counter):

_____ Front drafting preferred

Refrigerated Display Cases:

_____ Pastry case a must for displaying refrigerated pastries and desserts. A deli case is not the same as a pastry case!

Carts and Kiosks:

_____ Make sure all electronic components are U.L. approved.

_____ Make sure that all water storage containers, water lines, connectors, valves, pumps, etc., are N.S.F. approved.

CHAPTER 26

Selecting Your Vendors

Contents

CHAPTER 26

Selecting Your Vendors

Now that you have defined your concept, designed your lease space, planned your menu, and selected your equipment, it is time to make decisions about the products you will sell, and the vendors from whom you are going to purchase those products.

When opening a coffee business, one of the most important decisions you will ever make is the coffee you choose to serve your customers and the roaster you select to be your coffee vendor. Because there is an abundance of information for you to consider before you make this critical decision, we have devoted an entire chapter to this subject. [See Chapter 12—*Selecting the Right Coffee & Roaster*]

In this chapter we focus on selecting the vendors you will be relying on to provide your supplemental, non-coffee items.

Selecting Vendors For Your Baked Goods

Baked goods and coffee go hand in hand, both in the morning and evening.

Baked goods and coffee go hand in hand

As we touched on earlier, the basic question is whether you plan to do the baking yourself, or buy your goods from a vendor. Assuming you decide to simplify your life and your operation by not investing in the extra labor and equipment required to do your own baking, you will need to research who in your area will be able to provide you with quality products.

The local bakeries will usually be more than happy to bring you samples of their offerings. Look for a full-service bakery that provides muffins, bagels, scones, cinnamon rolls, and a variety of other goodies, as well as regular, consistent delivery.

Delivery schedules

Delivery is a big consideration.

Not all bakeries offer delivery service. You need a baker who is dependable, who delivers on a regular basis, and whose products are consistent in quality. You do not want to be without fresh baked goods for your morning customers because your baker failed to deliver as promised.

You need to be sure that your baker will be able to provide you with a.m. delivery

You may find vendors who are comparable on price and service, but some will prove to be more flexible than others with regard to their delivery schedules. Some vendors may only deliver to your area once or twice a week, others may provide you with service five days a week.

A vendor who can deliver any day of the week means you will always have the freshest baked goods, you can keep a smaller inventory on your shelf, and your unexpected needs can be met if you find yourself with a sudden heavy volume of business.

One other important point you need to address:

If your operation opens at 6:30 or 7:00 a.m., you need to be sure that your baker will be able to provide you with delivery, without failure, at that time. You do not want to be without baked goods during your prime hours of business.

Match the quality of your coffee

Try to match the quality of your baked goods to the quality of your coffee. You want to offer baked goods that **compliment the quality of your coffee**. and reflect the quality level defined in your mission statement.

Offer baked goods that are baked fresh daily

And, as we mentioned in Chapter 24—*Planning Your Menu,* you want to offer baked goods that are baked fresh daily.

Most coffee operations will have a basket on their counter where they offer their day-old baked goods at half price or at cost. The goal is to at least break even on your baked goods. A percentage of your customers will be looking for a value and will not mind that the baked goods are a day old. These items usually go very quickly.

Sometimes, large bakeries will offer a buy-back service, at least initially until you know what your use is going to be. They will credit you on day-old or two-day-old baked goods or will buy back some items. This is fairly typical of bread companies.

At one of our cart operations, we bought muffins from a company at a cost of 75 cents, and sold them for $1.25.

We could have bought the muffins for 60 cents.

But at that price, we would have had to pick the muffins up, and deal with any of left-over muffins that we did not sell. At the 75 cent price, the company would both deliver and pick up the unsold muffins every two days, and replace the ones which had not sold with fresh ones.

Because this was a cart operation, and the majority of sales were from coffee, we decided that it was more important to have fresh muffins with convenient service, than to make a larger profit from their sale.

Signature items

It can be advantageous to promote who you are buying your baked goods from, if that business is renowned in your area for their quality goods.

If you want an original item, or if you have a specific recipe for an item that you would like to offer, you can ask a bakery to contract bake for you.

If they will provide that service for you, it is a great way to offer a signature product.

We had one client in the Midwest who contracted to buy homemade pies from various women in her town. These pies soon became a popular attraction to her coffee bar. You could enjoy a wonderful cup of coffee with a slice of great home-made pie. She was buying the pies for about $3 each, cutting them into eight pieces, and selling them for $2.50 per slice. She not only made a very nice profit from her pie sales, but her coffee bar quickly became famous for these pies.

We should warn you that typically your health department will not permit you to sell an item that has not been prepared in a certified kitchen. There are usually severe fines and penalties for doing so. The women selling the pies we mentioned had to go through a certification process with the county enabling their kitchens to be health department certified.

Selecting syrups, chocolates, etc.

The same quality considerations apply to syrups, chocolates, and other food products that are combined with, or accompany, your coffee.

Don't compromise with less than the best.

Attend coffee trade or gourmet product shows

Many of your drinks will incorporate a flavored syrup or chocolate as an ingredient. It is important to taste test these products before making a decision.

A good way of doing this is to attend one of the coffee trade or gourmet product shows which occur in various locations across the country. You will find that most syrup and chocolate manufacturers will be there to promote their products.

The real cost is the cost-per-portion, and not the cost-per-bottle

A woman told us that she was very confused about choosing a syrup for her coffee bar until she went to a coffee trade show and was able to taste all of them within one day. It was very easy for her to choose the one that she felt was the best when she was able to taste all the brands side-by-side.

She would have had a much more difficult time coming to a decision without her coffee show experience.

If you are not able to attend a coffee show, you can call syrup or chocolate companies and have them send you samples.

- In choosing syrups this way, pick out several specific flavors that you are most interested in, like vanilla, hazelnut, and raspberry; and have all the companies send you the **same flavors**. Then when you are doing a taste test you will be comparing "apples to apples," so to speak.

One more consideration about syrups:

When you pick a vendor, make sure they will be able to provide you with the service you will need

- Make sure you pay attention to the portions each manufacturer recommends. Some manufacturers recommend a smaller portion of syrup per beverage. Many times this will provide the same flavor intensity as compared to a much larger portion of another manufacturer's syrup.

You have to consider the concentration of the product, because the real cost is the cost-per-portion, and not the cost-per-bottle. For example:

- If you are getting 50 portions of syrup from Brand A, and Brand A cost $7 per bottle, and only 25 portions from Brand B, at $5 per bottle, Brand A costs two dollars more than Brand B. But you are actually saving money by using Brand A. ($7 divided by 50 portions = 14 cents per portion; $5 divided by 25 portions = 20 cents per portion).

Too often, people just look at the bottom-line price.

The Challenges of Vendor Selection

Selecting vendors will present some challenges.

Certainly if you have a cart, kiosk, or drive-thru operation, you are going to have a bigger challenge getting a full-service vendor than if you have a sit-down coffee bar. This will be primarily due to the small quantity of products you will be able to order because of your limited storage area. Many companies require a minimum order for delivery. If your orders are small, it will be even less appealing to these vendors when you tell them you may require multiple deliveries per week.

So when you pick a vendor, make sure they will be able to provide you with the frequency of service you will need, and that they do not have a minimum order you will not be able to fulfill.

Also, ask the vendors you are considering if they will break up case quantities. Sometimes vendors will only sell you products by case lots. If you will only be using one bottle of banana syrup a year, you will not want to purchase and warehouse 12 bottles because it is the only quantity your vendor will offer.

Reputation is important

The reputation of the vendor is important.

- Do they have a long, established track record?

- Do they stock a quality line of products?

- Do they deliver on schedule?

- Do they make excessive mistakes in filling your orders?

Try to buy as many of your items as possible from one vendor

Nothing is more frustrating than placing an order for 30 items, and the delivery truck shows up with only 20 of them, and possibly 2 of the 20 items were not what you had ordered.

Many times you will not discover that a vendor has problems until you actually start dealing with them, but if you talk with other coffee bar owners, you can find out which vendors work well for them. *Who do they patronize? Who have they had problems with?*

If you have an operation that is open afternoons or evenings, and is serving desserts, look for a vendor that carries a line of frozen, high-quality desserts. Most major grocery purveyors such as Sysco, Alliant, Food Service of American and S.E. Rykoff will carry such a line. *Bindi* brand (imported from Italy) and *Sweet Street* both have excellent products that, when thawed, you would never know were frozen products.

Negotiating with vendors

We suggest you try to buy as many of your items as possible from one vendor. It will simplify your life and simplify your ordering.

If you are ordering cups from one vendor, chocolate syrup from a second, and napkins from a third, because you can save 25 cents here and 50 cents there, you have to ask yourself:

> *What's my time worth? What's my frustration worth?*

You can have much more buying power if you go to a single vendor and say:

> *I do not want to purchase my products from a dozen different vendors, and I'd like to buy all of these products from you; but I want a good price if I give you the lion's share of the business.*

Generally, we recommend that you create a list of all the products you are interested in—different flavored syrups, napkins, cups, straws, sugar, and everything else—and if you have two or three grocery vendors in your area, put your list out to bid with all of them so you can find out who is going to give you the best prices overall.

•*Note your high-use items*

Pay attention to your high-use items

When you are looking at vendors and thinking about prices, pay attention to your high-use items—the things you will use a substantial amount of, like cups, napkins and milk.

The cost of your high-use items is much more crucial to your buying decisions than most other factors.

You may not taste any difference in the flavor of 2% milk because of who you purchased from, but a better price for your milk could affect your costs dramatically. So make your considerations based on their bids of your high-use items. Do not get hung up if one vendor's price on Sweet 'n Low was a $1 more a box, but they are saving you real money on cups and napkins and other high-use items. Ask:

What am I going to use a lot of? Who can provide me with the best prices on those high-use items?

•Negotiating points

Establishing a good working relationship with your vendors is important. And do not hesitate to attempt to negotiate:

- Ask them to lock in prices for you for 30, 60 or 90 days. Many times they may be hesitant to do this because the prices they pay for the product fluctuate; but if they are hungry for the business, sometimes they may work with you.

- Ask them to notify you in advance when prices are going to be increased on your key items. You do not want to discover two months later that your price on cups has increased by $6 a case. This will allow you to stock up on certain items if the price is going to increase significantly.

What's your time worth?

- Find out if they will make a special delivery if you are in a pinch. If you run out of something, can you call your salesman and say,

I'm out of this item and I can't leave my store, can you drop off a case?

Will he run to his warehouse and bring you a case? Or will he say,

I'm sorry but your next delivery date is a week from Friday?

These are the little things that make a vendor invaluable. If they are hungry and if they want your business, they will be working hard to do many of these things for you.

Cash and carry

In addition to vendors who deliver goods to your doorstep, you may have the option of using cash-and-carry wholesale establishments. This is a wholesale store that you personally go to and do your own shopping once or twice a week. But again...you want to analyze,

What's your time worth?

If you could be spending the two or three hours per week marketing your business rather than running out to shop for supplies, is it worth the four dollars you have saved?

Vendor selection is, as we have said, very important and something that should be done in the planning stages, or while your operation is being built.

Take your time and make wise choices about the companies you will work with.

For more information on this specific subject, refer to the following books and videos from Bellissimo—800-655-3955.

- **Achieving Success in Specialty Coffee**

- **Everything BUT Coffee**

Chapter 26 Check List

Vendor Considerations:

All Vendors:

_____ Do they provide quality products which are consistent with your concept?
_____ How long have they been in business?
_____ Will they extent terms for payment?
_____ Will they guarantee prices for a specific period of time?
_____ Will they inform you of price increases?
_____ Do they anticipate discontinuing any of the product lines you have specified?
_____ Will they provide you with a special delivery of product in the case of an emergency?
_____ Will they provide you with references of other businesses they are servicing?
_____ Have them evaluate your product list to inform you of which products they stock, and to provide prices for each.

Coffee Roasters: [Note - This section is from the check list in chapter 11- *Selecting the Right Coffee & Roaster.*]

_____ Do they use only hard bean Arabica coffees?
_____ Do they offer espresso blends and varietals?
_____ How often do they roast each varietal and blend?
_____ Where did they attain their roasting knowledge?
_____ If they ship, is the shipping charge included in the price per pound or is it an additional charge?
_____ Will they provide you with samples for evaluation?
_____ Do they practice open dating? (Do they indicate on the package when the coffee was roasted?)
_____ Do they nitrogen flush their roasted beans and immediately heat seal them in foil packaging incorporating one-way valves?
_____ How long after you have placed your order will it take for your coffee to be shipped?

Bakers:

_____ Will they deliver daily?
_____ Can they deliver without failure by _____AM?
_____ Will they provide you with samples of their products for consideration?
_____ Do they offer all the products that you desire? (Bagels, scones, muffins, cinnamon rolls, Danish, croissants, brownies, cookies, cakes, pies, cheese cakes, breads, etc.)
_____ Do they offer any type of buy back or credit policy for unsold baked goods?
_____ Will they provide any custom baking services if desired?

Grocery Purveyors:

_____ Do they have a minimum order requirement? How much is it $_____?
_____ Will they break case lots?
_____ How many days a week do they service your area?

CHAPTER 27

Your Operational Systems

Contents

CHAPTER 27

Your Operational Systems

What are operational systems and why are they important?

Operational systems are basically paper tools that help control your costs and insure your operational efficiency.

These systems are very important because in managing a food or coffee operation, there are hundreds, perhaps thousands, of variables that have to be controlled on a daily, weekly, or monthly basis.

They free up your time so you can take care of other important management aspects of the operation

Most managers or store owners will discover that they must control numerous variables. Without the ability to delegate and monitor all the aspects of your operation with the aid of operational controls and systems, many details will be left unattended or go unchecked. Operational systems will allow you more time to manage effectively, and will alleviate much unnecessary stress.

You have a choice. Try to control a thousand variables, or control two dozen operational systems. Controlling the two dozen systems is much easier! If they are set up properly, and designed with an element of accountability, they will be very effective tools that will save you money, time, and frustration.

Operational systems can help insure the efficiency of your operation. They help insure that your costs are being controlled, and that you are not experiencing an element of theft.

And most importantly, they free up your time so that you can take care of other important management aspects of the operation, such as:

- Overseeing your operation.

- Financial analysis, goal setting, and planning.

- Evaluating and tracking business achievements.

- Marketing your business in the best possible manner.

- Evaluating long-range expansion plans.

Typical operational systems

We divide typical operational systems into two categories:

- Operational systems that aid and monitor employee production.

- Operational systems that function as management tools for owners and managers.

Operational systems for employee production

Install a variety of employee check lists

Many owners and managers do not realize the value of operational systems. Many are content to *fly by the seat of their pants*, so to speak. They run around their store 60 hours a week, trying to control every minor detail, and putting out **the same fires** multiple times hourly, daily, and weekly...for their entire careers.

Understandably, in due time, they burn out and become ineffective—and so usually does their store.

A check list for each employment position

The first operational system that we like to install consists of a variety of employee check lists. We usually break those down by shift and by employee designation. For example:

If you own a very small coffee bar and work alongside only a few employees, it is likely no one specializes in an individual solitary function. Everyone operates as barista, cashier, busboy, and dishwasher.

If you have a larger store, there is likely to be some specialization. For example:

- The cashier's responsibility might be making the initial contact with the customer, taking orders, conducting all cash transactions, stocking and serving pastries, weighing and bagging bulk coffee beans, etc.

This is an example of a set of responsibilities and duties associated with a particular job function. The barista position will have its own set of dedicated duties, primarily dealing with beverage preparation; bus persons, of course, will be in charge of clearing tables, maintaining the cleanliness and appearance of the customer seating area, loading dishes into the glass washer, and sweeping the floors.

A check list should be created for each shift

As you can see in this type of operation, multiple check lists are needed, one for each position in the operation. Typically, a check list should be created for each shift, with specific functions associated with the particular needs and timing of the business day.

Opening setup check list

An *Opening setup check list* might include everything that the opening person is responsible for in setting up the operation. The list might include:

- Stocking the pastries, filling all bean hoppers, making sure that the daily special is written up on the chalk board, plus any other functions that insure everything will be stocked, prepped, and set up for the start of a new business day.

Shift change check list

Next, we create a *Shift Change check list.* Unless your store runs only one shift, with the same employees all day long, typically you will have a period in the day when a shift change will occur—when the morning employees go home and the afternoon employees come in and work into the late afternoon or evening.

If you have late night activities or entertainment, you might even have three shifts a day.

Your way of making sure that employees working the next shift are not routinely disgruntled

A shift change check list assures that the morning employees have left everything stocked for the next shift and have done some basic store maintenance, such as: *Cleaned the fingerprints off the glass front door and pastry case; wiped down the tables; put the chairs back in place, restocked the pastry case,* etc.

A shift change check list is your way of making sure that employees working the next shift are not routinely disgruntled because they have to bear the brunt of all the restocking and cleaning from the shift before.

Closing check list

Finally, you will need to create a *Closing check list* for the end of the day. This list will concentrate on the cleaning and restocking chores that will be needed to prepare for the morning opening.

These three check lists are essential to make sure that, (1) everything is being maintained at its optimal level of performance and appearance, and (2), you have happy employees who do not have to confront each other (and you) over who is responsible for doing what.

The following is a partial example of one check list:

Cashier Shift Change Check List

1. Clean glass windows on pastry cases inside and out.

2. Restock all pastries and desserts.

3. Wipe down service counter with a damp clean towel.

4. Clean outside of biscotti and cookie jars.

5. Refill granita machine.

6. Restock any bulk coffee bins if below half full.

7. Dispose of brewed coffee if over 30 minutes old, brew new pot.

8. Empty trash can, don't forget to replace the liner.

9. Check the cash register tape, make sure there is a back-up.

We created these three check lists with our computer, printed them out, plasticize them (had them laminated), and then put them on a clipboard with a grease pencil. Employees are required to check off the items on their check list and then sign it. This procedure creates some accountability. For example:

Takes away the excuse of, Oh, I forgot!

- If, at shift change, the second shift arrives and then tells you about all the work that was left by the first shift, you can go back and review the shift change check list and see if the first shift employees checked everything off and signed it.

Perhaps they did not check everything off. Or perhaps they were not being truthful when they filled out their check list. But, in any case, it creates accountability and takes away the excuse of, *Oh, I forgot!* Forgetting is no excuse if it is all there in writing.

Periodic cleaning check list

Beyond the opening, shift change and closing check lists, you might want to have a *Periodic Cleaning check list* to specify certain cleaning chores that do not need to be done on a daily basis but on a weekly or monthly basis. This is a list that may specify that:

- On Mondays, upon closing, you need to clean behind and under the espresso machine with hot soapy water; once a month you wash down all the table tops with hot soapy water; and so forth.

This check list is another simple operational system to make sure the appearance of your store stays at a superior level on a continuous basis.

Cashier's shift reconciliation report

The employee has to account for the sales with the appropriate cash and receipts

Another typical employee operational system is the *Cashier's Shift Reconciliation Report*. Rather than having the cashier at the end of the shift say:

> *I'm done, I'm outta here!*

—and then run off leaving you to count out a starting change bank for the till, and trying to figure out why the recorded sales and cash do not balance—you make the employee responsible for those functions.

The cashier's shift reconciliation report is a very simple process where the employee has to account for the sales which were rung on the cash register with the appropriate cash and receipts.

If there is a discrepancy between recorded sales and the cash and receipts on hand, it can be addressed at that point in time.

If there is a cash shortage at the end of the shift, it is obvious where the problem lies

It makes it a lot easier for your bookkeeping in the morning because you simply need to verify the employees' reports with their envelopes of cash and receipts.

This system also allows your employees to realize when they are having a problem balancing.

You do not want a situation where you have no idea where the accountability lies with cash. For this reason, *it is always wise to have only one person operating the cash register during a shift*. In this way, if there is a cash shortage at the end of the shift, it is obvious to everyone where the problem lies.

It may not always be possible, but even you, as the manager or owner, should try not to have your hands in the till if you have a designated cashier for a shift. If they do not balance at the end of the shift, and you have been working the cash register also, they may question your accuracy or honesty as an owner or manager. But more importantly, if the till is off they are not now fully responsible.

Your employees need to be accountable for all of the different aspects we have discussed, and that will be the result with diligent execution of some well thought out operational systems.

Operational systems for management

We recommend a variety of daily and weekly operational aides for managers, including:

- *Manager's daily check list*

- *Daily order guide — Vendor ordering worksheet*

Cashier Shift Report

Cashier _____
Date _____ Shift _____

Cash	$ _____
Coin	+$ _____
Checks	+$ _____
Charges	+$ _____
Total Deposit	= $ _____

Register Tape Total	$ _____
Over Rings	- $ _____
Promos / Comps	- $ _____
Coupons / Discounts	- $ _____
Employee Meals	- $ _____
Paid Outs	- $ _____
Total Receipts	= $ _____

Cash Over / Short $ _____

Notes _____
_____
_____
_____

- *Labor control card — Employee time card recap*

- *Weekly employee performance contract*

- *Daily key item inventory*

Manager's daily check list

All the details necessary for optimal store performance

The *Manager's Daily check list* is one of several operational systems designed to assist the manager in attending to all the details necessary for optimal store performance. It lists duties that the manager is responsible for on a daily basis, such as:

- Ordering of product; store readiness inspection; review of the employee check lists; making bank deposits; analyzing the week-to-date financial performance, and so on.

Daily order guide

The *Daily Order Guide* is a management tool that frees you from trying to hold in your head all those order and delivery questions, such as: Who do I order from today? When does the product come in?

For a daily order guide, we created a sheet that looks like a schedule. It lists all the purveyors down one side of the sheet, and the days—Monday, Tuesday, Wednesday, Thursday, Friday—across the top. We placed either an "O" or "D" under the appropriate days—an "O" for an order day, "D" for a delivery day.

Daily Order Guide
O = Order Day / D = Delivery Day

Company	Mon	Tues	Wed	Thur	Fri	Sat	Sun	Phone #

Your daily order guide provides a quick ready reference for you and your employees

Many times you will order on Monday, and the order will arrive on Tuesday, but with some companies you might order on Monday and it will not arrive until Thursday. Your daily order guide provides a quick ready reference for you and your employees.

If you are running low on a product, you and your employees can look at the order guide and know when more product is coming. If it is going to be delivered today, you probably will not have to worry about it. But if the delivery date is three days off, you can take the appropriate measures.

Vendor ordering worksheet

To actually place the orders, you go from the daily order guide to the *Vendor Ordering Worksheet* or *Par List*. These forms list every product that you purchase from a specific vendor, and allow you to assess what is on hand, what has been ordered, and how much has been used between the periods in which you order.

From this information you will always know if the products which might be running in short supply will be arriving with your next order.

These forms list every product that you purchase from a specific vendor

The usage information will allow you to set "pars," the amount of product that should be stocked on your shelf, after a delivery, to assure a sufficient inventory until the next delivery.

Vendor Ordering Guide   Vendor_____

Product	Order Unit	Par	/		/		/		/		/	
			O.H. Use	Order	O.H. Use	Order	O.H. Use	Order	O.H. Use	Order	O.H. Use	Order

Employee time card verification

To help with labor control, one system that works quite nicely is a policy that requires all employees to have their time card signed by the manager at the beginning and end of their shift. The system requires that the employees bring their time cards to the manager for his signature immediately after punching in, and just prior to punching out.

This interaction allows the manager to assess if the employee was on time for work, or if they punched in, needlessly, prior to their schedule starting time, consuming extra labor dollars. It gives the manager a chance to pass along any important information to the employee, and provides an opportunity to inspect their personal appearance and readiness for work.

Making your employees responsible for informing you that their scheduled shift ending time has arrived will help you control your labor and prevent you from running over your allocated budget.

Most employees are very cognizant of when their scheduled shift conclusion is approaching

During the course of a busy day, it is often easy to lose track of time, and when a specific employee should be off the clock. If keeping track of this information is up to you and you forget, employees may not remind you, assuming that you are not ready for them to leave. They may also just conveniently forget, desiring a few extra dollars on their pay checks. Most employees are very cognizant of when their scheduled shift conclusion is approaching. For this reason, making them responsible for reminding you will greatly increase you chances of controlling your labor.

The other advantage of having them bring you their time cards at the end of a shift is that it provides you with an opportunity to check all the other details they are responsible for, such as the shift change check list, or closing check list. It also gives your employees the opportunity to respond and express concerns they may have had during their shift.

Labor control card

A *Labor control card* is a valuable tool which will also help you keep tabs on your labor.

It is a simple pocket size card that provides spaces for the names of your scheduled employees, the starting and ending times for their shifts, and a space for the actual hours worked.

If you calculate the time they have worked when they bring you their time card when they punch out, and move that data on to the labor control card, you will be able to immediately assess, by employee, if your actual labor is exceeding your budget.

Also, you will no longer have to collect time cards for calculation at the end of the shift.

Daily time card recap

At the end of the day simply move the data from the labor control card to the *Daily Time Card Recap*.

This form will allow you to compare your daily labor performance, and your cumulative weekly performance, to what you had budgeted. This time card recap will also provide you with a summary of total hours worked by each employee for a two-week pay period.

Labor Card

Name	Shift	Sch. Hours	Actual Hours
	( )		
	( )		
	( )		
	( )		
	( )		
	( )		
	( )		
	( )		
	( )		
	( )		
	( )		
	( )		
	( )		
	( )		
	( )		
	( )		
	( )		
	( )		
	( )		
	( )		

Employee Timecard Recap

Month_____   Year_____

Date											Reg. Hrs $	O.T. Hrs $	Tot. Hrs $
Day													
Employee	Rate												
Daily Totals													
MTD Proj. $													
MTD Actual $													

Weekly employee performance contract

The *Weekly Employee Performance Contract* is an ongoing employee development tool.

Its purpose is to continually provide your employees with goals to improve and enhance their performance, while providing you with a means of being involved in the goal setting process, and allowing you to evaluate their progress.

Provides employees with goals to improve performance

We suggest establishing a goal with every employee each week, and then evaluating their progress in achieving that goal the following week.

If they achieve their goal, a new goal should be determined.

If they do not achieve their goal, they should continue to strive to attain it for an additional week, or until it has been achieved.

The physical contract is simple. We had a rubber stamp made which we used on the back of our employee time cards. It says *Employee Contract* with a half dozen lines on which the goal can be written, and then a place for the employee's and manager's signatures.

The time card is the perfect place to write the goal because the manager can be reminded of the employee's goals when they bring their card to be signed at the beginning of the shift. The manager can in turn remind and enforce the goal with the employee on a daily basis.

Goals should be specific and kept simple.

Concentrate on one goal per week instead of several.

At this rate, in one year you should be able to improve 52 different areas of performance!

EMPLOYEE CONTRACT

I will only grind as
much coffee as will
be necessary to
prepare the next
two to three
customer orders.

_____

_____

_____

_____

EMPLOYEE *Bob Barista*

MANAGER *Mike Manager*

Try to avoid lofty ideals such as:

I will work on providing a friendly, attentive, attitude towards customers.

This goal leaves too much to interpretation. What is *friendly*? What is *attentive*?

A better goal to start on a path to friendly attentive customer service might be:

I will greet every customer within five seconds of stepping up to the counter with "Good morning, how are you today? May I help you?"

Your employee will have no trouble understanding exactly what you expect of them with this type of goal.

Keep in mind that goals can be applied to any employment position within the store and to any area of performance.

Provides you with criteria for assessing who deserves a wage increase

Another advantage to using the weekly employee performance contract is that it provides you with criteria for assessing who deserves a wage increase, and provides justification for increases should some employees become disgruntled because they did not receive one.

For example: If Bob comes to you complaining that Sally received a raise, but he did not, you can easily and graphically explain to Bob why he did not.

You see these cards Bob, these are Sally's, and she achieved and started on a new goal each week. But here are your cards Bob, it took you eight weeks to achieve your first goal, four weeks to achieve your next goal,

and so forth. End of discussion.

Some typical goals

Here are some typical goals for different job functions within a specialty coffee cafe:

Cashiers:

1. Greet every customer within 5 seconds of stepping up to the counter.

2. Welcome every customer and ask how they are doing.

   "Welcome to Java John's, how are you today!"

3. Thank every customer at the conclusion of the transaction followed by,

   "We'll see you tomorrow!"

4. Exercise care when handling money and balance to the penny every shift this week.

5. Keep the order counter wiped clean of coffee spills and pastry crumbs after each transaction if necessary.

6. Keep pastry case free of splatters, smudges, and fingerprints at all times.

Baristas:

1. Wipe clean the steaming wand immediately upon the conclusion of every steaming cycle.

2. Grind only enough coffee for the next two beverages.

3. Rinse and return the portafilter to the machine after each extraction.

4. Use a thermometer every time you steam milk and do not exceed 150 degrees.

5. Time your extraction once an hour, using a measured shot glass, ensuring a 1 ounce single extraction within 25 to 30 seconds.

6. Wipe clean the espresso machine and surrounding counter area after every beverage if necessary.

Bus Persons:

1. When customers have an empty cup or plate in front of them, ask:

   Are you finished? Can I get this out of your way?

   Remove those items if they indicate they are finished.

2. Make removing dishes and wiping clean table tops your number one priority. Begin clearing tables within one minute after the customers have left.

3. Brush crumbs from tables into the bus tub and not onto the floor.

4. Check to be sure that chairs are free from crumbs and other food, and positioned neatly back around the table.

5. Spot sweep the seating area floor on a regular basis, keeping it free of crumbs and other debris.

6. Keep the front door free of fingerprints—clean on a regular basis.

7. Check the restrooms once an hour to be sure they are stocked with soap, paper towels, toilet paper, and make sure counter tops and floors are clean.

Daily key item inventory

Another key to manager control is what we call the *Daily Key Item Inventory.*

If your cost of sales are running high, (your food cost, or your beverage cost) and you are not really sure why, it may be time to implement a daily key item inventory. This is not an inventory of everything in your store. It is an inventory of some of the higher cost, more desirable theft items.

Makes it possible to quickly determine if you might have a theft problem

Perhaps you are worried that somebody might be walking out the door with a gallon of gourmet chocolate syrup, or a five pound bag of coffee. The daily key item inventory makes it possible for you to quickly determine if you might have a theft problem. You simply take an inventory of a few key items at the beginning of the day or shift, and at the end of that day or shift. Compare the items which have been reduced in inventory against the quantities which have been sold as indicated by your cash register tapes. This allows you to identify if there is a huge discrepancy. For example:

If you know you are getting 50 shots of espresso out of a pound of coffee, and you take your cash register tape at the end of the day and calculate that 250 shots have been expended, then you know that the total amount of coffee which should have been used is about five pounds.

That means that your coffee inventory should not vary by much more than a couple of pounds at most.

If you discover 15 pounds of coffee are missing, then this is a definite indicator that you have a very serious problem on your hands. It is then time to start watching people to find out where the problem exists.

The operational systems for management are some of the most important and useful tools you will need for your business.

Taking the time and energy to set them up properly will help you monitor and control the readiness and quality of your operation. They will:

- keep your employees motivated and moving in the right direction

- maintain the cleanliness and appeal of both your products and your physical plant

- control your inventory and your costs.

And, they will save you considerable amounts of time, preventing you from becoming extremely frustrated.

 For more information on this specific subject, refer to the following book from Bellissimo—800-655-3955.

- **Achieving Success in Specialty Coffee**

Chapter 27 Check List

Employee Systems:

_____ Establish an *Opening Setup Check List* for each position in your operation.
_____ Establish a *Shift Change Check List* for each position in your operation.
_____ Establish a *Closing Check List* for each position in your operation.
_____ Establish a *Periodic Cleaning Check List* for each position in your operation.
_____ Establish a Cashier Check Out Procedure.

Management Systems:

_____ Establish a *Manager's Daily/Weekly Check List.*
_____ Establish a *Daily Ordering Guide.*
_____ Establish a *Vendor Ordering Work Sheet* for each purveyor.
_____ Implement a policy in which your employees must have their time cards signed by management, and must inform management when their scheduled shift ending time has arrived.
_____ Create a pocket *Labor Control Card* to help manage daily labor.
_____ Establish a *Daily Time Card Recap* to track and assess daily labor performance.
_____ Implement an *Employee Performance Contract* program of employee development.
_____ Conduct a *Daily Key Item Inventory.*

CHAPTER 28

Hiring & Managing Employees

Contents

Chapter 28 Contents - Page 2

CHAPTER 28

Hiring & Managing Employees

Choosing your employees may be the most important administrative decision you will ever make

A good employee is extremely hard to find.

Not unlike finding a pearl in an oyster, finding great people to work with you is a numbers game. To find those reliable, honest, competent, loyal, optimistic, cheerful, conscientious, flexible, dynamic, hardworking individuals, you will need to interview numerous applicants.

The reward is worth the effort. In fact, it is essential to the success of your business. Choosing your employees may be the most important administrative decision you will ever make. It is appropriate, therefore, that you commit the time and attention to recruiting and interviewing enough people to fill positions with individuals who will enhance your organization.

Once hired, your employees must be able to:

- Attract customers through friendly, attentive service, and by preparing and serving only the highest quality product.

- Perform their assigned responsibilities well and in a timely fashion while projecting confidence with a bit of charisma.

- Help you maintain the professional appearance of your business by contributing to its physical upkeep, and by maintaining a high level of personal appearance and a positive attitude.

- Be conscientious with your product to help maintain your budgeted costs.

- Be honest and dependable so that you can have time away from the hands-on portion of your business to perform the administrative, promotional, analytic, and planning functions which are so necessary to the success and growth of your business.

- Be optimistic and enthusiastic in their relationships with customers.

- Be a clear communicator with a good speaking voice.

Because you will be hiring employees for different levels of responsibility, in the following sections we offer procedures and techniques for recruiting for the following two levels:

- Entry-level employees, such as baristas, cashiers, cooks, bakers, and bus persons.

- Advanced-level employees, such as senior management and -supervisors.

Hiring good entry-level employees

In most cases the attributes you will want most in an entry-level employee are energy and personality.

Of course you want some intelligence; you want to make sure they can balance their till, make quality beverages, carry on an intelligent conversation, and so forth.

But personality is absolutely paramount in this particular industry.

To help you find those pearls, we recommend the following four-step process for attracting and qualifying quality entry-level employees:

- Writing an effective Help Wanted ad

- Conducting the initial phone contact

- Conducting a quick screening interview

- Conducting an in-depth interview

Writing the Help Wanted ad

Write or start your Help Wanted ad in such a way as to attract the desired candidates for the available positions while discouraging undesirable applicants.

Indicate that you have something desirable to offer,

- Title your ad with something like: *Gourmet Coffee Opportunity* or *Train to be a Skilled Barista!*, instead of *Espresso Preparer Needed* or *Help Wanted*. This will indicate that you have something desirable to offer, rather than being desperate for assistance.

- Mention in the ad the characteristics you desire in an applicant. Use terms like: *dependable, energetic, service oriented, must love hard work, immaculate appearance a must*. Applicants who know they do not possess one or some of these desired qualities, will oftentimes not bother to apply.

- In the ad, ask those who are interested in applying to call for an interview appointment. (It may not be realistic to ask them to send a resume if you are hiring for an entry-level position, or if you are bringing in someone from high school. Having them call for an interview appointment gives you a chance to do some pre-screening on the phone.)

- Set a time range for calling that works for you. Say: *Call for an interview appointment on Friday between 3 and 4 p.m.* If they call at 1 o'clock, you will know they cannot follow instructions.

The initial phone interview

In the initial telephone interview, describe the position and work required, available hours, starting wage rate, when you would need them to start, etc.

- Ask callers if these conditions are agreeable to them. The tone of their voice, and their attitude is as important as their answers to the questions.

The tone of their voice, and attitude is as important as their answers

- If you perceive any hesitation or disappointment on their part during the conversation, you may want to consider if the position is right for their needs.

- An obvious benefit of scheduling an applicant for an interview appointment is that it gives you a chance to judge their dependability by seeing if they will show up for their interview on time.

Quick screening interview

Look at interviewing applicants as a process. It is not just getting the applicants you select for interviewing in front of you—you are testing them by putting them through the process and seeing how well they respond over time.

Usually, a two-interview process is sufficient, but if it becomes appropriate, do not hesitate to call the final applicants back for a third interview.

A two-step interview process allows you to keep the first interviews short during the qualifying stages. Initial interviews need not last longer than three to five minutes after the candidate has filled out an application.

- When the applicants show up for their first interview, have a receptionist or aid there who can hand out application forms and keep things organized so you can give your full attention to the interview process.

- Some applicants are going to show up 15 or 20 minutes early and your help can manage the waiting room situation.

- In our experience, a receptionist serves another purpose, as well. We always tell the receptionist to watch for people who come in to fill out an application but have not brought along a pen or pencil. If somebody comes in and asks for a pencil or a pen, before handing it over, we usually instruct the receptionist to say something like, *Let me make sure this writes,* and then to make a scribble in the corner of the application. When we receive the interviewer's application, this scribble signals to us that this person did not show up prepared.

The purpose of this first interview is for you to determine if the position is right for them and, more important, to give you a chance to size up the applicant. Make note of the following:

Remember, they will probably never look better than they do at the time of the interview

- Is their personal appearance pleasant, clean, and neat? Remember, they will probably never look better than they do at the time of the interview.

- Do they make eye contact when speaking to you?

- Do they answer the questions asked of them?

- Are they confident and friendly?

- Do they smile?

During the first interview we generally ask the following questions:

- *Are you seeking a full-time or part-time position?*

- *Are the hours available acceptable for your needs?*

- *The starting wage is $____. Is this an acceptable wage to you?*

- *Does transportation to and from work present a problem for you?*

- *Do you have any other outside activities that might conflict with this work schedule?*

- *If hired, when would you be available to begin work?*

All we really try to determine in this first interview is: *Do we want to bring this person back to talk with us in-depth?* This is an evaluation based upon first impressions with a goal of pass or fail. To help you make this evaluation:

Do not discount the importance of your "gut feelings"

- Do not discount the importance of your "gut feelings" about a person. We all communicate with body language when we interact with others. Facial expressions and body movements which may last for only a fraction of a second are perceived by our subconscious.

- Listen to your intuitions, they will tell you a lot.

- Positive personal chemistry between you and the applicant is essential. If your personalities clash, you may want to consider if this is really the type of person you want to work with every day.

We usually conclude this phase of the interview process with the statement:

This is only a preliminary interview. We have more interviews to conduct and upon their conclusion we will be calling some individuals back for additional interviews. You will either be hearing from us within the next 24 to 48 hours, or you won't be hearing from us. Thank you for coming to this interview. We appreciate your time.

Remember, great people will normally be hired quickly

By concluding the interview with that statement, you will relieve yourself of the responsibility of having to call everyone back and answering uncomfortable questions as to why they did not qualify for a second interview. If they do not hear from you within several days, they will know they did not qualify. Make sure you have a phone number you can reach them at if you are planning to bring them back for a second interview.

If an individual appears to be that desired "pearl" you are seeking, schedule the next interview with them before they leave. Remember, great people will normally be hired quickly—you do not want to lose them to another job opportunity.

In-depth interview

The second interview will give you another opportunity to judge the applicant's personal appearance and dependability. If, again, they are on time and project a professional appearance, you can assume that the chances of this being a regular occurrence are great.

- Examine their application carefully. How long have they worked for previous employers? If short periods of time, ask why they changed jobs often.

- From our experiences we prefer applicants with no prior experience in this industry. We have found it to be much more difficult to change established habits and philosophies than to teach and instill new ones.

- If they are seeking this position as a second job, or are attending school and working, will they be able to commit the time and energy necessary to do all of these well?

- We like to ask multi-part questions that will require lengthy answers.

- Listen carefully to their answers, this is when you will gain important insights about your applicants.

- Ask multi-part questions to see if they will remember all that is asked of them. If they cannot remember a three-part question, will they be able to remember a complex six beverage order?

Here are a few of our favorite interview questions:

- *During your last year of employment, how many times would you estimate that you were late to work, and how many days did you miss due to illness?*

- *Tell me about the most physically demanding work you have ever done, and how long you worked at that job.*

- *Tell me about the most stressful or hectic work-related situation you have experienced, what happened, and how you got through that situation.*

- *As a person, what would you say are your three strongest qualities, and what are three areas in which you could make some self-improvements?*

Beware of the individual who cannot think of any areas in which they might need to improve

This last question has been one of the most productive at revealing potential short-comings in an applicant. Beware of the individual who cannot think of any areas in which they might need to improve. Have you ever met the perfect person? How well will this individual take constructive criticism if they think they are already perfect?

If you are still undecided after the second interview, schedule a third to make a determination between your final candidates. Putting your candidates through this rigorous process will many times reveal their true level of patience and eagerness for the available position. We have had candidates show noticeable annoyance at having to return once again. If this happens, we eliminate them from consideration.

Before we conduct a third interview or make a determination to hire an individual, we strongly recommend that you phone some of their past employers and personal references. Candidates that project desirable characteristics are sometimes skilled sales persons. Serious potential shortcomings might be revealed by those who have had firsthand experiences with them in the past.

Try these techniques for yourself, interview lots of applicants, and you will find those great people. They are out there, but you must spend the required time to search for them!

Legal guidelines

In preparing your list of interview questions, keep in mind that in today's business climate it is important that you follow legal guidelines with respect to what you may and may not discuss with your applicants.

Find out what legal guidelines apply to your interview situation

We advise that you find out what legal guidelines apply to your interview situation by requesting a copy of your state's legal hiring practices from your local or state Department of Employment or Bureau of Labor.

In Oregon, we have been informed by the Department of Employment that you can ask any question you like. BUT—and note the BUT— you may not discriminate on the basis of certain protected criteria, including religion, creed, national origin, sexual orientation, or marital status. And since you, the employer, will be required to establish that you did not exclude a candidate on the basis of a protected right, you would be wise to not ask the questions in the first place.

In some states you can safely ask about the applicant's age, ability to handle the physical requirements of the job, legal work status, availability during the hours you need covered, and job and educational experience. And you can ask questions that might elicit information that you would not want to ask with a direct question, like,

> *Are there any outside activities or responsibilities you can think of that might interfere with your ability to do the job?*

Barista salaries

Barista salaries vary in different parts of the country so you may want to check average salaries in your area. In Seattle, the city that usually sets the standard for the specialty coffee industry, beginning salaries start at around $6 an hour and go up to around $10. Because of the low wages, baristas generally depend on tips to get by. Of course, the wage for a qualified manager will usually be higher.

The old adage, *You get what you pay for* holds as true in staffing as anywhere else. Fair salaries and reasonable benefit plans go a long way in attracting and maintaining high performance associates.

Hiring good advanced-level employees

You get what you pay for

If you have a larger operation, you really need to find what we term "a real rock"— somebody who can be a trainer, accept responsibility and function as a member of your management team.

We have worked with many operations that have numerous employees but do not have that one key employee. We believe it is very important to develop and have a manager-type key employee— an operational-systems person upon whom you can rely to act in your place when it is appropriate and when you are not there. The most important trait is a management attitude. Your key employee has to be able to perceive, think, and process information from a management position.

Key employees are difficult to find, but there are certainly people out there who, regardless of what they do in life, conscientiously do their very best job. They treat their work as if it were their own operation, and as if the dollars were going to the bottom line for their own use.

When you lose these experienced employees, you will want to replace them with personnel who exhibit aptitudes and experiences that are a healthy cut above entry-level employees. You will need to shape your recruiting strategies differently.

Recently our company, Bellissimo Coffee InfoGroup, was faced with this very challenge. Our employee of nine months was heading off to San Francisco to attend graduate school. We had a few weeks to plan on how we would replace her, and what attributes we wanted in our new employee. This new person would not only have to learn the existing job, but be required to take on added responsibility in our small but growing company. We knew we would have to do a number of things correctly to find the person who would be right for this position.

The recruiting and qualifying procedure we followed was an expanded version of the four-step process recommended for entry-level positions, and included the following seven steps:

- Placing a great Help Wanted ad

- Screening the mail and resumes from applicants

- Making the initial phone contact with selected applicants

- Conducting the first interview

- Conducting the final interview

- Checking references

- Rating the finalists

Placing a great ad

No matter how many qualified applicants might be in your area, and no matter how attractive your job might be, bringing those people through the door for the interview is your first challenge.

In our case we wanted to let the reader know this was a position that offered advancement. We also wanted to convey that the person would be doing a multitude of tasks. We needed someone who had a background with various computer programs and an aptitude for sales. Conveying the fact that we were a small growing company, and that sales were involved in the position, we wanted to make sure the ad did not sound like the job would be selling encyclopedias door-to-door. We ran the following ad:

> *Young Dynamic Media Company—well established in national/ international markets, seeks energetic, inspired individual for multi-faceted tasks. Career potential unlimited. Computer/ marketing skills a must. 30-40 hours/wk. Possible travel. Send resume & cover letter to: Media Position, PO Box 5182 Eugene, OR 97405.*

We feel it is extremely important to add the part about the cover letter. If they do not take the time to produce a personalized cover letter for you when instructed to, no matter how great the application is…throw it away! Why? Because they did not follow instructions and the position obviously was not that important to them.

We placed our ad Saturday and Sunday on two consecutive weekends. We then waited to see how well we had done on describing our employment opportunity, and in enticing potential candidates.

Screening the mail

We were most fortunate in the applications we received. We received many from individuals who appeared to be highly qualified, and a minimal amount from entry-level candidates. The following points are areas we scrutinize when reviewing an application:

Did they include the requested cover letter and was it well thought out and written?

- The envelope/cover letter/resume: How neatly was the envelope addressed? Did they address the envelope in the way it was requested in the ad? Did they take the time to produce a label or type the address? (Look at the envelope, it is going to tell you a lot. We always staple the envelope to the back of the resume and cover letter so we can give it the attention it deserves.) Did they include the requested cover letter and was it well thought out and written? Was it personalized or an obvious form response? Is their resume neat and complete? What does the resume tell you about this person, their skills, their history?

- Time spent in each of their previous positions: If they have only worked three to six months at all of their previous jobs you should be cautious and concerned.

- What job experience did they have that would relate to the available position?

Did they give phone numbers for their references?

- Did they give phone numbers for their references? We feel if they really want you to call references they will make it as easy as possible for you to contact them. Upon reaching the reference of one individual that had not given us his reference's phone numbers, we were told, *What! He put my name down as a reference, that's unbelievable!* As you can imagine, what this former employer told us about this person was not complimentary.

- Length of time in the community. Did they just move here from across the country? Do they have any roots in the community or are they just hoping to get a job to enable them to stay in town?

The initial phone call

We now have a stack of resumes of what we hope are all "A" candidates for the position. We initially call each to do some phone screening, and do not offer an interview until we have asked them some basic questions, like:

- *Have you been looking for work long?*

- *What did you find of interest about this position which motivated you to send in a resume?*

More than anything this provides us with an opportunity to find out what their phone skills are like, and to learn a little about their confidence and background. If they are not home when called, we leave a message. How long does it take for them to get back to us? If they leave us a message, how thorough was the information?

After we screen our hypothetical stack of 12 resumes, we ask the eight who look the most impressive to come in for an initial interview.

The first interview

For the initial interview, we bring in all the applicants for what they are told will be a 10-minute interview. We schedule a full half an hour just in case we want to spend a little more time with any person we are really interested in. This way, if you know immediately when he or she walks through the door that this person is not right for the position, you can get out of the situation in just a few minutes without either party feeling uncomfortable.

First impressions are important. We bring a candidate in to make obvious initial observations. When they walk through the door we can make some immediate determinations by how they are dressed, if they smile, if they make eye contact, etc. Many times our first impression will tell us whether this person is going to work out or not.

Sometimes, after you talk to them for a minute or two, you might have a slightly different opinion; but dress is very important, as is their demeanor, eye contact, voice and speech quality, and you can judge all those things in the first minute. Always remember, as we have stated, that they are never going to look better than they do in the interview.

In this first interview, we tell them briefly what our company and the job is all about, and ask them how they think they will fit in. Be observant of their reactions and facial expressions as you talk about the position. We ask some basic questions, such as:

- *From the information we have related to you about this position, do you feel you could be comfortable in this work situation?*

- *What are your salary expectations?*

- *What about the hours we mentioned, are they acceptable to you?*

- *Do you have any outside activities which might conflict with your ability to give this position 100% of your effort?*

- *This position may require you to run some errands on a regular basis, do you have sound transportation and would this request present any concerns?*

- *If you could have your dream job today, what would you like to be doing?*

- *If an opening comes along in a few months for the position you just mentioned, would you accept it?*

- *Do you like and drink coffee? Do you feel you could become passionate about our product and our industry?*

Following each interview, we evaluate the candidate on a scale of 1-10. When all the interviews are finished, we schedule one hour to discuss the pros and cons of each applicant and why we gave them the rating we did.

The final interview

This is crunch time! We now have our eight job seekers narrowed down to four, and we need to make a decision. Here is the real challenge. Each applicant will usually possess certain and different attributes for consideration. If you have done your research correctly to this point, you will probably have four very qualified candidates in front of you and making the choice can be difficult.

We have developed the following system which we feel is very logical for making the final decision of whom to hire.

- We schedule each of the four finalists for interviews, allowing one hour for each.

- We tell them they will have a 45-minute interview, which will allow us 15 minutes between each to discuss our impressions.

- We try to ask each of them the same questions, the first being:

  If we could have been privy to your discussion with your (husband, wife, roommate, mother) after our first interview, what would we have heard you say about this job? And please be honest with us.

  Amazing what you will hear with this question. Also we might ask questions like:

- *Why do you desire this particular job, and why do you feel you would be an asset to our company?*

- *Tell us about the most important decision you have ever made in your life, why you made that decision and, knowing what you do today, what you would do differently if you had the chance to do it again.*

- *Tell us about the most challenging organizational project you have ever had, and describe in detail your methods and solutions to that project.*

- *Tell us about the most difficult relationship you have ever experienced with a co-worker or supervisor, what happened, and how you addressed that challenge.*

- *What types of things really annoy you in a work-related situation?*

- *Tell us about your short-term and long-term goals. What do you see yourself doing one year from now, and five years from now?*

- *Tell us the most stressful job situation you have ever encountered, how you dealt with it, and what you learned from it.*

- *What would you say are your three strongest qualities, and what are three areas in which you could make some self-improvements?*

Rating the finalists

In our particular case, after each interview we rated the candidate in the following 10 categories:

Phone skills:	7 *
Sales ability:	10
Mundane tasks:	8
Community stability/longevity:	8
Salary expectations:	8
Individual growth potential:	7
Child care expenses:	5
Office personality/fit:	9
Interest in product and industry:	8
Personal appearance:	7
Initial first impression:	8

*The numbers beside each rating category represents our value for the importance of that function in respect to the overall job, with 10 being very important, and 1 being unimportant.

We then rated each person separately in each category on a scale of 1 to 5, with 1 being low and 5 being high. We discussed why we gave each the score we did, added our two scores together and multiplied by the number value associated with each category to achieve an overall score.

For example:

> *Bruce felt that our candidate Carol would be very good on the phone— nice voice, quick thinker, and very responsible—so he gave her a 5. Ed was not quite as impressed and only gave Carol a 3. Between the two, Carol got a total of 8. We then multiplied that by seven (the rating of importance of phone skills to our office) and came up with, of course, 56.*

Objectively evaluate candidates using your head as well as your heart

We followed the same procedure for each category and, at the end of each interview, had a total for that applicant in each discipline. Adding together the individual category scores gave us the applicant's total score. The total scores for each of the applicants can then be used as a basis for making a final intelligent decision. This system may seem complex but it really is not. It is just another way for you to objectively evaluate candidates using your head as well as your heart.

Once again, be sure to check references before you make your hiring decision. Be perceptive of the attitude and enthusiasm that the past employers express about this individual. If they tend to be vague, or not overly excited, try to extract as much information as possible. Some companies have policies of not revealing any information about a past employee's performance. One question we like to ask is:

> *If given the chance, would you hire this person again?*

This will tell you a lot!

Managing employees

Once hired, managing your employees is probably one of the biggest challenges you will have in running a specialty coffee operation. One of the keys to successful management is having your employees understand from the beginning what is expected of them, and what your standards are. To accomplish this, you must have their job well defined.

You must have their job well defined

It also means that you have to spend time with them initially; you have to walk them through their job functions for at least several shifts, explaining and clarifying tasks. Managing employees effectively means that they must first be properly trained. [We will be dealing with employee training in detail in the next chapter.]

Have a written employee manual

A written employee manual, even a brief one, is a good place to start in defining the acceptable parameters of behavior and desired performance and goals of your business. Putting your expectations in writing leaves little doubt that the information has been conveyed to the employee.

Put your expectations in writing

We suggest you incorporate a page in the manual which the employee signs and returns to you. This page states that the employee has read and understands the performance criteria and policies of their employment. We also suggest that specific criteria for wage increases be included in your employee manual. Too often employees are under the impression that merely showing up for work qualifies them for a wage increase.

Avoid an adversarial relationship

It seems that, especially in our culture here in the United States, an adversarial relationship prevails between employer and employee. The employer is often perceived by employees as the enemy, and employees are seen by their employers as *the troops.*

What is really needed in this business is for you and your employees to work as a team.

You have to understand that—even though you own the business and have certain advantages, privileges, responsibilities, and decision-making powers that your employees do not—their job is equally as important to the success of the operation as is your function. They have to know that their contribution is ultimately critical. It is important they understand that you are depending on them to perform at a level necessary for that success. They have to feel that they are appreciated and consequently rewarded for their contribution.

You must create a culture of caring between you and your employees

A majority of employees will not mind working hard, but they must feel rewards will come back to them if they make the effort.

You must create a culture of caring between you and your employees. It is important for you to know something about their lives, and to understand their dreams and aspirations. Equally, they must understand you, your priorities and motivations.

When there exists a mutual attitude and desire to see each other succeed and be happy, you will have created an environment where your employees will be motivated to help you make your business flourish. By leading by example, and praising positive performance, you will create a culture of caring, professionalism, and pride in doing one's job well.

For some individuals this environment is more important and valuable than simple economic rewards.

Conduct periodic performance reviews

Regular periodic employee performance reviews should be incorporated so employees know exactly how they are doing. It is important to:

- Tell people not only what they do wrong, but what they do right. (This is a good time to review the *Employee performance contracts* that were established on the back of your employee time cards).

- Follow the basic principle, *Praise in public and punish in private.*

- Be consistent in how you deal with employees. Do not show favoritism for one employee over another. Employees would like to know daily that when they arrive at work your attitude will be consistent if their performance is consistent. (We all know managers who are "up" one day and then behave totally differently the next, which confuses employees as to whether they are doing well or not.)

- Follow an important premise: *Don't ask your employees to do anything you wouldn't do yourself.* If there is an undesirable job to be done that no one would like to do, the first time you can say, *Let's roll up our sleeves and do this one together.* Show them that you are not putting yourself on a level above them, and that you are willing to experience what they have to go through.

For example:

> You think an employee should get through his cleanup routine in 30 minutes, but he says,
>
> *Well, I can't do it in 30 minutes!*
>
> You can argue that you think it can be accomplished in 30 minutes, or you can roll up your sleeves and prove to him that with a little elbow grease, and some hustle, you can get it done in 20. At this point it will be difficult for him to convince you that it cannot be done in 30. This will also help build camaraderie between you and the employee.

Being honest with your employees about their performance level is important

Being honest with your employees about their performance level is important. When you see a performance or customer-service deficiency, you need to address that problem as soon as possible—but certainly not in front of the customer or another employee. At the first opportune moment, pull the employee aside and say, *Hey, I saw something today that concerns me a little bit and I want to talk with you about it.*

Many times, the employee's immediate reaction will be defensive. Always try to defuse this at the outset with,

> *I'm not getting down on you. I like you as a person but you need to do this for the well-being of the business, and for all of us. I don't want you to take this as a personal attack; it is constructive criticism which is intended to help you be better at your job. I want to help you be successful.*

Schedule team meetings

Your basic orientation—and one you have to instill in your employees—is that your operation needs to be a team effort, no different from a sports team. The entire staff needs to function as one collaborative effort to achieve common goals.

Regularly scheduled team meetings are vital to helping team members work together. When you first open your coffee bar, you should strive to conduct weekly meetings for your first two months. Then, when your team is functioning smoothly, you can reduce the schedule for a team meeting to every two weeks.

After about six months, you can reduce them to monthly meetings.

Make employee attendance at the staff meetings mandatory. Legally, you may need to pay your employees for attending, but the investment will be worth it. These meetings provide you and your employees with an opportunity to:

- Find out exactly what is going on

- Identify and resolve problems

- Air complaints and discuss options

- Offer suggestions for improvement

- Come to know and understand one another

- Clarify performance expectations

- Deal with changes in the operation as the business grows.

In our experience with team meetings, we have noticed that the usual outcome of a successful meeting is a level of calmness and an air of relaxation among employees. Before we began the policy of conducting meetings on a regular basis, relations could start to become stressful because employees were thinking things that had never been brought into the open and discussed. Remember that:

- It is vital that team meetings be constructive. A team meeting is not a "rag session." It is not an opportunity for you to sit down with your employees and beat them up and tell them how worthless they are. This is not a situation where the owner does the majority of the talking.

- Certainly there might be some performance deficiencies that need to be addressed. But you want the meeting to focus on two-way communication. Talk to your employees about challenges that the business is facing without getting specific about the financials. (Obviously you do not want to panic them or signal that you might be going out of business.) But do let them know what the goals and objectives are from your standpoint as an owner or manager, and what will be required to achieve those goals. Then, throw the meeting open by asking, *Who has some ideas on how we can achieve this?*

You may be amazed at the great ideas that flow out of your employees' heads.

• This may be a nice time to show them your appreciation by spending a few dollars on a couple of pizzas. A gesture of this sort will show them you care.

Your employees do not realize and are not aware of all the operational costs involved in operating the business. Team meetings provide a forum where you can explain these costs and help them to see you and your business differently. If you do not want your employees thinking you are rolling in money because you just bought a brand new van for the business, this forum will give you an opportunity to say,

> *You know, we just acquired a brand new van for our operation. We had to lease it. It didn't require that we put very much down, and it is something that is really necessary for our operation.*

You can clear up a lot of negative gossip and mistaken assumptions about your operation which are not true.

Team meetings are especially valuable in the beginning stages of the business when you have your sleeves rolled up and you are spending a lot of hours with your baristas to make sure they are trained properly. But later, you want to be able to use this time for long-term planning and budgeting. When you are no longer spending eight hours a day on site, but only four, you do not want your employees thinking that you are playing golf while they are making you rich.

Reward your employees

Always remember, working at your coffee operation may not be the most important activity in the lives of your employees. In most cases they simply wish to serve their time in a hassle-free environment and pick up their paycheck. Your employees generally do not have any delusions about achieving their fortunes and long-term security working for your business.

This does not mean that you cannot, or ought not, expect excellent performance from your employees. It does mean that you must understand what motivates them in order to manage them properly.

They should understand that as the business prospers, everybody will get rewarded. This concept is a very powerful tool. Present goals for your employees, such as, *When we get up to X cups a day, everyone is going to get a raise,* from this, they will be able to see themselves as part of a team motivated to achieve a common goal.

Looking back on some of the more difficult operations we owned which were located a long distance away from our offices, we think now it would have been wiser to have based pay raises on performance goals. This would have provided good motivation for them to build the business, and leave the money in the cash register. It is an alternative to an employee thinking, *We aren't going to get rewarded, so we might as well reward ourselves now.*

And, there are other ways of motivating your employees:

Praise employees when they do something exceptional

- Giving employee-of-the-month awards. Perhaps the award winner gets two pounds of coffee, or a free dinner at a local restaurant.

- Rewarding every employee with half-pound of coffee a week. (Coffee-awards also discourage theft.)

- Asking your employees for help rather than demanding performance.

- Saying *Please, Thank you, Excuse me,* are still great motivators. Especially saying *Thank you.* a term often forgotten. Try saying, *Thank you very much, good job today!* to each employee at the end of the day, if they deserve it.

- Praising employees when they do something exceptional (in front of other employees if possible).

Dealing with unacceptable performance

If employee problems are limited to one or two individuals and are minor in nature, an earnest personal consultation may be in order. Do the following:

- Ask the employee why *they* feel they are having performance problems.

* Design a solution together.

* Set a time limit in which improvement must be realized.

* Clarify what will happen if the employee shows no improvement.

Bad attitudes are like a cancer; they must be dealt with swiftly and seriously

In some cases it is just time for an employee to move on. We always ask employees who are not performing acceptably if they are unhappy with us, the job, or if they are having any personal problems which may affect their attitude and/or performance.

It is important that both you and the employee are happy and feeling that fairness exists. Employees who perform at unacceptable levels or who possess bad attitudes must be corrected as quickly as possible before they drive away business, or worse, affect other employees around them. Bad attitudes are like a cancer; they must be dealt with swiftly and seriously. If not eliminated or cured they can destroy the entire body, which is...your operation.

There are three reasons employees may not succeed:

1. They **do not know**

2. They **do not care**, or

3. they **cannot do**.

If they **do not know**, you can teach them.

If they **do not** care, you may be able to motivate them.

But if they simply **cannot do**—meaning the job is beyond their capabilities—you must replace them or restructure their position.

Firing—the last resort

If you have ever been responsible for the hiring of employees, then you have also probably been faced with the dreaded task of firing employees.

Even when an employee has driven you to the brink of insanity, and you know you will be happier and your business will be healthier after his or her removal, the anticipation of the potential confrontation is not a pleasant event to look forward to. It can create knots in your stomach and contribute to sleepless nights.

But how did the situation come to this point? How could this wonderful individual transform from the applicant you were anxious to hire, into the nightmare which haunts your life and business? Could this deterioration of performance, communications, and relations have been prevented? How do you know if this person is salvageable? And if not, how do you make the break as painless as possible for you as well as the employee?

Early problem recognition and response

In most cases there are symptoms which indicate that a problem is beginning to develop. The little things an employee does that irritate you are the first signs that greater problems may develop.

Performance deficiencies should be addressed constructively at their earliest recognition. Short of intolerable behaviors—such as theft, intoxication on the job, or blatant disrespect to customers or other members of your staff (including yourself)—many situations can be reversed.

Pre-firing guidelines

If employees do not understand exactly what is expected of them, then you must teach them. If they do not seem to care, then you must motivate them (with either the carrot or the stick, or both). But if they simply cannot do—if the duties of the job are beyond their capabilities either physically or mentally—then you must let them go.

Some guidelines to follow:

Never level criticism when you are angry

- When addressing performance deficiencies, counsel the employee one-on-one before or after their shift in a place where you can speak privately. Remember: *Always praise in public and punish in private.* Criticizing an employee's performance in front of others will only create an attitude of resentment. Humiliation will only make them unreceptive to any constructive criticism.

- Address specific areas of behavior or performance in detail and clearly specify the changes desired. If the employee becomes defensive during counseling, assure them this is not meant as a personal attack but as constructive guidance.

- Never level criticism when you are angry.

If no improvements are realized, then a more serious talk must occur. In this more-serious talk:

- Explain to the employee their role in the overall success of your business, and the importance of their performance as a member of your team.

- Do not conclude your counseling session until you have the employee's commitment to address the topics discussed.

- Draft a summary of the topics discussed and have the employee sign it so that a record of your counseling session can be placed in their file. This will prove useful should the problems not improve and the employee denies that certain specifics were ever discussed.

- Specify in what time frame the problems are to be addressed, and what action will be taken if they are not.

The last chance

How many chances should be given to a specific employee is up to you. The severity of the performance deficiency and the level of effort being made by the employee will influence that decision. Make sure of the following:

There should be no doubt left in the employee's mind when you determine that the next talk will be the last one

- Regardless of how many talks you have had, there should be no doubt left in the employee's mind when you determine that the next talk will be the last one. In other words, if their performance does not improve, they need to realize that you will have to terminate their employment.

- As before, be sure that you document each counseling session and have them sign it. This documentation will be your protection should they be terminated and decide to file a grievance with the Department of Labor.

If all the ground work has been properly laid, the employee will know exactly what is going to happen when you say, *Please come into my office, we need to have a serious talk.*

In some cases you may wish to terminate an employee without counseling. Perhaps you suspect an employee of theft but cannot catch them red-handed. To make that accusation without proof would be unwise. If all the indicators point to this person, you may discharge them without cause. Keep in mind:

- You do not have to state to an employee why you are terminating their employment.

- Having a witness to the termination may be wise if the process is not expected to be pretty. Have your assistant manager, supervisor, or some other key person sit in on the event. Should the employee file a grievance, a witness may prove critical to determining the truth of what was said.

We hope it is evident how important we feel it is to take your time in hiring good employees. Make time to manage them properly and do all you can to have them be a part of your team. Remember, your employees are one of the most important elements your business has to offer. They alone can be THE critical factor to success or failure of your operation.

Note: Above all, check with your local government and speak with your attorney about local, state and national laws governing employment.

For more information on this specific subject, refer to the following books and videos from Bellissimo—800-655-3955.

- **Achieving Success in Specialty Coffee**
- **Customer Service for the Retail Coffee Bar**

Chapter 28 Check List

Pre-hiring Considerations:

_____ Determine staffing needs (create sample schedules).
_____ Determine starting wage rates.
_____ Obtain hiring guidelines from your local or state Department of Labor.

Hiring Entry-Level Employees:

_____ Write help wanted ad.
_____ Conduct a brief phone screening and schedule an interview appointment.
_____ Conduct a quick screening interview.
_____ Conduct an in-depth interview.
_____ Check references.
_____ Hire.

Hiring Advanced-Level Employees:

_____ Place a great ad.
_____ Screen mail: envelope, cover letter, and resume.
_____ Conduct a phone interview; if you are interested in the candidate schedule an interview appointment.
_____ Conduct an initial interview.
_____ Conduct a final interview.
_____ Evaluate candidates using the point system.
_____ Check references.
_____ Hire.

Managing Employees:

_____ Create a written employee manual with a signature page.
_____ Personally train and work with your employees.
_____ Perform undesirable tasks with your employees the first time.
_____ Address performance deficiencies immediately.
_____ Praise in public, punish in private.
_____ Let your employees know they will be rewarded as you succeed.

_____ Conduct employee meetings on a regular basis.

_____ Treat your employees with respect, praise exceptional performance, and thank them for their contributions.

Unacceptable Performance:

_____ Determine if performance deficiency is a product of: _don't know; don't care; or can't do._

_____ Address performance deficiency with the employee in detail. Define the necessary employee actions and a timetable for correcting the deficiencies. Document counseling session and have employee sign.

_____ Be sure the employee knows when you have determined that a counseling session/warning will be the last.

_____ Have a witness present for the termination if it is expected to be difficult or problematic.

CHAPTER 29

Importance of Employee Training

Contents

Chapter 29 Contents - Page 2

CHAPTER 29

Importance of Employee Training

How important is training?

In our opinion it may be the most important job the coffee bar owner faces. Unlike many facets of management, training is ongoing. With the high turnover of employees in most food-service operations in the United States, it is essential to develop a structured training program and to stick with it.

A case in point

Bruce, back from a recent consultation with a client in Mexico City, told of a classic example of what happens in the absence of a training program.

Unlike many facets of management, training is ongoing

He was surprised as he visited the first of three coffee bars owned by our client. Visually the bar was quite impressive. The owner had studied coffee bars in the United States and had also visited many in Europe. Upon arrival, as Bruce stood at the entry of our client's bar, he saw a business that definitely reflected thoughtful design and an intense pride of ownership.

- There were large photographs on the walls of drinks prepared in cups embellished with his logo.

- The employees wore embroidered uniforms also proudly displaying his cafe's name.

- The pastry case was filled with both simple morning pastries and elaborately designed dessert cakes...you get the picture.

He was really impressed until the first customer walked up and spoke to the barista behind the counter who greeted him pleasantly and took his order.

Uno Americano, negro, (one American coffee produced through the espresso machine, no cream) the customer requested.

What happen next sent chills up his spine.

First, the barista dosed the coffee into the portafilter—only two-thirds as full as it should have been; also it was obvious that the grind was far too coarse. Then to make matters worse, she tamped very lightly. After pressing the button of her semi-automatic machine, into the 14-ounce styrofoam cup flowed the wicked extraction, 1 ounce...3 ounces...6 ounces...and finally, she stopped the machine at...believe it or not, 12 ounces! Yes, a 12-ounce extraction! She then topped it with 2 ounces of hot water.

He could not believe his eyes.

But, then how was she to know?

Was it her fault? Should this entry-level employee be expected to research correct brewing methods and drink preparation on her own?

Of course not!

This is your job as an owner because your bottom line will be the one that will suffer if you do not train your employees properly!

Espresso is a complex culinary art form

Making and serving espresso beverages is not like opening and serving a bottle of wine. With wine, as long as it is stored properly and allowed to breathe, you are pretty much drinking what the vintner has intended. The product was basically finished when it went into the bottle.

Espresso, on the other hand, is a culinary art form. Ninety percent of the quality of this beverage happens during preparation. Only by understanding the nuances of the preparation can your barista create a beverage worthy of its place as culinary art.

You can take the very best coffee beans and produce a product that is not drinkable. Great coffee beans and expensive machines do not assure a great product; they only provide the potential. You have to receive the proper training before you can create the quality beverage which will be the centerpiece of your business.

You can take the very best coffee beans and produce a product that is not drinkable

Remember, your employee's skills are critical.

In the same way that a steak house serving lousy steaks will not be successful, your espresso bar will flop unless you serve great coffee. So, it is vital to your success that you and your employees understand your product...completely!

We have said many times, that during our travels across the United States, we rarely receive a properly made espresso beverage. When we do, we are actually quite surprised!

When one receives a poorly prepared beverage, 95% of the time it will be the result of improper training.

Ninety-nine times out of a hundred, you will not get a job as a chef with a fine restaurant unless you have a degree from a culinary institute or possess extensive experience.

Unfortunately, in the specialty coffee industry, comparable training standards have not yet been established.

Many entering the specialty coffee industry have been told and taught that espresso is so simple to prepare that someone can train you to prepare it properly in just a couple of hours.

This is a widespread and fundamental misconception. It is simply not the case.

In the espresso coffee industry, we are dealing with all the complexities and subtleties of a gourmet product. We know of 30 to 50 variables which will determine whether you will produce a good, mediocre, or terrible beverage.

So, in the rest of this chapter we are going to take a close look at:

- Training your employees to properly prepare the product.

- Training your employees to provide excellent customer service.

- Defining your standards and expectations of employee performance.

The strange path of training in the United States

Training in the specialty coffee industry has taken an unfortunate and distressing path in the United States. This industry has grown so quickly that the proper training of would-be baristas has been scarce or nonexistent.

Who has been responsible for the training of our industry? The equipment salesperson.

Equipment companies, who have the most to gain initially from new business start-ups, have had this training burden thrust upon them. An unfair burden, we might add.

This responsibility has occurred, primarily, because those starting a business spend a significant amount on equipment and they expect training to be included. Furthermore, many equipment companies offer training as a carrot to entice the customer to select their machine over a competitor's. Because of this, most machine companies will, of course, match this offer whether they are actually qualified to teach beverage preparation or not.

While equipment companies are responsible for educating their customers about their products and are eager to see their clients' businesses grow, they should not be relied upon to provide answers to questions outside their areas of expertise.

If you were opening a restaurant and purchased a grill, would you expect the salesman who sold you that grill to teach you how to cook, or to design your menu? This analogy, unfortunately, fits that which occurs so often in the specialty coffee business. And it has populated the coffee industry with a great number of inadequately trained baristas.

Even if the equipment salesman knows all the nuances of proper preparation (which is a rare occurrence), the information is usually passed along to the owners in a brief initial training session. They may explain:

Here is the machine, here is how it works, and...oh yes, by the way, here let me spend a few minutes to show you how to pull a good shot of espresso and steam your milk...

In many cases after the owners have had their brief one- or two-hour training session, this inadequate learning curve really goes off the graph when these improperly-trained owners are left on their own with the responsibility of training their new employees.

We equate it to the children's game of "telephone," where you whisper a phrase to the person next to you and by the time it has passed around the room the information has become so distorted you can hardly believe it. It is downright scary...usually the message is hardly recognizable!

We know for a fact that there are actually a few companies selling machines that pride themselves on their great training programs, and, indeed, some do a great job. The problem is they **all** say they do a great job, and in our estimation less than 20% do. Or to put it another way, from our experience, **drink preparation of espresso-based beverages is below acceptable standards at 80% of the coffee bars operating in this country.**

So what is the answer?

Implementation of a proper and consistent training program in each and every coffee establishment.

Product Training

Training your baristas in the art of espresso preparation is an ongoing process that should start with at least a week of intensive training in such fundamentals as adjusting the grind, dosing and tamping the ground coffee, timing the extraction, visual determinations, and tasting the results. Equal effort and care need to be applied to the fundamental techniques of proper milk steaming.

Doing the training yourself

Obviously, there are a lot of different ways to teach your employees about how to properly prepare the product. If you have acquired the proper knowledge, have done a lot of reading, and have some practical experience with a person who really understands the product, you could teach your employees yourself.

Typically, the problem with doing it yourself is that it is very time consuming. It comes down to:

> *How well do you want to train your employees?*

> *Do you have big blocks of your time, or your manager's time, available for training?*

If you merely wish to teach them how to operate the machine and prepare the beverage, you can probably do that yourself.

It is important that they not only understand what to do, but also:

- Why they are doing it,

- How to troubleshoot problems,

- How to adjust all the variables that might be involved which could affect the product quality.

And it would be nice if they had some background information on the product.

The biggest problem with doing the hands-on training of your employees yourself, is time. If you just taught them the mechanics of preparing the beverage, perhaps you could train them in 6 to 10 hours. But our experience is that it is going to take 20 to 25 hours if you also want to provide them with all the background information. So ask yourself:

> *When I'm running all the other aspects of the business, do I have the 20 or 25 hours to invest in training employees, perhaps 5, 6 or maybe even 10 to 20 times a year?*

In the beginning of your business when you hire one individual, you may have the dedication to spend 25 hours to train this person. But what happens when you have three employees leave at the end of the school semester and you have three new people to train? Do you have 75 hours to train these three employees?

The answer is, *Probably not.*

Do these employees get trained as well as your first employee? *Probably not.* At this point, you will most likely start taking shortcuts. By the time you are training your eighth or ninth employee, you will have most likely lost your fire and passion for training. By then, training has become a drudgery. It will be reduced to an attitude of:

The problem with doing it yourself is that it is very time consuming

Oh boy, I've got to train another one! Let's just get through this as quickly as possible.

So doing the training yourself is not fair to your employees or your customers and will certainly rob you of valuable administrative time.

Video-training programs

We think video is the best and most efficient way to accomplish your training goals. With video training, each person is trained the same, with correct information which can be reviewed at the push of a button.

With video training, each person is trained the same, with correct information

Various video programs show how coffee is grown, harvested, cupped, blended, and roasted, allowing your employees to understand the product they serve. If someone asks them about a French roast, they will not think this is coffee grown in the hills surrounding Paris!

Using video, we have seen a better-trained employee, with the average training time for a barista reduced by 70%.

Most young baristas are from the television generation and this method communicates to them effectively.

We do not say this simply because we have created the industry's leading training video, *Espresso 101*. We created a video training tool because we knew it could convey the maximum amount of oral and visual information in a minimal amount of time. There is no replacement for hands-on learning, but video is a great tool for feeding your employees the fundamental information quickly and efficiently. It was our own operations with which we felt frustration and the need for such a tool, one that taught drink preparation correctly.

Video vs. books as training tools

There are excellent books on the market that can certainly teach you and your employees the nuances of proper coffee preparation. But, with regard to their usefulness as training tools, there are some limitations as compared to videos:

- Written information is more difficult to digest than video for the average 18-year-old, minimum-wage employee. You typically cannot hand them a book and expect them to read and digest it, coming away feeling excitement about the experience. In most cases it is not likely to happen.

A video's instructional messages are delivered with the same accuracy and passion every time

- It may take pages to describe in a book what can be seen and understood in seconds in a video, viewing a hands-on demonstration. It is unlikely that the reader will pick up on all the nuances and details that have been so carefully placed in a written text.

- A training video is something from which your employees can learn without your presence.

- A video's instructional messages are delivered with the same accuracy and passion every time, and are highly visual.

It was these comparative advantages of video over books that motivated us to create *Espresso 101.* We saw our training video as something that could be visual, and informational; a teaching instrument which could be as passionate and exciting as you yourself might have been the first time you did the training.

Although you could train an employee solely with *Espresso 101*, it is designed to go along with hands-on experience and mentoring by you. Basically, the video brings the employee about 80% along the required learning curve, and you then finish the training by reinforcing the principles with some supervised hands-on experience. In our opinion, your employees will be better trained after only a few hours, with the help of *Espresso 101*, as compared to 20 hours invested in training without this video.

Other uses of video training

Videos are useful training tools for preparing drinks because they visually demonstrate the steps involved in creating espresso drinks and how the finished product should look. A good video about drink preparation will cut the initial time spent on training.

Given the high turnover rate of specialty coffee employees, retailers can benefit from some training videos on another level. If, like *Espresso 101,* the video package includes a multiple-choice test, retailers can send the perspective applicant home with the video and then administer the exam to the applicant when they return to determine their level of interest in coffee and the job. A test can weed out applicants who are not serious about becoming baristas, thus avoiding the expense of hiring and training applicants who are not likely to work out on the job.

In summary, instructional videos provide a tool which will assist with initial employee training, and reinforce principles with existing employees. They will improve the quality of your staff and operation, which is essential to your survival as competition increases. Video training aids allow you to:

- Save substantial time expended on initial employee training.

- Reinforce skills and fundamentals with your existing baristas.

- Give new employees confidence behind the bar.

- Provide uniform and consistent guidelines for employees to follow.

- Provide a benchmark for evaluating performance at review time.

- Reduce cost of product demonstrations.

- Give you competitive advantage over other establishments that have not instituted regular training programs.

Other training resources

There are many other resources available for learning about the industry and/or training your employees. For example:

- Books abound on the subject of coffee. Your library should be filled with them.

- There are courses and seminars offered periodically throughout the year by the SCAA and other organizations.

- If you are a coffee bar owner you should be reading every coffee periodical (magazine) available. There is an amazing amount of useful information at your disposal. And, of course, there is the Internet...talk about information at your fingertips!

Unless you understand the product, how can you judge if someone else does?

- You can hire a consultant who understands the product to train your employees.

Perhaps the equipment salesperson can do the training, but you have to ask:

Does this person really understand the product?

And unless *you* understand the product, how can you judge if someone else does?

The customer service cost of hands-on training

Another obvious problem with trying to train employees on the job yourself is that you are under pressure to minimize the time spent in hands-on training.

If you are going to train an employee on the job, you have to be doing one of two things: You are either training outside of regular business hours or you are training during regular business hours.

If you are training outside of regular business hours, you are spending time (and money) creating drinks for customers who do not exist. Because no customer is standing there waiting for the drink, you are wasting product. Also, if you are already open for business and working 12 to 16 hours per day, how anxious will you be to spend additional hours training new employees?

If you train an employee during regular business hours, you find yourself trying to walk the fine line between proper training and customer service. You find yourself thinking,

> *Can I really let my customer wait longer while I'm explaining all these details to my new employee?*

It can become an awkward situation for you, your employee, and your customer. You have to ask:

> *Will the customer feel that they are getting a properly made drink when they know this is a learning situation? Does the employee feel pressured or nervous, with the customer watching and waiting? How much is the employee really absorbing and understanding under these circumstances?*

What we saw repeatedly in hands-on training situations was that when employees were feeling intimidated—which was common—they were not learning very well because they were anxious and fearful of making mistakes, and feeling self-conscious.

With video training, your trainees watch and learn in the comfort and safety of their own home, sitting on their own couch. In such a setting, they can more easily absorb and retain the information they need to know. If they do not fully understand a principle, they can rewind that section and watch it multiple times without being embarrassed or feeling intimidated.

Certainly, you would not want to be a customer waiting for your drink, overhearing the trainer tell the employee who prepared your beverage, *Well, that was pretty good John...we'll get it perfect next time!*

Proper preparation is the competitive advantage

It is amazing how many people in the business do not understand this beverage

If you are in an area where there is a lot of espresso and you want to gain an immediate competitive advantage over everyone else in your market place, just learn how to make the beverages properly. As we have said, the reality is very few operations do.

It is amazing how many people in the business do not understand this beverage. But as the public becomes better informed and educated as to what the beverage should and could taste like, more of them will gravitate to those places that do prepare the product properly. The places that do not prepare the product properly will have to scamper to understand the beverage if they want to retain some market share. Many coffee operations early to the market are now resting on their laurels. Do not assume because an established operation or established name is doing well serving an inferior product that you can or should do the same!

We read an article recently in which the author maintained that the average eight-year-old Italian youngster knows more about espresso and espresso preparation than 95% of the baristas working in coffee bars in the United States. We can believe it. Espresso is important to Italian society and is a product everyone takes seriously. They display knowledge, pride, and passion in their preparation of this product.

There are nuances which need to be understood and mastered to produce excellent espresso consistently

Anyone can learn to prepare espresso, but there are nuances which need to be understood and mastered to produce excellent espresso consistently. As we mentioned earlier in this chapter, the perfect espresso requires your barista to be in control of a number of preparation variables, each of which will affect the final outcome of the beverage.

In the United States, far too few roasters or equipment salespeople in the industry will stress the complexity and nuances of espresso preparation because many of them want the product to appear as simple as possible. They want to make espresso preparation sound like a "nobrainer." And while espresso preparation is not brain surgery, you need to understand and adhere to each of the nuances required to make this beverage properly.

The bottom line is, you have to care! If the shot is not correct, or you know it is not a particularly good pitcher of foamed milk, you have to care enough to be able to say:

No, I'm not going to serve this, I'll try again!

Customer Service

After you teach your employees how to make the product, you have to teach them the principles of customer service.

- They have to understand what it means to be a server.

- They have to understand that this is not a demeaning position.

So often in our culture, those who have a service-related job look at these functions as something that is beneath them. They think,

I'm nothing more than a servant!

And,

I have so much more potential.

But serving and service are what this job entails. You need to take pride in doing the job as well as it can possibly be done.

Instilling pride of performance

As we have said before, the attitude toward service in Europe and many other parts of the world outside of the United States is very different. Becoming a barista is a career position. People who work in coffee bars generally go to school to learn their craft and polish their art. They train extensively. They take enormous pride in what they do. They understand their customers will expect nothing less.

The baristas we interviewed in Italy were very proud to be part of this profession. They were baristas because they had a passion for coffee and a desire to work at that occupation. They talked about seeing themselves as a barista 10 years into the future. It was not the minimum wage interim position as it oftentimes is here.

Since we are not likely going to change our culture here in United States, we need to find ways to instill more pride in our employees.

Teaching your employees how to make artistic pours is of value from more than a marketing standpoint. It helps people take more pride and a greater interest in how they perform their job. It helps them to see the job as a skilled art form. (When we talk about *artistic pours,* we are talking about milk art—pouring hearts and rosette designs on top of the drinks.)

In the same way, when we see a barista who is flashy—who can flip cups and do other artful things—we have the impression we are seeing a person who has taken the time to become a proud master of his craft, someone who enjoys what he does.

Three types of customer experience

From the customer's vantage point, service-related experiences—whether they be in a clothing store or in a restaurant—come in three basic types:

- *The negative experience*—in which you get treated badly, you do not get what you asked for, you will never go back again, and you will probably tell 20 of your friends about the terrible experience you had there.

- *The zero experience*—which probably makes up 90% of your service experiences. There is nothing terrible about your zero experience, nothing bad happens. It is just that nothing memorable happens, either. It is:

  Hi. How're ya doin? Wha'd'ya want? Two-fifty.

  And maybe, just maybe...

  Thanks.

  And that is the whole experience. There is nothing that leaves you feeling good; nothing that makes you run to the office and say:

  Wow, you ought to see this guy I met down at Mocha Joe's! What a dynamo, and the coffee...best latte I've ever had!

  The zero-experience guy is quite unmemorable.

And then there is:

- *The positive experience*—The positive experience happens when someone goes out of their way to do something for you.

  They take the time to learn your name.

  They take the time to have a little conversation and they are genuinely interested in you and looking after your welfare.

  They recommend things on the menu for you to try that they personally believe in.

They go that extra step. They do not point to where the lids are, they put the lid on the cup for you. They ask if you need another napkin.

Your special requests are met with the enthusiastic reply:

Sure we can! You bet! No problem! I'd be more than happy to!

How to relate to your captive audience

We have always told our employees that while you prepare a drink, *you have a captive audience to work with*—especially in a small coffee bar.

For the well-trained employee, it is a perfect situation for teaching customers about your product, telling them why your product is better, and helping them to have a memorable experience.

Using your captive audience to advantage takes a lot of training, but it also will give your employees more pride in what they do.

Take advantage of that awkward time right after the customer places his order: you now have 25 seconds while the shot is being pulled, possibly another 35 seconds for steaming and foaming milk, and more time while you assemble the drink—you might have a minute plus tied up in the product preparation.

You can have a minute of uncomfortable silence, with people standing in line, or you can have a conversation.

There is no better way to promote your business and your expertise than to be able to talk about coffee. Most people like to talk coffee in the same way they like to talk about wine. This is all part of the service experience that is so important. For example you can:

- Talk about coffee trivia:

  Did you know that the pope blessed coffee declaring it a truly Christian beverage, because he himself loved coffee?

- Talk about why your coffee is so special:

  This blend is composed of 100% Arabica estate grown coffees. Do you know about estate grown Arabica coffees?

- Talk about the characteristics of the different varietals:

Our espresso is a blend of four beans: Kenya AA, Guatemalan, Brazilian Santos and Sumatran. Kenyan coffees tend to have characteristics in taste which are almost wine-like. Sumatran coffees have earthy overtones and substantial body. Guatemalans are typically high-acid bright flavored coffees....

- Talk about how important the nuances of preparation are to your coffee operation:

  Check out this crema! See this golden layer of foam on top? These are the released oils from the coffee, and this is where the majority of flavor and aroma will be found. This is what espresso is all about! This is what you should always observe no matter where you order your espresso.

We are fortunate in the coffee business. We are involved with an industry that is both sexy and glamorous. If you were selling somebody a mop bucket or a ladder, it would be difficult to get people excited about the galvanized steel or aluminum. But people are interested in coffee. They love to learn about it, savor it, and share their knowledge and experiences with their friends.

Additional customer-service strategies

Train employees to recognize every customer when they walk up

- Train employees to recognize every customer when they walk up to your operation with an enthusiastic, sincere greeting.

  Hi! How are you today? Want your regular grande decaf Americano?

- If you are busy preparing drinks and talking to a customer, and another customer comes in, break out of your conversation long enough to make eye contact and say, *Hi! Be right with you.* This puts the new customer's mind at ease, they know they are important and have not been ignored. They will be less apt to become impatient. This is important. You do not want people walking away from your operation feeling neglected. You want to capitalize on their presence, and realize that income in your cash register.

It is important to teach your employees how to suggest add-on sales

- Suggest add-on sales. If you have 100 customers visit your operation in a day, and you sell every one of them a beverage at $2, you have made $200. But if you can also sell half of those customers a pastry or a muffin, you could potentially make $300 or $400 a day. You have an excellent opportunity while you are preparing their beverage to say,

Have you tried our new chocolate-hazelnut biscotti? Have you tried our blueberry muffins? They were just baked this morning, and they are still warm!

It is important to teach your employees how to suggest add-on sales, make recommendations, and promote other events that you may be scheduling. Perhaps you are going to conduct an educational cupping session at the end of the month where your customers can learn about the flavor characteristics of different coffee varietals. Maybe you have scheduled some special entertainment for tonight. Your employees are the perfect vehicle to promote your forthcoming events to your customers.

More strategies for success

Every person behind your counter should be knowledgeable about every product you sell

- Every person behind your counter should be knowledgeable about every product you sell. If you are selling brewing equipment in addition to your beverages and food items, your employees should be adequately trained in the equipment's operation and use. Oftentimes employees do not understand even the basics about the products they are selling.

- Employees who have not been trained, or possess no experience in sales, will often be uncomfortable promoting a product. They feel as if they are being pushy and phony. Our suggestion to them is:

  Pick one product that you really like and practice selling it. We do not care which one it is. If you think the blueberry muffins are fantastic, then try to sell everyone a blueberry muffin. Once you become comfortable with the process, then you can sell other items as well.

- Personal recommendation means a lot to people. If you can say,

An important principle of sales is asking, Would you like one?

  The blueberry muffins are my favorite, and they are still warm today! I think you'd really enjoy one with your coffee.... Would you like to try one?

  Of course, a certain number of folks will say, *No, I just want coffee,* but some of them are going to say, *Sure, I'll try one.*

An important principle of sales is asking, *Would you like one?* You can talk about a product all day long promoting its attributes and benefits, but unless you ask the final magic question—*Would you like one?*— you will not enjoy the degree of the success you might otherwise realize.

You must pose this type of question to your customers so they are forced to make a decision...you must force them to say, *NO!*

Many people do not like to face any confrontation and will say—*Sure, I'll try one,* before they will put themselves in the uncomfortable position of having to say—*NO!* Try this technique yourself. You will be amazed how easy it is to sell.

- Get in the habit of doing as many extras for your customer as you can. Pamper your customers.

- Always plant the suggestion in the mind of your customer that they are appreciated and will return. Say: *Thanks for coming in...we'll see you again tomorrow.* Whether or not they are planning on coming back tomorrow, you have implanted the suggestion and reinforced the feeling that you value them as a customer and expect to see them again. It may register on a subconscious level, and a certain number of them are going to come back tomorrow.

It is all part of customer service and maximizing the quality of each customer's visit.

Defining Your Standards and Expectations

We have now discussed training your employees in the fundamentals of beverage preparation and customer service, but equally important is that your employees fully understand exactly what their job function entails. They need to know in clear and certain terms where your standards lie, and what you expect from them.

Clarify from the beginning what your expectations and level of standards are

If you do not define what you expect in advance, you will tend to relate these standards on the heels of criticizing their performance. You will be giving them the information they need *after* you see that they *have not* done something which meets your expectations.

Is it their fault that they did not perform according to your expectations? If you never made clear to them what your expectations are, it is not their fault. But they are certainly apt to feel that way when you say, *Hey, you forgot to clean under there, make sure you don't forget that next time!*

Clarify from the beginning what your expectations and level of standards are. For example: What happens if a customer does not like their beverage? Does your employee know how to handle this situation? Have you told them what your policy is if a customer is dissatisfied?

There are numerous considerations of this sort that need to be encompassed within your training. This is why big companies create policy manuals and procedures. It is why they have weekly sessions to review this information—so their employees understand what is expected.

Having your employees understand what is expected of them puts you in the position of being able to praise them for demonstrating what they have learned, rather than always criticizing and correcting their performance.

They must be rewarded for their team effort

As we made clear in Chapter 28—*Hiring and Managing Employees,* it is important for everyone to feel they are part of the team. They—and you—need to understand that achieving common goals will benefit everyone on the team. Very few people work strictly for fun. Most people work for income, and that is usually the primary motivator. It is important that you let them know:

If we do everything properly, if we prepare 100% of our beverages to high standards, if we deliver great customer service, we will see our business grow. As our business grows, we are going to create greater income. I want you to know that I recognize your importance as part of the team that creates our success. And you will be rewarded!

It is vital that they understand they are not going to be forgotten; that as the owner, you will not stuff your own pockets with the profits, forgetting about their contributions to your success. They must be rewarded for their team effort.

Make education an ongoing process

In terms of personal development, you are either improving or declining. There is no such thing as a plateau.

Education and training is part of your personal development. If you are not constantly in a learning mode, then typically you start to look for shortcuts, you cut corners and your performance starts to diminish. A consistent ongoing training program can spell the difference between diminishing and improving performance. You have to constantly monitor performance quality and reinforce training or you and your employees will fall into bad habits and your operation will begin to erode.

We think it wise, especially in medium- to large-size operations, to put your best barista in charge of your beverage preparation training program. Give your trainer every opportunity to read and study any information available, and review daily the practices of all the employees under them.

Hold regular sessions to review employees' skills and habits. Challenge your employees on an ongoing basis. This is important to their continued progress along their learning curve. Some ways to do this, are:

We need to take the importance of training much more seriously

- Purchase books about coffee and espresso, invite your employees to check them out and take them home to further their knowledge.

- Find good articles in your newspaper or trade journals about the coffee industry, and about what other successful operations are doing. Post these articles on the bulletin board in your establishment.

- Make your employees aware of training opportunities and educational materials during your monthly meetings.

For our wonderful specialty coffee industry to survive and prosper, we need to take the importance of training much more seriously.

Do not be fooled by a false sense of security because consumers (who have never tasted this beverage prepared to its utmost potential), sheepishly line up daily to await a cup of inferior brew.

Some day a few entrepreneurs may come to your neighborhood who really understand this beverage, and many customers will discover what they have been missing. We are afraid that if they do not, someday specialty coffee may be talked about as we now refer to the frozen yogurt craze.

After all, what is so special about paying $2.50 for a bitter brew, topped with bubbles that look like they should be in someone's bath?

 For more information on this specific subject, refer to the following books and videos from Bellissimo—800-655-3955.

- **Achieving Success in Specialty Coffee**

- **Customer Service for the Retail Coffee Bar**

Chapter 29 Check List

Training Related to your Products:

_____ Coffee as a product: botanical information, affects of roasting and blending, varietal flavor characteristics, proper handling and storage.

_____ Principles of brewed coffee.

_____ Fundamentals of espresso and espresso beverage preparation.

_____ Will you provide your employees with all the above mentioned information, or will you use some training tools for assistance?

_____ Information about all of your food items, their ingredients, and methods of preparation.

_____ Provide an understanding of all the other goods you will be offering for sale, including hard goods (be sure your employees understand how to use all of the different brewing devices, what information is covered in the books you are selling, etc.).

Training Related to Customer Service:

_____ Establish your philosophies and policies regarding customer service.

_____ Discuss the role and philosophy of providing excellent customer service.

_____ Discuss your policies as to how dissatisfied customers are to be compensated.

_____ Determine how this information will be related to your employees: Staff meeting? A service manual? Both?

_____ Conduct a preopening role-play session with your employees.

Your Day-to-Day Involvement in the Training Process:

_____ Create a schedule dedicating a block of time to train each of your employees.

_____ Create an outline/check list of the information and philosophies that you want to cover for each employment position.

_____ Create a method of evaluating your employee's understanding and compliance to the above mentioned information, philosophies, and procedures.

_____ Determine how new and future employees will receive all of the above mentioned information. Who will be responsible for training and evaluating them?

CHAPTER 30

Your Opening Day

Contents

CHAPTER 30

Your Opening Day

Your project is no longer in the dream and planning stage

Opening day is always an exciting time. It is also a time of apprehension because you know that now you have reached the beginning of your business operational cycle. Everything you have worked for is now on the line, and you will either realize success or

failure. Your project is no longer in the dream and planning stage. *Now* is what it has all been about.

It is not unlike a sports team. They train all year long, lift weights, practice plays, and run wind sprints, but it has all been in preparation for when the season starts, and for when the games begin.

In your business you have now started your season. And your goal is to make it to the playoffs, to the championship, because that represents profitability and that is why you are starting your business.

There has been a lot of long, hard work involved in getting to this day. You endured all the tests. You have put together the capital. You have found the location. You have completed your build-out... put in your cabinets, flooring, electrical, and plumbing. All your equipment has been purchased and installed. You have had all your permits approved by the appropriate bureaucracies. You have your occupancy permit. You have contacted the health department so they can conduct their initial inspection upon opening. The fire marshal will soon do his initial inspection. You have established your liability insurance, and your workmen's compensation coverage. Your menu is established. You have placed all of your initial orders and have enough product on your shelves to facilitate your menu. You have set up delivery and service schedules with your food purveyors, your linen company, and your garbage collection service. You have gone through the interview process and hired all of your employees. You brought them in for a session of pre-opening training. You have programmed your cash register. You are ready to open!

Why not throw a party?

Consider throwing a *By Invitation Only* party for your opening day. Before your opening, send out invitations to all the people you know—friends and relatives, people from the Chamber of Commerce, business neighbors, contractors you have worked with, your landlord, prominent business and community leaders—people of diverse backgrounds.

The goal is to expose as many people as possible to your new business

If you decide to do a *By Invitation Only* opening, plan on giving away your products. The goal is to expose as many people as possible to your new business. You want them to experience what you have created. You want them to get excited about it, and then go back out into the community and spread the good word. A percentage of them will provide you with a built-in clientele right from the beginning.

It is natural to think: *We can't afford to give away this much product!* Do not look at the retail selling price of the product you will be giving away, but look at the actual cost. If your cost of sales is 25%, this means that for every $100 of product you give away at menu prices, your actual cost is $25. How much advertising can you buy for $250 or $500? There is a lot more to be gained by getting a few hundred people through your door than from placing $500 worth of newspaper advertising which, if you are lucky, might attract a dozen people.

Of course we have understated the expense of a *By Invitation Only* opening if we only consider the cost of the product. Some expenses will be incurred in printing and sending the invitations, and for the labor it will require to service your guests. We still feel that it is a tactic worth doing that works very well. The immediate patronage which it can generate could take months to develop without this event.

Remember, you are going to have to reach the "break-even point" in your business. If you do not generate a sufficient level of sales in your first 90, 180, or 270 days, you may have to pour tens of thousands of additional dollars into your business to pay your bills and keep your doors open. The $500 to $1,000 you spend up-front to expose your business and attract paying customers, could be one of the wisest and most cost-effective investments you will ever make.

Another benefit of this event is that it allows you to field-test some of your operational systems in a comfortable and forgiving environment. It gives you an opportunity to take care of any glitches that may crop up.

Obviously, you will want to be as prepared as possible for your opening party. You do not want to invite a multitude of people and subject them to a terrible experience. Here again, a qualified consultant can help assure your event will be a success. Be sure that your employees have been properly trained, and that you have sufficient product on hand. Your guests have been invited to a fun opening featuring free beverages, pastries, and panini. They will most likely overlook minor operational glitches. Since it is a free, festive party, the odds are that everyone will be very forgiving and appreciative.

Preparing for your opening to the public

When opening day comes, there are some important things to think about.

First of all, you will probably want to schedule extra employees. You want to have enough staff on hand to take care of whatever volume might come through your door during your first week of operation.

The other reason you should have as many employees as possible working for the first several weeks is so they can acquire experience. This will allow you to train and develop your entire staff quickly. It will provide an opportunity to spend a significant amount of time with all your employees, instilling your values and philosophies about customer service and enforcing the levels of performance you expect.

Remember, it is easier to instill good habits than to change bad habits after they have already been established. It will also provide you with an opportunity to individually assess their performance. If someone does not appear to possess the necessary attitude or skills to meet your expectations, you can make the decision to expend extra energy in an attempt to develop them, or you can terminate their employment before you have invested significant time and expense.

Of course, all this labor should be accounted for in your projected labor budget. Setting up your projected budgets is the one thing you will need to complete before you open your doors, because once you are open you will be very busy. We highly recommend you estimate your sales and expenses for the first six months, and have your projected income statements for that period prepared before you open.

The next phase of your business starts here

You are now starting a new phase in your business' life.

It has seemed like such a monumental achievement just to put together all the pre-opening pieces. They are behind you now and you need to forget about them. You need to start with renewed energy to attack this new phase. It has now become your most important phase. It is what you have been working towards. To be in business. To start operating.

Once you open your doors, for all intent and purposes you can take those projections and forget about them

In Chapter 19—*Developing Your Business Plan*, we discussed the importance of having your projected income statements calculated—an idea of what you might produce in terms of sales and expenses.

Once you open your doors, for all intent and purposes you can take those projections and forget about them. They will be useful as a budgetary guideline, but from now on, you are dealing with the real world. If you projected that 100 people would come in on your first day, but only 25 show up, then this becomes the new reality of the situation and you have to be able to respond to it. What are you going to do to achieve those projections? How are you going to adjust?

Initially, you may have overstaffed so you could be sure of providing good service, and providing your employees with some valuable training time. But if your sales are falling far below your initial expectations, you may have to make some adjustments.

The days or weeks after opening day are also a valuable time to start debugging your operation. This is when you are going to find out if the way you planned your operations on paper—the flow in the work areas, the procedures you set up—are going to work properly. And if they do not, you need to make the necessary adjustments early, before you start to attract the high volume of business you hope for.

When to hold your Grand Opening

You do not want to be over-whelmed on your first day

After you have a week or two under your belt and your staff has settled into a set routine, understanding how to produce good quality drinks, understanding the principles of customer service—then it is time to start your promotional phase and announce your Grand Opening to the public.

Do not make the mistake of advertising and marketing a Grand Opening coinciding with your first day of operation. You do not want to be overwhelmed on your first day. You will probably be thankful if you only have to serve 50 beverages, because you will need some time to work out the glitches of your operation.

Two or three weeks after you have been open, when you start to feel comfortable with your operation, then it will be time to:

...you probably will not make money your first day, your first month, or perhaps not even your first three to six months

- do your grand opening promotion,

- hang your "Now Open" sign in your window,

- place some newspaper ads,

- possibly begin some radio advertising,

- send someone around to the surrounding businesses to start handing out To Go menus and coupons, and

- personally introduce yourself to your neighbors, letting them know you have opened, and that you offer superior quality products and friendly service.

You need to recognize that you probably will not make money your first day, your first month, or perhaps not even your first three to six months. Obviously you want to minimize the amount of time your business will loose money, but this may be inevitable at first.

You need to allocate significant capital in reserve to help pay all or a portion of your expenses until your business actually does become profitable.

Clear your schedule so you can dedicate time to meet your customers and work with your employees.

It is absolutely essential that you spend the majority of your time working with your employees, and meeting your customers, during the first days and weeks after your business has opened. You should not be in your office performing administrative and clerical duties during your operational business hours.

You need to observe and teach

- You need to be involved where the interaction occurs between your employees and customers.

- You need to establish your goals and standards for beverage preparation and customer service.

- You need to observe and teach.

Details such as establishing your bank account, linen delivery and trash pick-up services, operational and clerical systems, all should have been completed well in advance of opening.

You need to establish a block of time outside the hours you will be open for business for paying bills, calculating payroll, taking inventory, creating income statements, and other similar functions.

...strive for quality from the beginning

Operationally, you need to strive for quality from the beginning. If you do not, the word will travel quickly. You do not want those who have visited your business saying, *That place has a lot of problems! It took forever to get my drink, and it wasn't very good, and their employees didn't seem to know what they were doing!*

- You need to keep in mind and practice the basics we have discussed.

- You need to be well prepared before you open your doors for business.

Understand that you have entered a new phase in the life of your business.

You need to apply more energy, and work harder, than you have in any of the previous phases. Your season has now begun, and your goal and focus should be doing whatever it takes to win the championship.

Chapter 30 Check List

Preopening Check List:

_____ All construction is complete?

_____ All the necessary permits for the completed construction were filed and final inspections have been approved?

_____ All business licenses and permits have been obtained or applied for?

_____ All health department and fire department specifications have been met and those agencies have been informed as to your anticipated opening date so they can facilitate their final inspections?

_____ All utilities, including your phone service, have been established? Have you had your business name and number added to the phone book?

_____ All of your major equipment has arrived, been installed, tested, and is operating properly?

_____ All smallwares have been purchased, washed, and are in place and ready to be used?

_____ Your signs and menus are completed and installed?

_____ Your cash register(s) have been programmed to facilitate your menu?

_____ Banking services have been established: business checking account; merchant credit card account and terminal; starting supply of change?

_____ Payroll services have been established?

_____ Janitorial, linen delivery, and trash pickup services have all been established?

_____ Your office has been setup; all your files and forms are in order?

_____ All your operational systems have been created and are ready to be implemented?

_____ Have you projected daily sales, and created a weekly employee schedule for your first four weeks of operation?

_____ Have you created six months of projected income statements?

_____ All your beginning inventory has arrived and has been stored properly?

_____ Your coffee order has arrived?

_____ Frozen products that will be used in a thawed state have been removed from the freezer and placed in the refrigerator 48 hours prior to being needed?

_____ Orders have been placed and delivery arranged for your pastries, dairy products, and other perishable items? (They should be scheduled to arrive the day before you open.)

_____ Employees have been hired, and have gone through an initial orientation and training session?

_____ Opening advertising game plan has been established; all ad materials have been created, and instructions for their implementation have been given to the various media?

_____ Invitations have been sent to those who will be invited to your complementary preopening party?

PART III- Being Successful

Contents

CHAPTER 31

Marketing Your Business

Contents

CHAPTER 31

Marketing Your Business

You may have the greatest business in the world, but if few people know about it, you will not be successful. You may have great coffee, friendly, attentive employees, a beautiful ambience in your coffee bar, but if people do not patronize your establishment, it will fail.

If people do not patronize your establish-ment it will fail

Marketing your business properly is one of the most important skills you will need to learn and master.

If you take the attitude:

> *We have a great operation, and people will stumble upon us or automatically hear about us...*

you can be in for a long wait. Chances are you will not survive that wait financially. You have to ask yourself:

> *Why am I in business?*

You will need to make people aware of your existence

Presumably, the primary reason you are in business is to make money. To make money you will need customers coming through your door to purchase your products. You can accomplish this goal through sound marketing practices.

There are a variety of marketing strategies you can use.

One of the strongest marketing strategies, and the one that will gain you long-term success, is word of mouth advertising. People who come into your coffee bar, and have a wonderful experience...good service, good product, go out and tell their friends about the great place they have found.

But when you initially open up your doors, you will need something to jump-start your business. You will need to make people aware of your existence.

In this chapter we will look at a number of different ways to accomplish this goal. The proper marketing strategy for your business will depend upon the type of operation you have, where it is located, the type of clientele you wish to attract and, of course, your marketing budget.

Develop a marketing plan

Before you invest your marketing dollars, take the time to generate a marketing plan that defines your marketing objectives and strategies. If you followed the instructions in Chapter 19—*Developing a Business Plan*—you will have already completed much of the work needed to create an up-to-date marketing plan. Your plan should:

- *Define your target market.* Use the demographic data you gathered in your earlier research to identify the specific audience you want to attract to your business.

- *Analyze your competition.* Find out what they are doing to promote their operations, and create a strategy to improve and differentiate your plan.

- *Define your marketing objective.* Set specific goals to achieve with your marketing plan. For example: *I want to increase my sales to the office workers in this building by 30% over the next three months.*

- *Enlist professional help.* Once you have determined what you would like your marketing dollars to accomplish, consider having an ad agency or media buyer review and refine your plan to ensure that it will achieve your requirements. Consider using a professional graphics artist to assist with the layout of your promotional materials.

- *Select your media.* Your advertising dollars should be spent on media that will suit your marketing needs, and are cost effective.

- *Determine your advertising budget.* Acquire information about the costs for various forms of advertising. This information can be obtained from your ad agency, media buyers, and media rate cards. Determine your budget and assess the effectiveness of different media combinations.

Your budget for advertising should be analyzed as a component of your income statement. Consideration must be given to sales that the advertising is expected to produce, as well as the impact this expenditure will have upon your bottom line.

Typically, 2% to 5% of gross sales are expended on advertising by food-service operations. Your percentage may be higher in the early months of the life of your business. This will be due to two factors:

1. Your level of sales will be relatively low in the beginning, so the dollars spent on advertising will appear high when compared as a percentage of sales.

2. During the initial campaign to expose your business, you will need to advertise with greater frequency and in multiple media.

- *Explore cost-cutting options.* Attempt to trade your goods and services for the advertising you desire, or at least for a portion of that expense. In many instances you will find you can trade a certain dollar amount of food and beverages in exchange for advertising. Bartering for services can be very cost-effective. Remember, if you exchange $400 of product (at menu prices) for services, and your cost of goods is 25%, your actual expenditure is $100.

- *Be involved in the design and preparation of ad materials.* Make sure your ads project the character and image of your operation in an accurate and effective manner.

- *Measure the results and make revisions.* Use coupons, customer feedback, and other means of measuring the effectiveness of your ad campaign. Compare the results with your marketing targets. Make modifications in your program and then measure what happens when you make the adjustments.

With experience, you will learn how to evaluate and modify your marketing strategies to gain and maintain optimum performance.

Flyers

If you are located in a core downtown area surrounded by a large population of businesses, or in a residential area with a large number of houses, apartments, and condominiums, then a promotional flyer may be an effective marketing strategy.

Your flyer should prominently display the name and logo of your business, and include your entire menu with prices. Be sure to highlight any house specialties, promotions, and special events.

Be sure that your flyer includes your hours of operation phone number, address, and possibly a small map showing your exact location.

Promotional flyers may be an effective marketing strategy

Place a coupon on the bottom as an incentive. We suggest that you put an expiration date on the coupon corresponding with the distribution of your next flyer. Be sure to instruct your employees to honor all your coupons, even if they have expired. Never forget why you created the coupon in the first place, to get people through your door!

Distribute your flyers on a weekly basis initially. You can cut back to a monthly basis when your customer base is established. Try to print your flyer on a different color paper each time. Change your coupon offerings each time. The goal of multiple distributions is to reinforce the fact that your business exists. Every time you distribute a new flyer it will be a reminder of your business.

Depending upon your situation, you can try different strategies for getting your flyers to your audience, such as:

- Putting them in plastic bags and hanging them on doorknobs.

- Delivering them personally to offices.

- Having an employee pass them out in high traffic locations.

- Asking offices if you can post them on their break room bulletin board.

Flyers can be an effective way to market your business without spending a lot of money.

You can utilize the graphics from our clip-art programs (*Bellissimo's "Sip Art"*) to cost-effectively put together beautiful and effective flyers. It should cost a minimal amount to photocopy your flyer on brightly colored paper, plus a couple hours of labor per week, or month, for the distribution.

If you do not have a computer, or any artistic or graphic abilities, utilize the services of a professional to create your flyers. We had a client who traded a certain dollar value of beverages every month to a graphic designer who worked in the building next door, in exchange for these services. Perhaps you may have an employee who is capable of taking on this project. Regardless of how you create your flyer, it must look professional!

Make your flyer fun. Try asking trivia questions about coffee on your flyer and offer 25 cents off if your customers can supply the correct answer. These responses, along with the returned coupons, are a good way of judging the effectiveness of your flyer marketing.

Logos and graphics

We discussed the importance of incorporating a logo and quality graphics on your printed presentations in Chapter 19—*Developing a Business Plan.* If you followed our recommendations, you should now have a well-designed logo you can use on your promotional flyers and print ads. If you did not, then by all means, have one created now.

It is important for your business to have a professionally produced logo

It is important for your business to have a professionally produced logo. You may not have to spend a considerable amount of money for professionally designed work, but the results must look professional. If you shop around, you should be able to have a logo produced for between $500-$1,500. It is worth every penny! This will be your identity. If your logo does not look professional, potential customers will have a difficult time believing that any other aspects of your operation will be.

You are going to be competing against major coffee operations that— judging by outward appearances—are doing a first-rate job. They are successful companies because they have perfected their marketing strategies. You have to compete with them. And you can learn from what they have done.

The major corporations have professionally produced logos which create strong images. In the same way, your great logo can create the image you want for your business.

While you may never have the marketing budget that they do, you do have an important advantage. You can possess a better understanding, and be able to adapt easier to your specific market. You should be more in tune with your clientele. You can certainly produce a better quality product, and provide a superior level of customer service.

More guerilla marketing options

Guerilla marketing is the method of promoting your business without using conventional means or media, and without spending a significant amount of money. These methods are usually executed by you or your employees. Flyers are a prime example of guerilla marketing.

There are other things you can do in your immediate surrounding business area by way of guerilla marketing besides just distributing menus, flyers, and coupons. For example:

- *Explore the possibilities of cause-related marketing.* Consider adopting and supporting a cause that both you and your customers are deeply concerned with. Find out what your customers care about—world peace, hunger, AIDS, homelessness, the environment, etc.—and think of ways you and your business can partner in support of your shared beliefs. Many times the parent organization for these causes will produce literature in which they thank their sponsors. This is another great way of getting your name out in print to individuals who have never visited or heard of your company. This kind of partnering with the worthy causes that your customer base supports, amounts to productive marketing at costs you can afford.

- *Consider the possibilities of in-house events,* such as live musical entertainment, poetry readings, meet-the-author hours, and similar activities. Such events can be scheduled as "specials" or as regular events. Marketed either way, both draw old and new customers and build your reputation in the cultural life of your community. Several thoughts we would like to pass on about live entertainment: Try to find talented individuals who are seeking exposure and are willing to perform for no money, or are willing to exchange their services for products. Be sure to have them audition first— you do not want any unpleasant surprises!

We read an article in a recent periodical about a café owner who was disgruntled about his experiences with live entertainment. He marketed the events well and always had a packed house. Unfortunately, the clientele who came in occupied his tables for hours but seldom purchased anything. He created a clever solution. He charged a $5 entry fee, which was in exchange for $5 of "Java bucks" which could be redeemed in his store. His patrons felt as if they were getting value for the entry fee (as opposed to a straight cover charge), and the owner was getting what he wanted, paying customers.

- *Call your Welcome Wagon.* They will distribute your coupons or promotions to people who are new to the area. Provide them with coupons, flyers, and information about your business, and tell them you want to be in their Welcome Wagon packages.

- *Join the Chamber of Commerce.* Chamber members tend to support each other, and the chamber offers members an opportunity to speak about themselves and their businesses. It is a great time to meet and talk with people who are involved in the civic affairs in your area. Tell them about your new business, and invite them to visit.

- *Actively network with the other business owners.* Go to their places of business. Make a personal connection. Introduce yourself as the owner of your business. Find out a little bit about them and how long they have been in the area. Provide them with a brochure and a menu. Tell them what your goals are. Think about offering a special discount to the business owners in the immediate surrounding area to encourage their patronage. Many times other business owners may be receptive to a joint promotion which can be mutually beneficial.

  For example:

  One coffee bar owner we know provided coupons to a local music store which featured a wide selection of CDs. The music store promotes the fact that if you buy a CD, you will receive a coupon good for a complementary espresso beverage at the coffee bar. The promotion is an enticement to buy a CD. It also brings a number of individuals through the door of the coffee bar who have not previously visited. This type of networking benefits both businesses.

- *Carry a pocket full of your business cards.* Whether you are at the gas station, supermarket, bank, or post office, it seems there

Carry a pocket full of your business cards.

is always an opportunity to talk about your day and what you do. This is the perfect time to promote your business. Give one of your cards to the people you meet, and invite them down to see your store. You can always handwrite on the back, *Good for one complementary espresso beverage*, as an incentive.

Your overall marketing program needs to implant your business identity in the public's consciousness in positive ways. It should include a variety of strategies.

Here are just a few ideas you may want to consider:

- Donate items or incentives to auctions or fund raisers that are going to be on TV to reach a wide, mass audience.

- Sponsor a 5-K Run for your favorite charity and put your logo on the T-shirts of the participants.

- Have your employees participate in an Environmental Clean-up Day or other event that brings some positive press to your business.

- Sponsor a cultural event in your community and provide the coffee. (We did this for "A Tour of Beautiful Homes & Gardens" and they put our name in front of the thousands of people who participated.)

You need to get your finances out of the red and into the black as fast as possible

All of these steps will help you build that core business. You want 100 or 200 customers to come into your establishment 15 to 25 times a month so you can have those guaranteed core sales.

You need to get your finances out of the red and into the black as fast as possible, and the way to do this is to have numerous customers coming over your threshold on a daily basis.

There are many ways to market your business, and you need to pick the most applicable ones for your operation. A coffee business that we owned was on an arterial street en route to a junior college (JC). We advertised in the JC newspaper, and put flyers with coupons on cars in the JC parking lot. We also supplied a nearby grocery store with a supply of our flyers and offered discounts to the employees in exchange for stuffing a flyer into every bag of groceries at the checkout stand.

As you have seen, there are a variety of ways to promote your business and not spend a lot of money.

Newspaper ads and news items

Depending on what type of business you have and where you are located, you may wish to consider newspaper ads. This advertising can be costly, and it can be difficult to measure your return. One way is to include a coupon in the ad offering customers half off or a two-for-one on their next drink or coffee purchase. In this way, you can measure the response by counting the coupons as they are cashed in.

Alternative newspapers can work well

One problem with newspaper advertising is that readers have to find your ad among the many others, and then respond to it before it will have any impact. Given the number of pages and competing material on the page, newspaper ads are not as likely to find your audience as some other advertising options. Consider newspapers other than the costly "daily" in your town. Many of the specialty free and low cost alternative newspapers can work well. With one of our operations we found a monthly newspaper called "The Comic News", which primarily featured political cartoons. For the money, this was our best advertising source, and we were surprised by the strong response we received from these particular coupon ads.

Tying in your ad with a news release announcing some newsworthy event that is about to happen at your coffee bar (or one that just did), can be a more productive path. If you have some writing skills and a little knowledge of how to prepare a news release, you can do this yourself, or you can hire a publicist to do it for you. If you want to do it yourself, here are a few guidelines:

- Focus your news release on a genuinely newsworthy item— some event that is unique to you or your business and will be of interest to the readers of the newspaper. Have you won a special award? Performed a noteworthy service in your community? Scheduled some newsworthy entertainment in your coffee bar? Planned a Grand Opening? The more unique, the more interesting, the better!

- Put the most important eye-catching part of your news event into the lead paragraph.

- Edit your news release until your writing is tight and concise. Limit it to a single page of double-spaced typewritten text (250 words or less).

- Include all the relevant facts. The release should answer the five W's: Who? What? When? Where? and Why?

- Go to your local public library and ask your reference librarian for a newspaper directory that lists all the newspapers in your locality (*Bacon's Newspaper Directory* is a good one). Make a list of their names, addresses, and phone numbers.

- Purchase the papers on your list (or find recent copies of them in the library's periodical room) and review them to note which papers actively cover your area of interest. Make a short list of the relevant newspapers. Check various sections of the papers (business, restaurant reviews, entertainment) and add the names of relevant reporters, reviewers, and section editors to your list.

- Call (or contact in person) each of the relevant newspapers and ask to speak to one of your target reporters, reviewers, or editors. Introduce yourself, tell them about your news release and ask them how you can help them do a better job of covering your business.

Take advantage of the media contacts you may have already made in the community, and use this news event to make some new ones. Always invite them to your café for a firsthand experience.

Radio commercials

Radio can be a good advertising medium but it also tends to be expensive. One limitation of radio is that people generally have what the radio industry refers to as *station listener loyalty*. If you like listening to classical music, chances are that you will only listen to the one or two channels in your area that play classical. So if you are not advertising on the classical channel, you are not reaching that audience. If you want to reach several different audiences with your radio ads, you have to place them on several stations, and that can be extremely expensive.

If you are located near a college or a university, radio may be an effective means of reaching your target market because most college kids are going to listen to rock, rap, top 40, or whatever else is popular, and you can often advertise on a single station to get the desired crowd. A campus station might prove to be both successful and economical.

Another venue for radio advertising that might be less expensive is to target nonprofit radio stations and offer sponsorships. You may want to sponsor a jazz hour or National Public Radio (NPR). It is a good way of promoting your business in a noncommercial way, and will boost your image as a supporter of public radio.

TV advertising

Television advertising, as a rule, is very expensive and typically not suitable for a single small operation. It might be cost-effective if you have a number of operations in one city or area. On the other hand, you may be able to place ads fairly inexpensively with your cable affiliates.

If you want to advertise on a network station—ABC, CBS or NBC— you probably are going to find that you will pay upwards from $75 to $80 dollars for a 30-second spot in a bad time slot, and up to $800, $900, $1,200 for the same ad in a prime time slot. So, you probably will not be able to afford TV advertising.

On the other hand, if you can commit to a small advertising schedule, a network affiliate may produce a 30- or 60-second ad for you (which usually becomes your property) at no cost. You can then take it to your local cable provider later for broadcasting at a rate you can afford.

We found we could advertise on the local TV cable affiliate for as little as $10 to $15 a broadcast. For $500 we were able to run 50 30-second ads on channels like ESPN, the Family Channel, Lifetime, MTV, and CNN. If there was something especially newsworthy happening which could warrant long-term coverage, we would usually request a significant number of our mix to be broadcast on CNN. Under these circumstances TV ads become fairly cost-effective.

Billboards, buses and other options

Billboards can be highly effective, especially if you have a drive-thru location on a busy thoroughfare, on the morning in-bound side of the street. Advertising on billboards and buses are certainly not your least expensive options, but we have noticed that in our area many small, independent coffee bars are advertising on buses and billboards.

The key to the success of your billboard ad is to have your billboard located a block or two ahead of your operation, so drivers will be alerted before they get to your location.

Likewise with bus advertising. You want to put your ad on buses that travel the same arterial that your coffee bar is located on. The ad is not likely to benefit your business if the bus never travels to your side of town.

Other advertising options to consider:

- We have had manufacturers of real estate or campaign signs produce signs for us to place on the median strip between the highway and the sidewalk. (You want to check with the city to make sure that your sign is not in violation of the sign ordinance.) Put an arrow on it with a message, like, *Turn here for Portland's best espresso.*

- Capture people's attention with brightly colored helium balloons tied to your cart or drive-thru.

- Try something crazy like making a big coffee bean outfit, or a big suit that looks like a giant cup of coffee. Put a person inside and have them hold a sign reading *Turn here for great coffee!* (There is a business in our town that sells tropical fish. The owner's son dresses up in a big fish suit every Saturday and stands at the road and points to his dad's store. We guess it must be working for him because he keeps doing it!) At the very least, it is certainly drawing attention to the business.

Signs

Your primary exterior sign, which identifies your business and includes your logo, should be professional in appearance, as large as possible, and easy to read. In addition to your primary business sign, you may wish to incorporate a number of other signs to announce the identity, character, or special offerings of your business. The appearance of your signs can attract or repel potential customers before they ever reach your front door. You should explore your sign options and calculate what your budget will allow. You have lots of options, and some of the newer ones, like edge-lit acrylic signs, are unusually attractive and effective in drawing attention to your business.

If allowed by city policy, among your least-costly options are:

- A-frames are inexpensive and effective in attracting walk-by traffic. They can work either as temporary signs for when you are getting started, or as a supplement to your permanent sign.

- Banners are effective in attracting attention. They can be big and elaborate, and their cost is comparatively minimal.

- Chalkboards also fit tighter budgets, but may or may not blend with the ambiance of your operation.

For larger budgets, consider:

- Wet erase boards back-lit by fluorescent bulbs which create a neon-like effect.

- Edge-lit signs have a fixed light source at the base of the sign which illuminates both the bevelled edges of the frame and your customized logo or word on the sign proper (*Espresso, Cappuccino, Tony's Place*). The rest of the frame and sign remain translucent while the message part glows in the eye-catching color of your choice.

- Back-lit exterior signs that are fixed to the building's exterior can be effective but costly.

For other options and costs in your area, check with your local sign people. Before you spend money and time on any signs, be sure to check your local sign codes and restrictions.

Have your ads hit their target

Regardless of what type of advertising you do, make sure your advertising is hitting the mark so people will understand what it is you are selling, and who you are selling it to.

We have all seen clever ads on TV that have no identifiable connection to the product they are advertising. Five minutes later you can remember all the clever things about the ad, but you can not remember what the advertisement was selling.

In your advertising you want to make sure that:

- You are not trying to convey too much information in too short time period.

> • The ad establishes the key points you want to get across.
>
> • Anyone looking at the ad will know what you are selling and who is selling it.

Pay attention to the bigger picture

You need to realize that marketing is not just your print ad and your visuals but a host of other things as well, such as:

- The ambience you have created inside your bar

- Your logo on cups

- Your employees' uniforms and the T-shirts that identify your business

- All the other little strategies and gimmicks that remind your target audience of your existence, and the uniqueness of your operation

Advertising does work. It would not be a present-day billion dollar industry if it did not. You have to spend your advertising money wisely. You have to do many things right.

We can not say enough about the advantages to be gained by taking lessons from the big boys. Look at what the successful major companies in America are doing, and adapt some of their advertising ideas and concepts to fit your own situation and budget.

Think of marketing as exercise

An analogy for you to think about is one between marketing and exercise.

Suppose you want to get in shape so you go to the health club, push some weights, and then go home and look in the mirror. Of course, you can not see any improvement, so you think: *This isn't working.* For exercise to work, you have to make a commitment and follow through day after day, week after week, and month after month. Then and only then will you be able to evaluate the results.

Marketing works in the same way.

You must have a consistent advertising program in order to see results

You have to promote yourself and your business every day, week, and month. Do not make the mistake of placing one or two ads, and then jump to the conclusion that they did not do anything for your business. You must have a consistent advertising program in order to see results.

If you open your eyes and explore, you will find many ways to market your business that are both inexpensive and effective.

For more information on this specific subject, refer to the following books and videos from Bellissimo—800-655-3955.

- **Achieving Success in Specialty Coffee**
- **Espresso 501**

Chapter 31 Check List

Materials Needed to Prepare a Marketing Plan:

_____ Do you have a professional logo developed?
_____ Do you have a hard copy of your menu including appealing descriptions of your items?
_____ Do you have access to some high quality coffee graphics?
_____ Have you establish a relationship with a good graphic artist who can create your marketing materials for you?

Developing a Marketing Plan:

_____ Define your target market.
_____ Analyze your competition and what they are doing in terms of advertising.
_____ Define your market objectives; what specifically do you want your marketing program to achieve?
_____ Determine your marketing budget.
_____ Have a professional evaluate your marketing plan.

Select your media; what can you buy for your budgeted funds?

_____ Your daily newspaper
_____ Alternative newspapers
_____ Radio
_____ Cable television
_____ Direct mail
_____ Bill boards, busses, and signs
_____ Guerilla marketing: menu/coupon distribution, press releases, sponsoring civic or charitable events, etc.

Evaluate Your Marketing Results:

_____ Did your marketing plan achieve the desired result?
_____ How might you improve or change your marketing plan?

CHAPTER 32

Customer Service

Contents

CHAPTER 32

Customer Service

The success of your specialty coffee business will be dependent upon many variables, the two most important being product quality and customer service. We have already discussed in detail the variables necessary to create superior espresso and coffee beverages. We touched on principles of customer service during our chapter on employee training, but let us now address the important subject of customer service in greater detail.

You and your employees' attitudes, will be major factors in attracting and building a loyal clientele

Unless you are buying coffee from a vending machine, your interaction with the people who prepare and serve you your beverage is a significant portion of your experience. Their interaction can either enhance or detract from that experience. In this business, when you are serving someone their morning cup of coffee, you must realize that, in many cases, you may be the first human that this person will come in contact with that day. When someone visits your business outside of those early morning hours, you may well represent a needed and important break from their hectic daily activities. You and your employees' attitudes, your standards of customer service, your ability to make your customers feel comfortable, appreciated, and pampered, will all be major factors in attracting and building a loyal clientele. You and your people can either be the highlight of your customers' day...people they look forward to seeing, or just another typical, cold and impersonal product-for-cash transaction.

Most people...unless their photo is on display in the Post Office, will like to be recognized; they want you to care. When you can remember a customer's special drink, when you are able to greet them by name, and remember something you had talked with them about upon their last visit, you have then mastered a valuable principle of customer service.

A superior service attitude and beverages of uncompromising quality are the foundations of success in this business

We are living in an age which is very impersonal, leaving many people feeling isolated and unappreciated. The only positive aspect of this sad state of affairs is that it provides you with an opportunity to be different than most corporate coffee bars.

You can possess a significant competitive advantage in this business, if you make a commitment to care. Seek out quality employees, people who are upbeat, have great personalities, happy attitudes, and are eager to serve other people. Show them the rewards of service, of making someone's day. Teach them to take their eyes off themselves and to put them on the needs of others.

If you can accomplish these goals, you will have created an atmosphere and attraction that the giants of this industry cannot compete with. A superior service attitude and beverages of uncompromising quality are the foundations of success in this business.

Clarify your mission statement

As an owner, you must make sure your staff understands your mission statement as it relates to the customer. Your mission should be to satisfy your customers' needs (within reason), sending them away happy and eager to return.

When real-life customer situations are bogged down by policies and procedures, your employees can miss the primary goal, which is: *Make the Customer Happy!*

For example: Telling a customer that they cannot use a coupon because it has expired. This, of course, defeats the coupon's fundamental purpose—to attract customers and capture their willingness to buy. It is better to accept that coupon, even if it is a year old. The only purpose of putting an expiration date on the coupon is to elicit a response within a certain period of time. If a customer presents a coupon that expired two months ago and you say, *I'm sorry, this coupon has expired,* you will only upset the customer and defeat the intended purpose of the promotion.

Customer service basics

Think in terms of three customer service components that, when combined with quality products, will result in a successful sale:

1) The first impression

2) The person selling the product

3) The lasting impression

When all three components are recognized and properly attended to, you will be providing complete and effective customer service.

When we talk about customer service we are referring to some simple basic rules, such as:

- Greet the customer with a smile.

- Learn the names of your customers.

- Relate to every customer as an individual.

- Recognize people coming in by making voice and eye contact, even when busy.

- Acknowledge the presence and patience of customers waiting in line.

- Maintain a pleasant and friendly attitude.

- Thank them for coming in and invite them to come again.

- Go that extra mile at every opportunity.

Excellent customer service means asking questions and giving people choices.

Is this for here or to go?

Would you like cream and sugar?

How many sugar packets?

Would you like skim or regular milk?

Would you like a single or double shot?

Would you like whipped cream?

How about chocolate?

How about a flavored syrup?

Would you prefer cinnamon?

Would you like any of our fresh baked goods to go with that?

Would you like a straw?

Can I put a lid on that for you?

Would you like a napkin?

Good customer service is doing whatever is needed to keep the customer happy

Good customer service is doing whatever is needed to keep the customer happy. Developing good customer service requires training in new skills, and lots of practice. You know you have done your job when your customer utters those most cherished words:

I'll be back!

Dealing with problematic customers

At some points in your career, you are going to have to face the customer who is difficult. When a customer is basically rude, curt, and inconsiderate, your response is likely to be negative. You may say to yourself,

What an idiot! I'm not going to give this guy the time of day.

Kill them with kindness

What you need to remember is that this person still has money in his pocket, and he may have friends who are not like him.

The way to deal with people like this is not to ignore them, or to make them more upset. The solution, we feel, is to kill them with kindness. The probability is that this is a person who is basically miserable and in considerable pain.

More often than not, if you can put up with their idiosyncracies and their personalities, an amazing thing could happen. You may win them over!

And while this may sound like a negative outcome (since the last thing you want is this awful person coming back every day), the chances are good that, if you can send them away happy, when they come back you will find they are not a big problem anymore. Their attitudes have changed because you have accepted them into your world, when no one else would.

It is amazing how kindness moves people from hostility to friendliness. Oftentimes customers who start out being problems blossom into friends. And when this happens, they come back on a regular basis and add their money to your cash register, and their good will to your reputation, which is what your business is all about. We have seen this strategy work successfully in numerous situations.

The customer is always right

Customer service is the attitude that the customer is always right.

> *If they tell you their blueberry bagel does not have enough blueberries in it, then give them another blueberry bagel, a different flavor, or a refund.*

> *If they tell you their coffee drink is not hot enough, pour it back in the pitcher and warm it with the steaming wand.*

> *If they want their milk scalded to 180°, explain to them what this does chemically to the milk, but if they still insist...then scald their milk.*

The bottom line is you have to give the people what they want.

When things go wrong

Subscribing to the principle, *The customer is always right*, raises a question:

> *How do you compensate people who are not being taken care of as well as they should be?*

This is a policy concern that you need to think through as an owner and make clear to your employees. For example, consider the following scenario:

> *There are now 15 to 20 people waiting in line for their coffee drinks at your coffee bar. Some of your customers who are standing in line are growing more impatient and irritated with each moment. You know it is unacceptable that they should have to wait so long, but what do you do about it?*

You need to establish a policy ahead of time

We have all had dining experiences where our order was fouled up. Perhaps the kitchen forgot to prepare one of the entrees on your order, and the rest of your party is eating while one person waits 20 minutes for their food. When it finally arrives, everyone else is done eating. The outcome is always burdensome and frustrating, resulting usually in customer dissatisfaction, loss of respect for the service staff, and possible loss of future business. To make matters worse, no one even offered an apology!

You need to establish a policy ahead of time, for dealing with these potentially costly situations in a timely fashion. It is important to set up a policy of compensation that empowers your employees with the freedom to make corrective decisions when you are not there, or to get you involved in making those decisions when you are. You want an employee to be able to say to that customer,

> *I'm sorry you had to wait so long for your drink, there will be no charge today.*

Even though the customer may respond with, *Oh, that's not necessary, it's okay, I understand*, you want to be able to say:

> *No, really. When you come in here we want you to be served in a timely fashion. I don't feel good about how long you had to wait, so please, have today's coffee on us.*

This kind of sincere caring, and generous response, will win you customers for life.

Something like a love affair

You need to think of your customer service as a love affair between you and your customers. You express this love for your customers by caring about their welfare, and by serving them to the best of your abilities.

This is why it is so important to search for the right employees with service-oriented attitudes. If you hire someone who is not deeply concerned about other people, and who may feel that customer service is demeaning, the love affair is not going to flourish.

If you are conducting a love affair, you try to do everything possible to make your beloved happy; you buy flowers, candy, listen to them, open the door of the car. Making that person happy becomes your goal in life. Their welfare is always in your thoughts.

In customer service, you express your caring for your customers with thoughts like:

Today I am going to spread as much good will as possible. I will be personally interested in every person I come in contact with today. I will make sure that every person gets the best product and service possible. I will let them know how much they are appreciated, and will definitely invite them back.

All of these behaviors are saying:

You are important to me and I care about you.

If you can do these things with every customer, you will be successful. Love your customers, your business will prosper...and on a personal level, you will establish gratifying relationships with your customers.

For more information on this specific subject, refer to the following books and videos from Bellissimo—800-655-3955.

- **Achieving Success in Specialty Coffee**
- **Customer Service for the Retail Coffee Bar**

Chapter 31 Check List

Training Related to Customer Service:
[Note- this first section comes directly from the Chapter 29 Check List.]

_____ Establish your philosophies and policies regarding customer services.

_____ Discuss the role and philosophy of providing excellent customer service.

_____ Discuss your policies as to how dissatisfied customers are to be compensated.

_____ Determine how this information will be related to your employees; staff meeting? a service manual? Both?

_____ Conduct a preopening role-play session with your employees?

Additional Customer Service Objectives:

Create specific standards for the following:

_____ Customer greeting

_____ Policy related to special requests ("sure we can!")

_____ Being perceptive to what the customer may need and providing it without being asked (napkin, lid for a beverage, a beverage tray for multiple drinks, etc.)

_____ How to conquer the problematic customer with a positive attitude.

_____ A commitment to making every customer happy.

_____ Letting every customer know that they are genuinely appreciated and inviting them to return.

Motivating Your Employees to Provide Excellent Customer Service:

_____ Set the example as the owner or manager by providing superior customer service to every customer.

_____ Place a "gratuity cup" next to the cash register and have them take note of the results!

_____ Give an award and prize monthly to the employee who exhibits "excellence in customer service".

_____ Praise employees who deliver excellent customer service (preferably in front of other employees).

CHAPTER 33

Merchandising in Your Business

Contents

CHAPTER 33

Merchandising in Your Business

The specialty coffee business is highly dependent upon volume. The number of customers who purchase products from your business on a daily basis, and the amount of money they spend on each visit, will determine whether your business will succeed or fail.

This is not the type of business where one customer will come in and make a purchase costing thousands of dollars. This business is not like owning an art gallery or automobile dealership where the sale of a single item can create significant income.

The success of your business will be dependent upon attracting a significant number of customers on a daily basis, and then maximizing the amount they spend upon that visit. If on the average, 100 people visit your establishment every day and spend approximately $2 on a coffee beverage, your gross income for that day will be $200. If you can get half of those individuals to buy a muffin in addition to their coffee, and you sell your muffins for $1, you will realize an additional $50 in sales every day. This may seem like a fairly insignificant amount of extra income, but if we multiply these potential daily incomes by a 30-

day operating month, the accumulative effect is significant.

$200 per day X 30-day business month = $6,000 gross income

$250 per day X 30-day business month = $7,500 gross income

The extra $1,500 of income produced by selling a $1 muffin to every other customer could make a difference between being able to pay your rent or not...or perhaps paying yourself or not!

Before you ask, *Where can I get more customers? How can I entice more people to come into my store?* you need to ask yourself:

Am I maximizing the dollars I can get from every customer who comes through my door presently?

This is the goal of merchandising.

What is merchandising?

It may help for you to think of merchandising as an art form. Like any other art, there are rules and conventions governing what you can do, but there is also room for individual expression, innovation and creativity. In this chapter, we will pay attention to the rules and conventions. But never forget that merchandising is also an art form to which you, the artist, will be bringing your expressive and creative energies.

Merchandising is what you do inside of your store to entice them to buy

Merchandising differs from advertising in that advertising is external, and merchandising is internal. Advertising is the thing you do, outside of your store, to attract individuals to your location. Once they come through your door, merchandising is what you do inside of your store to entice them to buy.

Merchandising is the practice of presenting all the products you have in your store to your customers so they can see what you have to offer. Merchandising is also the art of enticing your customers to purchase more than they had originally intended on buying when they first walked in.

Successful merchandising is of critical importance to the success of your business because it will maximize your sales. It will motivate many of your customers to purchase additional items. These items may include pastries, desserts, sandwiches, salads, candies, bulk coffees, teas, books, T-shirts, coffee brewers, cups, or anything else that you may have to offer.

Do not forget that the reason you brought these items into your store was to generate extra income from their sale. If your customers are not aware that you have these items, or if they reject them because they are poorly presented, they will not bring you any benefit.

Important factors of successful merchandising

Store design and layout

You have to start making considerations about merchandising while you are designing the physical layout of your store. The location of your pastry cases, display shelves, coffee bins, service counters, and seating areas, should be analyzed and determined during the early design phases of your space. The costs can be great if you fail to anticipate your merchandising needs in the beginning.

Anticipate your merchandising needs in the beginning

Once you decide which products are most important to your overall concept, and which have the greatest margins of profit, you can make decisions on their placement and how much space to devote to each. Will they require floor space, counter space or wall space?

Try to gather information from suppliers of display equipment about the various methods of displaying and marketing each product. Observe and take note of the methods that other successful retailers in your area are using to display similar products. With all of this information in hand, you can plan a display system that best suits your tastes and will work for your situation.

Positioning add-on sale items

A common mistake that we often see is positioning add-on sale items out of view of customers

A common mistake that we often see is positioning add-on sale items out of view of customers who are waiting in line. Customers who are waiting to buy beverages are excellent prospects for pastries and other impulse items, but the add-on sales are not likely to happen if those items are not within plain view. Your pastry case—and perhaps, your bulk bean bins—should be positioned so customers are exposed to those products before arriving at the cash register to close their transaction.

You want your quick-sale items situated on a traffic path *prior to* the point of the cash transaction.

Have you ever walked into an espresso bar to buy a coffee and you did not notice the pastry case until *after* you had gone a step or two

491

beyond where you had bought the coffee? By then, you have concluded your purchase, walked away, and the next customer is already placing their order. At this point it will be awkward to cut back into the line and say, *Oh yes, by the way, I'd like that croissant, also!*

In terms of positioning, ask yourself:

- *What do I want to sell with the beverage?*

- *Are these items positioned so that the customers can see them before they get to the cash register?*

- *Are they positioned prior to where the customers place their order and make their purchase?*

On a recent consulting job, our client's beautiful pastry case was the first thing we saw as we walked into his café. During our visit, we could see customers walking in—probably thinking about buying a coffee—but their eyes were being drawn to the pastry case. As they made their way to the counter to place their order, we could almost see their minds working:

> *Maybe I should get a cinnamon roll, those lemon bars sure look good, maybe some chocolate-chip cookies—I want something to go along with my coffee!*

Because of the thoughtful placement of this piece of equipment, we observed that our client was doing 50% of his business in pastries.

Take advantage of visually appealing items

There are two ways to promote the sale of companion products: through effective display merchandising, and actual sales presentation.

For an effective display, take advantage of the items that have the greatest visual appeal. Make sure that these items can be easily seen, so that they might attract people and stimulate their interest.

Position visually appealing items...within immediate view of the customer

Position visually appealing items—like granita machines—within immediate view of the customer. Brightly colored granitas, turning in their cylinders, will catch your customer's eye as they walk up to your counter. A granita machine tucked away in a corner, where most people will not even see the product, will definitely cost you sales.

Hard goods such as brewing devices, ceramic cups, books, and T-shirts, need to be positioned where customers will notice them, but where you can also keep an eye on them so they will not become easy targets for theft.

Hard goods are generally not impulse-sales items, so it may not be advantageous to place them where items like pastries and candies should go. People standing in line for coffee will probably not be thinking, *Gosh, I need that $350 espresso machine, I better buy it now!* Your customers will need to give this type of item some thoughtful consideration before being prepared to make a purchase. A good place to locate non-impulse items is an area adjacent to your customer seating. These items will attract interest and provide something for your customers to look at while they are enjoying their beverages.

Remember the 80-20 rule

The 80-20 rule states that 80% of your sales comes from 20% of your inventory selection. It is very important for you to understand which items are included within this 20% category. This should not be a challenge if your cash register has preset keys for each item you sell. You should be able to access information from your cash register on a daily and periodic basis, and it should be able to provide you with data in terms of units sold and total income for each item. You should try to constantly improve the variety and quality of your products which fall within your 20% category. Try new and unique items to see how they will mix with your current inventory, and to judge their popularity.

80% of your sales comes from 20% of your inventory

Some typical products which usually fall into the 20% category are:

- Biscotti, cookies, brownies, and candies. (Try to locate these in jars or on displays near your cash register.)

- A variety of whole-coffee beans (varietals and blends).

- Bulk and prepackaged specialty teas.

- A variety of quality baked goods (hand out free samples to introduce these products to your customers).

- Small-size bottles of gourmet flavored syrups (so your customers can purchase their favorite flavors for making Italian sodas and flavored lattés at home).

- Double-insulated travel mugs.

- Gift baskets and boxes featuring a combination of the products listed above. These can include some select hard goods as well, such as, a ceramic cup(s), a French press coffee maker, or a mocha pot.

When considering companion products to add to your inventory, ask yourself:

- Does this item fit within my existing product line?

- Can I afford the expenses involved in marketing it?

- Can I set up a display effectively so that the item will sell itself?

- Is there enough profit margin to compensate for spoilage or breakage?

- Is this an impulse item that will increase my average ticket sale?

- Does this item fit within the theme of my operation?

- *Will it bring me new customers?*

Signs

Signs attract people's attention

Attractive, well placed, easy-to-read signs are critical to successfully merchandising your business. Signs attract people's attention. They should be bright, colorful, with large letters, using fonts which are easy to read, and artistically attractive.

It can be very helpful to incorporate graphics onto your signs. A picture of coffee beans on a sign over your bulk bean area will help to convey an accurate message. In our travels, we have seen many creative and exciting applications of graphics to signs. A coffee operation in Portland, Oregon, uses a local artist to create beautiful coffee-related drawings on a number of large chalkboards. Some of these are used as menu boards, others for daily and weekly specials.

Do not be afraid to allocate some money... for signs

Do not be afraid to allocate some money from your merchandising budget for signs. Your sign should catch the attention of everyone who walks into your business, and they should motivate a response. Here are some areas where effective signs will help you accomplish your merchandising goals:

Instructional and directional signs

We often see people wander into a coffee bar unsure where they are supposed to order, or where they should pick up their beverage. Simple as it sounds, hang signs that read: *Order Here* and *Pick Up Here*.

Not all problems involving customer confusion are as obvious or as simple. Consider, for example, a trend that we have observed among some of the newer coffee bars. It began with the gradual discovery that they were losing business because people who only wanted brewed coffee had to wait in the same line as those folks who wanted espresso beverages. Because espresso beverages take longer to prepare, the customers who wanted brewed coffee became impatient and would leave.

These clever entrepreneurs gave this challenge some real thought and designed a solution to this problem. They set up two order stations— open counter spaces—one on each side of the cash register. Over one was a sign that read: *Order Espresso Beverages & Pastries Here.* Over the other was a sign reading: *Order Brewed Coffee Here.*

When a customer stepped up to the brewed coffee sign, the cashier knew immediately that he was going to be handling a high-priority quick sale. This is similar to the grocery store philosophy of the "8 items or less" check-out line.

You may wish to place your brewed coffees in pump pots that are readily accessible to the customer. They can pay in advance and receive their cup from the cashier, or help themselves and then pay on the "honor system." However, we believe that as an industry we must educate our customers to understand that gourmet 100% Arabica coffees are very different from the institutional coffees we used to consume. It is very difficult to employ the "bottomless cup" philosophies of the past with a high-end product. Should you decide to provide refills, we suggest that you charge 50% of the first cup price. In other words, if your brewed coffee costs $1.50, charge 75 cents for a refill.

Menu signs

The next and most critical piece of signage in your espresso bar is your physical menu.

The sign(s) for your menu should be in plain view, easy to read, and categorized so you see:

- Hot Coffee Beverages

- Frozen & Iced Beverages

- Teas, Chai, Hot Chocolate

- Baked Goods, Pastries & Desserts

- Salads and Sandwiches

And whatever else you might be serving that fits into a category.

It is also important that your menu lists not only the beverage or item, but also a brief description. (See sample menus in Chapter 24—*Planning Your Menu.*) People who are not coffee aficionados and see a list of drinks with names like Espresso, Macchiato, Espresso Con Panna, Cappuccino, Latté, Mocha and Brevé, can become very confused and intimidated about ordering. Many people often order an espresso and think they are ordering a cappuccino or latté. It is only when they get their 3/4 ounce shot of espresso that they discover their error. They did not understand that an espresso is just the straight shot.

Descriptions of the beverages on your menu serve to avoid this kind of confusion and increase customer awareness and satisfaction.

Point-of-sale signs

Point-of-sale signs are small signs placed on the group of items that you are selling. Such as:

- pastries in the pastry cabinet (*Lemon bars - Fresh & Tangy - $2.00*)

- bulk coffees (*Kenyan Coffee - A delicious full-bodied coffee with wine-like characteristics—$6.50 for 1/2 pound*)

Some knowledgeable wine store merchants hang signs on certain bottles of wine which include their personal endorsement and talk about how good these particular bottles are. When we are looking at a lot of different wines, and we are not sure which ones may be good, we find these signs to be very helpful. The recommendation from a knowledgeable owner is extremely helpful and appreciated. They can tell us what foods go well with a particular wine, and gives us a description of the its characteristics.

The same applies to coffees. There are certain coffees which are better suited for drinking at different times of the day, some particular brewing methods, and some are more appealing to certain taste preferences. You can use signs to describe to your customers the varietals and blends which are best suited for these particular brewing methods, occasions, and palates.

Do not assume that people will automatically know what you are selling

Do not assume that people will automatically know what you are selling. You have to tell them. You will not be able to verbally communicate to every customer everything that you have to sell. Because of this, generating point-of-sale signs for each of your products is important.

Spend a little money. Generate some signs with your computer, have them photocopied onto some colored card stock, then have them laminated between clear plastic. This will create a durable sign which is professional in appearance.

Signs for special promotions

Musical events, author book signings, and poetry readings are all special events which you will want to advertise with signs inside your café, and in your windows.

Keep in mind that a good way to promote add-on sales is by informing people about how to use your products. This can be accomplished by conducting some free informational classes.

In addition to your signs promoting these events, use flyers and hand-out menus to make announcements like:

Free cupping classes will be held on the first Saturday of each month from 9 to 11 am. Come join us and taste the finest coffees from around the world, and learn how to prepare them properly!

Other ideas for classes:

- *Home espresso making*

- *Selecting, storing, and preparing coffees*

• *Cooking, baking, and dessert making with coffees*

If you are thinking of conducting classes, keep in mind that there are some fine videos available. You can set up a VCR, play a video that will entertain and educate your customers about coffee, and then answer any questions they may have. Bellissmo's video, *The Passionate Harvest*, is perfect for this purpose.

By involving your customers in activities that you conduct in your store, they will become better educated. This will have a positive effect upon your business. Your customers will understand that you possess a knowledge and a passion for your product, and that you care enough to give them information they can use. By educating your customers, and getting them excited about this product, they will gain confidence that they can prepare it properly at home, and they will consume more product.

Organization and presentation

Effective merchandising in your specialty coffee business requires that all your products need to be attractively displayed and artistically arranged.

Your products need to be attractively displayed

The truth of this statement was vividly brought home to us on a recent consulting job. We saw a selection of beautiful high-end pastries being displayed within their original packaging. It gave them the appearance of a product which had been purchased from the supermarket. It was obvious they were not freshly baked.

On the first day of business, very few of these excellent pastries were sold. When we brought our client's attention to this situation, he removed them from their box, placed them on little individual doilies, and arranged them attractively in the display case on ceramic plates. Immediately, they began selling. The next day, they were selling as fast as our client could put them in the case.

Proper presentation requires that your products look fresh

Our client later told us that he sold 480 of those little pastries in one week!

Leaving them in the original boxes did absolutely nothing for their appearance. Merchandising those pastries properly made all the difference in the world.

Proper presentation requires that your products look fresh. You cannot have pastries in your display case that look stale. And there is nothing that looks worse than having pastries wrapped in cellophane, unless you are selling them from a cart, or they are being sold as day-old.

(NOTE: As we described in Chapter 25—*Choosing and Buying Equipment,* there is an important difference between a refrigerated deli case and a pastry case. A pastry case costs more money, but for a very good reason. Typically a pastry case will circulate a lower flow of humid, cold air, which keeps your pastries from drying out, curling up, and looking like pieces of leather.)

Keep your products well stocked

It is also imperative that you keep your products well stocked. Nothing is less appealing than buying the last of something. A full bin of coffee beans has much more visual appeal than a bin which is almost empty. A basket piled high with fresh bagels is much more inviting than a basket which only contains two. We have all seen pictures on the news of stores in impoverished third-world countries which have almost no product on their shelves to sell. Was it a very appealing picture?

Everything you are selling must be kept clean and constantly organized

As well as arranging your products attractively, your physical equipment has to be attractive also. Fingerprints and frosting stuck to the glass of your pastry case, dirty biscotti jars, milk crusted on the steaming wand of your espresso machine, coffee oil residues on the inside of your bulk bins...none of these are appealing. Your equipment and inventory, including hard goods, are all going to require constant monitoring, rearranging and priming. Everything you are selling must be kept clean and constantly organized.

Convenient packaging

Providing convenient packaging of bulk items adds to their presentation and customer appeal. For example, if you are offering Ethiopian coffee on special this week, consider prebagging some of it in 1/2- and 1-pound bags. Having prebagged coffee available makes it convenient for your customers and, because they do not have to wait for the coffee to be weighed and bagged by your cashier, your sales should increase.

Employee-customer interaction

The final key ingredient to successfully merchandising your business is your employees. We talked a little about this in Chapter 32—*Customer Service,* but it merits re-emphasizing here. Your employees need to understand and master two customer-relations skills:

1. Develop the habit of being observant.

2. Make recommendations and suggestions.

These are simple skills.

If you see a customer paying special attention to something in your store, perhaps it is on your counter, or in your pastry display case, or they have picked up a piece of merchandise from your hard goods shelf, do not be afraid to ask:

Can I answer some questions for you? Are you familiar with that? Let me tell you about that!

Your employees have to be knowledgeable about the products you sell

For your employees to have this type of interaction with your customers, they will have to be knowledgeable about the products you sell. You need to conduct some training sessions with your employees to teach them about all of your products. Then check out:

- *Have they tasted all your beverage and food items and are they familiar with their ingredients and methods of preparation?*

- *Have they tasted all your bulk coffee offerings, your varietals and blends?*

- *Can they describe their flavor characteristics and suggest the best method of brewing for each?*

- *Do they have a thorough understanding of all your hard goods?*

- *Can they explain how to use a French press, a mocha pot, your home espresso machine?*

- *Do they have hands-on experience on these pieces of equipment? Have they ever even seen them out of the boxes? Can they tell your customer about the warranty?*

We suggest that you take each of your pastries and cut them up into small pieces and have all your employees taste them.

Find out what ingredients are in each one. We guarantee that you are going to have customers asking about that.

What's in that Tiramisu bar?

What is a Tiramisu bar? It could be anything. It probably has coffee flavoring, chocolate, and marsala or rum, but what else is in it? Does it have eggs in it? This customer may have allergies and is concerned about the ingredients. You will need to alert your employees to these types of customer concerns and train them so they are knowledgeable.

Type out a description sheet of your items and have it available under the cash register or somewhere else where everyone will know where it is. If they do not have the information memorized, at least they can refer to a description sheet to answer questions. The last thing you want an employee to do is tell a customer that there are no nuts in an item, but in reality there are, and the customer who is allergic to nuts has a violent allergic reaction after eating that item.

Sales presentations should be short and well thought out

It is vital that your employees realize that their job responsibilities go well beyond taking orders, dispensing beverages and collecting money. It includes becoming knowledgeable, effective merchandisers. If a customer is purchasing bulk coffee beans and would like you to grind them for their use at home, the question you should ask is

How do you brew your coffee at home?

Will your employees know what the recommended grind is for this specific method of brewing? This also creates another opportunity to talk about alternative brewing methods—methods that you just happen to sell the equipment for.

Have you ever tried using a French press? It's a wonderful method. It is probably faster and easier than the method you are using now, and the best feature is that it produces an extremely smooth cup of coffee that will never be bitter!

Sales presentations should be short and well thought out. Identify the key points for each item. Write them down so your employees have a reference for every item. The results will be that you will sell significantly more than an occasional pound of coffee.

For more information on this specific subject, refer to the following books and videos from Bellissimo—800-655-3955.

- **Achieving Success in Specialty Coffee**

- **Customer Service for the Retail Coffee Bar**

Chapter 33 Check List

Important Factors of Merchandising:

_____ Is your food service equipment placed so that impulse purchase items are located along the walking path to where orders are taken or items are purchased? (Pastry cases, bulk coffee bins, etc.)

_____ Are typical food items that would be purchased with coffee located near the point of purchase? (Biscotti, cookies, candies, etc.)

_____ Are visually appealing items within direct view of the customer? (Granita machine, beautiful desserts, attractive hard goods, etc.)

_____ Are items conveniently packaged to encourage a quick sale? (Coffee beans weighed out into 1/2 and 1 pound bags, etc.)

_____ Do you ever create attractive gift baskets of assorted products to take advantage of holidays?

_____ Are items which are not a quick impulse purchases located where your customers can see them, and think about them, while seated in your establishment?

_____ Are your items attractively displayed, and are your displays well stocked and maintained to create the maximum appeal?

_____ Do you have attractive, easy-to-read point of sales signs to promote the products you have available for sale?

_____ Are your signs descriptive and/or educational?

_____ Do you offer samples to your customers of food or beverage items you are trying to promote?

_____ Do your employees make recommendations, and do they try to market the products to your customers?

_____ Are your employees observant to a customer's interest in a product, and do they attempt to offer assistance?

_____ Do you conduct and promote any instore activities which might increase your sales such as special entertainment or educational seminars?

CHAPTER 34

Record Keeping

Contents

CHAPTER 34

Record Keeping

Few small businesses maintain good and accurate records

Record keeping is a necessary evil. Not many people really enjoy spending hours and hours accumulating data. As a consequence, few small businesses maintain good and accurate records.

The problem with such a lackadaisical approach is that it could come back to bite you somehow...sooner or later.

In this chapter we will first look at why you need to keep accurate records and then review the types of records you will be needing.

[NOTE: See Appendix 1 for sample records and forms]

Why Keep Records?

Following are five sound reasons for establishing and maintaining sound and accurate records:

- for day-to-day operations

- for business performance analysis

- for forecasting, budgeting and planning

- for tax liability purposes

- for legal protection

III. Being Successful

Day-to-day operations

You cannot run a sound business without knowing what your cash receipts are on a daily basis, how much product you are ordering, using, and have on your shelf.

Business performance analysis

You will not know how your business is performing if you only generate a profit and loss statement at year's end.

To measure how well your business is performing, you need to keep accurate expenditure and income records on a daily and monthly basis. These will include:

- **Purchases, operating expenses, accounts payable** and other expenses that perhaps do not come in by invoice or purchase order, such as rent, utilities, and cash purchases.

- **Daily sales receipts.** You need to know daily how many dollars are coming into your cash register. More specifically, you need to be able to track how much came in for which items.

  (Be sure you have a cash register that is programmed with item presets—specific keys on your register that are designated for each menu item which allows your register to generate a tally of what items have been sold on a daily, weekly, and monthly basis.)

In addition, you will want to know:

- how much of your sales receipts actually filters down to the bottom line as profit for that day,

- how much of it went to pay outs,

- how much of it was not collected in cash because of coupons, discounts, etc.,

- if your register is balancing out every day, on every shift.

  (If it is not, you may be able to pinpoint which particular shift or employee is your problem.)

Forecasting, budgeting, and planning

You need accurate records to be able to forecast, budget, and plan properly. Without good records, you are trusting to luck that you are in reality making a profit.

You need accurate records to be able to forecast, budget, and plan properly

You need to know, for example, what your sales totals were during the last three months and how much they increased or decreased from month to month to best predict what the future of your business will be.

Accurate forecasting is important in setting your menu prices. Unless you know what you are paying for your product, and are taking into account price increases in the cost of that product, you will not know if your menu is priced out properly, or should change. If you are not making money, without proper records and checks, you will not know if it is because your prices are too low, or because you have a theft problem.

Tax liability purposes

Accurate record keeping is obviously important for tax liability and legal purposes. If you ever get audited by the IRS, you will want to have good solid records to substantiate that your numbers are indeed correct.

Legal protection

You will need to accurately document what happens in two types of situations which have potential legal consequences for you.

If you ever get audited by the IRS, you will want to have good solid records

1. **Employee corrective actions.** Recurring problems with employees need to be documented on paper. If you counsel a poorly-performing employee a half a dozen times before dismissing him but it is not documented, you could have a problem if he complains to the Department of Labor. [See Chapter 28—*Hiring and Managing Employees.*]

2. **Customer accidents and complaints**— If a customer slips and falls in your store, you want to document the event, even though they may tell you they are fine.

   Record all the relevant information, perhaps in a manager's log book, making sure that your report lists names, addresses, phone numbers, description of the incident, plus any recollections you and your employees remember, such as, *She walked out of the store without a limp.* Similarly, you want to document all complaints that have been registered by customers, noting which employees were on duty at the time.

You want to make sure that none of these situations come back to bite you in a legal situation later and, if they do, that you have something documented to support your position.

Income Statement-Your Business Report Card

Producing a monthly income statement is essential to the success and growth of your business.

Producing a monthly income statement is essential to the success and growth of your business

Not unlike a student's report card, your income statement evaluates the present performance of your business, and your progress along the road to your short-term and long-range goals. Business owners should generate a review of their business performance on a regular basis, typically the first day of every month for the month that has just passed. Operations that are experiencing cost control problems, may want to generate a mid-month income statement as well.

What is an income statement?

Income statements are also referred to as profit and loss statements (P & L's).

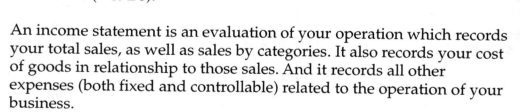

An income statement is an evaluation of your operation which records your total sales, as well as sales by categories. It also records your cost of goods in relationship to those sales. And it records all other expenses (both fixed and controllable) related to the operation of your business.

It allows you to determine whether or not your business is making money.

It may or may not include depreciation expense, and it does not include your equity in assets, stock, etc. These subjects are elements of your business balance sheet, which evaluates your total worth in the business at a particular point in time.

An effective income statement should not only recap your past month's business performance, but also provide goals for all of your sales, cost of sales, and expense categories, to measure your performance against.

Prior to the beginning of each month you should establish ideals or projections for all income statement categories. Only by doing this will you be able to evaluate your business performance during the course of the month, and determine if your business is on the desired course to complete its financial mission. It is too late after the month has passed to wish you had reacted to an expense that may be over budget.

Measuring your ideals against your actual performance

Effective management means keeping close tabs on how the business is doing in relationship to its projected performance. A timely reaction to a given problem or situation is important in the course of the month to achieve your desired profitability.

Measuring your ideals against your actual performance should be accomplished by comparing the two as a percentage of sales. Only then, will you actually see if you are over or under budget. Cost of sales categories are always divided by the sales they created. All other sales and expense categories should be divided by total sales to arrive at a percentage.

Generating an income statement

We start the process of generating an income statement by creating a form which will list: *all sales, cost of sales,* and *expense categories.* (See example *Income Statement* at the end of this chapter).

Next we need to project our expected performance for each one of these categories.

If your operation has already been open for at least several months, these numbers should be fairly easy to establish. Simply average past monthly data for each category to establish an average. Take into account any trends which may be occurring within your operation (example: if sales have been increasing 5% per month, then you should assume this trend will continue and adjust your next month's projected sales to reflect this trend).

511

If you have not yet opened for business, you will need to create some estimated guesses for projected sales. Be sure to conduct some careful research to estimate cost of goods and expenses.

Projecting sales

Estimating sales is one of the most difficult tasks because so many variables may come into play.

How visible and attractive is your physical location?

How convenient and accessible is your location?

Estimating sales is one of the most difficult tasks

How much traffic, either walk-by or drive-by, passes your establishment daily?

How much built-in clientele either works or lives adjacent to your location?

In our work with clients, we project sales after analyzing all of the above.

If, for example, we determine that your combined potential daily market is approximately 5,000 customers, we project that you may attract as many as 1% of those customers on an average daily basis in the first or second month of your business. Your potential market may be as large as 5% to 15% of these 5,000 individuals on a daily basis.

How fast and how large your customer base may grow is dependent upon your product quality, customer service, marketing efforts, and the surrounding competition.

So let us say:

- *You plan to average 50 customers per day in your second month of operation. Multiply the 50 expected customers times the number of business days you will be open during the month.*

  If your coffee operation is open 30 days next month, then you will be expecting 1,500 transactions (50 x 30 = 1,500).

Next, we need to estimate approximately how much each customer may spend. For typical coffee/espresso and morning pastry operations we might determine sales per customer as follows:

- *Average beverage purchase is $1.80 x 1,500 customers = $2,700 in beverage sales for the month.*

In addition to beverage sales we will estimate that every fifth customer will order a baked good at an average price of $1.

- *Fifteen hundred customers divided by 5 (every fifth customer) = 300 baked goods sold x $1 = $300 in food sales.*

If no bulk beans, hard goods (brewers, cups, etc.), or any other products or services are sold from this operation, then total sales would be the sum of these projected beverage and food sales:

- *$2,700 + $300 = $3,000.*

Projecting costs

To project the estimated costs associated with sales, you will need to determine your ideal beverage and food costs, and your projected menu mix.

Determining projected expenses for your new business start-up will require research and investigation.

You will need to determine your ideal beverage and food costs

Fixed expenses are fairly easy. Your *rent* is, of course, X amount of dollars. The same is true for *insurance, permits and licenses, monthly bank charges, loan payments and interest,* etc. These costs are generally determined and static; usually you cannot impact or reduce these expenses.

Controllable expenses are what the term implies; they can be impacted by your efforts. Controlling these expenses along with your cost of goods is where you have the opportunity to maximize your bottom line.

Labor is the largest controllable expense. Smart operators watch their labor expense daily and weekly and react to stay within budget.

Other controllable expenses, such as *office supplies, repair and maintenance, small wares, laundry and uniform, telephone,* etc., can also be estimated and controlled.

We highly recommend keeping a running monthly ledger for each of your controllable expense categories. By entering each expenditure daily, on its appropriate ledger, and maintaining a month-to-date running total, one can easily determine if budgets are being maintained. If an unexpected costly repair occurs exceeding your monthly repair and maintenance budget by $150, you can begin to analyze where else in your business you might be able to save money to make up the difference. In chapter 37—*Budgets & Cost Controls,* we will discuss expense and cost controls in much greater detail.

Keep in mind no matter how carefully you have done your research and made your projections, with new business start-ups—once you open your doors—you now must deal with reality. If the reality of your business performance does not meet your ideals, then you either need to reestablish your goals or devise a different game plan to achieve your intended goals.

One thing is certain:

If you have no goals, and do not generate a report card of your business performance on a regular basis, it will be highly unlikely that you will be able to control your business effectively and maximize your returns.

Producing an accurate income statement in a timely manner can be time consuming and tedious; however, it is absolutely essential to the overall success of your business.

For more information on this specific subject, refer to the following book from Bellissimo—800-655-3955.

- **Achieving Success in Specialty Coffee**

DISCLAIMER

Please understand that the following two pages of financial projections are "best-guess" estimates. Bellissimo, Inc. cannot guarantee that the following financial estimates, can or will be achieved, if or when you open for business. These financial estimates do not, and are not intended to, guarantee your business success.

These financial estimates are based upon our personal experiences gained as a result of owning and/or operating food service related businesses during the past 25 years. The estimates provided represent industry typicals, and should be used only as a model to assist with financial planing.

If you do not fully understand the following eight pages of financial statements, or have any questions, call Bellissimo at (1-800) 655-3955, or contact your attorney and/or accountant.

Sample Income Statement

The Fictitious Coffee House

For the month of:_____, 20__

	Projected		Actual	
Gross Sales				
Food	593	5.1%	625	5.5%
Coffee Beverages	9,120	77.8%	8,955	79.5%
Other Beverages	1,263	10.7%	1,042	9.3%
Bulk Coffee	425	3.6%	510	4.5%
Hard Goods	318	2.7%	125	1.1%
Sales Tax Collected (X%)	X			
Promos/Comps				
Net Sales	$ 11,719	100%	$11,257	100%
Cost of Sales				
Food	326	55%	353	56.4%
Coffee Beverages	1,641	18%	1,629	18.2%
Other Beverages	303	24%	279	26.7%
Bulk Coffee	255	60%	306	60.%
Hard Goods	159	50%	65	52.%
Total Cost of Sales	$ 2,684	22.9%	$2,632	23.4%
Gross Profit From Sales	$ 9,035	77.1%	$8,625	76.6%
Expenses				
Wages	3,500	29.9%	3,645	32.3%
Payroll Taxes / Benefits				
Payroll Taxes	420	3.6%	437	3.8%
Employee Meals	100	.8%	100	9.%
Total Labor Costs	$ 4,020	34.3%	4,182	37.1%

Controllable Expenses

Smallwares	50	.4%	32	.2%
Laundry / Uniform	50	.4%	50	.4%
Office Supplies	50	.4%	18	.2%
Printing	100	.8%	78	.7%
Promos / Comps	0			
Repairs & Maintenance	25	.2%	42	.4%
Paper & Chemical	497	4.2%	476	4.2%
Phone	100	.8%	86	.8%
Utilities	350	2.9%	324	2.9%
Garbage Service	50	.4%	50	.4%
Janitorial Service	0			
Sales Tax Payable (X%)	X			
Cash over / short	30	.3%	44	.4%
Advertising	500	4.3%	385	3.4%
Misc.				

Fixed Expenses

Rent	1,250	10.6%	1,250	11.1%
Loan Payments	0			
Interest	0			
Business Insurance	75	6.0%	75	.7%
Bank Charges / Discounts	25	.2%	25	.2%
Licenses & Permits	21	.2%	21	.2%
Professional Fees	80	.7%	80	.7%
Total Expenses	**$ 7,273**	**62.1%**	7,218	64.1%
PROFIT / LOSS	**$ 1,762**	**15%**	1,407	12.5%

Chapter 34 Check List

Establish Record Keeping Systems for:

_____   Invoice purchases

_____   Cash purchases

_____   Operating expenses

_____   Daily sales and receipts

_____   Bank deposits

_____   Tax payments and deposits

_____   Employee hours worked and wages paid

_____   Employee corrective actions and counseling sessions

_____   Customer accidents and complaints

_____   Monthly income statements

Note - Many of the financial related record keeping systems will be discussed in chapter 37- *Budgets and Cost Controls,* and forms for tracking sales, expenses, and producing income statements can be found in Appendix 1.

CHAPTER 35

Tax Liabilities

Contents

CHAPTER 35

Tax Liabilities

Ignorance is no excuse

When it comes to taxes, the first thing you need to realize is the government wants their money and the government is going to get their money. Ignorance is no excuse, and if you do not know what taxes are due and when, you will have major problems.

No matter how you may feel about paying taxes, taking care of your business's tax liability is your responsibility.

Get professional help

As we suggested earlier, you should hire professionals to help you stay on top of your tax situation.

Hire pros to help you stay on top of your tax situation

Hire a competent bookkeeper to handle your payroll, someone who is familiar with your type of retail operation, who understands and knows federal, state, and local tax liabilities.

Definitely retain a CPA for advice on financial and tax matters, and for handling your end of the year taxes, your appeals to the IRS, and any other more complex tax matters.

The importance of making timely payments

It is absolutely critical to make your tax payments in a timely manner. It is amazing how quickly the interest on unpaid taxes and the penalties for late payment can accumulate.

The IRS may seize your bank account

Even more costly is the battering to your peace of mind from all the threatening letters and phone calls that you will receive from the IRS, state, and local tax collectors, if you ignore these items. If left unattended, they may seize your bank account and will take their money out of it.

You will not want to develop a red-dot file with the federal government or the state as someone who is constantly having tax problems.

Typical tax liabilities

Typical tax liabilities that you need to be concerned with in a retail business are:

Federal payroll taxes

Federal payroll taxes are assessed on a quarterly basis but you are required to make an estimated payment on a monthly basis. Following are the form numbers by which the various taxes are identified:

- **940**—federal unemployment tax, also known as FUTA.

- **941**—taxes withheld from your employees' income from wages, tips and other compensation, to cover Social Security and Medicare taxes.

Other federal taxes

Other federal taxes you may see, are:

- **945**—taxes on pensions if you are successful long enough and you have a pension program for your employees.

- **1042**—withholding tax on foreigners. If you have someone working for you who is not a US citizen and has a green card, you might be responsible for filing a 1042.

State and local taxes

In addition to federal withholding taxes, you will probably be liable for state and local payroll taxes, such as:

- State withholding tax

- State unemployment tax

- State worker's compensation assessment

Each state and local jurisdiction is unique

In addition, there could typically be county or city taxes related to parking districts, street improvements, sewer assessments, the rapid transit district, etc.

Here again is the value of working with a professional who already understands all the federal and state taxes. They can call you to explain tax matters and send you the paperwork, and all you need to do is send in the money you owe. It simplifies your life incredibly.

Naturally, it is not possible for us to know every jurisdiction that you may be dealing with. Each state and local jurisdiction is unique. Every county is different, every city is different, so wherever you are, you need to check with your local tax officials.

State and/or local sales taxes

Other taxes you may have to pay are state and local sales taxes. In Oregon, we do not have sales taxes. However, in most states where sales taxes are levied, the merchant is responsible for collecting them and paying them back to the state on a monthly basis.

It might be wise to establish a separate bank account—an *Impound Account*—into which you can deposit these collected taxes. This will assure that when it is time for you to make your payment, the collected taxes will be there.

Individual or corporate income taxes

Another tax that you are responsible for is income tax. This tax is usually paid at the end of the year, when you are confronting your individual or corporate income tax returns.

It is important to keep in mind that the government and the state are not always right. So, do not be afraid to question authority!

In fact, we have been amazed at how many times we have received threatening messages from the government or the state even though the taxes had been paid and everything had been properly filed. It was their error, and when that happens, you must respond with the proper paper work and records.

You have to prove to them that they are mistaken.

If you think you have paid the tax, by all means defend your position.

Here again is the advantage of working with a bookkeeper or CPA. You can call them and explain the situation, and then fax them the notice so they can handle it for you.

We have found that 8 times out of 10, it was a mistake, or a problem at a clerical level with the government. Our bookkeeper was usually able to handle the entire situation very smoothly.

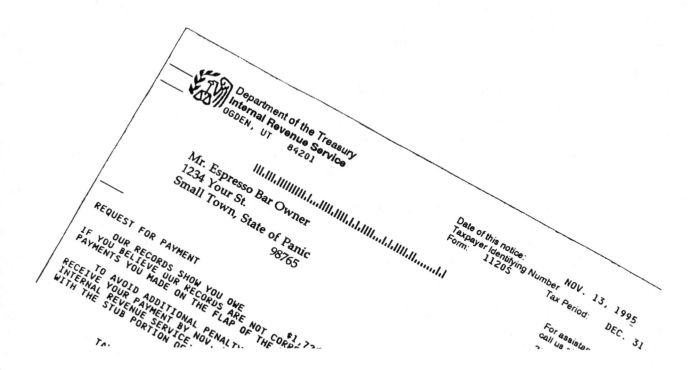

Chapter 35 Check List

Tax Considerations:

_____ Retain a qualified bookkeeper and/or a C.P.A. to handle your tax preparation and reporting for you.

If you do not choose to use a tax professional, then conduct research to determine which of the following taxes and related reports you will be responsible for:

_____ 940- federal unemployment tax

_____ 941- federal employee withholding tax for Social Security and Medicare

_____ 945- federal tax on pension funds

_____ 1042- federal withholding tax on foreign employees legally working in the United States

_____ State sales tax (payment of taxes you collected on the sale of your merchandise)

_____ State employee withholding tax

_____ State unemployment tax

_____ State worker's compensation assessment

_____ Local taxes (city or county taxes)

_____ Individual or corporate income tax

CHAPTER 36

Risk Management

Contents

CHAPTER 36

Risk Management

What is risk management?

Risk management is reducing your exposure to the risk of losing everything you have. First and foremost, speak with your business attorney about all risk issues.

Making sure you are protecting yourself and your business

It is making sure that you are protecting yourself and your business by having an adequate amount of insurance. And it is making sure that you do not have any dangerous conditions existing within your operation that will contribute to a potential liability situation.

The one thing you need to be aware of when owning a business in the United States is that anyone can attempt to sue you at any time, for **anything**.

They do not have to appear before a board to prove that they have a valid reason.

In many other countries, you actually have to prove that you have suffered an injustice (or have a case) to sue for damages.

Insurance

We recommend that you work with a reputable insurance company and a professional that you trust. Here are **some** of the types of insurance that you should ask about.

Fire insurance

If you are leasing your space, the landlord will probably be carrying fire insurance on the building. Make sure that the building is insured for fire.

Personal property insurance

A personal property insurance policy will provide coverage for your equipment, furnishings, and inventory.

If your building burns down, and the landlord's fire insurance does not cover any of the contents of the building, your personal property insurance should compensate you for your destroyed belongings.

It is also important to check to see if your insurance covers your losses if a theft occurs, and if it encompasses losses from natural catastrophes, such as floods, earthquakes, volcanos, hurricanes, and tornados.

Business liability insurance

One of the most important insurance policies you will need to carry in your business is called business liability insurance. This will help protect you in the event that one of your customers is injured in your store, or is injured by your product, or the action of one of your employees.

Seek the counsel of your insurance professional

How much insurance should you buy?

You will want to seek the counsel of your insurance professional for this advice, but when we established liability insurance for one of our locations, our agent highly recommended that we protect ourselves with one million dollars worth of coverage.

What happens if you get sued for five million and you only have a one million policy? Well, that is a possibility, and indeed the consequences would be devastating if you lost your case and were found negligent. But your insurance company would probably send out their battery of high powered attorneys to fight your case, because they will not want to pay the one million. That is your protection, and the reason you want to carry such a substantial level of coverage.

But if you only have $100,000 worth of coverage, your insurance company may decide that paying the plaintiff is cheaper than the potential legal costs. So if you get sued for five million, and the plaintiff wins, guess who gets to pay the other $4,900,000?

Business income insurance

Another kind of insurance which you may want to consider is called business income insurance. This insurance can be fairly expensive, but if it is ever needed, it can be invaluable.

- What happens if you have a fire in your store and it will take 180 days to rebuild? The contents of the store may be covered by your personal property policy, the building by the landlord's fire insurance, but what happens to your paycheck...your income?

- How is your family going to live day-to-day?

- And what about your employees? Do you want to retain them, or will all of your employees leave, and will you have to hire and train an entirely new staff when you reopen?

Business income insurance can guarantee your personal income, and the policy might also cover your employees' income, until you are back in operation.

Personal disability insurance

Personal disability insurance is something you may want to consider if you are the key person responsible for operating your business. As with business income insurance, this policy can supply you with income, should you become disabled.

Typically, personal disability insurance is cheaper than business income insurance while still assuring that you have a paycheck.

Also, there is a variation of this insurance to protect your family or business partner should you become permanently disabled. If your business partner does not possess your operational expertise, and you become disabled, your entire business may be at risk. There should be policies that will pay off any long-term debts such as loans for the purchase of a building or equipment.

Eliminating hazardous situations

A major part of risk management is making absolutely sure that you have eliminated any potentially hazardous situations within your store. This could be any situation that could cause harm to your employees or customers.

Compliance with codes and regulations

You and your employees must make sure that you are in compliance at all times with all the codes and regulations that govern your business. You need to operate on the assumption that there are sound safety reasons for the existence of these codes and regulations.

Make sure you are in compliance with all the codes and regulations

If you have an emergency EXIT door and the fire code says that nothing should obstruct access to the emergency EXIT door, then by all means do not put anything in the way that could become an obstruction. Imagine someone trying to travel through choking smoke to get out of your burning building, and they run into a table you had put in the hallway en route to this emergency exit. If this person is injured, or dies, you may be liable because you were not in compliance with codes and regulations which were designed to ensure the public's safety.

Warnings and disclaimers

You will no doubt have some situations for which you may want to issue warnings and disclaimers. These might be written, or they might be related verbally.

If one of your employees is giving a customer a Caffé Americano, you must train your employee to say,

This is extremely hot, so be very careful.

Because of a recent lawsuit by a customer who was burned by hot coffee at a well-known fast food franchise, many companies have now printed disclaimers right on their cups.

We thought it was amusing when we walked by a lawyer's office located in an old historic building, and he had placed a sign with a disclaimer on the door saying:

These stairs are old and rickety, proceed at your own risk.

He was protecting his interests, and so should you.

Lawsuits, etc.

There are a lot of people out in this world who are looking to get rich quick, without working. There are, unfortunately, many unscrupulous people who are looking for a reason to sue someone in hopes of making an easy buck. Believe it or not...some of them are attorneys.

There are a lot of people who are looking to get rich quick

We know this from personal experience.

We had a product with a name which was similar to the name of another product owned by another company. It was a totally different product, in a totally different product category. We had a registered federal trademark on our product's name.

One day we received a letter from an attorney demanding that we discontinue using this name, or pay $5,000 for the right to continue to use it. Upon a thorough investigation, we discovered that this attorney's entire practice consisted of reviewing registered names. He would approach what he felt was the strongest of the two companies, when he found that either the company's product or the name of their product was similar to another. He would send them a letter which read something like this:

> *I am an attorney, and recently while conducting some research I discovered another company who is using a name for their product which is very similar to your registered trademark. I believe that this situation may constitute an infringement upon your rights. I certainly believe that it is not in the best interest of your company to have at risk the unique identity of your product with that of a competitor's.*
>
> *My firm specializes in trademark infringements, and I am confident that with your permission, we can persuade this other party to discontinue the use of the name which is similar to yours. If we achieve this protection of your name, our customary fee would be $2,000.*
>
> *Another possibility is to seek $5,000 in compensation from these potential violators in exchange for your permission for their continued use of this similar name. This may be the most advantageous alternative. If we prevail in this action, we would retain our $2,000 fee for services from the award, and you would be the beneficiary of the remaining $3,000.*

Yes, there are actually attorneys who base their entire practice upon these types of actions.

Trademark protection

The water of trademark registrations, business names, and the like can get very clouded and murky. You need to talk to professionals and consult an attorney that specializes in this work with ANY questions you might have.

If you create a unique name, logo, or slogan for your product or company, you can legally exclude others from using it by registering it for trademark protection...provided it is not already in use.

A registered servicemark is a trademark that applies to services rather than products. If you are, or are expecting to engage, in interstate commerce (business in more than one state), you can apply for federal trademark or servicemark.

Both trademarks and servicemarks should offer protection from competitors; they let your customers and your competitors know that you are the sole provider of these particular goods and services.

The registration process generally takes at least 12 months to complete, and begins with a formal application, prepared and filed by your trademark attorney, with the United States Patent and Trademark Office (USPTO).

There are both benefits and responsibilities that are attached to trademark laws, and a lack of awareness of these can create problems that you will want to avoid. **So we recommend that you consult a trademark attorney before you proceed**.

Chapter 36 Check List

Insurance Considerations:

_____ Establish a relationship with a reputable, qualified insurance agent.

With the advise of your agent, assess your needs for each of the following insurance and obtain the appropriate coverage:

_____ Fire insurance
_____ Personal property insurance
_____ Business liability insurance
_____ Business income insurance
_____ Personal disability insurance
_____ Ask your agent if they would recommend any additional insurance not listed above.

Potential Liability Concerns:

_____ Are you in compliance with all agency bureaucracy codes and regulations? (fire department, O.S.H.A., etc.)
_____ Have you provided all necessary warnings and disclaimers to any potentially hazardous conditions or situations?
_____ Have you verified that your business name, and any names you have applied to your products, are not infringing upon a registered trade mark?

CHAPTER 37

Budgets & Cost Controls

Contents

Chapter 37 Contents - Page 2

CHAPTER 37

Budgets & Cost Controls

Budgets

To be successful, you must budget out every expense related to the operation of your business.

To be successful, you must budget

If you do not have a budget set up in advance, you will have no goals to strive for. You will not know what it is that you are trying to achieve. You will be operating from a gut instinct instead of a carefully prepared plan, and you may find that at the end of the month you have not made any money, or certainly less than you should have.

A good place to start creating your budget is with a projected *Profit & Loss* statement for the month. It should reflect your answers to these important questions:

- What am I anticipating in sales?

- What will my cost of goods be? (Cost of goods is the actual dollar value spent on the products you sold.)

- What should I spend on my controllable expenses? (As the name implies, these are expenses that you actually have some control over such as: *labor, utilities, office supplies, repair and maintenance,* etc.)

- What will my fixed expenses be? (These are expenses you have no control over, such as: *rent, insurance, loan payments, bank service charges,* etc.)

- And finally, if I subtract my cost of goods and all my expenses from my anticipated sales, what is left over? Will I make money, or loose money? And, if I am going to loose money, what can I do to correct this situation?

You need to generate realistic monthly budgets for all of these items, and then you need to achieve those budgets.

A running ledger

We suggest that you create a running ledger.

- Set up a separate page for each of your expense categories.

You will immediately know how much you have spent

- On each ledger page, leave a column for recording individual expense transactions, and a second column for a "month-to-date" accumulation of your expenses.

- Every time you pay an expense, record the invoice or receipt on the appropriate expense ledger, add that expense to the cumulative total of all previous expenses for that month, and then post that total in the month-to-date column.

You will immediately know how much you have spent, in this expense category, at this point in the month. By comparing this total with your budget for the month, you can quickly assess if you are on track to achieve your goal.

Let us look at a simple example:

Suppose you have allotted $100 for *Operating Supplies* , items such as steaming pitchers, thermometers, ceramic cups, etc.

If on the 10th of the month you spend $80 for two cases of cups because your supply was running low, you have now expended 80% of your budget for the month.

If later in the month you create a list of additional items that you need, and the total expense for those items will be $60, you will need to consider the following:

- According to your budget, you only have $20 left to spend.

- Do you really need all of those items now, or can $40 of those items be purchased next month?

- And if you do need all of those items now, is there another category of expenses where you can save $40 so your **total expenses** will not be over budget at the end of the month?

One caution on budgets: You do not want to become so focused on your bottom-line that you sacrifice essentials. Of course you want to achieve your goals, but if you start sacrificing customer service, product quality, store cleanliness, or tools which are needed by your employees to achieve these other fundamentals, then you will be hurting your overall operation.

Your budgets need to be realistic and responsive to your operating situation. You need to react to the events happening in your real world. If your sales are significantly surpassing your projections, and you are having a fantastic month, then obviously you will probably need more products and more labor.

Controlling your cost of goods sold

Your two most critical controllable expenses on a monthly basis are your *cost of goods sold* and your *labor expense*. These two categories may consume two-thirds of your total income, and it is essential that you control them well.

Your *cost of goods sold* are often referred to as the *cost of goods* or *cost of sales*. These costs represent the actual dollar value of the products which were sold. They include all your food items, beverages, bulk beans, and hard goods (cups, home brewing devices, T-shirts, or anything else you sold to customers).

Because your paper products and chemicals (paper cups, napkins, dish washing detergent, etc.) are also directly related to the cost of the sales of these items, they can also be considered a cost of sales, but they are handled differently from an accounting standpoint, and will be addressed later in this chapter.

Do not become so focused on your bottom-line that you sacrifice essentials

Your two most critical expenses on are your Cost of goods sold and your Labor expense

Your cost of goods should be calculated by category (food, beverages, bulk beans, hard goods, etc.) so that if there is a cost problem you can determine where it is happening. You can create as many categories as you like.

For example:

- You can analyze all beverages together to achieve one cost calculation, or

- break beverages into separate categories: coffee beverage, juices, other beverages.

This will let you know exactly where a cost problem may exist.

Your total cost of sales will usually represent 25% to 35% of your total income

You will need to keep in mind that if you are going to calculate multiple categories, you will need to track sales, purchases, and inventories separately for each category. It will be important to decide this before you program your cash register or POS system. Typically, a good register system will let you group items by category and will provide you information about how many of each item was sold, with category totals.

Your total cost of sales for all categories combined will usually represent 25% to 35% of your total income.

We are always amazed that when we ask coffee bar owners what their cost of sales are running, many have absolutely no idea. Furthermore, they do not even know how to calculate their cost of sales, or know what their *ideal cost of sales* should be.

There are many things involved in controlling your cost of sales, and the procedures to assess these costs on a weekly or monthly basis can be time consuming and tedious. But expending the effort to determine this information is essential if you want to attain or maximize profitability.

Determining your ideal costs

Before you calculate your present food, beverage, bulk coffee, or hard goods cost, you need to know what your *ideal* for each of those costs should be. If you do not establish ideal costs, you will have no way of knowing if your actual costs are excessive.

To calculate an ideal cost of sales for a specific category of sales, you need to know two things:

1. The exact cost of every item you sell (including ready-to-serve products you purchase for resale, such as bagels, muffins, cookies, candies, etc.).

2. How many of each item you sell over a specific period of time (typically a calendar month).

Calculate an accurate ideal cost

You must calculate the cost of every menu item, and each variation of that item. For example, you probably sell lattes, but how many sizes do you offer? How many are singles and how many are doubles? How many have a flavored syrup added? The cost of each variation of this beverage is different, and you need to know the cost of each to calculate an accurate ideal cost.

We recommend that you create some work sheets listing:

- The quantity of each ingredient used in each variation of every menu item.

- Leave a blank space beside each ingredient. You will need to enter an exact cost for each portion of every ingredient.

- After you have created your work sheets, print out a working set from your computer or make photo copies of your typed originals.

- **Do not write on your originals**. You will need the original masters for future use.

The costs for the ingredients will change, and because they are the components of your menu items , you will need to recalculate your ideal costs periodically (usually once or twice a year).

Sample work sheet for cappuccino variations

MENU ITEM	INGREDIENTS	QTY.	COST
Cappuccino (8 oz.) 8 oz. / single	Espresso beans Milk 	8 grams 3 oz. Total	____ ____ ____
8 oz. / double	Espresso beans Milk 	16 grams 3 oz. Total	____ ____ ____

III. Being Successful

MENU ITEM	INGREDIENTS	QTY.	COST
Cappuccino (12 oz.)			
12 oz. / single	Espresso beans	8 grams	_____
	Milk	5 oz.	_____
		Total	_____
12 oz. / double	Espresso beans	16 grams	_____
	Milk	5 oz.	_____
		Total	_____
Cappuccino - (Flavored - 8 oz.)			
8 oz. / single	Cappuccino	8 oz./single	_____
	Syrup	3/4 oz.	_____
		Total	_____
8 oz. / double	Cappuccino	8 oz./dbl.	_____
	Syrup	3/4 oz.	_____
		Total	_____
Cappuccino (Flavored - 12 oz.)			
12 oz. / single	Cappuccino	12 oz./single	_____
	Syrup	1 oz.	_____
		Total	_____
12 oz. / double	Cappuccino	12 oz./dbl.	_____
	Syrup	1 oz.	_____
		Total	_____

After you have completed work sheets for all your menu items and their variations, you must next calculate the cost of the portion of each ingredient used in each item.

For example:

A gallon of milk is also 128 ounces. If you divide the price of a gallon of milk by 128 you have calculated the cost per ounce.

Multiply the number of ounces used for each milk based beverage by that cost per ounce and you will have determined your cost of the milk for each beverage. (Remember, if you are making an 8-ounce cappuccino, one ounce of the cup will be filled with espresso. You will not need 7 ounces of milk to top off the cup since the volume of milk will at least double in the steaming process. You will probably only need to use about 3 to 3 1/2 ounces.)

In a similar fashion, break down the costs of all your other ingredients.

- We recommend using 50 8-gram shots to determine your cost for a single shot of espresso (you may actually get about 56 8-gram shots from a pound of coffee beans, but we have allowed for a loss of 6 shots per pound for test shots, unusable extractions, and spillage).

- Most full-size syrup bottles will hold 25 ounces. You may actually have to perform some tests to determine the cost of some ingredients. It may be necessary to dispense an entire can of aerosol whipped cream to determine how many beverages you can top with a typical can.

One final note on calculating the cost of individual menu items:

- We do not recommend factoring in the cost of your cup, napkin, stir stick or straw into your beverage cost. We prefer to track the cost of paper products as a separate cost. By keeping the two expenses separate, you may better analyze which of your costs are out of line.

Calculating menu mix

The next essential step in calculating an ideal cost for a specific cost category is determining the menu mix. This is the total number of each menu item/ variation that you have sold over a period of time.

Different menu items will have different costs

This is an important factor when determining an ideal for a cost of sales category because different menu items will have different costs.

For example only:

If you sell a shot of espresso for $1, and your cost of producing that shot is 10 cents, then your cost reflected as a percentage of sales is 10%.

But if you sell a caffe mocha for $2, and your cost is 50 cents, then your cost for that mocha when reflected as a percentage of sales is 25%.

Because the cost will vary between each menu item when analyzed as a percentage of their selling price, knowing exactly how many of each item was sold is essential in determining an overall ideal cost.

This will not be difficult to determine *if your cash register is set up with item presets* (a specific key on your register for each menu item and all of its variations).

Your cash register should be able to produce a report which is a breakdown of what has been sold on a daily basis, or for an entire week or month.

- If you are recording daily item sales, create a form for each category of sales with 31 columns, one for each day of the month, and a list of all your menu items within that category.

- List your menu items on the form in the order they appear on your cash register tape report.

This will make the daily recording of items sold a very easy process. At the end of each month add up the daily totals for each item to assess the total sold for the month.

- Multiply the total number of each item sold for that month by that item's corresponding cost.

- Add together the total costs for every menu item sold.

The resulting dollar figure represents the total dollar amount of product that should have been used in achieving the sales for that category. This total is your *ideal cost* in terms of dollars.

- Divide this number by the total sales for the category, and the resulting number is the cost reflected as *a percentage of sales.*

We should caution you that because you have determined an ideal cost for one month, it does not mean that it will remain your ideal for the following month. If the number of each item sold changes significantly from month to month, then your ideal cost will also change.

We had mentioned earlier that you should recalculate your ideal cost once or twice a year. But when you first open, we recommend that you calculate an ideal every month for a period of several months to determine if there is any significant fluctuation in your ideal cost created by inconsistencies in menu mix.

We can now move on to calculating our actual cost of sales for a specific category for this same period. When we complete this process, we will know if our cost is in line with our ideal, or if we have some cost problems.

Calculating cost of sales

Cost of sales for a specific category is the actual dollar value of inventory that you have expended over a select period of time to produce the sales for that category during that same period.

The formula for calculating a monthly cost of sales for a category is:

Cost of sales is the actual dollar value of inventory that you have expended

Beginning inventory—the total dollar value of all products on hand on the first day of the month (same as last months ending inventory),

plus purchases—the total dollar value of all products purchased during that month,

minus ending inventory—the dollar value of products left on hand at the end of the month, equals—the cost of sales (or the cost of goods sold).

Cost of Sales Formula:

Beginning Inventory + Purchases - Ending Inventory = Cost of Sales

To calculate your monthly cost of sales for a specific category you will need to do the following:

- Count all product on hand, after business hours, on the last day of the month.

  This ending inventory for the month just concluded will also be the beginning inventory for the next day, the first day of the new month.

- After you have counted all of your inventory, multiply each product by its corresponding unit price.

Be sure that, if you are counting coffee by the five-pound bag, when you multiply the number of bags counted, you use the cost associated with a five-pound bag and not the price per pound. If you do not multiply the quantities counted by the correct unit price, then your indicated total value for that item will be incorrect.

- Add together the total value of each product on hand to get a dollar value for your entire category inventory.

- Next, you will need to add up the invoice totals for all products purchased over the month.

  Be sure that if an invoice from your vendor includes items for other cost categories, you only record the dollar value of the items applicable to the category you are working on.

- Now take ending inventory on the last day of the month as you had the previous month.

You now possess all the necessary information to process through the inventory formula to determine your cost. (If you have not yet opened for business, or are still in your first month of business, then the total of your initial inventory purchases will be your beginning inventory value.)

Do not be alarmed if your actual cost is higher than your ideal

Divide your cost of sales for the month by the corresponding category sales for that same month. You have now determined your cost of sales as a percentage of total sales for the category.

Example:

If the cost of goods is $2,000 divided by their related sales, which in this case we will say is $10,000, your cost of sales equals 20% of your total sales for that category.

Ideal vs. actual cost of sales

You can now compare your ideal cost with your actual cost. Do not be alarmed if your actual cost is higher than your ideal. If it were a perfect world you would be able to achieve your ideal, but it is not...and you will not!

Mistakes happen, drinks are misprepared, old pastries are thrown away, and milk is spilled. As long as your costs are within a percent or two of your ideal, you probably do not have a serious problem. Your actual cost should never be lower than your ideal and if it is, you have probably made a clerical mistake in counting, calculating your inventory, or in recording your purchases.

Another factor which should be mentioned which might make your costs look as if they are out of line, is product which has been given away or consumed by employees.

- Be sure that all beverage promos and products consumed by employees are rung-up on your cash register at normal retail prices.

The total of these items can be backed-off of your cash receipts as an expense so that your till will balance at the end of each shift. It is important that these items are accounted for as a sale so that an accurate calculation of your cost of sales can be achieved.

But what if your actual cost is significantly higher than your ideal? What if it is 5% to 10% over your ideal?

You may have a serious waste, portioning, theft, or clerical problem.

Let us move on to discuss why you might be having, or appear to be having, a cost problem.

Finding and solving cost problems

So you have determined that your cost assessment needs some work.

Many times you will discover that it is a combination of factors

How do you find out where the product is going?

Many times you will discover that it is a combination of factors that have affected your costs.

Let us now look at common reasons why your real costs can be significantly higher than your ideals, and some suggested solutions.

<u>Problem</u>	<u>Solution</u>
1. **Over-portioning /waste.**	Actively observe and supervise your employees. Retrain if necessary.
2. **Theft—product being given away, or transaction not being rung on cash register and revenue being taken.**	Conduct key item inventory after each shift (weigh coffee or count desirable theft items after each shift and compare to register item report of product sales). Determine if there is a pattern between employees working and product missing. Create a policy that every sale must be accompanied with a cash register receipt. This will help discourage employees from ringing up "no sale" and then pocketing the cash.
3. **Invoice for product(s) not received.**	Create a merchandise receiving procedure. If employees are receiving deliveries, have them check-off each item on the invoice, verifying their presence upon delivery.
4. **Missing invoice(s) (this will make your food cost appear to be low).**	Implement the use of an invoice receiving log on which all invoice information is recorded upon delivery.

5.	**Errors in inventory count.**	Review your inventory counts to assess if all items on the shelves are reflected in your physical count. Verify that you counted by the units specified on your inventory sheets.
6.	**Errors in inventory calculations.**	Review your inventory sheet calculations— item count totals; correct unit prices; correct multiplication of item counts by unit prices; correct addition of page totals.
7.	**Errors in recording of purchases.**	Review your purchases journal—all invoices properly recorded to correct expense categories? No double entry of invoices? All product that was paid for was received?
8.	**Review/revise ideal food cost.**	Is the amount of each ingredient specified in the ideal food cost work sheets realistic? Have unit prices for products you purchase increased, but not been reflected in your ideal food cost calculations?

What Do People Buy?

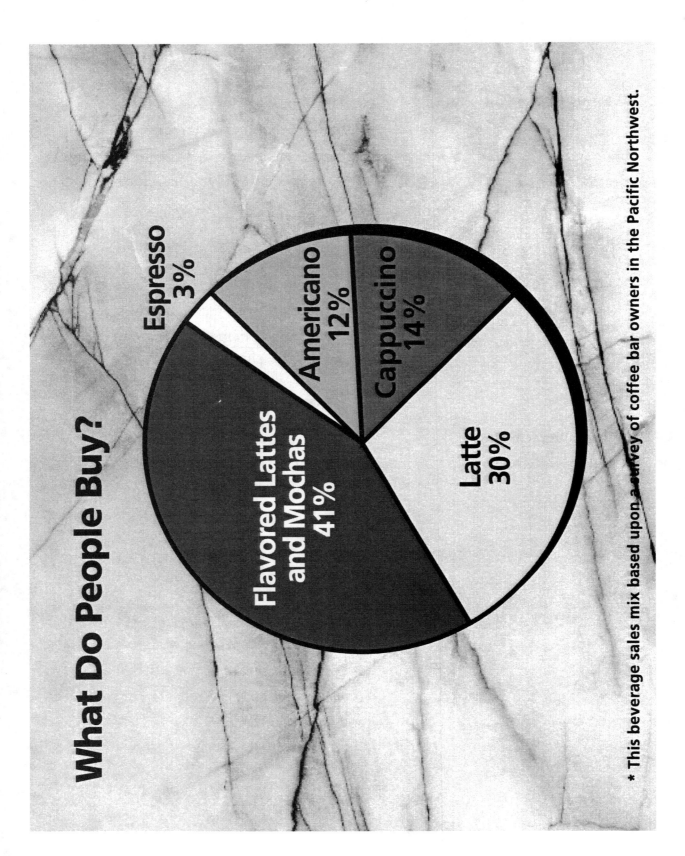

Espresso
3%

Americano
12%

Cappuccino
14%

Flavored Lattes
and Mochas
41%

Latte
30%

* This beverage sales mix based upon a survey of coffee bar owners in the Pacific Northwest.

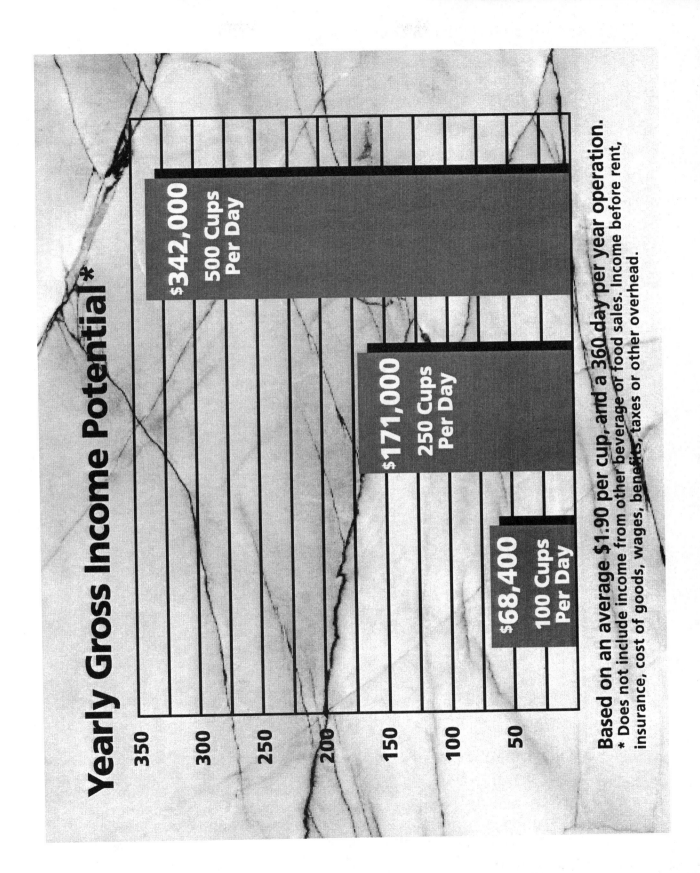

Yearly Gross Income Potential*

$342,000
500 Cups Per Day

$171,000
250 Cups Per Day

$68,400
100 Cups Per Day

350 300 250 200 150 100 50

Based on an average $1.90 per cup, and a 360 day per year operation.
* Does not include income from other beverage or food sales. Income before rent, insurance, cost of goods, wages, benefits, taxes or other overhead.

Paper and chemical as a cost of sales

Earlier we mentioned that because the expenditure of inventory of paper products and chemicals is directly related to product sales, these items can also be analyzed as a cost of sales.

The dollar value of inventory used is determined in the same manner as it would be for any other category—beginning inventory, plus purchases, minus ending inventory, equals the dollar value of inventory used.

The difference lies in the fact that paper products and chemicals are not sold to your customers; they are a cost associated with the sale of other items. You will not find a category on your cash register report that will indicate *paper and chemical* sales.

So when you want to analyze your paper and chemical usage as a percentage of sales, what do you divide it by?

> • Use your *Total sales*.

You cannot realistically determine an ideal cost for paper and chemical usage, so this percentage figure is only useful for monthly comparisons.

NOTE: See Appendix 1 for a variety of office forms for your use and directions for how to use them.

Controlling Labor Cost

The single largest monthly expenditure

Your labor expense will often be the single largest monthly expenditure in your business. Controlling your labor expense is critical and requires two actions:

> • You must actively manage your staff, and
>
> • you must track on paper (or in your computer) your daily labor expense in relationship to your budget.

Active staff management

Actively managing your staff means that you must work with them, constantly supervising until they understand what your performance expectations are. They must develop a sense of urgency to help you save your valuable labor dollars.

Will they inform you promptly when the rush is over so you might make a decision on sending someone home early?

Do they understand that it is their responsibility to inform you?

Do they stay productive?

Are they always thinking: *What next? What else could I be doing?*

Equally as important,

Do they tell you when they are overwhelmed?

Do they come to you when they are really busy and tell you they need more help?

They need to understand that helping you manage their labor includes getting another person involved when needed, so that customer service will not suffer. Getting your employees in this mind set is not difficult if you make it a priority, and remind them regularly.

Planning and monitoring your labor dollars on a daily basis

The second aspect to managing your labor is to have it well planned out on paper, and to monitor your progress on a daily basis.

You must first determine the total number of dollars you wish to expend on labor for the month. Be sure that this number is realistic and achievable.

Have it well planned out on paper

We would all like to expend a fraction of what we are spending on labor in our businesses, but we must first make sure that we have sufficient labor to provide good customer service and maintain the physical upkeep of our operation. Remember: poor customer service and a dirty operation will only contribute to decreasing sales, and eventually the demise of your business.

The key is to write an aggressive, realistic schedule for the month, and then manage your labor to achieve your budgetary goals. We might add that if your actual sales are exceeding what you projected for the month, it would be acceptable, maybe even expected, that your labor will also increase in order to service the additional business.

The key is to not let your labor exceed your projected labor dollars as a percentage of total sales. In other words:

If your labor is projected to be 25.5% of total sales of $15,000, then it certainly should not represent a higher percentage of sales if you achieve $19,000 in sales for that same month. If anything, the percentage should be lower.

Creating a weekly budget

Once you have determined the amount of labor dollars you desire to spend for the month, divide that amount by the number of weeks in the month to determine your weekly budget.

Now you can begin to create and cost out some weekly schedules.

We use a form we call a *Weekly Labor Projection Worksheet*. (See example in Appendix 1.) This control form allows us to write a weekly schedule and provides spaces to record projected hours to be worked, and dollars expended, for every employee each day. We can easily total projected hours and dollars for each day of operation, and a total for the week.

Once the budget has been achieved, then the scheduled shifts can be written up on a posting copy for the employees.

Calculating daily costs

Now that you have achieved a labor goal for each day, and the total week, you must calculate your actual daily expenditure of hours and dollars.

- From their time cards, calculate the actual hours worked by each employee every day.

  We enter these numbers on an *Employee Labor Log* (see example in Appendix 1) which creates a daily and period recap of hours and dollars expended. This form will also provide the necessary information to produce payroll.

- A total of daily dollars expended can be achieved by multiplying the number of hours worked by each employee, times their corresponding wage rate.

- Then add together the dollar amount expended on each employee to achieve a total for the day.

This form has two very useful lines of information to assist you in controlling your labor. They are:

- *MTD Projected $* (month-to-date projected labor dollars), and

- *MTD Actual $* (month-to-date actual labor dollars).

MTD Projected $ represents the sum of all projected daily labor dollars at any given point in that month.

MTD Actual $ represent the accumulation of actual labor dollars spent at any given point in the same month.

By comparing your Actual MTD to your Projected MTD you can easily assess on a daily basis whether your expenditures are over or under, and by how much.

You need to react on a daily basis

Monitoring your labor on a daily basis will give you the opportunity to take action and recover dollars spent above your budgeted goal. If you look at yesterday's labor and realize that you expended $10 more than was allocated, then you can try and save $10 in labor today, or over the next couple of days, to get back on track with your budget. It will be too late to look at your actual labor for the first time at the end of the month, only to discover that you were hundreds of dollars over your budgeted goal. You need to react on a daily basis.

Monthly recap

Finally, you should summarize your labor performance for each week on a *Monthly Labor Recap* (see example in Appendix 1). This allows you to monitor your labor performance on a weekly basis, and to analyze how you are doing in relationship to the budget you set for the month.

You will discover that controlling your labor is not difficult if you will take the time to train your staff, and to do the necessary 20 to 30 minutes of daily paper work to assess your situation.

Physical Cost Controls

In addition to paper controls, there are other control areas to consider, such as physical controls. When we talk about physical controls, we are referring to techniques that prevent product from walking out the back door in the employees' backpacks or being given away without money being collected for it.

We highly recommend that you equip your back door with an alarmed emergency breaker bar. This will still provide the necessary exit for an evacuation in the event of a fire, but it will not allow an undetected employee exit. This is a good physical control, a strong deterrent to theft.

Reducing temptation

Most people are basically honest, but...

In our own operations, it was standard practice to forbid coats and back packs to be stored in the back of the premises in close proximity to where the products were stored; it was too much of a temptation.

Most people are basically honest, but if you create a tempting situation, even the most honest person may steal from you. So the key is to minimize the temptation. Do not set yourself up to be a victim. Employ some common sense policies.

In the United States, we have the same lack of checks and balances existing in coffee bars that is typical in liquor bars: *the same person dispenses the product and collects the money.*

In Europe, they have a different system. Not only do you pay for your beverage before you receive it, but usually you purchase it from a cashier, and then present your receipt to the barista who will prepare it. This is an effective check and balance.

"Building a bank"

The problem with having the same person dispensing the product and collecting the money is that it offers a great opportunity for theft.

The technique used to steal money is referred to as "building a bank."

What typically happens is:

> The customer walks up and places an order, the cashier opens the drawer on the register without ringing the sale, and collects the appropriate amount from the customer. The cashier makes a mental note of that amount, or keeps track of it in some other way.

> At a later point in time, the employee takes the money from the cash register. If the employee has kept an accurate record of the money which was collected but not rung up, and then removes exactly that amount from the register, there is a good chance that the money in their cash drawer will balance with the register report at the end of the shift.

560

The owner or manager may never be aware that this theft is occurring.

There are a few indicators that may help you determine if this theft might be occurring.

- Examine the detail tape from your cash register and look for an excessive amount of "No Sales."

Of course, if a customer has requested change for the pay phone, or a newspaper, or if your cashier has opened the drawer to survey their change supply, the "No Sale" key would be used. But if there is an excessive amount of "No Sale" transactions indicated, you may want to question why.

- Another indicator will be if your costs begin to escalate.

This will be a more difficult factor to analyze because unless your cashier is stealing substantial amounts of money, the impact on your costs as a percentage of sales may be minimal. Also, there are many other factors which can contribute to an increase in costs like: waste, spoilage, over portioning, clerical errors, etc.

There is a variation of building a bank where a "No Sale" will not be indicated on the cash register tape. This happens when:

- The cashier does not close the cash register drawer between transactions. This works well if there are a number of customers being served simultaneously or in rapid succession.

Be aware of any peculiar notes or tallies you may see your cashier making.

We saw one situation where the cashier kept track of the number of dollars which had not been rung up by using stir sticks. They had two coffee cups along side of the cash register, one full of stir sticks, and one that was empty. Every time they would not ring up a transaction, they would move one stick to the empty cup for every dollar they had stolen.

At the end of the shift, it was an easy process to count the sticks and remove the appropriate amount of money from the cash register.

If you feel an employee may be stealing from you by building a bank, one thing that you can do is a surprise mid-shift reconciliation of the cash drawer.

- Take an "X" report (a cash register report that will provide you with total sales at that point without resetting the register) and count the drawer.

   If the drawer is significantly over the amount indicated on the report, it could mean that your cashier was in the process of building a bank.

Do NOT accuse them

Of course, do not accuse them of doing this. You will not want to put yourself in a potentially precarious legal situation. But at least you will know what is happening, and you can deal with it in another way, at another time.

Another method of testing an employee's honesty is to bait the cash drawer.

- Put $20 too much in the drawer at the beginning of the shift and see if the employee reports a $20 overage upon the completion of their check-out.

   If they do not, you have a good indication of this person's honesty.

You will, of course, want to confront them, but once again, say nothing. The important point is that you have verified your fears and you can deal with the situation later under another pretense.

Installing a receipt system

One way you can deter theft from an employee who may be building a bank is to implement a policy that a receipt is to be presented to every customer upon the completion of their cash transaction.

Implement a policy that a receipt is to be presented to every customer

This system is especially useful if you have a cart or kiosk, and you will not always be there. By offering an incentive, your customers help you police this policy. Place a sign which reads:

   If you do not get a receipt with your drink, your drink is free!

and attach it to the customer's side of the cash register.

You can further enhance this system by linking it to a contest with the receipt serving as the entry form. For example:

   We had a rubber stamp made which provided spaces for the customer's name, address, and phone number. The barista would ring up the sale, then stamp the back of the receipt and hand the receipt to the customer. The customer would fill in the requested information, and then drop the receipt in a fish bowl on the counter for an opportunity to win prizes at a weekly drawing.

Of course this promotion was also marketed on a large sign which was in direct view of the customer. It was another incentive for the customer to want a receipt, and also gave the coffee bar owner an ongoing supply of customer data that they could use for direct mail marketing.

Other controls

Other controls include taking measures such as:

- Counting cups—which we do not regard as very useful.

For example:

The New Mexico client with the fish bowl had two coffee bars. One coffee bar had "to-go" cups only, which made cup counting fairly easy. But the other coffee bar had both "to-go" and ceramic cups, which made it impossible for them to do cup counts that were very meaningful.

Other problems are that errors are made with beverages, double cupping is often used for Americano, and occasionally someone will ask for a cup of water. If the cup count is off by 10 cups per shift, how do you know what is really happening?

- Keeping track of your coffee poundage is a more accurate method of assessing the number of beverages being sold.

If you have a cash register with preset keys where every beverage and every variation of a beverage is recorded, at the end of a shift you can analyze how may shots of espresso and cups of brewed coffee were sold.

If you are using the formula of 50 to 56 shots of espresso per pound, and 37 8-ounce cups of brewed coffee per pound, it is not difficult to calculate how much coffee should have been used. If your remaining coffee inventory is significantly less than anticipated, you may have a potential problem.

If indeed you are coming up short on product, you may need to implement a *key item inventory* which we discussed in chapter 26— *Your Operational Systems*.

Setting up budgets and controls may seem overwhelming, but they are essential if you want to make money. You will have to dedicate a block of time on a daily, weekly, and monthly basis to analyze all the data, and then record and calculate the information. The operational systems which were discussed in chapter 27 will help you manage the details of the day-to-day administration of your business so that you can find this time.

Be aware that,

> *Running your business without budgets and controls is like driving across the country without maps and signs; it is highly unlikely that you will get to your desired destination.*

 For more information on this specific subject, refer to the following book from Bellissimo—800-655-3955.

- **Achieving Success in Specialty Coffee**

Chapter 37 Check List

Note—many of the forms necessary to achieve the following budgets and controls are located in Appendix 1.

Recording Purchases:

_____ Create a running ledger for each of your expense categories. (Use a book of ledger paper; dedicate one page to each category. Be sure to include your budget for each category on the log.)

_____ Record all invoice purchases on *Vendor Invoice Logs*, (set up a separate log for each vendor).

_____ At the end of the month combine the totals from each Vendor Invoice Log on the *Vendor Invoice Summary*. (This will provide you with your total invoice purchases for the month.)

_____ Record operating expenses that are not vendor invoices, and are not cash paid-outs, on the *Expense Log*. (This is where you will record items such as rent, utilities, bank service charges, etc.)

_____ Record your daily cash-paid outs on the *Daily Paid Out Log*. (Since these paid outs are typically for the same type of items you purchase from your vendors, the totals from this log are added to the Vendor Invoice Summary.)

_____ Transfer the total purchases from your Vendor Invoice Summary as follows:

1. Those purchase which are related to *Cost of Sales* categories should be posted to the *Cost of Sales Worksheet*. 2. All other purchase can be posted directly to the *Income Statement*.

_____ Transfer totals from the expense log directly to the income statement.

Controlling Cost of Goods (or Cost of Sales):

_____ Determine the exact cost for every item you sell. (Be sure to include every item variation also.)

_____ Create a log so that you can record the daily quantity sold for each menu item and all of its variations.

_____ Multiply the monthly total of each item sold times its corresponding cost. Add together all of the item totals to achieve and *Ideal Cost* for what was sold, in terms of dollars.

III. Being Successful

_____ Calculate an actual cost for product used during the month for each of your Cost of Goods (Sales) categories. (Use the *Cost of Sales Formula* to determine your actual cost.)

_____ Divide your ideal dollars costs and your actual dollars costs, or each Cost of Sales category, by the total sales generated in those categories, to obtain a cost as a percentage of sales.

_____ Compare your ideals to you actual costs as a percentage of sales and determine if you have a cost problem. If so, refer to the problem/solution section of this chapter.

Controlling Labor:

_____ Determine a monthly budget for labor and divide by the number of weeks within the month.

_____ Using the *Weekly Labor Projection Worksheet,* write a schedule which fits your weekly budget.

_____ Record your daily labor expenditures at the conclusion of each day on the *Employee Labor Log.*

_____ Transfer your totals for each week to the *Monthly Labor Recap.*

Other Controls:

_____ Secure your back door with an alarmed breaker-bar.

_____ Keep all desirable theft items in a locked store room or cabinet.

_____ Implement a policy of no jackets or backpacks in the back of the house.

_____ Have your cashier issue a receipt to every customer upon the completion of the transaction.

_____ Conduct occasional mid-shift reconciliations of the cash register drawer.

_____ Conduct key item inventories.

CHAPTER 38

How to Achieve Profitability

Contents

CHAPTER 38

How to Achieve Profitability

One reason you may choose to create your own business is because you desire to have control over your own destiny, and your own income potential. To control your own income potential, you need to understand that achieving profitability does not happen on its own. You have to achieve it by understanding and executing the basic fundamentals.

Achieving profitability does not happen on its own

If you are already open and operating, you will have made some of the fundamental decisions discussed in this chapter. But because they are an integral part of the equation for achieving profitability, we will discuss their importance again. If you have made poor decisions which may hinder your ability to realize a profit from your operation, you may need to take the appropriate actions to correct this situation.

In this chapter, we will not be going into detail on these fundamentals, but we will touch on the basics...and refer you to the chapters that will provide you with this detailed information.

The Fundamentals of Profitability

Understanding your product

First, you must obtain a total understanding of coffee.

If you were going to open a fitness center, you would need to be familiar with the physiology of the human body and principles of proper nutrition. If you were going to open an automobile repair shop, you would have to understand the mechanical functions of an automobile.

You must have an extensive knowledge of coffee

You are going to open a specialty coffee business, and you must have an extensive knowledge of coffee and all the information necessary to select, prepare, handle, and store it properly. This information is not only essential for preparing an appealing product which will attract your desired clientele, but will also be necessary for you to select purveyors and equipment wisely. (See Chapters 2 through 14—*Your Product.*)

Great location

Location is of the utmost importance to just about every retail business. Location is especially critical in the food-service industry. In the specialty coffee business you will hear the incantation:

The three most important things to your success are: Location, Location, Location.

A great location will help offset a lot of mistakes and challenges

If you have a great location, it will help offset a lot of mistakes and challenges. However, not only do you need to find a great location, you must be able to convince the property manager or owner that you are the best possible candidate for that location. Your business plan and your ability to sell yourself and your concept will be essential to achieving this goal. And, finally, you must be able to negotiate a lease which will provide the necessary conditions for you to succeed. (See Chapter 19—*Developing a Business Plan,* Chapter 20—*Finding a Great Location,* and Chapter 22—*Negotiating a Lease.*)

Attractive, immaculate physical plant

The next thing you need is an attractive, immaculate, and efficient physical plant. You will need to have the necessary capital to remodel, equip, furnish, and decorate your space. You will need to obtain permission and approval from the various government agencies to execute your plan. And, you will need to make wise decisions about the contractors you will use, and the equipment and furnishings you will purchase.

Your café, drive-thru, kiosk, or cart must be appealing to people

Your café, drive-thru, kiosk, or cart must be appealing to people, creating the desire to visit your location...and to purchase your products and services. (See Chapter 15—*Your Financial Resources,* Chapter 23—*Design & Construction of Your Coffee Bar,* Chapter 21—*Codes, Permits, & Red Tape,* and Chapter 25—*Choosing and Buying Equipment.*)

Superior product quality

Provide a superior product

The best way to attract customers and stay ahead of your competitors is to provide a superior product. This means sourcing and purchasing the best quality products, and then preparing them properly on a consistent basis.

Serving the highest quality products possible is your best insurance against losing customers to a competitor. If you position yourself, from the beginning, with mediocre, inferior products, then the best you will do is to serve glorified mediocre, inferior products.

Chapters 1 through 14 were designed to improve your understanding of coffee, and how to prepare quality espresso beverages. **Do it right from the start!** (See Chapter 24 — *Planning Your Menu,* and Chapter 26 — *Selecting Your Vendors* for essential information on obtaining, preparing, and presenting quality products.)

Excellent customer service

Have employees who will attract customers

Excellent customer service is essential. This is a people business, and your customers are not purchasing your product from a vending machine; they are purchasing them from your people.

One of your big advantages is to have employees who will attract customers; dynamic people who are committed to friendly customer service. You must be able to find the people who possess positive, energetic attitudes, and then train and manage them effectively. (See Chapter 28—*Hiring and Managing Employees,* Chapter 29—*Importance of Employee Training,* and Chapter 32—*Customer Service.*)

Maintaining a high level of operational performance

Maintain high levels of performance on a daily basis

Of course, you can teach your employees to produce a quality product and to provide excellent customer service, but it is critical to maintain those high levels of performance on a daily basis. You must keep your store immaculate, and you must attend to all the daily administrative functions.

How do you manage these hundreds of details without forgetting any of them? By creating and using some efficient operational systems. (See Chapter 27—*Your Operational Systems.*)

Marketing and merchandising your business

Present everything that you have to sell

If customers do not know about your business, and if you cannot motivate them to visit, you will not be successful. When they do visit your location, you must attractively present everything that you have to sell to entice them to buy as much as possible. (See Chapter 31—*Marketing Your Business,* and Chapter 33—*Merchandising in Your Business.*)

Budgeting and controlling your costs

Once you are generating sales, you need to maximize your profit from those sales.

Maximize your profit from sales

Establishing budgets and controlling your costs is essential to this objective. You need to accurately estimate your sales and expenditures, and then achieve those objectives so that you will obtain your desired level of profitability at the end of the month. You must create a method to monitor your financial performance on a daily and weekly basis to make sure you are on track. (See Chapter 34—*Record Keeping,* and Chapter 37—*Budgets and Cost Controls.*)

Having sufficient operating capital

Have enough capital in reserve

One of the fundamental reasons that people fail in this business is insufficient capital. They run out of operating capital before they can achieve profitability.

It is critical that you have enough capital in reserve to operate your business until you are making money. (See Chapter 15—*Your Financial Resources.*)

Becoming a student of the business

Obtain substantial knowledge and expertise

In order to execute all the fundamentals necessary to be successful in the specialty coffee business, you will have to obtain a substantial amount of knowledge and expertise. You will need to become a student of this business. You will need to stay in a constant mode of learning and self development.

There are no such things as plateaus—you are either growing or regressing. Unless you stay in a constant mode of self-improvement and growth, you will be moving in the other direction. You need to take advantage of all the educational resources and embark on a program of improving yourself, and your business, on a month-to-month basis.

Educational resources

There is an enormous amount of available knowledge about the specialty coffee business for a relatively small amount of money. For $125 to $150 a year, you can subscribe to the five or six major coffee periodicals. It makes for fascinating reading at home during your evening hours; you will pick up great ideas, see what other operators have done, and become informed on what is happening "now" in our industry.

Some periodicals are aimed at the roaster and green bean buyers, others are targeted specifically at specialty coffee retailers. As a retailer, it is important for you to understand what is happening with your product, where coffee prices might be headed, and what the consequences for your business may be if there is a problem in a producing nation.

You need to keep in touch with what is happening

We are living in a world of constant flux where conditions change very quickly. You need to ride this wave of change by keeping in touch with what is happening on a daily and monthly basis.

You need to learn how to address challenges in your business, and a good way to do this is by learning about what other people have done. See how they addressed similar challenges, how they dealt with obstacles and problems, and what they did to achieve profitability. When you learn from other people, you will not have to reinvent the wheel every time you set out on a new project or task. More importantly, you will not have to make the same costly mistakes they did.

Other great sources of education are books and training videos. You can find books about the coffee business, managing, marketing, and improving your business skills. And of course there are countless books with formulas for improving yourself as a person.

Training videos can make your life a lot easier and save you valuable time. With our own training video, *"Espresso 101,"* you can train an employee better and faster than you could by yourself with hands-on training. You can save valuable time and money by taking advantage of the technology and innovations that others have invested their capital and expertise in, developing such aids for your use.

Seminars, classes, and trade shows are excellent sources for valuable information about products, management techniques, and personal development. They are also excellent environments for discovering what other businesses and entrepreneurs are doing. When you learn

When you learn from other people you will not have to make the same costly mistakes they did

from other people you will not have to reinvent the wheel every time you set out on a new project or task. More importantly, you will not have to make the same costly mistakes they did.

Of course, it is not enough to just discover this great information and these promising techniques. You need to apply your new understanding and knowledge and put it to practical use on a daily basis. You have to develop a plan for how you are going to apply this knowledge to achieve the maximum return.

And that is what we will be covering in the next chapter on *Goal Setting & Business Planning.*

 For more information on this specific subject, refer to the following book from Bellissimo—800-655-3955.

- **Achieving Success in Specialty Coffee**

CHAPTER 39

Goal Setting & Business Planning

Contents

CHAPTER 39

Goal Setting & Business Planning

The Big Picture

You need to establish what you want to obtain from your business during the initial planning stages.

Most people's goal for getting into business is to make money, and to have control of their own income and destiny.

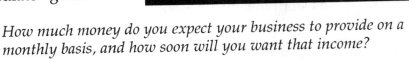

You will need to establish milestones and define a time schedule

But you must establish more specific "immediate" goals.

How much money do you expect your business to provide on a monthly basis, and how soon will you want that income?

Will the business you are planning, and the market you intend on targeting, provide you with this income?

These are, of course, important questions, but you also need to have a far more reaching vision of what you want your business to achieve over the course of its life. You will need to establish milestones along that path, and define a time schedule for reaching each of them.

Very few businesses put together ongoing business plans

Unfortunately, what may happen after you open your business is that you will become so entrenched in the day-to-day operation that you will lose sight of the big picture. You may find yourself ending each year in the same place where you started, and you will not understand why you have not moved any closer to that grand vision you had initially.

The key to achieving your vision is to set goals and have a business plan for achieving those goals.

Most businesses will put together a business plan before they open. But very few businesses will put together ongoing business plans because they get mired down in the day-to-day activities.

Understanding which factors are within your control

First, you need to look at the variety of factors affecting your business and know which factors you can control, and which factors you will have no control over. If coffee prices suddenly double, or if the surgeon general releases a report stating that coffee may increase the risk of developing cancer, these are factors influencing your business over which you have no control.

But there are a great many things that you can control in your business, such as your marketing, menu, product quality, customer service, store design, cleanliness, etc.

Setting Specific Goals

You will need to establish a long-term goal for your business, and then break that goal down into a number of short-term goals that will serve as stepping stones along this path to your ultimate destination.

Long-term goals

Long-term goals are what you want your business to achieve over the next three to five years. You might have certain *financial goals* that you want to achieve; *sales goals, profitability goals, expansion goals.*

All of these are typical long-term goals in a business.

Short-term goals

You need to break down your long-term goals into multiple short-term goals. If your coffee bar is generating $10,000 a month in sales now, and in five years you want it to produce $25,000 a month, you have to determine how you are going to move from your present sales level to your desired level.

Your answers to this question will define your short-term goals. You need to create a plan of action which can be measured in increments.

Example:

> If you have a two story house and you want to get from the first floor to the second floor, you cannot jump from the first floor to the second.
>
> You have to use a staircase.
>
> And then you have to proceed up those stairs, one step at a time. The first step helps you get to the second step, the second step helps you to the third, and so on.

This may seem like an obvious, remedial concept, but it is amazing how many people expect their business to just jump to the next level. It does not work that way. You need to define the steps that will get your business to the next level.

The process involves breaking down the five year objective for your business into annual, monthly, and finally weekly and daily goals.

The result will be a timetable for achieving your long-term vision.

Determining if the goal is realistic

Once you set up your periodic goals, and the timetable for achieving them, you can assess if your goals are realistic and attainable.

You may have to change your goals if it becomes apparent that they are unrealistic

You may have to change your goals if it becomes apparent that they are unrealistic. Or, your other alternative is to create a more aggressive plan for achieving them.

You will need to reevaluate your goals periodically.

If your results are exceeding your goals, you will need to raise your expectations and set more challenging goals.

If it becomes obvious that you will not achieve your goals, you may want to adjust them to a more modest level.

Creating and implementing a plan

What specific actions are going to be taken

The next step is creating and implementing your plan. This means deciding what specific actions are going to be taken on a daily, weekly, and monthly basis, who will be responsible for executing them, what the expected results will be, and who will accumulate the data and analyze the progress.

If your goal is to increase sales by $2,000 a week, and you want $400 of that to result in net profit, how will this be accomplished?

- *Will you attract new customers?*

- *Will you increase the frequency of visits by your present customers?*

- *Will you strive to increase your average sale?*

You may need to accomplish all of these objectives.

- *But how many new customers will you need, and how will you attract them?*

- *How will you get your present clientele base to visit more often, and how many more times a month will you need them to visit?*

- *How much will you need to increase your average sale to every customer, and how will you accomplish this?*

These are the types of questions that your plan needs to address.

Once you have created a plan which answers all of these questions, you have to take into account the affect of your plan on your net profitability.

- *If you will be increasing your marketing efforts, what will the additional expense of this campaign be?*

- *If you will be running some in-store promotions to entice your present clientele to increase their frequency of visits, what will the additional cost of this promotion be?*

Remember, your goal was not only to increase sales, but also retain 20% of those sales as net profit.

You must analyze the costs associated with your plan to be sure that it will achieve the desired result.

Focusing on the steps and evaluating your progress

Next, you need to focus on the individual steps.

If your goal this week is to raise your per customer revenue by 50 cents, you need to determine what specific action will be taken to accomplish this goal.

- *Will your cashier or barista suggest a double shot for a fuller, more robust coffee flavor in your customer's beverage?*

- *Will they ask your customers if they would like a biscotti or muffin to accompany their coffee?*

- *Will they suggest a half pound of coffee for your customers to enjoy at home?*

You must be able to evaluate the progress

You will need to inform your employees of your goal, and emphasize the importance of their participation in achieving this goal.

You will need to teach them the necessary techniques to achieve this objective.

You will need to reinforce and monitor their actions, so this goal will remain a priority in their minds.

And, you must be able to evaluate the progress on a daily and weekly basis, and provide everyone with feedback as to how they are doing.

Goals achieved? What next?

Finally, what do you do once you have achieved your goals? The answer is twofold:

First, you evaluate the results of the entire goal setting and achieving process that you have just been through. You do this by looking at the process and its results—both as a whole and in detail—and you ask and answer the following questions:

- *What did we achieve?*

- *What did we learn?*

- *What could we have done differently?*

- *How can we do it better next time?*

- *How realistic were our goals?*

- *Were they the right goals?*

And so forth.

And then, it is time to establish new goals and generate a new action plan and repeat the entire process over again. In this way you will guide and grow your business along its ongoing journey to new heights of accomplishment.

 For more information on this specific subject, refer to the following book from Bellissimo—800-655-3955.

- **Achieving Success in Specialty Coffee**

Chapter 39 Check List

Goal Setting:

_____ Establish what you want your business to accomplish and over a specific period of time.

_____ Set a long term goal that will define the growth which will be necessary to move your business from its present level to your desired objective.

_____ Break your long term goal down into a series of short term goals.

_____ Create a plan for achieving your short term goals. Define how these goals will be achieved and what role each staff member will play in achieving them. Analyze the actions and results which will be necessary on a daily basis.

_____ Review your plan and determine if it can be accomplished, and if your goals are realistic.

_____ If it is determined that your goals are not realistic, readjust your goals or your plan.

_____ Inform your staff as to your goals, plans, and their role in relationship to these.

_____ Implement your plan

_____ Assess the results on a daily, weekly, and monthly basis, and keep your staff informed of your progress.

_____ When you have achieved your goals, evaluate the entire goal setting process and the results which were achieved.

_____ Establish new goals and a new plan.

CHAPTER 40

Business Expansion

Contents

Chapter 40 Contents - Page 2

CHAPTER 40

Business Expansion

Expanding a single coffee bar into a multi-location business can be an exciting and profitable venture. The lure of profit, growth, and personal satisfaction works its magic on many coffee entrepreneurs; for others, the added investments of time, money, and headaches may not be worthwhile.

Typically, the first thing people think of when considering business expansion is opening additional locations. But there are other expansion options as well. In this chapter, we look at:

- Different options for expanding your business

- Reasons for considering business expansion

- Concerns and problems of expansion

- The options of franchising and partnering

Types of Business Expansion

Opening additional locations

The most obvious way to expand your business is to open additional locations.

If your market will support additional locations, and if you have enjoyed success with your first operation, you may want to consider this option. We will be exploring the pros and cons of business expansion throughout this chapter.

Enlarging your present facility

Perhaps you have just outgrown your facility, the capacity of your machine, or your seating, and you are actually losing business because your customers have to wait too long, or there is no place for them to sit.

The first thing you may want to consider is enlarging your present facility

The first thing you may want to consider is enlarging your present facility. You need to obtain more square footage so your business can continue to grow.

You can think about moving to a larger location, or expanding into a space next door, or building onto your present building.

Adding new elements to your present concept

We had a client in the Virgin Islands who had a successful pizza operation and then added a second operation selling espresso, sandwiches, and pastries. In essence, he already had a small restaurant to which he added another element to achieve greater overall profitability.

He took over the space next door (which was available), developed an espresso bar operation, and then added it to his pizza restaurant by removing a large proportion of the wall between the two spaces. In this way, he doubled the size of his facility and added a separate business.

The two concepts—since they are both basically Italian in character—complemented each other very nicely. Together, they formed a symbiotic relationship that allowed both businesses to benefit from each other.

The first week he was open his pizza sales were up 25% and coffee sales were strong. People ordering pizza came over and bought pastries and coffee after they had their lunch or dinner. He also noticed a number of clients who stopped in for coffee came back later to have dinner in his pizza operation.

There are numerous options for expanding your business, such as:

- If there is a demand for fresh roasted coffee in your community and there is not a local roaster, you can do some micro roasting in your store.

- If you already have a roasting operation and wish to expand your market, you might consider adding a mail order service to boost your bulk coffee retail sales. There are a number of mail order possibilities to consider, such as setting up a coffee of the month club and/or a web page site on the Internet.

- You may want to expand by taking on additional retail items. Perhaps you are in a small community where there is no outlet for specialized brewing devices like home espresso machines.

- Cyber cafés are becoming very popular. If you are near a college, there will no doubt be a supply of students who do not have a computer and need some place to do their work, or surf the Net. Cyber cafés rent computer time.

- In some small communities there are a limited number of copy shops. Adding a photo copy machine and a couple of computers presents a profitable opportunity.

- Laundromats and coffee bars are a good combination. It gives people something to do and a place to socialize while waiting for their laundry.

Adding an additional "twist" to your present concept

Another reason for expansion would be the addition of a new dimension to your business

Another reason for expansion would be the addition of a new dimension to your business that will require an additional location.

Perhaps you own an existing successful cart operation located at a university, but you see an opportunity and market potential to establish a drive-thru on a major traffic artery. Since you have already acquired the operational experience, the situation would allow you to expand your business without hurting the sales at your other location.

Or perhaps you have an in-line café in a shopping mall, but you find a space in a large office building downtown where you may be able to establish a cart or a kiosk. Viable opportunities that will not negatively affect your first operation should be investigated when considering business expansion.

So, as you can see, a number of different ways exist to expand your business by offering services and products that are needed or desired.

Franchising or partnering your concept

A final way of expanding your business if you have a very successful concept is through franchising or partnering.

If you have multiple units already up and running, and are enjoying a healthy level of profit, others may see value in your concept and be interested in purchasing a similar operation. You can consider either franchising your concept, or partnering with other people. (We discuss both these options later in this chapter.)

Insufficient Reasons For Business Expansion

You need more money

The obvious reason to expand your business is the potential to make more money. But one thing you do not want to consider is expanding your business because you are making insufficient income in your first operation.

You do not want to compound the problem by repeating your errors

If your first operation is just squeezing by, or losing money, this is not a good reason to open a second operation. What you need to do is fix the first one.

Perhaps this means moving to a new location, troubleshooting the operation, or marketing the business—whatever it takes to make it profitable.

The last thing you need is two operations that are not making money. Chances are you have made some mistakes and bad decisions with your first operation. You do not want to compound the problem by repeating your errors.

Maybe a larger space will generate more income?

One of the most foolish business decisions we have ever witnessed was by a gentleman who took over a café and made a major investment by adding additional booths and tables. The café's problem was not insufficient seating capacity, it was insufficient sales volume. He did not need more tables and chairs, he needed more customers to fill the tables and chairs which often sat empty.

You have to make sure that your customer demand exceeds your capacity before you consider enlarging your physical operation.

You will be competing with yourself

If you have a population base that will support additional operations, then by all means consider opening more businesses. But if you are in a limited market where you will split the sales between your two locations, with twice the overhead, you will only be competing with yourself.

Concerns About Business Expansion

When you are considering expanding your business, there are a number of concerns you will want to address, such as:

Key personnel

One major consideration has to do with key personnel. Who is going to run this new business?

If you do not have good people who can help you, you cannot expect the same kind of success you enjoyed in your first operation. You only have so many hours that you can devote to your business, and if you have to divide that time between two operations, both are likely to suffer. To consider a second location, you must have a manager to assist you.

Whoever he or she may be, this person has to be rock solid and someone you can trust. They should preferably have food-service management experience, with a proven track record of success, or at least be extremely trainable.

Market opportunities / location availability

You must honestly ask yourself, does the market opportunity really exist?

Are good locations available?

What is the long-term growth potential?

Operational systems

Is your existing business set up well, with good operational systems, so that the success of your expansion is not totally linked to **your presence** and operational expertise?

If the only reason your business is profitable is because you are spending 70 to 80 hours a week running it hands-on, how will you possibly run two?

If your business is not set up with strong operational systems that will allow someone else to duplicate what you are doing, then you will have problems in controlling all the aspects of a second operation.

To achieve quality and consistency in two operations, training and quality control procedures are absolutely essential.

Headaches vs. additional income

One final concern are all those headaches you will be dealing with by owning a second location. You will have to weigh these against the amount of additional income you will be gaining.

What is really going to be the net gain

Perhaps the most important consideration in opening a second location is overhead. How long will it take for the second operation to pay its own way? And how long will the first shop be able to sustain the overhead of the second?

Certainly, it is going to be more demanding to run two operations. So you really have to ask yourself:

- *How much additional income am I really going to generate?*

- *How much will my established operation have to suffer while I am opening and managing my second?*

- *What is really going to be the net gain after the additional investment, monthly expenses, and taxation?*

- *Will it really be worth my time and the headaches to run two operations?*

Duplicating successful fundamentals

When you open additional operations, do not forget those fundamentals that brought you success the first time. You put all the elements together properly—great location, attractive physical plant, good people well trained in customer service, quality product, etc. Now you have to duplicate these same principles and invest the same energy into every one of your new operations.

Do not forget those fundamentals that brought you success the first time

You cannot sustain yourself with the glow of success from your first operation. If your second operation has a mediocre location, you cannot rely on the fact that you now have strong name recognition to overcome this weak fundamental.

Do not risk your first operation by making bad decisions with your second operation.

Franchising or Partnering Prerequisites

The final options for business expansion are franchising or partnering your concept.

Before you consider doing this you will need to demonstrate the following:

A proven track record

The necessary "proven track record" that says you are ready to franchise or partner with someone to open additional operations, is generally recognized in the industry as a minimum of three to five profitable, up-and-running units. But sometimes it may take as many as ten.

Of course, this is not always true.

You may find someone who will buy a franchise from you even though you only have one operation turning marginal profit...it does happen. But the average intelligent investor will want to see a proven commodity before they are going to pay you a franchise fee and give you a percentage of their gross revenue.

A cookie-cutter concept

A franchise operation usually requires what we call a "cookie-cutter concept." In other words, every operation needs to be the same. With the cookie-cutter concept, you are duplicating all the elements of success—your store design, systems, menus, etc.

Potential buyers look for this in a franchise. They do not want every unit to be a new innovation.

They will buy your franchise because you already have a proven track record of success, and you can provide them with these same proven elements.

Franchising vs. partnering

Franchising and partnering are two different ways by which you can help other people to open and operate businesses and derive income from helping them.

Franchising is the most common option, and the one that comes most readily to the minds of most people.

The other option is partnering.

Each has some advantages.

In Chapter 16—*To Franchise or Not to Franchise,* we talked about the advantages and disadvantages of *buying* a franchise. But if you are trying to *create and sell* your own franchise concept, there are some very real additional challenges to face.

Expense and headaches

One of the challenges of franchising your operation is the expense of doing all the legal paperwork. Franchising can be **very** costly and complex. Certain legal considerations may come into play, like protection of the franchisee, and having exclusive rights to certain franchise areas, or having a certain number of units within an area.

We were told by a leading national franchise attorney that generally there is a honeymoon period after you sell a franchise to someone. For the first year, things generally go pretty well. The franchisees are still excited about their new business, and if they are not making money yet, they are sure things will get better.

But from that point on, you may start to have some problems. You might have a great concept, but that does not guarantee that your franchisee will be as competent, dedicated, or passionate an operator as you are. And if your franchisees are not enjoying the same level of success as you, their tendency is not to look at themselves and ask,

What am I doing wrong?

They are more likely to think,

I've been sold a bill of goods.

At this point, you may be dealing with a lot of hostile feelings and possibly a lawsuit.

If your franchisees are not enjoying the same level of success as you...

Risking your image and losing control

You can risk your image with franchising and lose your control.

Your franchisee has paid for the right to use your concept and name, but what if they do not maintain the quality?

What if they keep a dirty store?

What if their employees are not as friendly and customer-oriented as yours?

The customer may not know or care that it is a franchise. They may think that this franchise coffee operation is the same as your coffee operation. If they receive bad customer service or a product of poor quality, they are going to assume that your operation is also operated the same way.

Do you really want to work with these people?

Ask yourself:

Do I really want to work with these people?

In a franchise situation, most often if a buyer "bellies up to the bar" and has the money, and wants to buy a franchise, you have to sell them a franchise.

But you must consider if they are people you can work with. You have to ask yourself:

- *Do they have the same passion for the product?*

- *Do they have the business expertise?*

- *Are they going to damage my good name?*

- *Am I really going to benefit from selling my operation to these people?*

Partnering

An alternative to franchising is partnering. It is another way to expand that has certain advantages over franchising.

Partnering is when someone buys into your business and becomes a part-owner with you. However, you can still maintain control.

Typically, you will want to own 51%, and sell them 49%.

Once again, check with your professionals

They put all the up-front money into their unit. You provide the start-up and operational expertise, the sources for the equipment and products, and the ongoing training and operational support.

You take your percentage off the top just like a franchiser would. The difference is that you have avoided the franchise paperwork, and you retain ultimate control because you own 51% of the business.

You can always buy them out if they are not operating profitably and are hurting your good name.

You must once again check with your professionals, especially your attorney, about their feelings on the benefits of franchising or partnering, given your particular situation.

Careful consideration and well thought-out planning is vital to the success of your expansion plans. All your options should be examined equally. If you can justify expansion, then by all means go ahead and do it. But realize that a lot of people are happier running one very successful operation, than trying to manage several.

 For more information on this specific subject, refer to the following book from Bellissimo—800-655-3955.

- **Achieving Success in Specialty Coffee**

APPENDIX 1

Operational Forms

Index of Forms

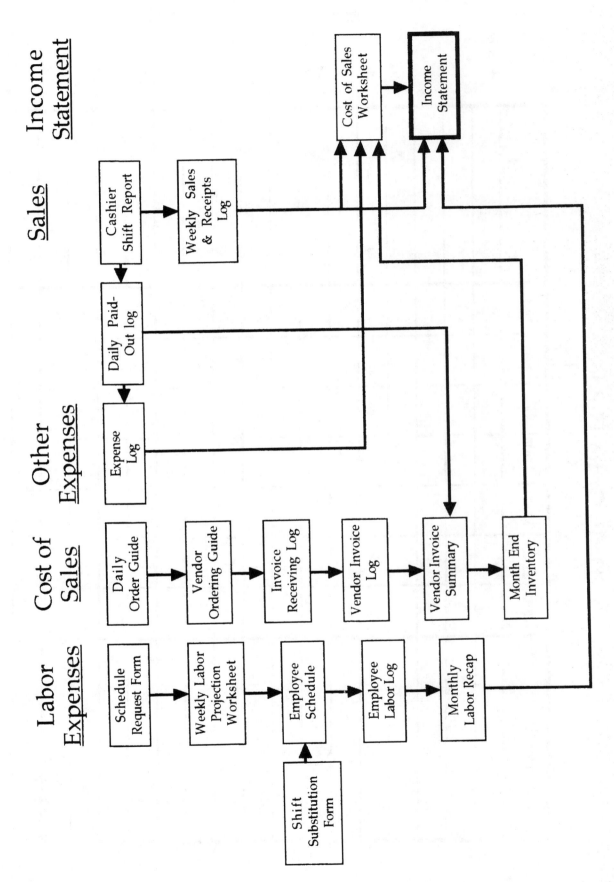

Daily Order Guide

O = Order Day / D = Delivery Day

Company	Mon	Tues	Wed	Thur	Fri	Sat	Sun	Phone #

Vendor Ordering Guide

Vendor _____

Product	Order Unit	Par	/ OH Use	Order	/ OH Use	Order	/ OH Use	Order	/ OH Use	Order	/ OH Use	Order

Invoice Receiving Log

Day / Date	Vendor	Invoice #	Invoice $	Received By	Logged

Vendor Invoice Log

Month _____ Year _____ Vendor _____

Inv. Date	Invoice Number	Invoice Total	Pay Date	Check Number	Food	Coffee Beverage	Other Beverage	Bulk Coffee	Hard Goods	Paper / Chemical	Small Wares	Laundry & Uniform	Other	Description
TOTALS														

Vendor Invoice Summary

Month_____ Year_____

VENDOR	# of Inv.	Total Purchases	Food	Coffee Beverage	Other Beverage	Bulk Coffee	Hard Goods	Paper / Chemical	Small Wares	Laundry & Uniform	Other	Description
Paid Outs												
TOTALS												

Month End Inventory

Cost of Goods Category_____ Month_____

Location_____

Page_____

Year_____

Item	Inv. Unit	Count	Unit Price	Total $

Page Total

Cost of Sales Worksheet

Location_____   Month_____   Year_____

Food
  Beginning Inventory $_____
  Purchases   + $_____
  Ending Inventory   - $_____
  Cost of Goods   = $_____

Coffee Beverages
  Beginning Inventory $_____
  Purchases   + $_____
  Ending Inventory   - $_____
  Cost of Goods   = $_____

Other Beverages
  Beginning Inventory $_____
  Purchases   + $_____
  Ending Inventory   - $_____
  Cost of Goods   = $_____

Whole Coffee Beans
  Beginning Inventory $_____
  Purchases   + $_____
  Ending Inventory   - $_____
  Cost of Goods   = $_____

Hard Goods
  Beginning Inventory $_____
  Purchases   + $_____
  Ending Inventory   - $_____
  Cost of Goods   = $_____

Paper & Chemicals
  Beginning   Inventory $_____
  Purchases   + $_____
  Ending Inventory   - $_____
  Cost of Goods   = $_____

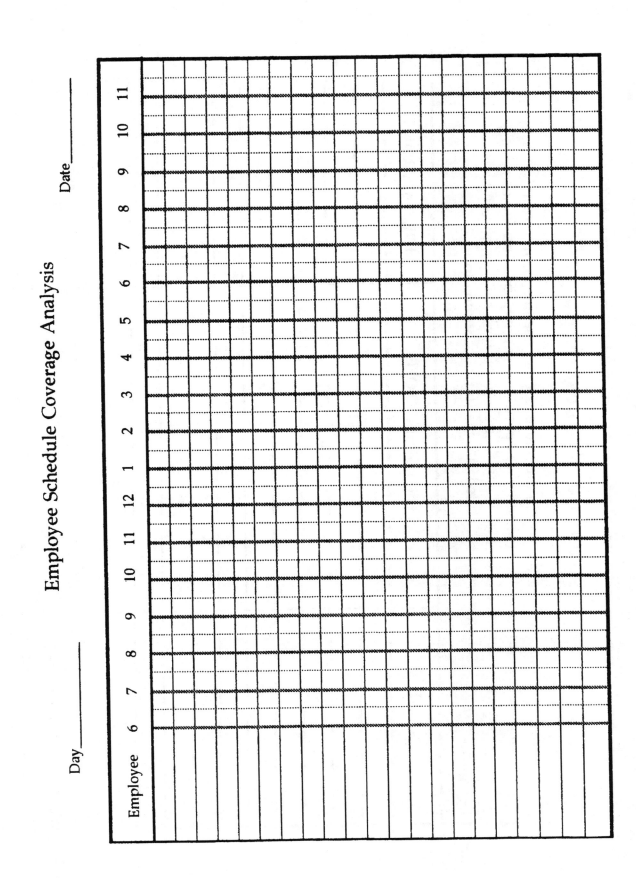

Employee Schedule Coverage Analysis

Day_____   Date_____

Schedule Request Form

Use this form to request time off in the future. Do not use this form to request time off on a schedule which has already been posted. You are responsible for all shifts you have been scheduled for. If you desire time off for a shift which you have already been scheduled, use the shift substitution form.

NAME	DATE(S) DESIRED OFF	MGRS. APPROVAL

Weekly Labor Projection Worksheet
Week beginning Monday / / - ending Sunday / /

Employee	Wage Rate	Mon. hrs	Mon. $	Tues. hrs	Tues. $	Wed. hrs	Wed. $	Thurs. hrs	Thurs. $	Fri. hrs	Fri. $	Sat. hrs	Sat. $	Sun. hrs	Sun. $	Total hrs / $
Total Hrs / $																

Shift Substitution Form

Use this form when someone else will be working your scheduled shift.
All substitutions must be approved by management.

SCHEDULED EMPLOYEE	SUBSTITUTING EMPLOYEE	SHIFT INFORMATION			MANAGERS APPROVAL
		DAY	DATE	TIME	

Employee Schedule

Week beginning Monday / / - ending Sunday / /

Employee	Mon.	Tues.	Wed.	Thurs.	Fri.	Sat.	Sun.

Labor Card

Name	Shift	Sch. Hours	Actual Hours
	( )		
	( )		
	( )		
	( )		
	( )		
	( )		
	( )		
	( )		
	( )		
	( )		
	( )		
	( )		
	( )		
	( )		
	( )		
	( )		
	( )		
	( )		
	( )		
	( )		
	( )		
	( )		
	( )		
	( )		
	( )		
	( )		
	( )		

Employee Timecard Recap

Month_____ Year_____

Date															Reg. Hrs $	O.T. Hrs $	Tot. Hrs $
Day																	
Employee	Rate																
Daily Totals																	
MTD Proj. $																	
MTD Actual $																	

Monthly Labor Recap

Month_____   Year_____

Week of / Department	/ – / Proj (H/$)	/ – / Act (H/$)	/ – / Proj (H/$)	/ – / Act (H/$)	/ – / Proj (H/$)	/ – / Act (H/$)	/ – / Proj (H/$)	/ – / Act (H/$)	Total Proj (H/$)	Total Act (H/$)
Management $										
Total Hours										
Total Dollars										
+ or – Hours										
+ or – Dollars										

Expense Log

Month_____ Year_____

Page 1

PAYEE	Inv. Date	Inv. #	Pay Date	Check #	Invoice Total	Wages/ Salaries	Payroll Taxes	Office Supplies	Printing	Repair & Maint.	Phone	Utilities	Garbage Service
1													
2													
3													
4													
5													
6													
7													
8													
9													
10													
11													
12													
13													
14													
15													
16													
17													
18													
19													
Paid Outs													
Totals													

Expense Log

Month _____ Year _____

	Janitorial Service	Sales Tax Payable	Advertising & Promos	Rent Charges	Loan Payments	Interest Payments	Insurance	Bank Charges	Licenses & Permits	Professional Services	Other	Description
1												
2												
3												
4												
5												
6												
7												
8												
9												
10												
11												
12												
13												
14												
15												
16												
17												
18												
19												

Daily Paid-Out Log

Month _____ Year _____

Date	Payee	Chk # or Cash?	Total Purch.	Food	Coffee Bev.	Other Bev.	Bulk Coffee	Hard Goods	Paper / Chem.	Small Wares	Laundry & Unif.	Office Supp.	Printing	Repair/ Maint.	Other $ / Description
TOTALS															

Cashier Shift Report

Cashier_____

Date _____ Shift _____

Cash $ _____
Coin   +$ _____
Checks   +$ _____
Charges   +$ _____
  Total Deposit   = $ _____

Register Tape Total $ _____
Over Rings   - $ _____
Promos / Comps   - $ _____
Coupons / Discounts   - $ _____
Employee Meals   - $ _____
Paid Outs   - $ _____
  Total Receipts   = $ _____

Cash Over / Short $ _____

Notes_____

_____

_____

_____

Weekly Sales & Receipts Recap

Month _____ Year _____

															Week Totals	MTD Totals
DAY																
DATE																
Cash																
Coin																
Checks																
Charges																
Total Deposit																
Register Tape Total																
Over Rings																
Net Sales																
•Food Sales																
•Coffee Bev. Sales																
•Other Bev. Sales																
•Bulk Bean Sales																
•Hard Good Sales																
Promos / Comps																
Coupons / Discounts																
Employee Meals																
Paid Outs																
Total Receipts																
Cash Over / Short																

Income Statement

Location_____

For the month of:_____ Year_____

| | Projected | | Actual | |
	$	%	$	%
Sales				
Food	-------	----	-------	----
Coffee Beverages	-------	----	-------	----
Other Beverages	-------	----	-------	----
Bulk Coffee	-------	----	-------	----
Hard Goods	-------	----	-------	----
Sales Tax Collected	-------	----	-------	----
Promos/Comps	-------	----	-------	----
Total Sales	-------	----	-------	----
Cost of Sales				
Food	-------	----	-------	----
Coffee Beverages	-------	----	-------	----
Other Beverages	-------	----	-------	----
Bulk Coffee	-------	----	-------	----
Hard Goods	-------	----	-------	----
Paper & Chemicals	-------	----	-------	----
Total Cost of Sales	-------	----	-------	----
Gross Profit from Sales	-------	----	-------	----
Expenses				
Wages				
Management	-------	----	-------	----
Employee	-------	----	-------	----
Payroll Taxes/ Benefits				
Payroll Taxes	-------	----	-------	----
Employee Meals	-------	----	-------	----
Total Labor Costs	-------	----	-------	----

(continued)

Controllable Expenses
   Small Wares
   Laundry/ Uniform
   Office Supplies
   Printing
   Promos/ Comps
   Repairs & Maintenance
   Phone
   Utilities
   Garbage Service
   Janitorial Service
   Sales Tax Payable
   Cash over/ short
   Advertising
   Misc. Expenses
Fixed Expenses
   Rent/ Payment
   Loan Payments
   Interest
   Business Insurance
   Bank Charges/ Discounts
   Licenses & Permits
   Professional Fees
   Depreciation

   Total Expenses

Profit / Loss

Year to Date

Barista's Beverage Quick Reference Guide

Beverage Name & Description	Regular (shot)	Large (shot)	Grande (shot)
Espresso *(use demitasse cup)* An extracted straight shot(s) of coffee.	Single (1 1/2 oz.)	Double (3 oz.)	N/A
Caffe Americano A straight shot(s) of espresso with the addition of hot water from the espresso machine.	Single	Single*	Double
Cappuccino A straight shot(s) of espresso combined with a velvety milk foam.	Single	Double	N/A
Caffe Latte A straight shot(s) of espresso combined with steamed milk, topped with 1/2 inch foam.	Single	Single*	Double
Flavored Caffe Latte follow same procedure as Caffe Latte but add flavored syrup directly to extracted shot(s) of espresso and stir before adding milk.	Single	Single*	Double

(Typical amount of syrup added)
1/2 oz.   3/4 oz.   1 oz.

| **Caffe Mocha** Follow same procedure as Caffe Latte but add chocolate syrup or powder to espresso & stir before adding milk. Top with whipped cream and chocolate garnish. | Single | Single* | Double |

(continued)

Beverage Name & Description	Regular (shot)	Large (shot)	Grande (shot)
Café Ole Extract a shot(s) of espresso. Fill the cup to the half way level with brewed coffee. Add steamed milk & top with whipped cream.	Single	Single*	Double
Espresso Macchiato *(use demitasse cup)* Extract a shot(s) of espresso. Top with one spoon of velvety milk foam.	Single	Double	N/A
Espresso con Panna *(use demitasse cup)* Extract a shot(s) of espresso. Top with a dollop of whipped cream.	Single	Double	N/A
Breve Follow same procedure as Caffe Latte substituting half & half for the milk.	Single	Single*	Double

Lungo (long shot): A term which refers to the volume of the shot, Typically a 1 1/2 ounce single shot.

Ristretto (short shot): A term which refers to the volume of the shot, Typically a 3/4 ounce single shot.

*This beverage size is price calculated for a single shot. The customer should be offered an additional shot for a more robust coffee flavor for an additional charge of _____.

Iced Beverages
The following beverages may also be served iced upon the customer's request: **Americano; Caffe Latte; Flavored Caffe Latte; Caffe Mocha; Café Ole; Breve.** Flavored lattes & mochas should still have the syrup or chocolate combined with the hot espresso first and then stirred. Pour espresso into a cold cup, fill with ice, add cold milk directly from the milk carton.

Set-Up / Production Guide

Item	Inventory Unit	Daily Par Level							On Hand	Needed
		Mon	Tues	Wed	Thur	Fri	Sat	Sun		

APPENDIX 2

Industry Resources

Coffee Industry Trade Publications

Fresh Cup Magazine
P.O. Box 14827
Portland, OR 97293-0827
Tel: 503-236-2587 / 800-868-5866
Fax: 503-236-3165
www.freshcup.com

Specialty Coffee Retailer
250 S. Wacker, Suite 1150
Chicago, IL 60606
Tel: 312-977-0999 / 856-786-7293
Fax: 312-980-3135
www.specialty-coffee.com

Tea & Coffee Trade Journal
26 Broadway, Floor 9M
New York, NY 10004
Tel: 212-391-2060 / 800-766-2633
Fax: 212-827-0945
www.teaandcoffee.net

The Gourmet Retailer Magazine
3301 Ponce de Leon Blvd., Suite 300
Coral Gables, FL 33134-7273
Tel: 305-446-3388 / 800-397-1137
Fax: 305-446-2868
www.gourmetretailer.com

Fancy Food Magazine
20 N. Wacker Drive, Suite 1865
Chicago, IL 60606
Tel: 312-849-2220
Fax: 312-849-2174
www.fancyfoodmagazine.com

Coffee & Beverage Magazine

P.O. Box 54583
1771 Avenue Road
Toronto, ON M5M 4N5
Canada
Tel: 416-784-3831
Fax: 416-784-1283
www.coffeeculture.net

Planet Coffee

Via Fortunio 1
Trieste, 34141
Italy
Tel: +39 040 9380764 / +39 040 9380891
Fax: +39 040 945101
www.planet-coffeemagazine.com

Coffee & Cocoa International

2 Queensway
Redhill, Surrey RH1 1QS
United Kingdom
Tel: +44 1737 768 611
Fax: +44 1737 855 470
www.dmgworldmedia.com

Tea & Coffee Asia

Lockwood Trade Journal Co., Inc.
SNC Tower Unit 11E
33 Soi 4 Sukhumvit Road, Klong Toey
Bankok 10110
Thailand
Tel: +66 2 656 9394/5
Fax: +66 2 656 9396
www.teacoffeeasia.com

Beverage Retailer

307 West Jackson Ave.
Oxford, MS 38655
Tel: 800-247-3881 / 662-236-5510.
Fax: 662-236-5541
www.beverage-retailer.com

VirtualCoffee.com

Web 'Zine, on-line magazine for the coffee consumer
www.virtualcoffee.com

Forum Café
 Forum Cultural del Café
 C/ Fontanella, 21-23, 2a planta
 08010 Barcelona, Espana
 Tel: +93 412 20 90
 Fax: +93 317 04 62
 www.forum-cafe.com

Coffee Industry Associations

Specialty Coffee Association of America (SCAA)
One World Trade Center, Suite 1200
Long Beach, CA 90831-1200
Tel: 562-624-4100
Fax: 562-624-4101
www.scaa.org

National Coffee Association
15 Maiden Lane, Suite 1405
New York, NY 10038-4003
Tel: 212-766-4007
Fax: 212-766-5815
www.ncausa.org

Coffee Association of Canada
855 Don Mills Road, Suite 301
Don Mills, ON M3C 1V9
Canada
Tel: 416-510-8032
Fax: 416-510-8044
www.coffeeassoc.com

Brazil Specialty Coffee Association
Cx. Postal 30 - 37130-000
Alfenas - Minas Gerais - Brazil
Tel: +55 35 3292 1880
Fax: +55 35 3291 9077
www.bsca.com.br

Specialty Coffee Association of Europe (SCAE)
Brook Meadow Cottage
Mid Holmwood Lane
Dorking, Surrey, RH5 4HE
United Kingdom
Tel: +44 1306 743524
Fax: +44 1306 743527
www.scae.com

627

Coffee Industry Tradeshows

Contact the following organizations for current show dates and locations:

NASCORE
P.O. Box 14827
Portland, OR 97293
Tel: 503-236-2587 / 800-548-0551
Fax: 503-236-3165
www.freshcup.com/nascore

SCAA Conference & Exhibition
Specialty Coffee Association of America (SCAA)
One World Trade Center, Suite 1200
Long Beach, CA 90831-1200
Tel: 562-624-4100
Fax: 562-624-4101
www.scaa.org

Coffee Fest
P.O. Box 1158
9655 SE 36th St., Suite 101 A
Mercer Island, WA 98404-1158
Tel: 206-232-2982 / 800-232-0083
Fax: 206-236-5241
www.coffeefest.com

NCA Annual Convention
National Coffee Association
15 Maiden Lane, Suite 1405
New York, NY 10038-4003
Tel: 212-766-4007
Fax: 212-766-5815
www.ncausa.org

**International Food & Beverage
Restaurant, Bar and Hospitality Show**
307 West Jackson Ave.
Oxford, MS 38665
Tel: 800-247-3881 / 662-236-5510
Fax: 662-281-0104
www.restaurant-marketing.net

Major International Shows:

The Canadian Coffee & Tea Expo
P.O. Box 54583
1771 Avenue Road
Toronto, ON M5M 4N5
Canada
Tel: 416-784-3831
Fax: 416-784-1283
www.coffeeculture.net

European Specialty Coffee Conference & Exhibition
Specialty Coffee Association of Europe (SCAE)
Brook Meadow Cottage
Mid Holmwood Lane
Dorking, Surrey, RH5 4HE
United Kingdom
Tel: +44 1306 743524
Fax: +44 1306 743527
www.scae.com

Coffee International Conference & Exhibition
Coffee & Cocoa International
2 Queensway
Redhill, Surrey RH1 1QS
United Kingdom
Tel: +44 01737 855 294
Fax: +44 01737 855 470
www.coffeeinternational.co.uk

Tea & Coffee World Cup Exhibition & Symposium / Asia, Europe
Tea & Coffee Asia, Lockwood Trade Journal Co., Inc.
SNC Tower Unit 11E
33 Soi 4 Sukhumvit Road, Klong Toey
Bankok 10110
Thailand
Tel: +66 2656 9394/5
Fax: +66 2656 9396
www.tcworldcup.net

Coffee Resource Directory

A complete directory for the following coffee industry categories can be found under "Coffee Resources" on the Web site **www.coffeeuniverse.com**. This site is updated on a weekly basis.

Coffee Business Categories:

Apparel/Uniform

Baked Goods

Biscotti

Bottled Beverages

Brewing Equipment Home

Brewing Equipment Commercial

Café Design/Construction

Cart/Kiosk Manufacturer

Cash Registers/Computer Systems/P.O.S.

Chocolate/Cocoas

Cleaning Products

Coffee Accessories

Coffee Houses/Cyber Cafes

Coffee Roasters

Coffee Bar Candies

Consultants

Cooking & Heating Equipment

Display Fixtures

Drive-thru & Mobile Espresso Structures

Espresso Equipment Commercial

Espresso Equipment Home

Espresso Machine Service/Repair/Parts

Flavors/Condiments

Franchises

Granita Products/Mixes/Smoothies

Graphic Design/Logo Development

Green Bean Coffee Import/Broker

Grinders

Interior Design/Furniture

Mail-order Coffee

Menu Board/Signage

Miscellaneous Coffee Organizations/Groups/Services

News Groups

Organic Coffee

Packing Equipment & Goods

Paper Products

Private Labeling

Professional Organizations

Professional Services

Publications

Refrigeration Equipment

Publications

Refrigeration Equipment

Retail Merchandise

Roasting Equipment

Shipping/Storage

Small Wares

Syrup

Tea Accessories

Tea Importers/Brokers

Tea/Chai Distributors

Trade Shows

Training Materials/Education

Travel

Water Filtration

Glossary of Terms

AA or AAA	Grade indicators associated with large size green coffee beans.
Acidity	Sharp, bright, vibrant quality related to the flavor of coffee. A sensation of dryness that the coffee produces under the edge of the tongue.
Aftertaste	Lingering taste on the palate after the coffee is swallowed.
Aged Coffees	Green coffee beans which have been carefully held in warehouses for several years in order to reduce acidity and increase body.
Air Roaster	Also known as a "fluid bed roaster" or a "Sivetz roaster." A machine which roasts green coffee beans as they tumble on a current of hot air.
Americano	Beverage made from espresso combined with hot water, producing a gourmet version of an "American-style" cup of coffee.
Arabica	The species of coffee which is highest in quality and possesses superior characteristics of flavor and aroma; typically grown between 2,000 and 6,000 feet in elevation.
Aroma	The sensation created by the gasses escaping from freshly ground or brewed coffee which contributes to discerning flavors.
Automatic Espresso Machine	A variation of a semiautomatic espresso machine which has been calibrated to release a specified amount of pressurized brewing water through the ground coffee.
Back Flushing	Process of cleaning an espresso machine by forcing water backwards through the group head.

Balance	A coffee characteristic in which flavor, aroma and body are in symmetry.
Barista	(Italian for bartender) An expert with a professional level of understanding in making espresso and espresso beverages.
Batch Roaster	A mechanical roasting machine that roasts a given quantity of coffee at one time (a batch).
Bean Hopper	A storage container which sits above the burrs of a grinder and where gravity feeds the whole roasted coffee beans into the grinding mechanism.
Bitter	Describes a taste perceived near the rear of the tongue, sometimes associated with over-roasting or over-extraction. A slight bittersweet characteristic is typical of dark roasted coffees and is appealing to some consumers.
Blend	A mixture of two or more varietals.
Boiler	A pressurized tank within an espresso machine in which water is heated to produce steam, and which heats an exchanger containing the brewing water.
Brevé	Any milk-based espresso beverage in which half & half is substituted for milk.
Body	The sensation of viscosity, heaviness, thickness, or richness that the coffee produces in the mouth.
Caffé	Italian for coffee.
Caffé Americano	See Americano.
Caffé Latté	See Latté.
Caffeine	Natural chemical stimulant found in coffee.
Char	Charcoal-like flavor characteristic found in very dark roasted or over-roasted coffee beans.
Coffeol	Oil-like substance created during the roasting process which gives the coffee its flavor.

Cappuccino	An espresso-based beverage consisting of approximately 1 part espresso and 4 parts wet milk foam.
Complexity	The perception of multiple flavors and taste sensations.
Creamosa	An Italian soda with the addition of a small amount of half & half to create a gourmet cream soda.
Crema	A dense golden brown layer of frothed coffee oils which float on top of a properly extracted espresso. This foam is where the majority of flavor and aroma exist.
Cupping	Tasting procedure used to determine the quality of a roasted coffee.
Decaffeinated	Coffee with 97% of the caffeine removed from the whole bean.
Demitasse	A small cup, usually porcelain, with a 2 to 3 ounce capacity; used for serving espresso.
Doppio	Italian for "double"— see Double.
Doser	The component of an espresso grinder that dispenses servings of ground coffee to the portafilter.
Double	Double shot of espresso using 14 to 16 grams of ground coffee to produce 1 1/2 to 3 ounces of espresso.
Drip Method	Method of brewing coffee in which hot water settles through coffee grounds.
Dry Process	A process of drying whole coffee berries and then removing the fruit from the seed with a mechanical husker.
Espresso	A method of brewing in which hot water is forced under pressure through finely ground coffee, creating a coffee extract.
Espresso Machine	Equipment for producing espresso coffee and its beverages. The machine must produce a group head pressure of 130 pounds per square inch, and maintain a temperature of 192° to 198° Fahrenheit to produce the desired extraction. It must also produce prolonged steaming power to heat and froth milk.

Espresso Lungo	(Italian: long) 1 1/2 ounces of espresso extracted from 7 to 8 grams of coffee in approximately 25 to 30 seconds.
Espresso Macchiato	See Macchiato.
Espresso con Panna	(Italian: with cream) Straight shot of espresso topped with a small amount of whipped cream.
Espresso Roast	A very dark roasted coffee, almost black in color. Typically those coffees which are represented as espresso roasts are actually too dark to produce the best espresso.
Estate Coffee	Coffee from a medium sized plantation or a group of cooperative growers.
Extraction	The process of forcing pressurized water through ground coffee to produce espresso.
Filter Basket	The metal perforated cup which fits inside the portafilter and holds the ground coffee.
Filter Method	Method of brewing in which water settles through the ground coffee contained within a filter.
Finish	The aftertaste of a coffee which lingers on the palate after it has been swallowed; the length of the finish is directly related to the body of the coffee.
Flavored Coffees	Roasted coffee beans which have been sprayed with a flavor extract, or brewed coffee or espresso which has been flavored with an extract or flavored syrup.
Flavor	The overall perception of the coffee in your mouth. Acidity, aroma, and body are all components of flavor.
Foamed Milk	A velvety, small-celled foam which is created when hot steam and air are injected into milk.
French Press	A device used for infusion brewing; also known as a plunger pot. Coarsely ground coffee is covered with hot brewing water and allowed to steep for several minutes. The grounds are then forced through the water and trapped at the bottom of the cylindrical pot by a screen filter attached to a plunger.

French Roast	Coffee roasted to a very dark brown or almost black color.
Fully Automatic Machine	A fully automated espresso machine which grinds, doses, tamps the coffee, extracts the espresso, steams and foams the milk, and dispenses finished espresso beverages.
Full-City Roast	The darkest roast of a bean without oil budding onto its surface; typically a deep chocolate-brown in color.
Grandé	(Italian: large) Typically an espresso-based beverage served in a 16-ounce cup, using a minimum of 14 grams of coffee.
Granita	(Italian: little granules) A dense, slush-like, fruit or coffee flavored beverage.
Green Coffee	Coffee before it is roasted. The name refers to the greenish tint of the unroasted bean.
Grinder	1. Blade Grinder—an inexpensive homestyle coffee grinder that batters the roasted coffee beans into pieces with a spinning blade. 2. Burr Grinder—an apparatus with corrugated, rotating blades, that mills roasted coffee beans, and is adjustable. Possesses the capability of producing a variety of ground coffee consistencies.
Group	The component of an espresso machine which includes the group head and the portafilter.
Group Head	The component of the espresso machine which holds the portafilter, and from which the brewing water is dispensed.
Hard Bean Coffee	Term used to describe dense, slow maturing, high altitude coffee beans which are considered to be superior in quality.
Heat Exchanger	A tube within the boiler of an espresso machine in which the brew water travels and is heated.
High-Grown	Coffee beans grown at an altitude of 2,000 feet or more. The term is usually associated with high quality Arabica coffees.
Iced Espresso Beverages	Espresso-based beverages served cold over ice.
In-line	A term used to describe an espresso bar or coffee cafe.

Italian Roast	See Espresso Roast.
Italian Soda	Cold soda or sparkling mineral water poured over ice and combined with a flavored syrup.
Kiosk	A portable espresso operation, commonly multi-sided, with a more upscale and permanent appearance as compared to an espresso cart.
Knock Box	Container into which the spent grounds from the portafilter are disposed.
Latté	(Italian: milk) A condensed name for the caffé latté, which is espresso combined with steamed milk, topped with a thin layer of milk foam. A flavored syrup can be added creating a flavored latté.
Light Roast	Roasted beans which are cinnamon to light chocolate-tan in color, producing a sharp, acidic taste.
Macchiato	(Italian: marked) Espresso marked with a dollop of steamed milk foam on top (typically 1 teaspoon).
Macchinesti	Professional trainer and technician of espresso preparation.
Medium Roast	Coffee beans roasted to a medium or milk chocolate brown color. Also known as "American roast."
Mild	Term used to describe a coffee lacking any overriding characteristic.
Milk Thermometer	A thermometer used to monitor the temperature of milk during the foaming and steaming process.
Mocha	Espresso with steamed milk and flavored with chocolate (syrup, sauce or cocoa); usually topped with milk foam and/or whipped cream.
New Crop	Green coffee beans delivered for roasting within a short period of time after picking and processing. New crop coffees will typically be higher in acidity and possess greater aroma.
Organic Coffee	Coffee that is grow without the use of pesticides or herbicides.

638

Over-extraction	Term used when water remains in contact with the ground coffee for too long a period of time, or excessive water is poured through the ground coffee, resulting in a bitter extraction.
Peaberry	One small round bean which develops in the cherry (as opposed to the normal two). These are many times segregated from the other beans and typically command a higher price for their favorable flavor characteristics.
Percolation	Method of brewing coffee in which boiling water is forced up through a tube and then filters through ground coffee.
Portafilter	Part of an espresso machine that fits into the group head which holds the filter basket and the ground coffee.
Pyrolysis	The chemical transformations that occur within the bean during the roasting process which contribute to the compounds that create aroma, flavor, and body.
Rancidity	A rancid taste in brewed coffee resulting from spoiled coffee oils.
Recovery Time	The amount of time an espresso machine needs to recover between extractions/steaming to produce sufficient temperatures for proper operation.
Richness	Describing a satisfying fullness in flavor, body and acidity.
Ristretto	(Italian: restricted) A short shot of espresso achieved by stopping the machine partway through extraction. Typically, a 3/4 ounce single extraction occurring in 18 to 20 seconds.
Roast	Process of cooking coffee beans in which the sugars, starches, and fats within the coffee bean are caramelized and the coffee oils are created.
Robusta	Species of coffee which grows best at lower elevations. It possesses the least amount of flavor and aroma, and the highest content of caffeine.
Semiautomatic Machine	Electronic espresso machine that uses a pump to push water through coffee grounds. The brew cycle must be started and stopped by the manipulation of a control.

Short	A term typically used to describe an 8-ounce size beverage. beverage
Short Shot	See Ristretto.
Soft Bean Coffee	A term which typically refers to lower altitude, fast maturing coffees from soft porous beans; contains less acidity and flavor.
Sourness	Taste associated with unripened or overly acidic coffees; reminiscent of unripe fruit.
Specialty Coffee	Gourmet coffee consisting of the top 10% of quality Arabica beans.
Specialty Coffee Association of America	(SCAA) An organization of specialty coffee retailers, wholesalers, and roasters.
Steamed Milk	Milk heated to 140° to 160° Fahrenheit with the steam wand of the espresso machine.
Steam Wand	Used to steam and froth milk. It is a metal tube attached to an espresso machine which expels pressurized steam from the machine's boiler.
Steamer	Espresso-free drink, usually a combination of steamed and/or frothed milk with flavored syrup.
Supremo	A term applied to Colombian coffees that signifies a large bean size.
Swiss Water Process	A specific water decaffeination process that incorporates no chemical solvents in removing the caffeine.
Syrup	Sweet, thick, flavored liquids added to a beverage.
Tall	Typically refers to a 12-ounce beverage.
Tamper	Hand-held tool used to pack espresso coffee in a portafilter.
Under-extraction	Term used to describe the failure to extract all of the coffee's flavor, leaving it behind in the coffee grounds. Occurs when hot water passes too quickly through the coffee, or if the water temperature is insufficient.

Vacuum-Filter Method	Method of brewing in which a vacuum pulls the water through ground coffee.
Varietal Coffee	Unblended coffees from a specific country or growing region.
Tamp	Process of compacting ground espresso coffee in a portafilter.
Viennese Coffee	1. Refers to a drip or filter brew method using a Viennese Roast or Light French Roast. 2. Brewed coffee topped with whipped cream.
Whole Bean Coffee	Coffees which are in a whole bean form and have not been ground.
Wet-Processed	Process of removing the coffee berry's skin and pulp by a soaking and washing process before drying occurs.

642

Bellissimo Products and Services

Consulting

www.espresso101.com

Bellissimo is dedicated to the growth and success of the specialty coffee industry. The focus of our consulting division is to assist individuals in all aspects of creating new coffee businesses and to provide counseling beneficial to existing operations. Our worldwide client list includes Fortune 500 companies as well as American and international entrepreneurs.

Why are Bellissimo's Coffee Business Consulting Services Different?

Bellissimo differs from most industry consultants in that we only sell educational products and expert advice. We do not represent, or have any contractual agreements with, coffee or equipment companies. Our only objective is to maximize your chance for success. We work for our clients with the same passion as if their businesses were our own.

Many in the coffee industry call themselves consultants, but in most cases their primary occupations are directly related to equipment or coffee sales. Will the information they provide you with really be unbiased? What experience do they possess in coffee-business start-ups and operations? Are they really qualified coffee-business consultants?

Our team possesses over 30 years of combined experience in retail business ownership, food-service management, and specialty coffee. We fully understand every aspect of creating and operating a coffee business. Much of this expertise is included in this 700-page coffee start-up/operational manual.

643

We have assisted major companies in developing specialty coffee programs nationwide. Over the past 10 years, we have helped nearly 300 individuals with the creation of their coffee businesses and assisted numerous established operators solve problems. We have personally owned retail coffee bar, coffee cart, coffee drive-thru and coffee kiosk operations.

Bellissimo is the most highly respected company within the specialty coffee industry as a source for high-quality, award-winning educational and training products. We offer personal support and the finest coffee educational materials available to help enhance your chance for success. We have references who will validate our credentials as qualified coffee-business consultants. The Specialty Coffee Association of America, NASBEV, *Fresh Cup Magazine*, *Coffee & Beverage Magazine* (Canada) and numerous respected companies frequently refer individuals to us for assistance with the creation or refinement of their coffee businesses. Client references are available upon request.

The Advantages of Using a Qualified Consultant

Creating a winning concept is essential to optimize your chance for success. We have watched the specialty coffee industry grow from its inception. We know what typically works, and what does not. We understand how to help our clients position their coffee businesses so they will have a competitive advantage for years to come.

Choosing the right location for your coffee bar, coffee kiosk, coffee cart or coffee drive-thru may be the most important decision you will ever make in the life of your business. Your location must attract a high volume of customers, yet the cost of remodeling, equipping, and debt servicing that location must maximize your chance for success. We can help you evaluate and choose the right location.

Designing an efficient and attractive store is critical to optimizing sales and minimizing expenses. A good ergonomic store design will ensure that your products can be produced efficiently, with a minimal amount of labor. Good store design should also attractively present your products to the consumer, enticing them to buy. We design dozens of coffee bars each year.

Selecting the best equipment and products can be a confusing process. Which manufacturers produce superior equipment? Which distributors are reputable and provide good customer service? Who consistently roasts and blends the finest coffees? Who produces high-quality food products with proven customer acceptance? Which new products can provide you with a competitive advantage? We can guide you to the best in our industry!

Hiring the right people and training them properly is the key to your success. Your store, equipment and products are only tools. It is your employees who will differentiate you from your competition. Will they provide superior customer service? Will they understand how to properly prepare and handle your gourmet products? How will you find the right people and train them properly? We can help.

Managing thousands of variables that are essential to profitability is typically the most difficult challenge faced by the business owner and manager. We possess years of food-service operations experience. We can help you create operational systems and teach you the fundamentals of food-service business management. Don't let your business control you, learn how to control your business!

Avoiding costly or fatal business mistakes is what our services are all about. In many cases, the investment made in a coffee consultant by our clients actually results in an overall savings of thousands of dollars. Typically, we can help you select a better location, negotiate a more advantageous lease, purchase equipment for less, get your business open faster, turn a profit sooner, and eliminate many common costly mistakes.

Reducing the anxiety that is commonly associated with a coffee business start-up is one of the real benefits of working with a qualified coffee consultant. Having a guide who has traveled the path before, who can lead you through a "mine field" of potential mistakes, can provide you with peace of mind.

The Bellissimo Mission Statement

Bellissimo is dedicated to providing high quality education materials, personalized business consulting and custom media production for the specialty coffee industry. We have no hidden agendas; we offer only unbiased, quality information and services. Bellissimo believes KNOWLEDGE IS PROFIT.

What Our Coffee Consulting Clients Say

"Bellissimo gives 110% as business consultants! They each possess an extensive background in assisting others in opening and operating successful coffee establishments. Their passion for coffee and product knowledge is reflected by their tremendous support to their clients."
—*Ruth Wong, Maui, HI*

"Anyone opening a coffee operation knows how expensive it is. Of all the money we spent to open our coffee house, the dollars we spent with Bellissimo were among the most useful. Without Bellissimo, our opening could have been a disaster. But with their help we were able to handle the high traffic, and their continuing support keeps us running smoothly. Thanks Bellissimo!"
—*Bill Clark, 101 North Coffee Roaster & Cafe, Eufaula, AL*

"We own two successful drive-thru operations, but when it was time to think about further business expansion, we called Bellissimo. They were not only able to help us evaluate potential locations, but provided us with valuable suggestions on how we might increase sales and profitability in our present operations. We were a bit hesitant about using a consultant at first because of the expense, but truthfully, the insights they provided to us were invaluable. We highly recommend Bellissimo to anyone starting a coffee business, or to those who are already in the business and need assistance in fine tuning their operations. They truly possess the knowledge and experience to help you maximize your chance for success."
—*Ryan and Chad Corbin, Salt Lake City, Utah*

"I had heard about the video 'Espresso 101,' so I called Bellissimo and bought it and the book *Bean Business Basics*. Both were well worth the money! After looking over the available consultants, I decided to hire Bellissimo to help me with the many facets of opening my business, including planning my menu, selecting products, vendors and equipment, and financial projections. One of the best things we did was to have Bellissimo come to Webster to train our staff. Because of Bellissimo, we were much better prepared and our staff knew what they were doing before we even opened the doors. Hiring Bellissimo as a consultant and for our opening/training was well worth the money and a great alternative to opening a franchise operation."
—*Chuck Durand, Earthtones Coffee House, Webster, NY*

"Simply put, I could not have opened my coffee shop without the help and support I received from Bellissimo."
   —*Dan Robinson, The Western Coffee Bar, Fort Collins, CO*

"Bellissimo has the vision, expertise and experience to identify a viable location. They saved me thousands of dollars. I think they're the greatest."
   —*Cindy Ludwick, OH*

"...We believe working with Bellissimo to be our single wisest investment made to date! They are terrific!"
   —*Jana Eisenberger, Spring Lake, NJ*

"...Thank you for all your effort and exhibition of creativity in assembling our business plan and bar design. Without this plan I don't believe we would have had a chance for our location."
   —*John Shane, Richmond, VA*

"...Using their expertise in the coffee industry, they [Bellissimo] saved us thousands on our equipment purchases by directing us to the best companies to do business with..."
   —*Brian Johnson, Denver, CO*

"Bellissimo saved me from making a lot of mistakes when I opened my first coffee bar. They helped me in all aspects of getting open, from store design and menu preparation to equipment procurement and training my staff. I couldn't have done it without them. Bellissimo is truly the leading expert of coffee business management."
   —*Tom Elliott, Java Junkies, Virginia Beach, VA*

"The cost of engaging Bellissimo and bringing them to Singapore was insignificant compared to what we gained. I cannot put a dollar value on the service we received from Bellissimo, and I will always be thankful that I brought Bellissimo to Singapore for the opening of my café."
   —*Burso Tan, Ragtime Cafe, Singapore*

Our Services Include:

> Concept Development
> Equipment Selection
> Location Selection
> Vendor Selection
> Business Plan Development
> Advertising & Marketing
> Operational Systems
> Goal Setting
> Plumbing & Electrical
> Health Department Dialog

> Logo Development
> Beverage Preparation
> Staff Hiring and Training
> Menu Planning
> Café Design
> Merchandising
> Management Training
> Business Expansion
> Specifications
> Grand-Opening Assistance

Top Industry Professionals Speak

"I can't tell you how many readers I've sent to Bellissimo for its consulting services and training books and videos. Bellissimo knows the coffee industry and has invaluable resources to help owner-operators build a profitable business."

—*Sue Gillerlain, Editor,* Specialty Coffee Retailer

"Bellissimo is one of the most comprehensive resources for information regarding successfully owning and operating a coffee business. The first thing anyone starting a coffeehouse should do is call Bellissimo. The industry would not be the same today if we didn't have all their educational materials. Thanks for all your hard work!"

—*Connie Blumhardt, Director of Sales,* Fresh Cup Magazine

"Bellissimo serves the specialty coffee industry in a unique and essential manner. If you turn to Bellissimo for products or consulting, your chances for success in coffee will increase tenfold."

—*Jan Gibson, Executive Director, North American Specialty Coffee, Tea & Beverage Retailers' Expo*

Bellissimo Videos

Call 800-655-3955 to Order

The Passionate Harvest—$79.95

An historic video for the specialty coffee industry! This 60-minute video is the definitive film chronicling coffee from seed to cup.

Shot in Guatemala, Brazil, Kona and Ethiopia, "The Passionate Harvest" takes a detailed look at the inner workings of the diverse processes involved in coffee production, emphasizing the enormous amount of effort and care required to produce quality coffee, and highlighting some of the issues and decision points that affect final cup quality and character.

2001 Telly Award
2001 Summit Award
2001 Communicator Award

Platinum Award 2001 Houston Worldfest Film Festival

Espresso 101—$89.95

"Espresso 101" is the award-winning professional video training tool for you and your employees. This tape will cut the normal 20-hour employee-training cycle down to three or four hours. This tool pays for itself with the first employee trained.

Each package includes a study guide, multiple-choice test with answer key, barista diploma and a durable library case. Available in Spanish.

Winner of 3 Fresh Cup Magazine Spressy Awards

Espresso 501—$69.95

This 75-minute video is an advanced course in coffee and espresso for the specialty coffee industry professional. The perfect companion piece to the award-winning video, "Espresso 101", "Espresso 501" provides a detailed understanding of the variables essential to create a superior espresso beverage experience.

Winner Summit Creative Award

Everything BUT Coffee—$69.95

Learn how to maximize your business sales by offering a variety of complementary foods and beverages. Now coffee business owners and their employees can gain a comprehensive understanding of the non-coffee-related aspects of the business.

Free Bonus Section: This tape includes the entire contents of "Customer Service for the Retail Coffee Bar." Keep your customers coming back using the sure-fire methods outlined in this video.

Winner 2001 Telly Award

649

More Bellissimo Videos

Spilling the Beans—$39.95

A complete video overview of the specialty coffee business. Spend 40 minutes with the experts learning about investment, profit potential, cost factors, location considerations, and much more.

"Don't even consider specialty coffee as a new business or even an add-on to your present business until you, your banker, your accountant and your staff review this tape. Excellent information!"

—*Ward Barbee, Publisher,* Fresh Cup Magazine

Caffé Latte Art—$49.95

This instructional video by David Schomer is for the professional. Learn to pour hearts and rosettas in your cappuccinos and lattes. These special techniques will set your coffee operation apart from the rest...your customers will return for that extra touch.

"Using this tape has given me a competitive marketing edge over my competition. My employees learned to make artful pours in no time."

—*Rosanna Romeo, Palazzo Espresso*

Customer Service for the Retail Coffee Bar—$39.95

Next to your product, excellent service is your most important asset.

Build sales and insure customer loyalty by teaching your employees the fundamentals of superior customer service. This exceptional video will illustrate the psychology, attitude, and mechanics of good customer service. It will teach the viewer how to suggestive sell, be perceptive to customer needs, and to deal with difficult customers in a positive way.

"Customer service is a lost art. If you don't treat your customers like guests, they'll spend their time— and money—elsewhere."

—*Bruce Mullins, Vice-President, Coffee Bean International*

650

The Complete Dr. Illy—Milan Interview—*$49.95*

Spend 73 minutes with the father of the modern-day espresso industry! In this video filmed at the Four Seasons Hotel in Milan, Italy, Ernesto Illy shares his expansive knowledge of specialty coffee and his optimistic philosophy for the future of the beverage.

Dr. Illy has been the chairman of illycaffè S.p.A. of Trieste, Italy since 1963 and is well known in the specialty coffee industry, both for his expertise and for the positions he has held in many international coffee organizations.

The Art of Coffee—*$24.95*

This video teaches the home consumer proper handling and preparation of coffee in a wide variety of techniques. Educate your customers about the exciting world of coffee from seed to cup. Great for gift baskets! Stock this tape near your bulk beans and hard goods.

(Wholesale pricing available in lots of 10.)

Specialty Coffee Shops—*$49.95*

An information-packed 60-minute tour of some of the world's most successful specialty coffee stores. This behind-the-scenes visit provides tips, insights, and strategies from top retailers around the country.

Learn from professionals about personnel management, operations, merchandising and the latest innovations and trends in retail. Benefit from hundreds of stimulating, exciting, profit-generating ideas.

An Evening with the Experts—*$99.95*

A two-video set that includes interviews with five of the specialty coffee industry's most highly respected professionals. It explores in detail factors related to green coffee production, roasting and blending, beverage preparation, marketing, and the industry's future. Spend an evening learning from Dr. Ernesto Illy, Mauro Cipolla, Ted Lingle, Don Holly, and Ken Davids. The ultimate coffee information video set.

Bellissimo Books

Opening a Specialty Coffee Drive-thru—$129.95
($99.95 if you have already purchased *Bean Business Basics*)

A concept-specific supplement to *Bean Business Basics*. Finally, valuable information about opening and operating an espresso drive-thru. Designed as a companion piece to *Bean Business Basics*, this manual covers aspects of concept planning, location selection, drive-thru construction, bureaucratic considerations, and day-to-day operations. Includes estimated start-up costs.

"In a maturing specialty coffee market, the days of opening a retail operation on a lark are over. Success belongs to those whose passion for quality coffee is matched by solid business practices. Ed Arvidson and Bellissimo long ago established a reputation for helping their clients with both. In this new book, Arvidson breaks down a deceptively simple concept—the coffee drive-thru —to its essential business elements, providing a detailed start-up guide for a market niche that remains relatively untapped in many areas."

—*Mike Ferguson, Communications Director, Specialty Coffee Association of America (SCAA)*

Achieving Success in Specialty Coffee—$69.95

Each of the book's 23 chapters is written by an expert in specialty coffee, an industry that elicits from its producers, promoters, and purveyors emotions as strong as the brew itself. In this invaluable book, the most knowledgeable individuals in specialty coffee share their enthusiasm and expertise with the established or new-to-the-market retailer who is serious about operating his or her specialty coffee business at an elevated level and achieving maximum profitability. Marketing, customer service, staff training, equipment function/maintenance, and product information are just some of the areas discussed in-depth to help retailers devise their own personal strategies for success.

"*Achieving Success in Specialty Coffee* is equivalent to having 23 mentors ready, willing and able to help the specialty coffee retailer achieve business success. While reading this book, I felt as though I was talking with the authors. The information provided in each chapter is well organized and encourages the reader to take action. Congratulations Bellissimo on another success!"

—*Linda Smithers, President, Susan's Coffee & Tea /*
Past President, (SCAA)

Other Books from Bellissimo

Coffee Information

The Coffee Book: Anatomy of an Industry / Dicum and Luttinger $14.95
Up-to-date facts and figures about the coffee industry.

The Great Coffee Book / Castle & Nielsen $15.95
Practical information on choosing, brewing, and tasting. Over 30 coffee recipes!

Espresso: Ultimate Coffee / Davids $15.95
An entertaining and practical guide to espresso.

Espresso Quick Reference Guide / Janssen $17.95
New edition contains more than 1000 recipes, coffee trivia, latest how-to techniques; a great book!

Coffee / Davids $15.95
This informative book is a guide to buying, brewing and enjoying coffee.

Espresso Encyclopedia / Marino & West $12.95
An A to Z encyclopedia about espresso. For the professional or home connoisseur.

Espresso Professional Techniques / Schomer $27.95
Identifying and controlling each factor in perfecting espresso coffee in the commercial application.

The Perfect Cup / Castle $15.00
A great book on coffee and espresso, features a roaster/retailer section.

Coffee Technology / Sivetz & Desrosier $94.95
Comprehensive information on coffee roasting.

Espresso! / Monaghan & Huffaker $16.95
General beginner's overview to starting and running your own specialty coffee business.

Home Coffee Roasting / Davids $15.95
This book is entitled Home Coffee Roasting but provides invaluable information to anyone interested in the art of roasting coffee.

Coffee Basics / Knox & Huffaker $17.95
A wonderful book teaching the reader the fundamentals of good coffee and espresso, bean to cup.

All About Coffee / Ukers $109.95
This is THE classic! Unavailable for years, this book is a must for the library of anyone in the coffee business.

The Birth of Coffee / Lorenzetti $45
A pictorial visit to countries of origin.

Great Good Place / Oldenburg $14.95

A vision for revitalizing public places.

Coffee Cupper's Handbook / Lingle $27.95

A systematic guide to the sensory evaluation of coffee's flavor.

The Little Book of Coffee / Flammarion $12.95

Everything you want to know about coffee in one handy volume.

History

The Devil's Cup / Allen $25s

An entertaining travelogue retracing the spread of coffee, searching the globe for its historical and cultural significance.

Coffee: The Epic of a Commodity / Jacob $18.95

The 1998 reprint of the classic 1939 text. Covers a 1000 years of legend, lore, romance, drama, and tragedy as coffee became a world commodity.

Uncommon Grounds / Pendergrast $18

A fascinating history of coffee in the context of colonialism, the rise of mass production, modern-day media and marketing.

Coffee, Sex & Health / Bersten $14.95

A history of anti-coffee crusaders & sexual hysteria.

Tea

The Book of Tea & Herbs / The Republic of Tea $12.95

Appreciating the varietals and virtues of fine tea and herbs.

Tea: Essence of the Leaf / Slavin & Petzke $14.95

A book on the life and lore of tea. Includes enticing photographs, evocative poetry and prose, and an array of tempting recipes.

Tea Basics / Rasmussen & Rhinehart $16.95

A comprehensive tea book, covering the origin and history of tea; selection, blending, brewing, tasting and storage; harvesting, processing and grading.

Serendipitea / Podreka $16

A guide to the varieties, origins, and rituals of tea.

Design

Cafés & Coffee Shops II / Pegler $39.95

A pictorial tour of U.S. coffee bars.

Cafés & Bistros / Pegler $49.95

A pictorial tour of coffee bars and small restaurants.

Café Design / Pegler $49.95

60 new design solutions.

Coffee Clip Art

Approximately 100
original images per volume

The original volume, all
the basic coffee images.
Includes holidays.

More great coffee images.
More cups and includes
coffee borders.

Newest volume with
highly creative coffee
illustrations.

```
· DAILY SPECIALS
· MENUS
· FLYERS
· ADVERTISING
· POINT OF PURCHASE
· WEB DESIGN
· LABELS
```

49^{95} each on
floppy disks

109^{95} CD-ROM with
all three
collections

Available for PC/Windows
and Macintosh

More New Media

Countries of Origin

Decorate your coffee bins and label your bags with this collection of exciting images associated with various coffee-producing countries. Formatted to easily create labels and signs!

$79 95 on floppy disks

$179 95 CD-ROM with Sip Art 1, 2, 3 and Countries of Origin

Available for PC/Windows and Macintosh

New!

Movin' Sip Art
Animated Coffee Clip Art for the Web!

Jazz up and add movement to your Web site with this collection of distinctive and lively cups, beans and coffee machines. These images will make your Web site dance! 50-plus images.

$69 95 on CD-ROM

Available for PC/Windows and Macintosh

Bellissimo Specials

Start-up 3 pack—$249.95 (Regular value: $330)
Bean Business Basics, 700-page book • **Espresso 101**, training video
• **Spilling the Beans**, business overview video

Start-up 4 pack—$299.95 (Regular value: $400)

Bean Business Basics, 700-page book • **Espresso 101**, training video
• **Espresso 501**, advanced training video • **Spilling the Beans**, business overview

Start-up 5 pack—$349.95 (Regular value: $470)

Bean Business Basics, 700-page book • **Espresso 101**, training video
• **Espresso 501**, advanced training video • **Spilling the Beans**, business overview • **Everything BUT Coffee and Customer Service**, employee training videos

Next-Step 3 pack—$159.95 (Regular value: $210)

Espresso 501, advanced training video • **Everything BUT Coffee and Customer Service**, employee training videos • **Achieving Success in Specialty Coffee**, marketing and operational manual for the established retailer

Espresso Perfetto

Complete interactive barista training program from Italy!

This interactive training approach allows you to go one-on-one with your computer to learn about coffee and proper barista techniques. Program includes inter-active CD-ROM and companion print reference manual. Developed by Roberto Pregal of Brasilia, s.r.l., this new training tool includes video clips from Bellissimo's Espresso 101.

Manual: $59.95

CD-ROM: $129.95

Both: $179.95

Bellissimo on the Web

espresso101.com Coffee business resources from Bellissimo Coffee InfoGroup. If specialty coffee or espresso is in your future or your current business, visit Bellissimo Coffee InfoGroup! Bellissimo is the specialty coffee industry's most highly respected resource company, providing high quality coffee books, coffee videos, personalized coffee business consulting and custom media production for the specialty coffee industry.

coffeeuniverse.com Explore the hottest coffee Web site in the galaxy! This out-of-this-world site contains information about every aspect of coffee, and includes more than 3,000 industry-related links. A visit to Coffee Universe will fill your black hole with knowledge!

virtualcoffee.com Coffee's hottest Web 'zine! Virtual Coffee is the on-line magazine coffee consumers turn to for the latest definitive information about specialty coffee. Every issue contains columns by the industry's foremost experts, up-to-date news on industry events, trends, products and people, insightful features on the world of coffee, photos, links, reviews, tips and much more!

Coffee-Business.com

coffee-business.com Coffee business overview for retailers and new start-ups. How do I make my specialty coffee business work? What do I need to know to open my own specialty coffee business? Coffee-business.com answers your coffee-business questions.

coffee*i*nfo.com

coffee-info.com Your coffee information gateway! Whether you are presently in the coffee business, planning to open your own coffeehouse, or just interested in little brown beans, coffee-info.com in your gateway to the information and resources you need.

Stock Images from Coffee Images, LLC

Unique, one-of-a-kind coffee photographs, period pieces and original artwork.
For more information go to
www.coffeeimages.com

These extraordinary images and collections represent and characterize all aspects of coffee culture through the last century. Use them for your advertising and promotions.

Coffee Images, LLC images and collections are available via the Internet at Web site: **www.coffeeimages.com**. Check Web site or call 866-374-6868 for pricing.

"If you have photographic or image needs for advertising, catalogs, your Web site—even art for your walls—there is no collection of coffee images that can touch this huge image bank."
—Bruce Milletto, President, Bellissimo, Inc.

Notes

Notes

Notes

Notes

Notes

Notes

Notes

Notes

Notes